kimi ni todoke
From Me to You

Vol. 8

Story & Art by
Karuho Shiina

Volume 8

Contents

Story Thus Far

Sawako Kuronuma has always been a loner. Though not by choice, this optimistic 15-year-old can't seem to make any friends. Stuck with the unfortunate nickname "Sadako" after the haunting movie character, rumors about her summoning spirits have been greatly exaggerated. With her shy personality and scary looks, most of her classmates will barely talk to her, much less look into her eyes for more than three seconds lest they be cursed. Drawn out of her shell by Shota Kazehaya, the most popular boy in class, Sawako is no longer an outcast. And with her new friends Chizuru and Ayane, she's finally leading a more normal teenage life. In December, Sawako spends Christmas with her friends for the first time. The first number she enters into her new cell phone is Kazehaya's.

Winter break starts and Sawako plans to visit a shrine on New Year's Eve. Chizu and Ayane encourage her to ask Kazehaya to go with them and then learn that New Year's Eve is Sawako's birthday. They put makeup on Sawako and leave Sawako and Kazehaya alone together. Sawako has a good time with Kazehaya on New Year's Eve, but can't bring herself to give chocolate to him on Valentine's Day...

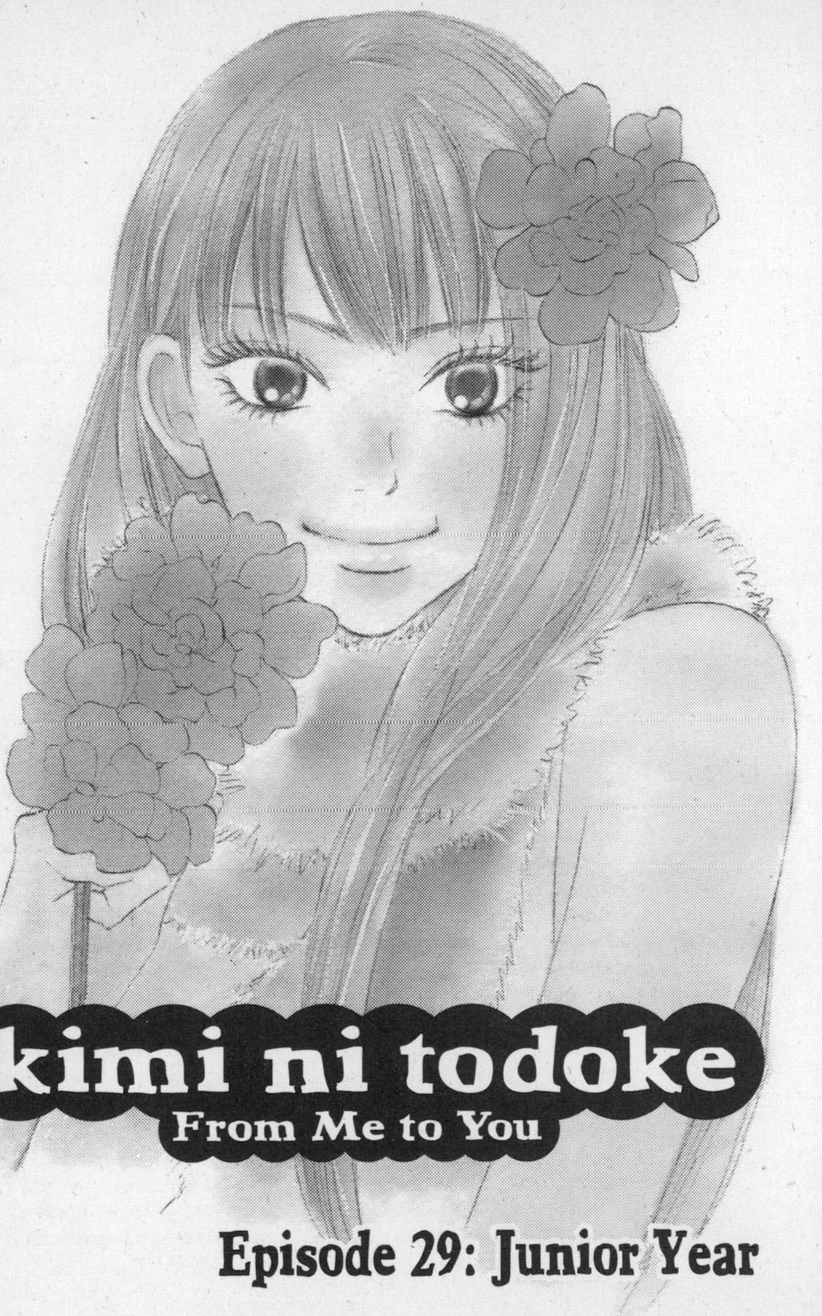

kimi ni todoke
From Me to You

Episode 29: Junior Year

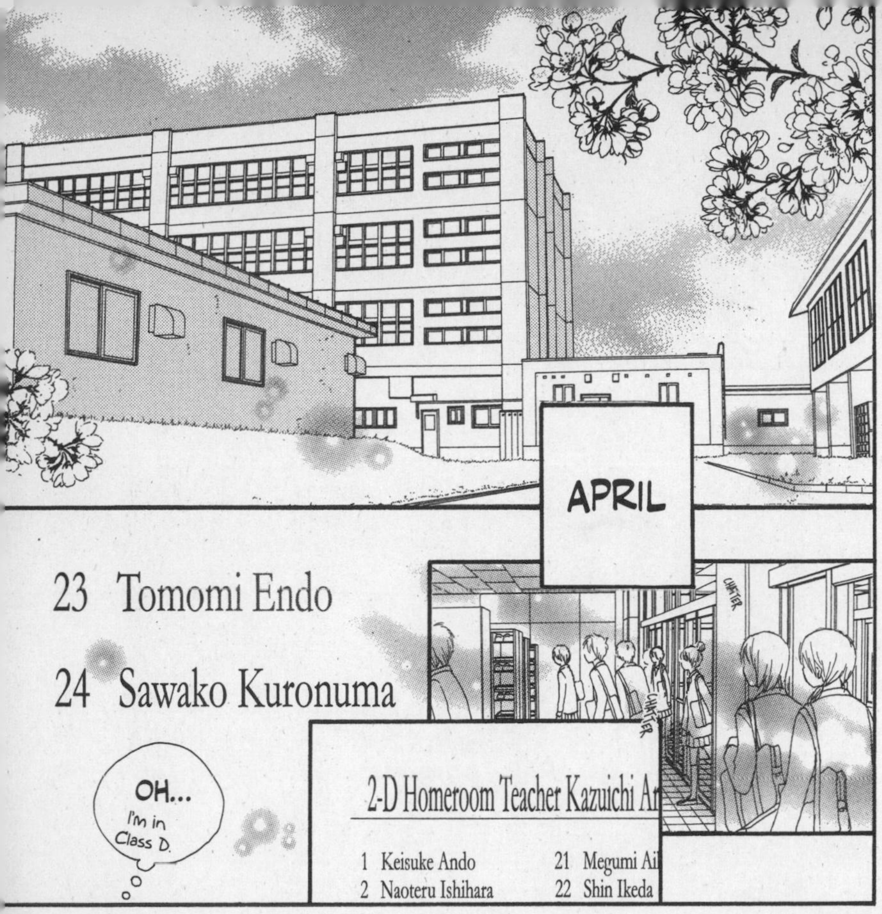
APRIL
CHATTER
CHATTER
2-D Homeroom Teacher Kazuichi Ar
1 Keisuke Ando
2 Naoteru Ishihara
21 Megumi Ai
22 Shin Ikeda
23 Tomomi Endo
24 Sawako Kuronuma
OH... I'm in Class D.

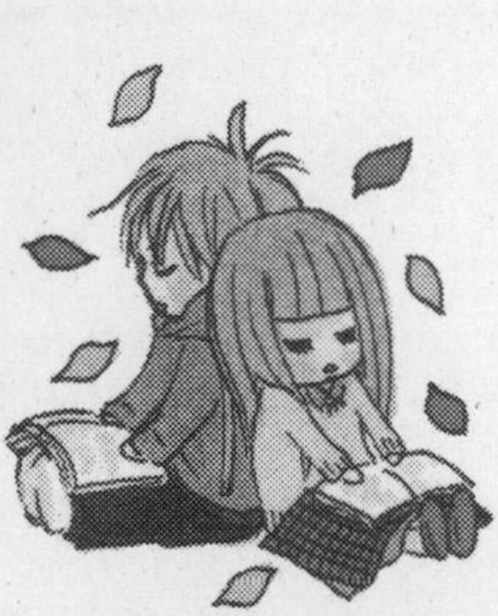

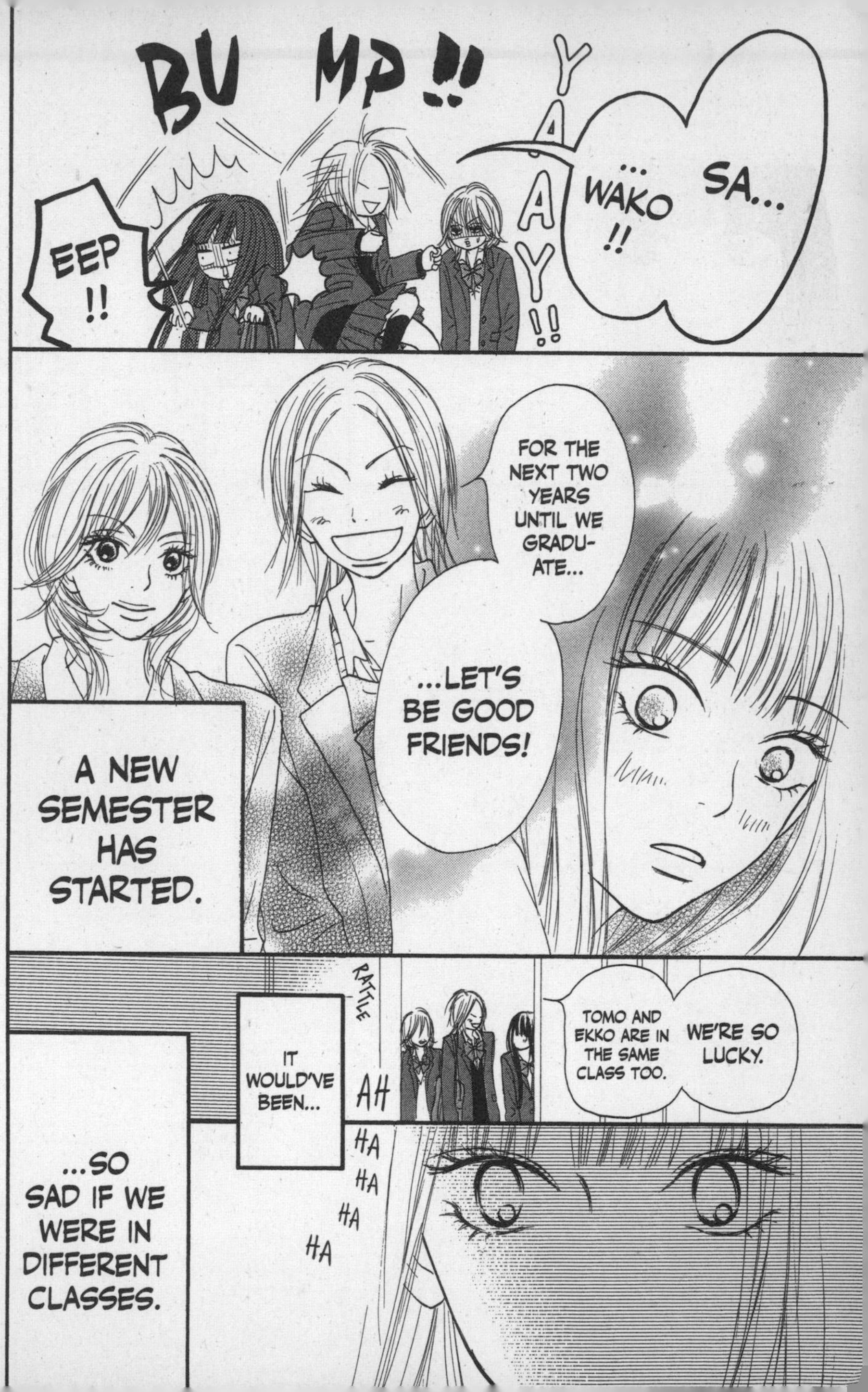
SA... ...WAKO!!
YAAAY!!
BUMP!!
EEP!!
FOR THE NEXT TWO YEARS UNTIL WE GRADU-ATE...
...LET'S BE GOOD FRIENDS!
A NEW SEMESTER HAS STARTED.
WE'RE SO LUCKY.
TOMO AND EKKO ARE IN THE SAME CLASS TOO.
RATTLE
AH
HA HA HA HA
IT WOULD'VE BEEN...
...SO SAD IF WE WERE IN DIFFERENT CLASSES.

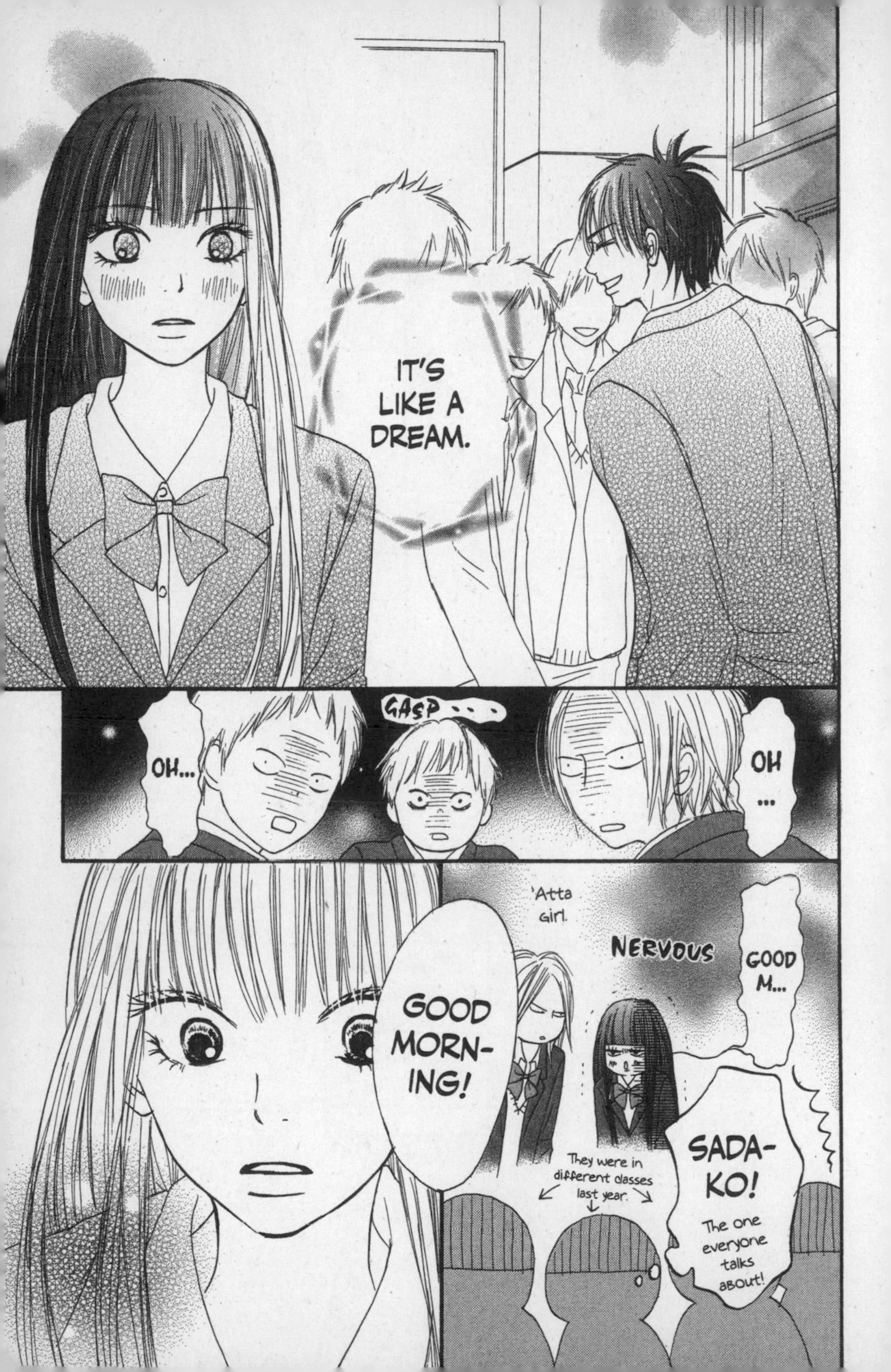
IT'S LIKE A DREAM.
OH ...
GASP . . .
OH...
GOOD M...
NERVOUS
'Atta Girl.
SADA-KO!
The one everyone talks about!
They were in different classes last year.
GOOD MORN-ING!

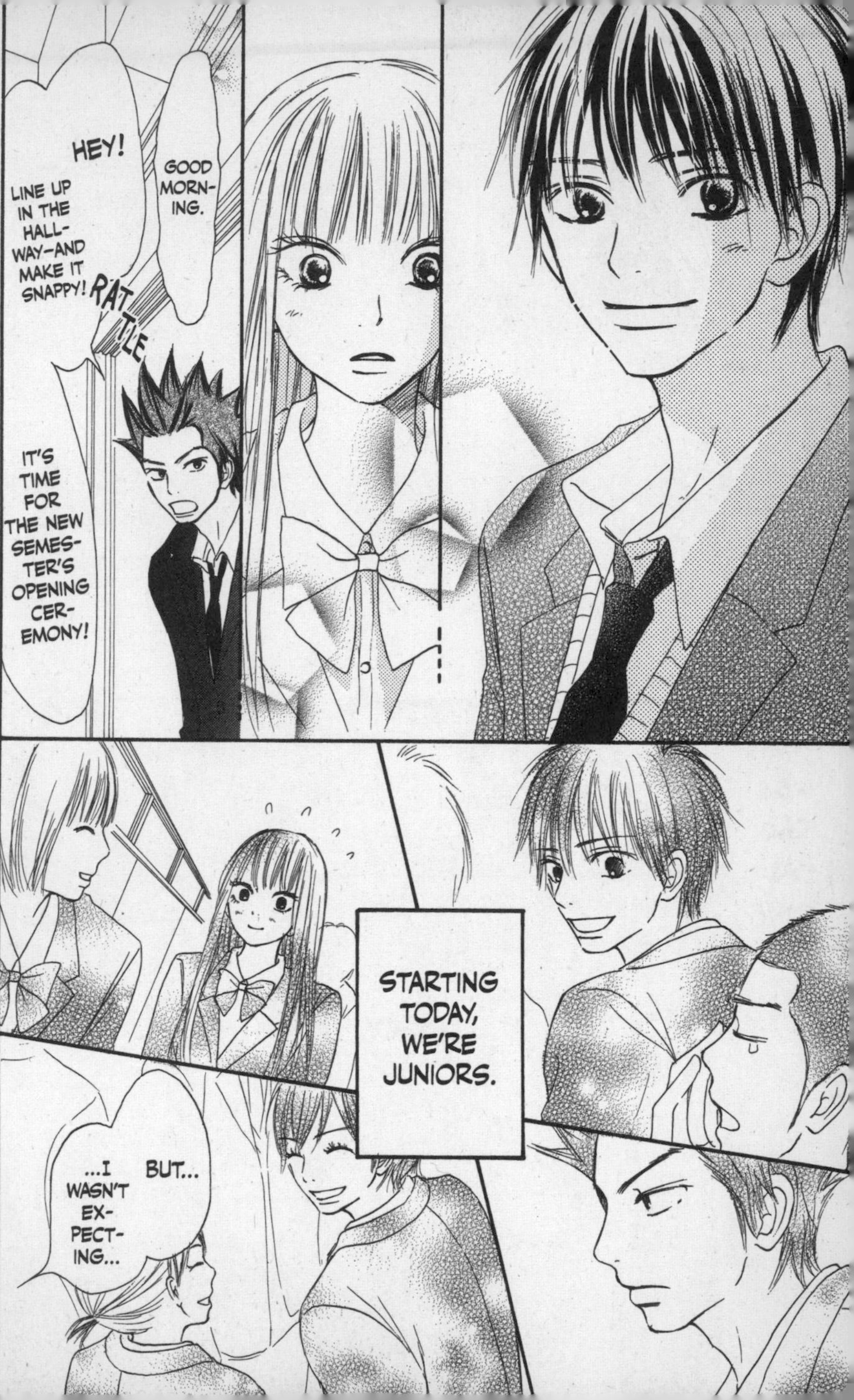
GOOD MORNING.
HEY!
LINE UP IN THE HALLWAY—AND MAKE IT SNAPPY!
RATTLE
IT'S TIME FOR THE NEW SEMESTER'S OPENING CEREMONY!
STARTING TODAY, WE'RE JUNIORS.
BUT...
...I WASN'T EXPECTING...

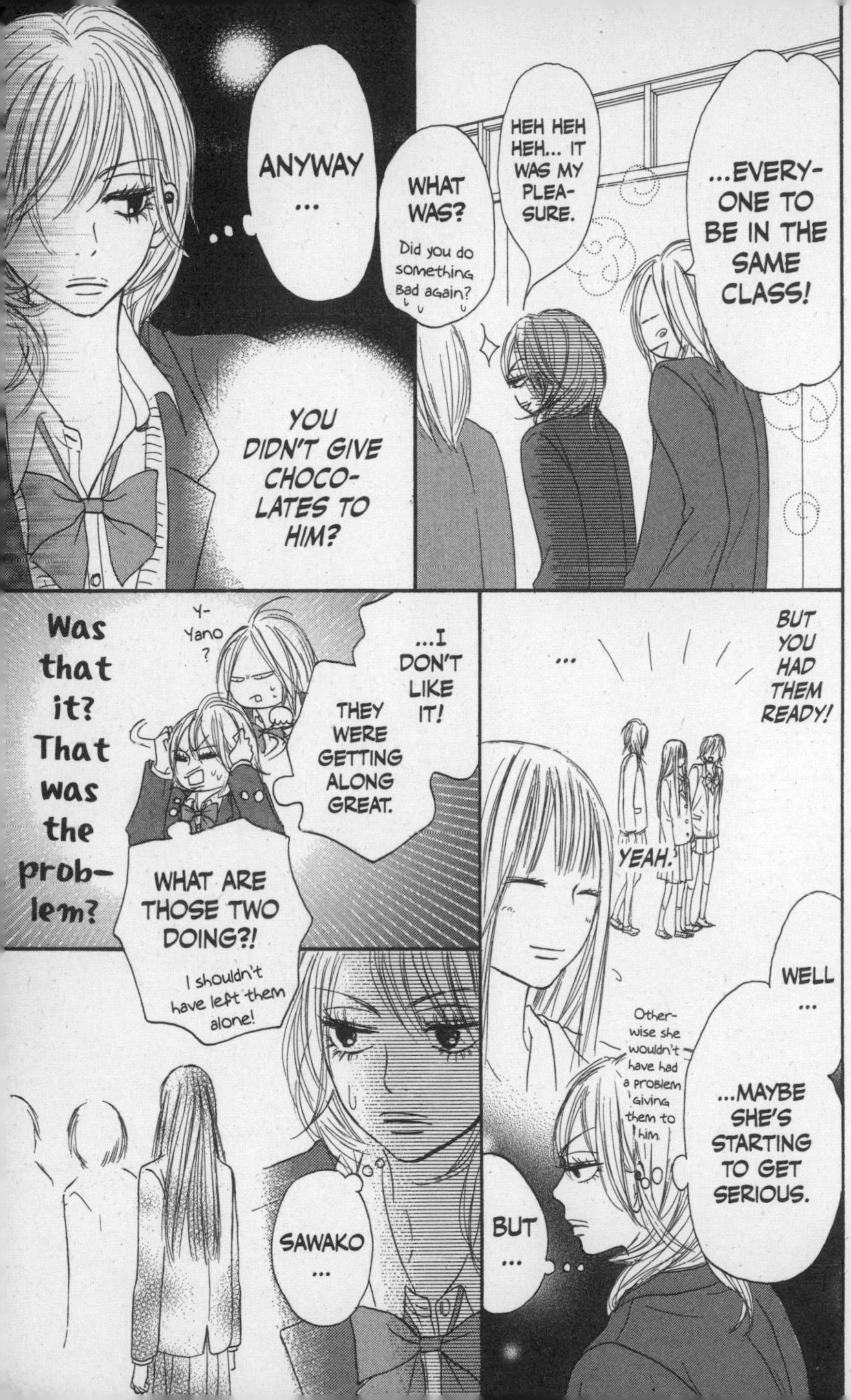
...EVERY-ONE TO BE IN THE SAME CLASS!
HEH HEH HEH... IT WAS MY PLEA-SURE.
WHAT WAS?
Did you do something bad again?
ANYWAY ...
YOU DIDN'T GIVE CHOCO-LATES TO HIM?
BUT YOU HAD THEM READY!
...
YEAH.
WELL ...
...MAYBE SHE'S STARTING TO GET SERIOUS.
Other-wise she wouldn't have had a problem giving them to him.
BUT ...
...I DON'T LIKE IT!
THEY WERE GETTING ALONG GREAT.
Y-Yano ?
Was that it? That was the prob-lem?
WHAT ARE THOSE TWO DOING?!
I shouldn't have left them alone!
SAWAKO ...

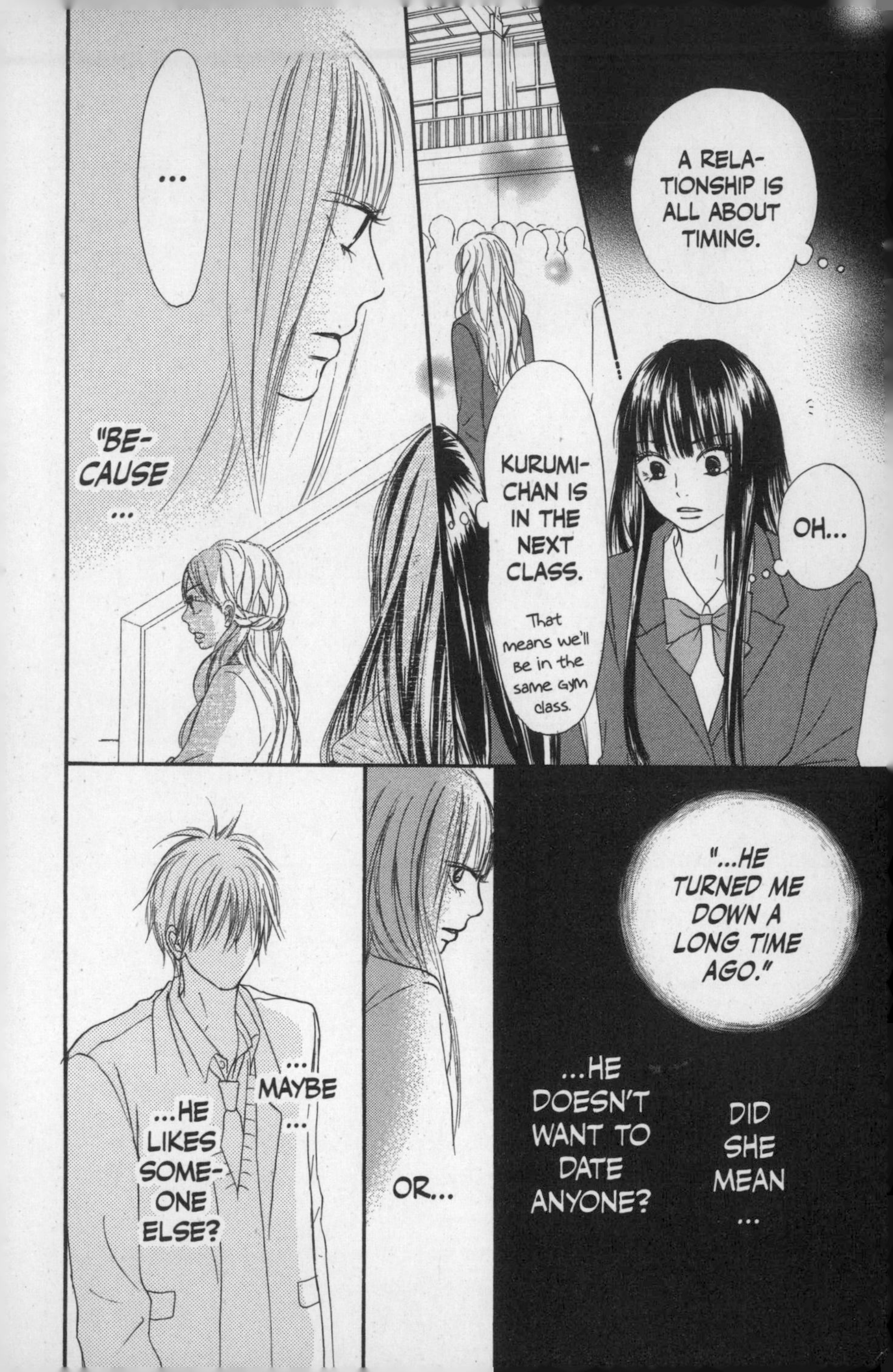
A RELATIONSHIP IS ALL ABOUT TIMING.
OH...
KURUMI-CHAN IS IN THE NEXT CLASS.
That means we'll be in the same gym class.
...
"BECAUSE ...
"...HE TURNED ME DOWN A LONG TIME AGO."
DID SHE MEAN ...
...HE DOESN'T WANT TO DATE ANYONE?
OR...
... MAYBE ...
...HE LIKES SOMEONE ELSE?

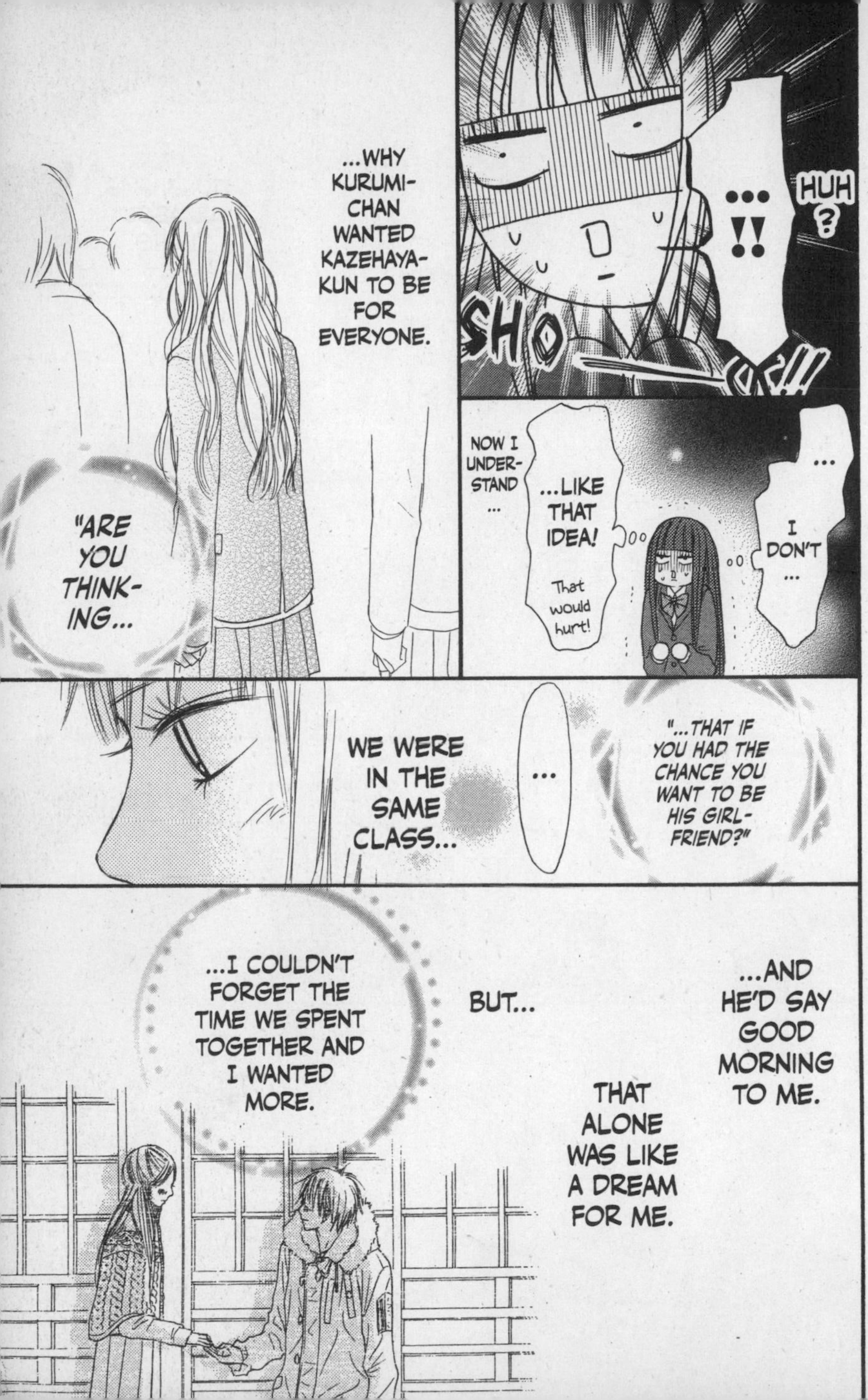
HUH?
...!!
SHO
...
I DON'T ...
...LIKE THAT IDEA!
That would hurt!
NOW I UNDER-STAND ...
...WHY KURUMI-CHAN WANTED KAZEHAYA-KUN TO BE FOR EVERYONE.
"ARE YOU THINK-ING...
"...THAT IF YOU HAD THE CHANCE YOU WANT TO BE HIS GIRL-FRIEND?"
...
WE WERE IN THE SAME CLASS...
...AND HE'D SAY GOOD MORNING TO ME.
THAT ALONE WAS LIKE A DREAM FOR ME.
BUT...
...I COULDN'T FORGET THE TIME WE SPENT TOGETHER AND I WANTED MORE.

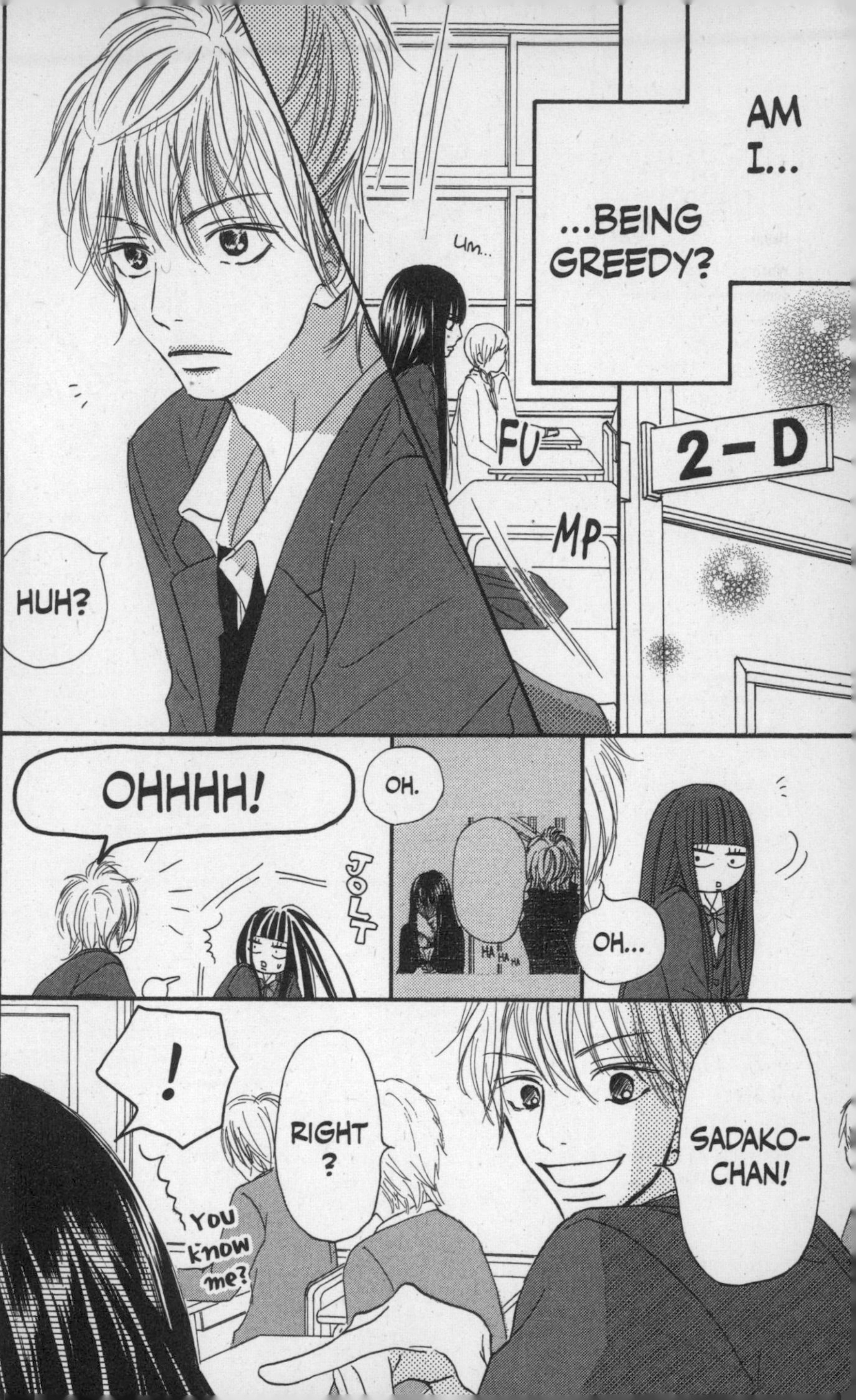
AM I...
...BEING GREEDY?
2-D
FU MP
Um...
HUH?
OH...
HA HA HA
OH.
OHHHH!
JOLT
SADAKO-CHAN!
RIGHT?
!
YOU know me?

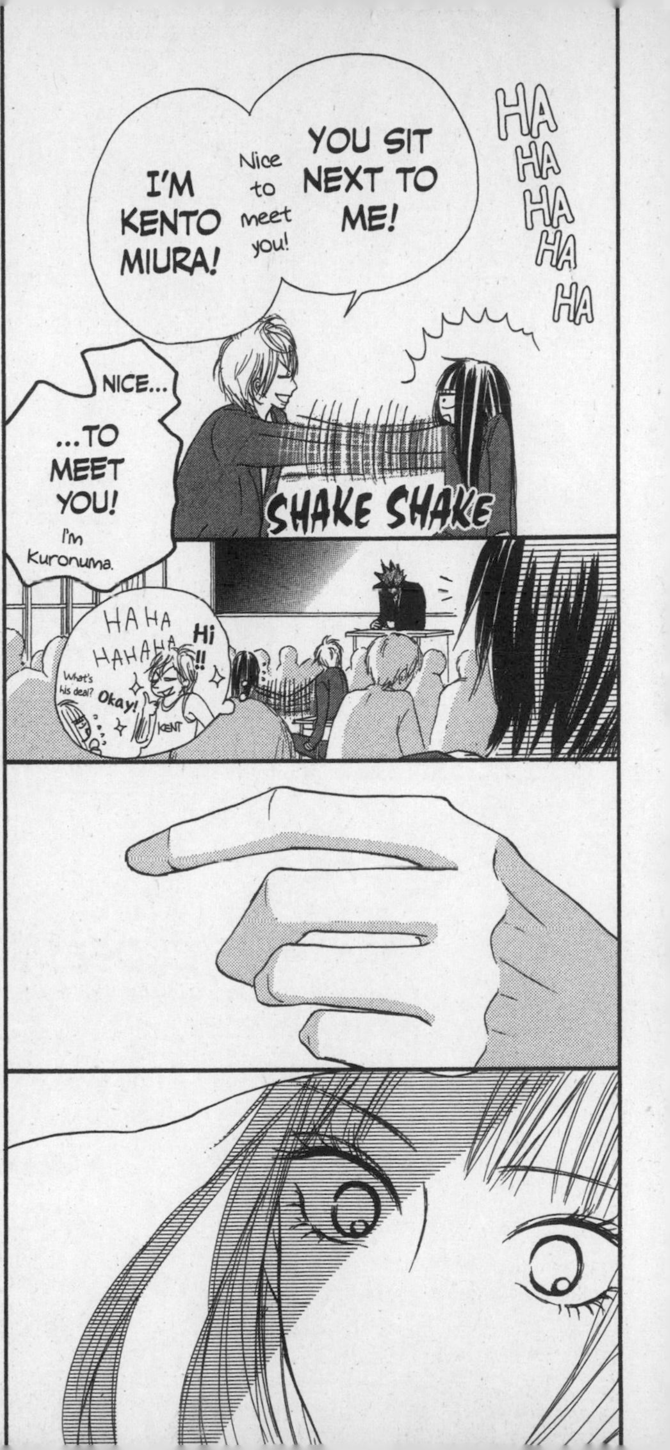
HA HA HA HA HA
YOU SIT NEXT TO ME!
Nice to meet you!
I'M KENTO MIURA!
NICE...
...TO MEET YOU!
I'm Kuronuma.
SHAKE SHAKE
HA HA HAHAHA
Hi !!
Okay!
What's his deal?
KENT

KARUPIN on JAPAN 1

Hello!

Whenever I see commercials for Noboribetsu Hot Spring, it always sounds like they're saying Rodriguez Hot Spring.

I haven't been to a hot spring for a while.

I want to sink into the water. I don't care if it's Rodriguez or whatever.

How are you?

This volume's structure is a little irregular (I'll explain why in the next volume), but please stick with me.

On a completely unrelated note, I realized something recently...

I don't like blood.

Oh...

I mean, I never gave needles and blood donations much thought until recently.

But I had the chance to donate my blood and...

To be continued... →

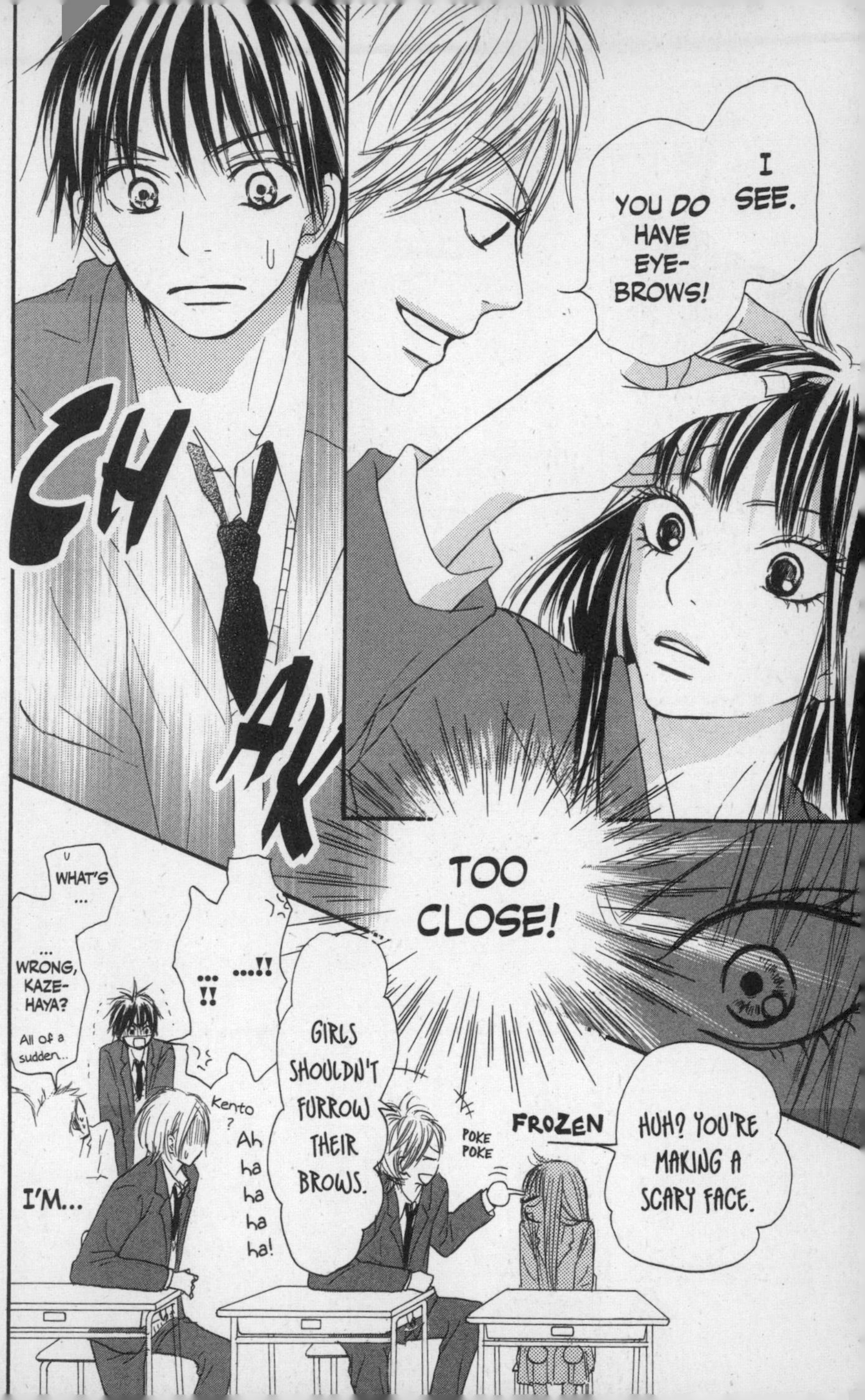
I SEE.
YOU DO HAVE EYE-BROWS!
CHAK
TOO CLOSE!
HUH? YOU'RE MAKING A SCARY FACE.
FROZEN
POKE POKE
GIRLS SHOULDN'T FURROW THEIR BROWS.
Ah ha ha ha ha!
...!!
...!!
Kento?
WHAT'S ... ... WRONG, KAZE-HAYA?
All of a sudden...
I'M...

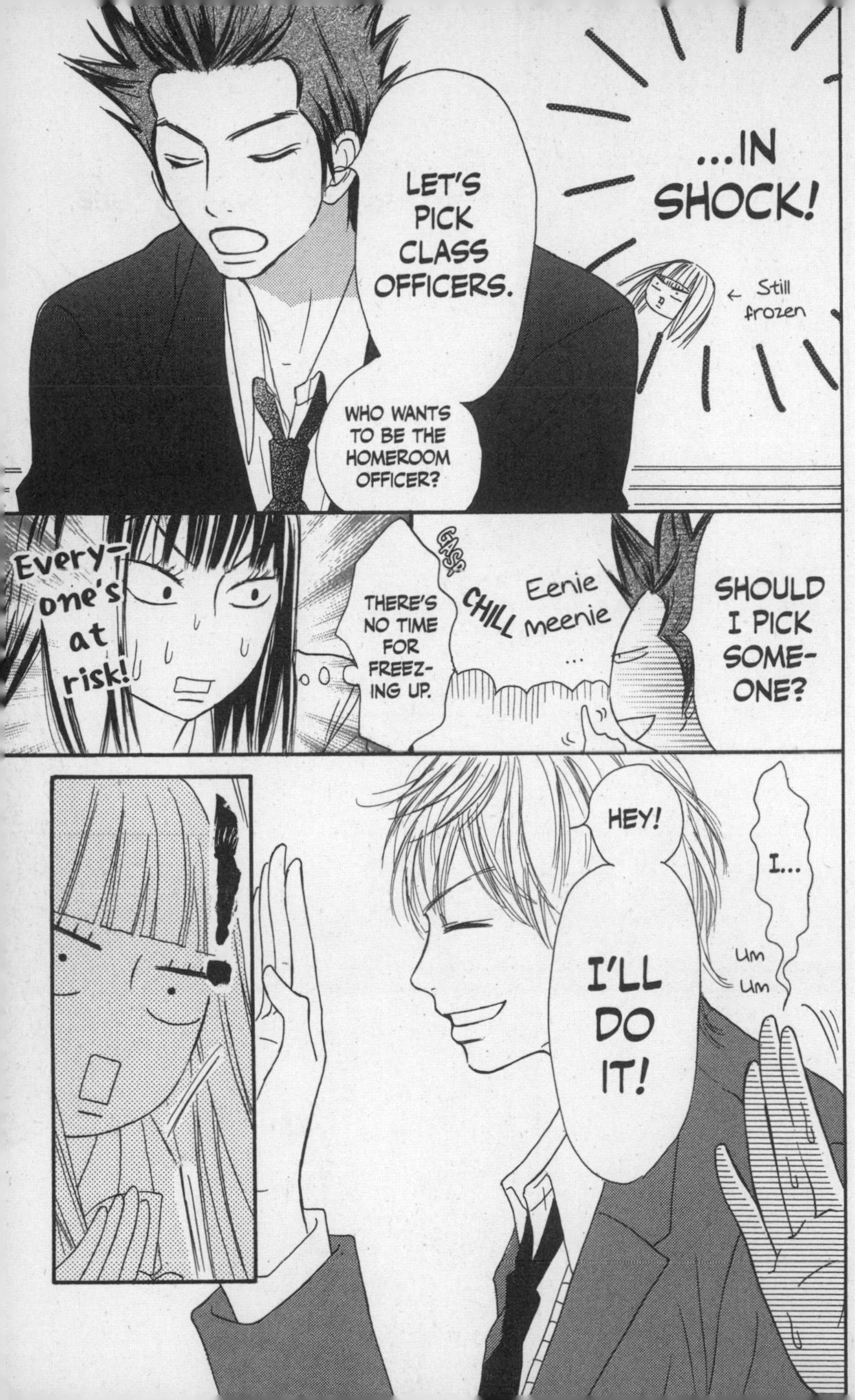
...IN SHOCK!
LET'S PICK CLASS OFFICERS.
← Still frozen
WHO WANTS TO BE THE HOMEROOM OFFICER?
SHOULD I PICK SOME-ONE?
Eenie meenie
...
CHILL
GASP
THERE'S NO TIME FOR FREEZ-ING UP.
Every-one's at risk!
I...
Um
Um
HEY!
I'LL DO IT!

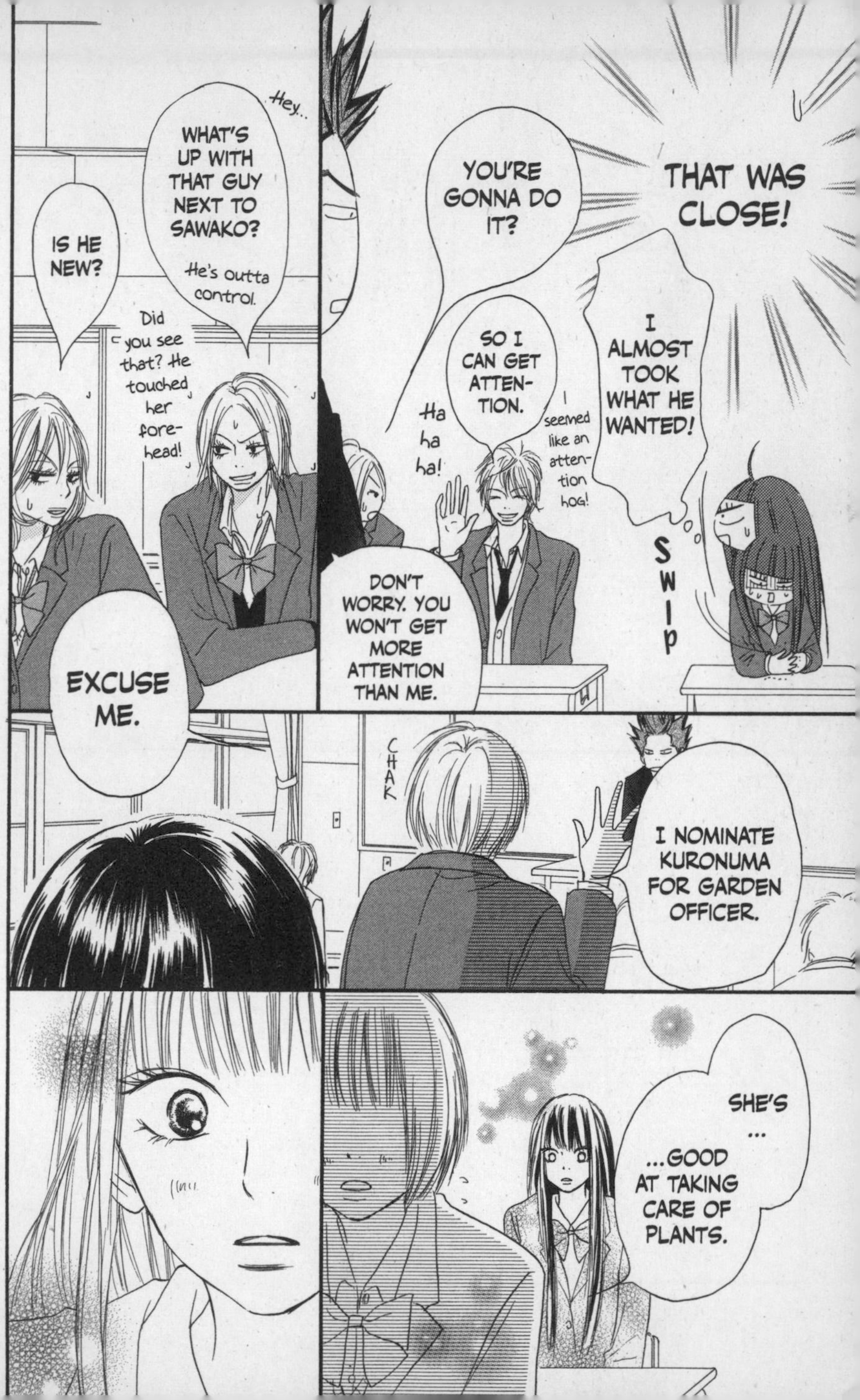
THAT WAS CLOSE!
I ALMOST TOOK WHAT HE WANTED!
Swip
YOU'RE GONNA DO IT?
SO I CAN GET ATTENTION.
I seemed like an attention hog!
Ha ha ha!
DON'T WORRY. YOU WON'T GET MORE ATTENTION THAN ME.
Hey..
WHAT'S UP WITH THAT GUY NEXT TO SAWAKO?
He's outta control.
IS HE NEW?
Did you see that? He touched her forehead!
EXCUSE ME.
CHAK
I NOMINATE KURONUMA FOR GARDEN OFFICER.
SHE'S ...
...GOOD AT TAKING CARE OF PLANTS.

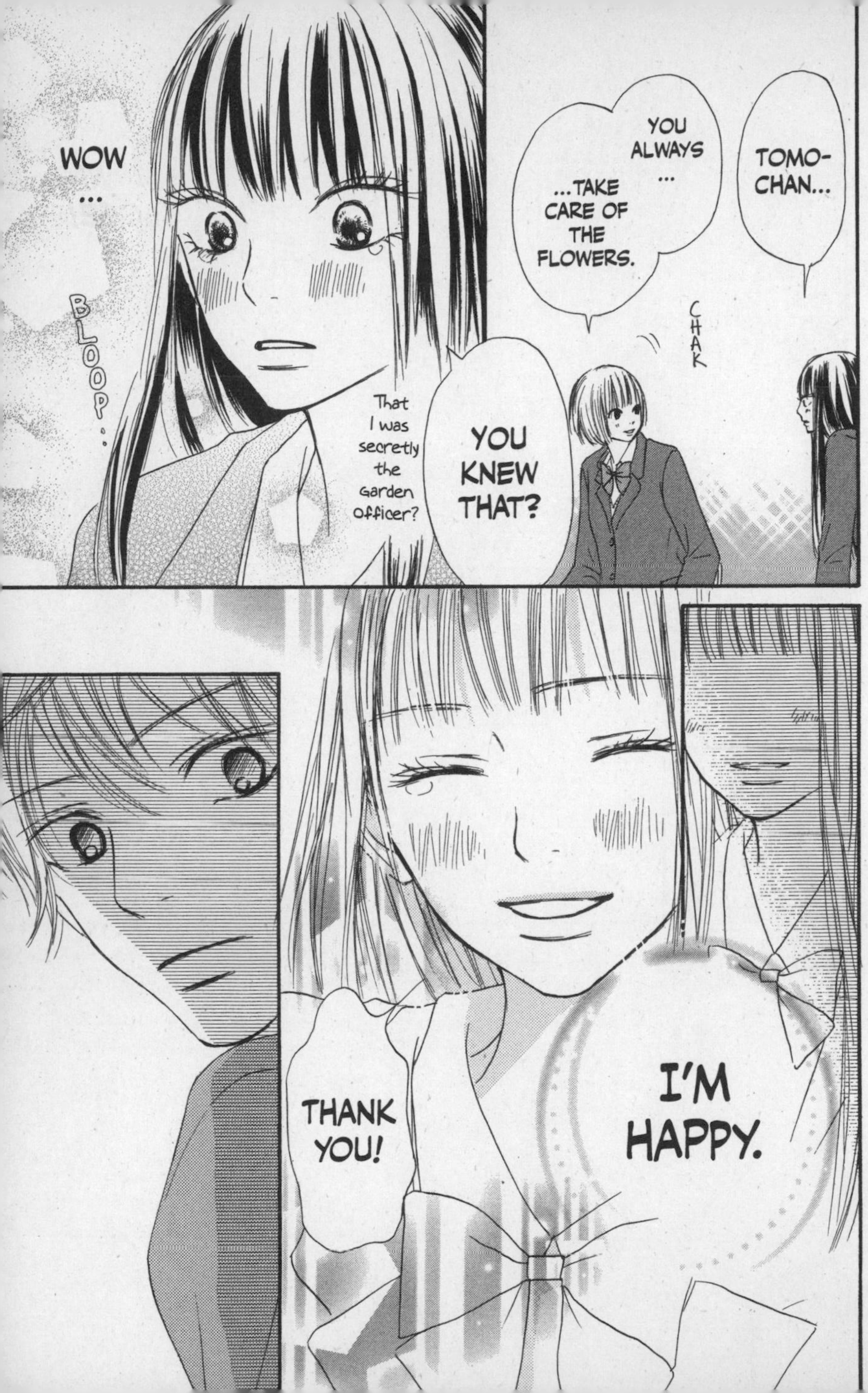
TOMO-CHAN...
YOU ALWAYS ...
...TAKE CARE OF THE FLOWERS.
CHAK
YOU KNEW THAT?
That I was secretly the garden officer?
WOW ...
BLOOP..
I'M HAPPY.
THANK YOU!

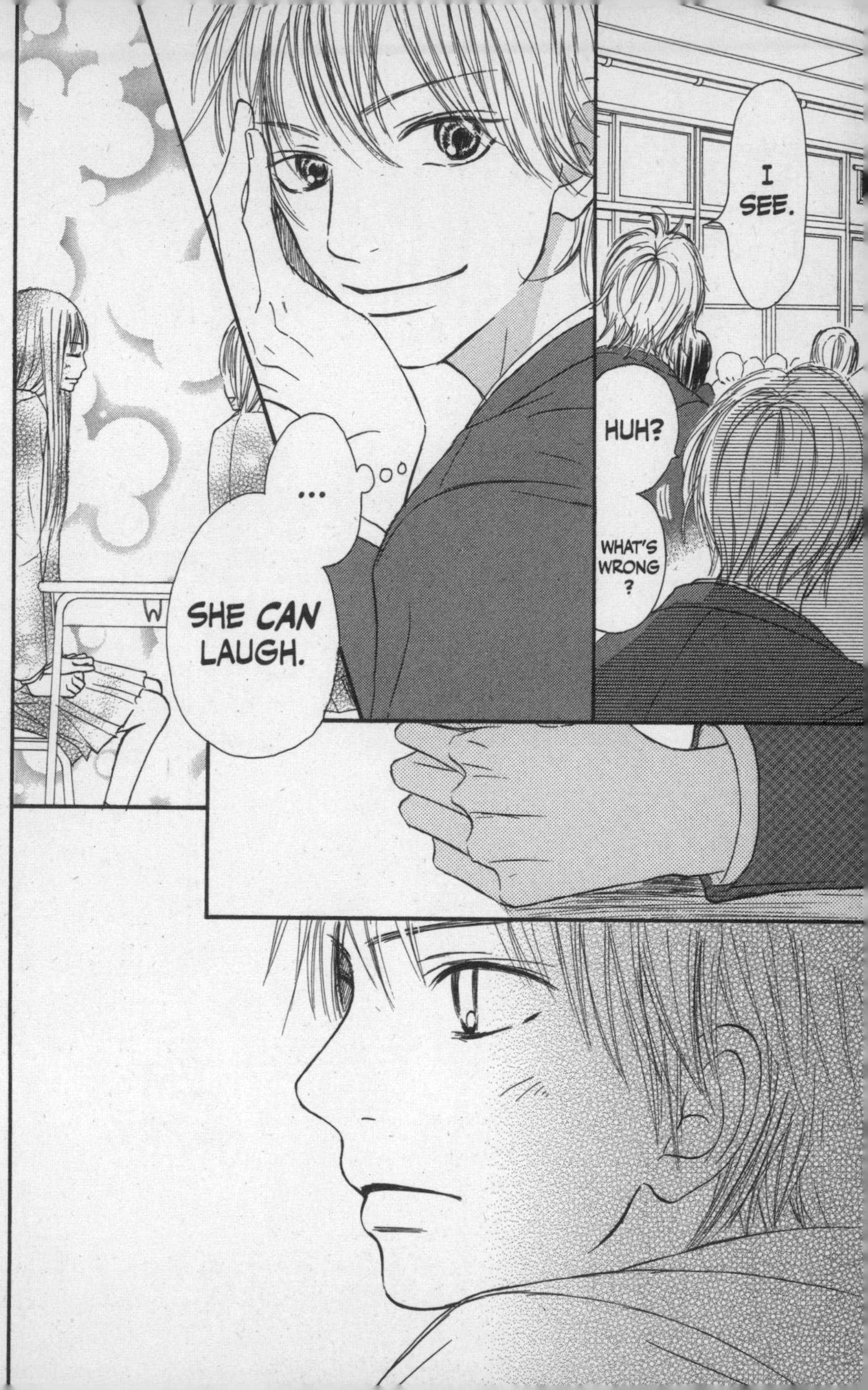
I SEE.
HUH?
WHAT'S WRONG?
...
SHE CAN LAUGH.

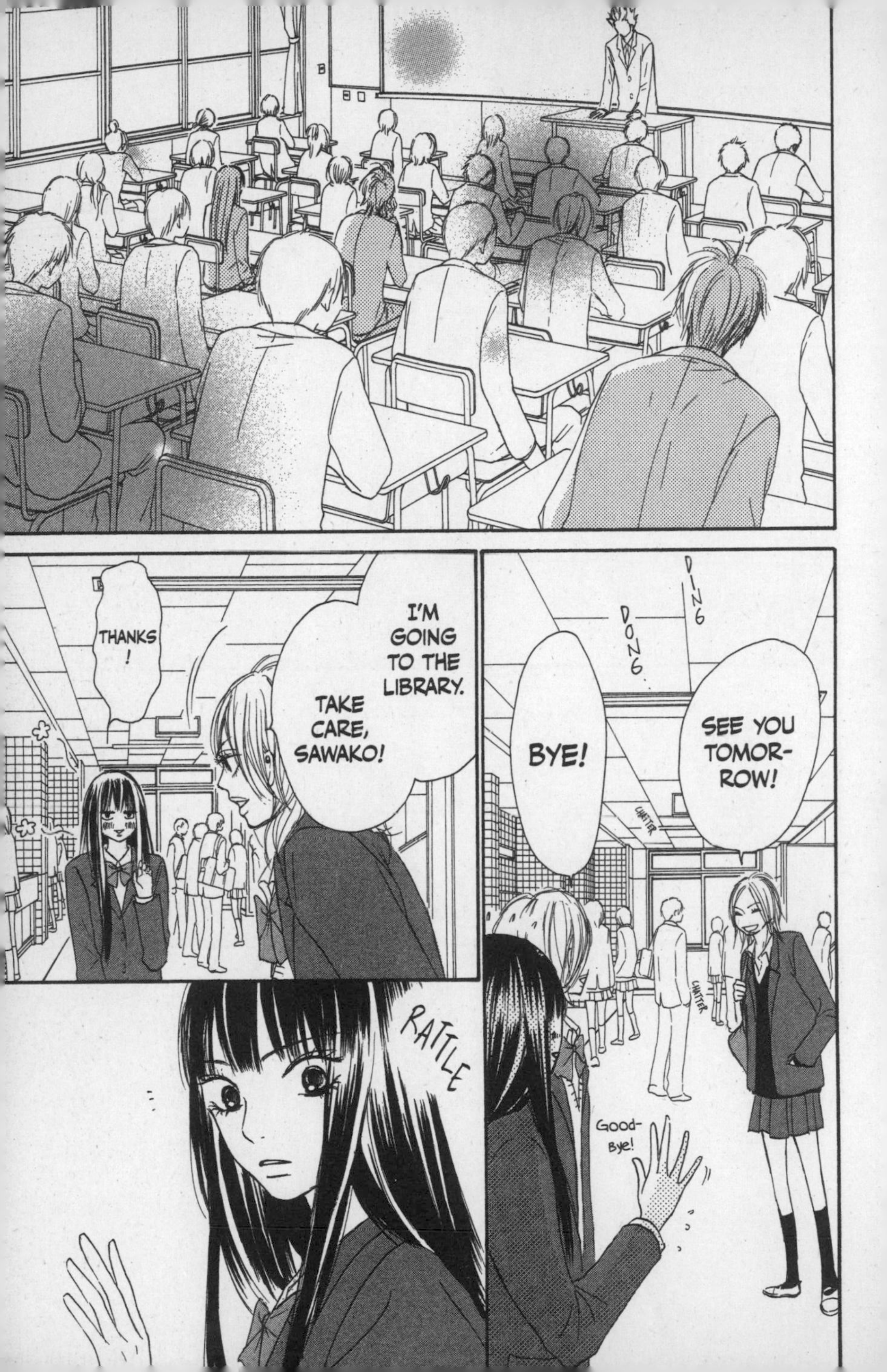
DING DONG
SEE YOU TOMORROW!
BYE!
CHATTER
CHATTER
Good-Bye!
I'M GOING TO THE LIBRARY.
TAKE CARE, SAWAKO!
THANKS!
RATTLE

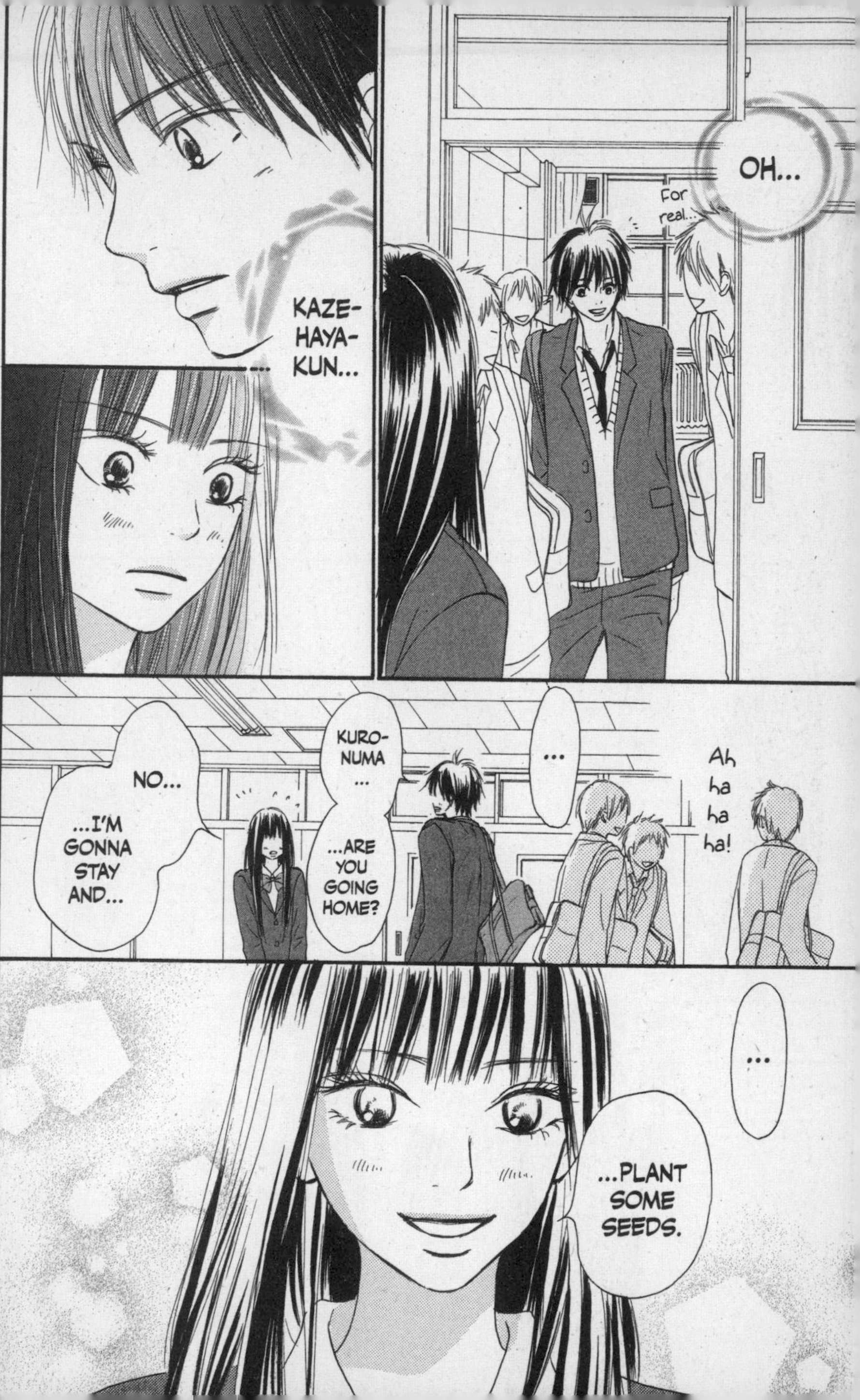
OH...
For real...
KAZE-HAYA-KUN...
Ah ha ha ha!
...
KURO-NUMA ...
...ARE YOU GOING HOME?
NO...
...I'M GONNA STAY AND...
...
...PLANT SOME SEEDS.

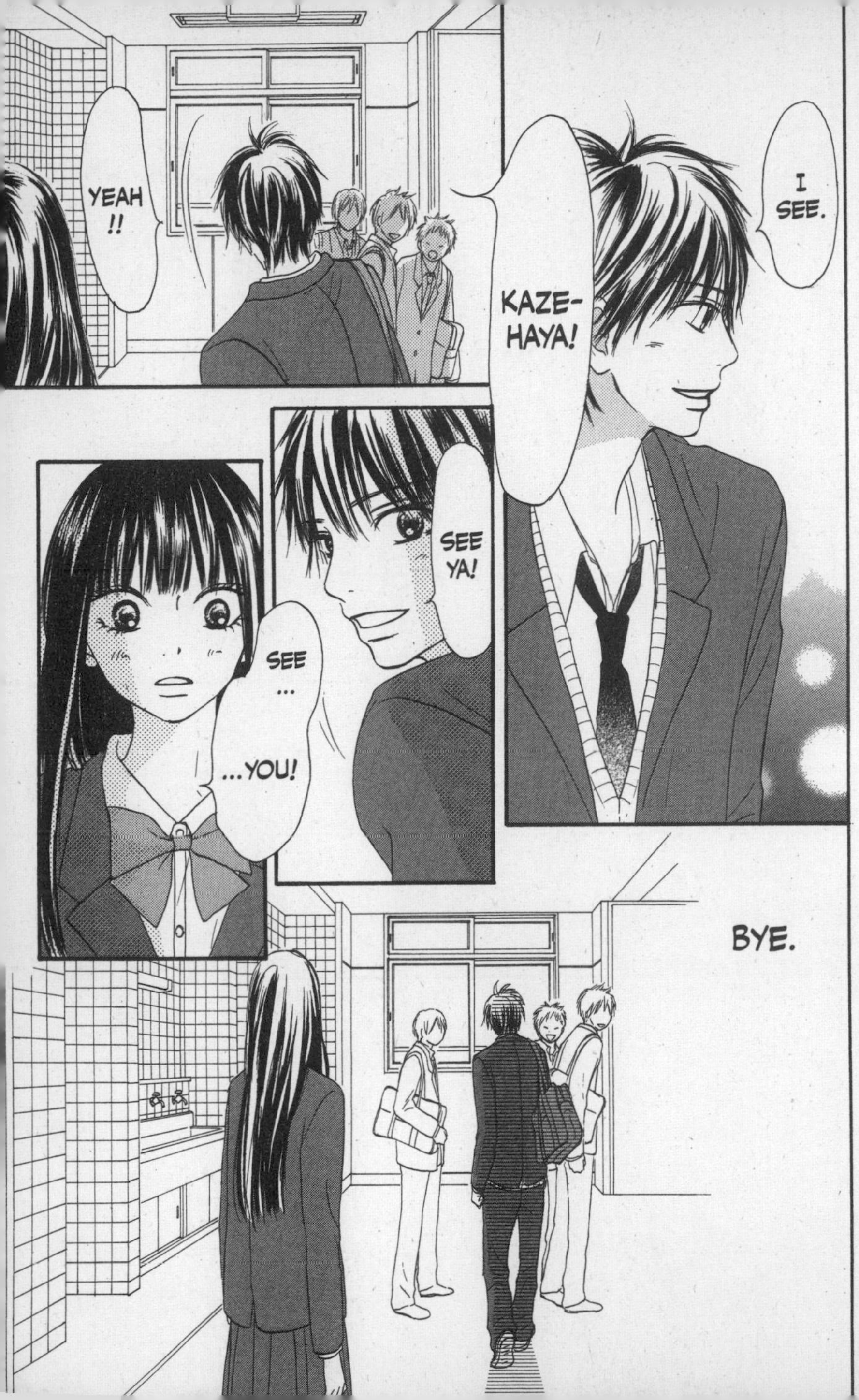
I SEE.
KAZE-HAYA!
YEAH!!
SEE YA!
SEE ...
...YOU!
BYE.

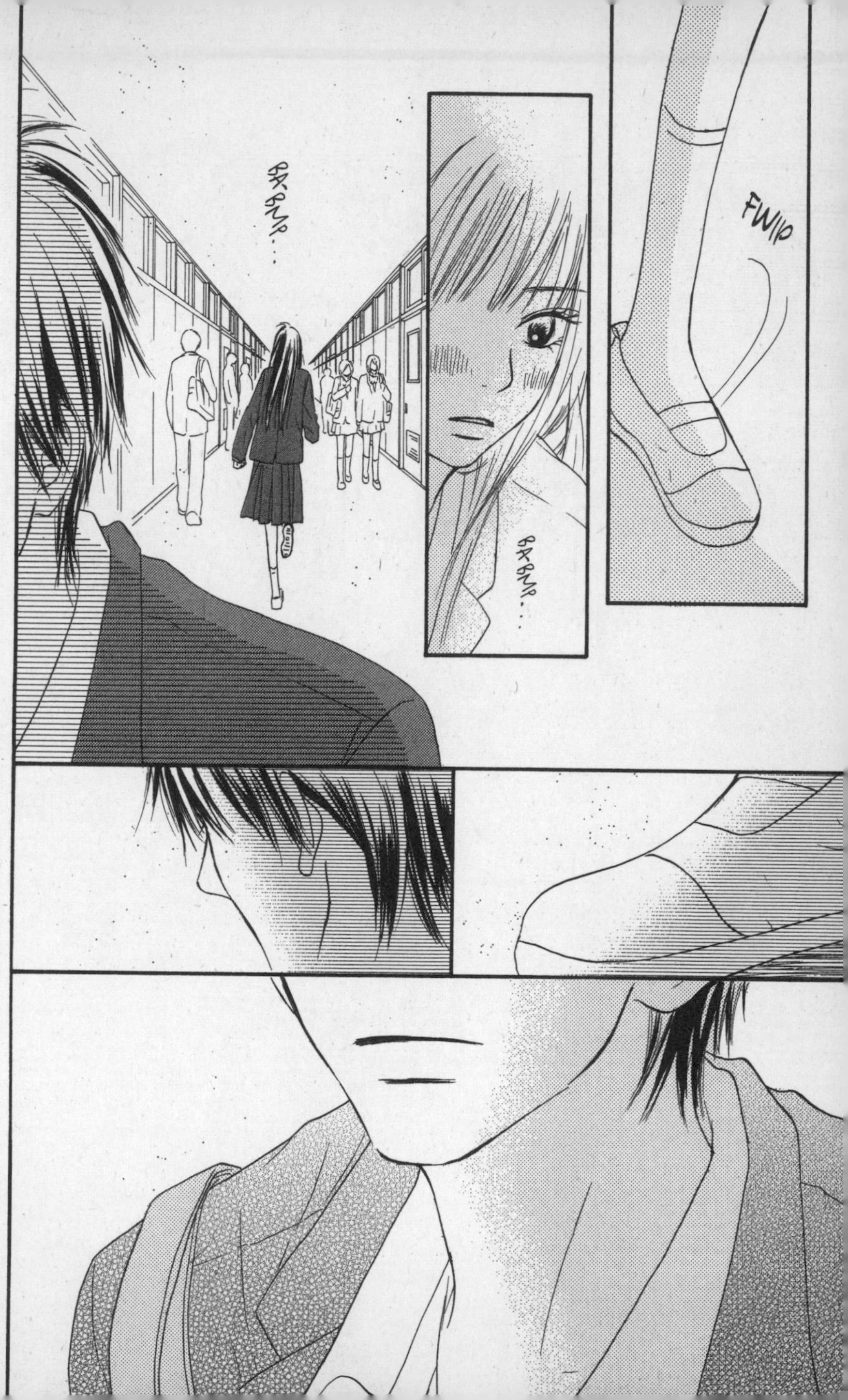
FWIP
BA-BMP...
BA-BMP...

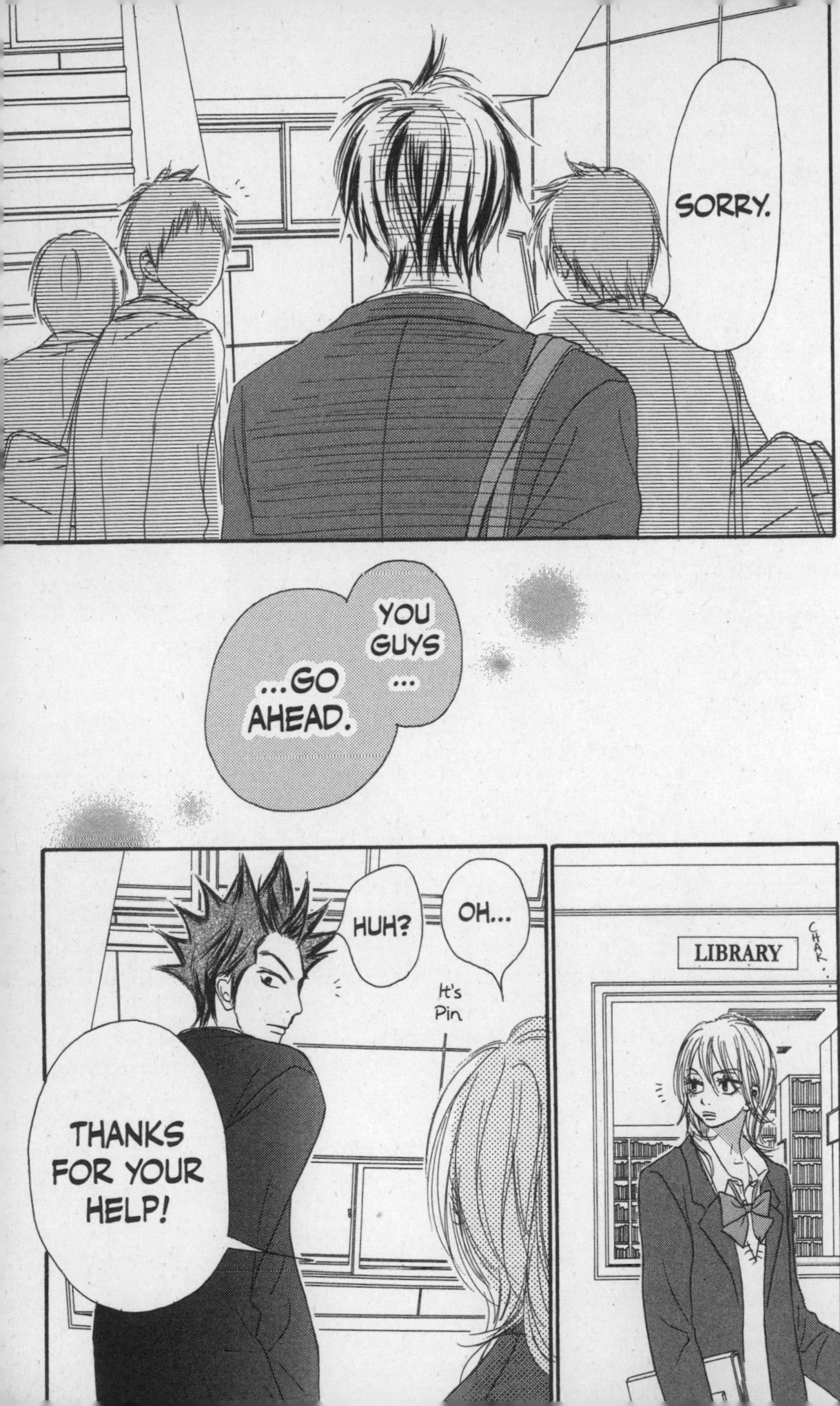
SORRY.
YOU GUYS ...
...GO AHEAD.
LIBRARY
CHAK
OH...
HUH?
It's Pin
THANKS FOR YOUR HELP!

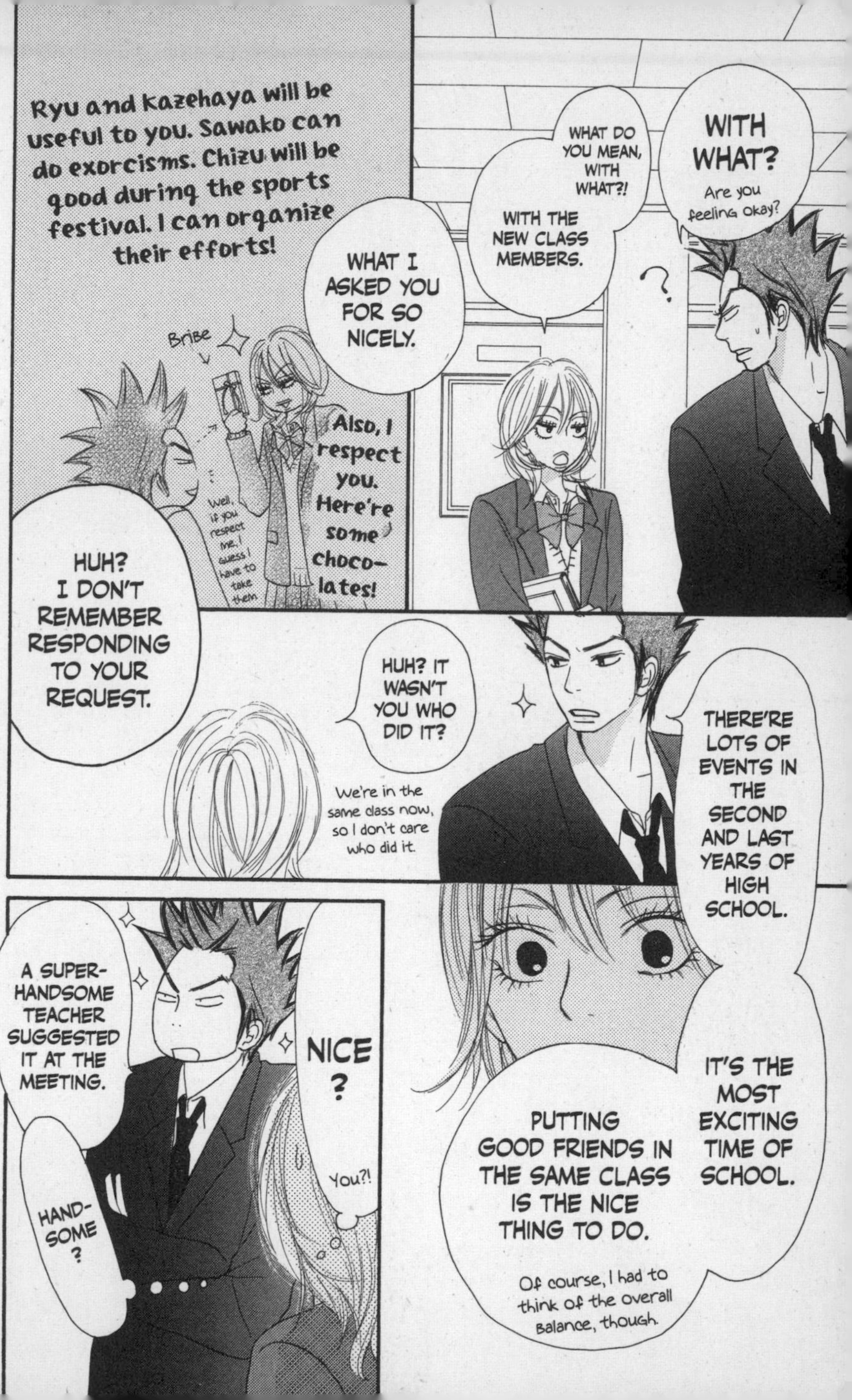
WITH WHAT?
Are you feeling okay?
WHAT DO YOU MEAN, WITH WHAT?!
WITH THE NEW CLASS MEMBERS.
WHAT I ASKED YOU FOR SO NICELY.
Ryu and Kazehaya will be useful to you. Sawako can do exorcisms. Chizu will be good during the sports festival. I can organize their efforts!
Bribe
Also, I respect you. Here're some chocolates!
Well, if you respect me, I guess I have to take them
HUH? I DON'T REMEMBER RESPONDING TO YOUR REQUEST.
HUH? IT WASN'T YOU WHO DID IT?
We're in the same class now, so I don't care who did it.
THERE'RE LOTS OF EVENTS IN THE SECOND AND LAST YEARS OF HIGH SCHOOL.
IT'S THE MOST EXCITING TIME OF SCHOOL.
PUTTING GOOD FRIENDS IN THE SAME CLASS IS THE NICE THING TO DO.
Of course, I had to think of the overall balance, though.
A SUPER-HANDSOME TEACHER SUGGESTED IT AT THE MEETING.
NICE?
You?!
HAND-SOME?

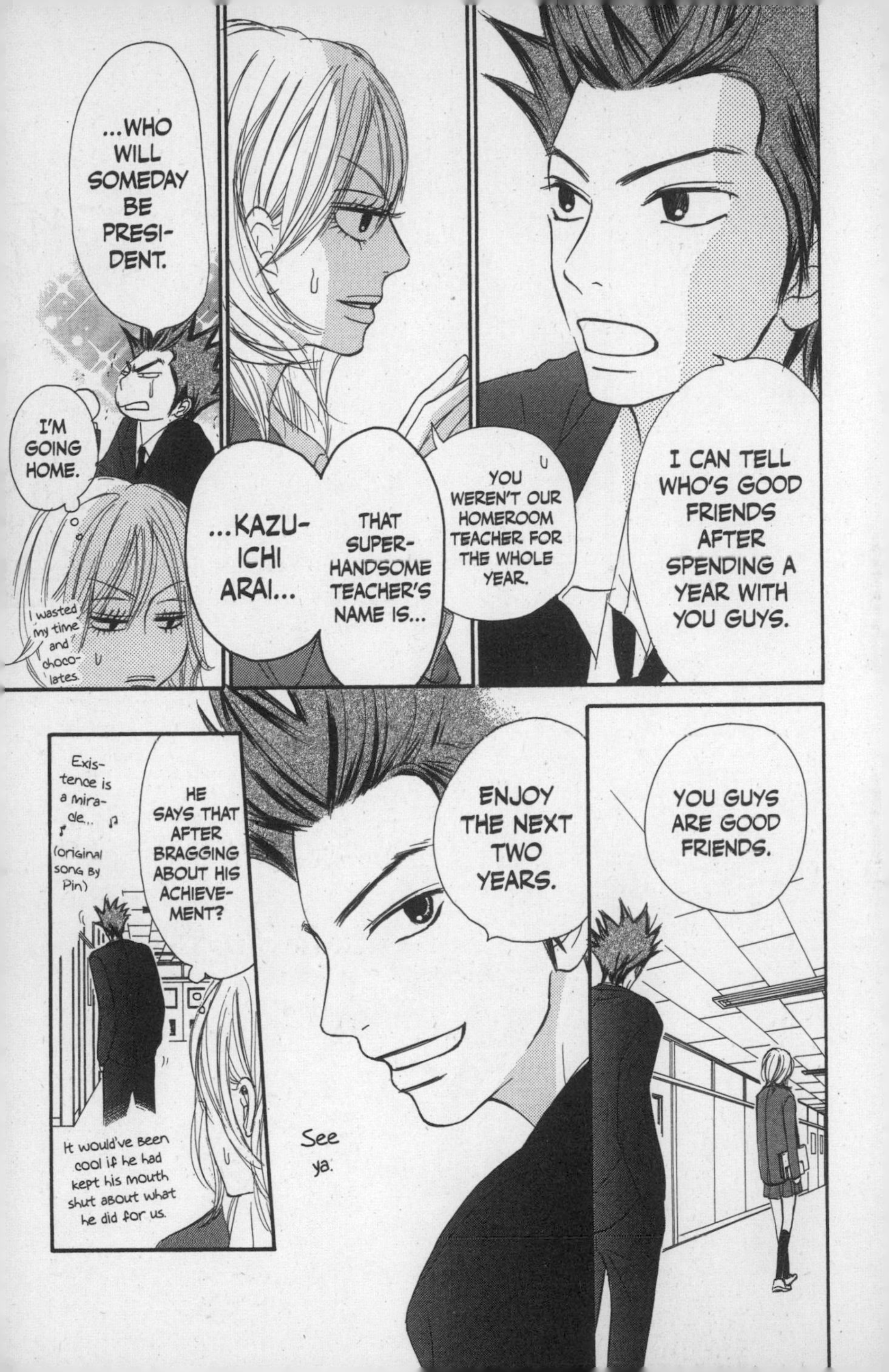
I CAN TELL WHO'S GOOD FRIENDS AFTER SPENDING A YEAR WITH YOU GUYS.
YOU WEREN'T OUR HOMEROOM TEACHER FOR THE WHOLE YEAR.
THAT SUPER-HANDSOME TEACHER'S NAME IS...
...KAZUICHI ARAI...
...WHO WILL SOMEDAY BE PRESIDENT.
I'M GOING HOME.
I wasted my time and chocolates.
YOU GUYS ARE GOOD FRIENDS.
ENJOY THE NEXT TWO YEARS.
See ya.
HE SAYS THAT AFTER BRAGGING ABOUT HIS ACHIEVEMENT?
Existence is a miracle... (original song by Pin)
It would've been cool if he had kept his mouth shut about what he did for us.

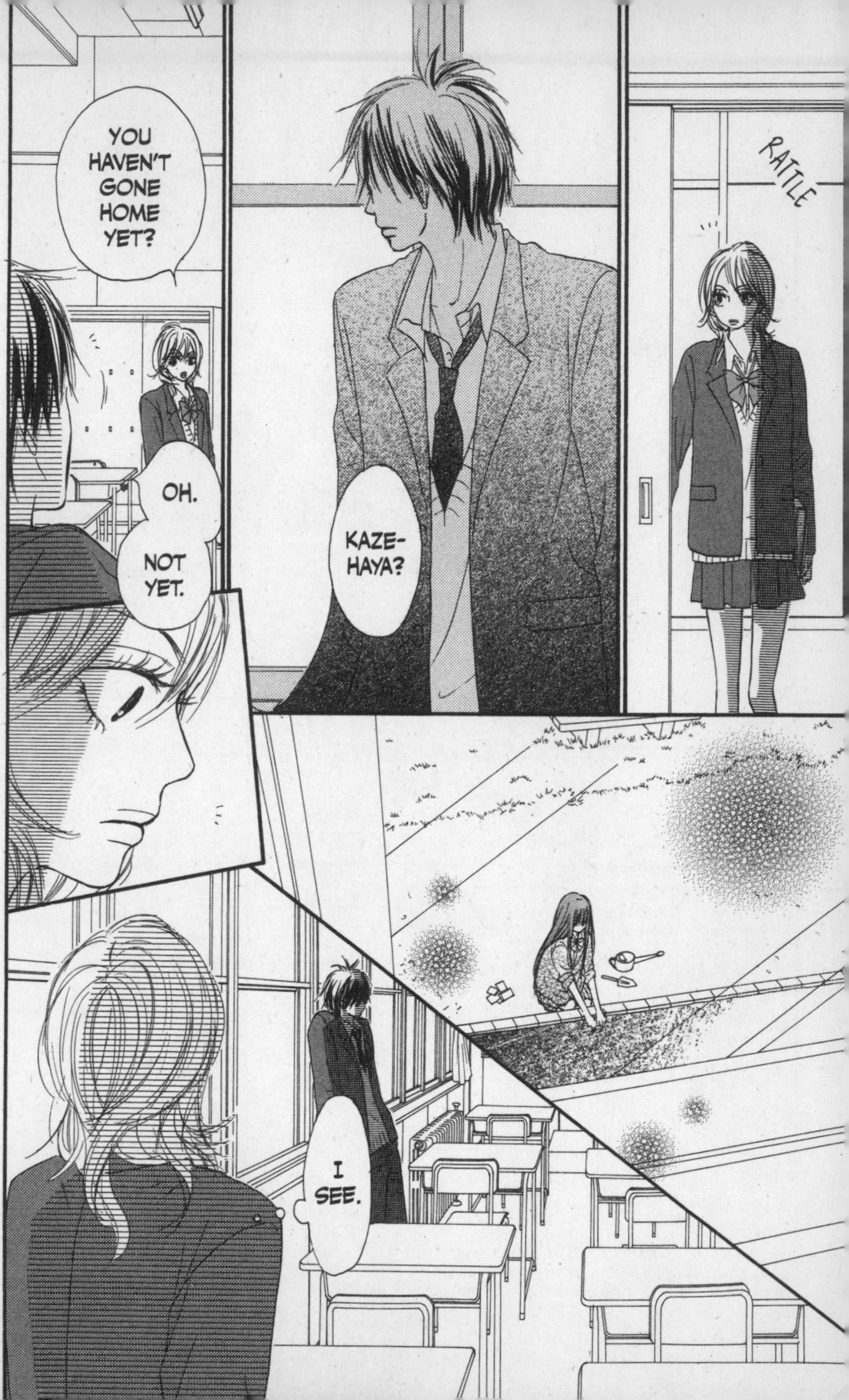
RATTLE
KAZE-HAYA?
YOU HAVEN'T GONE HOME YET?
OH.
NOT YET.
I SEE.

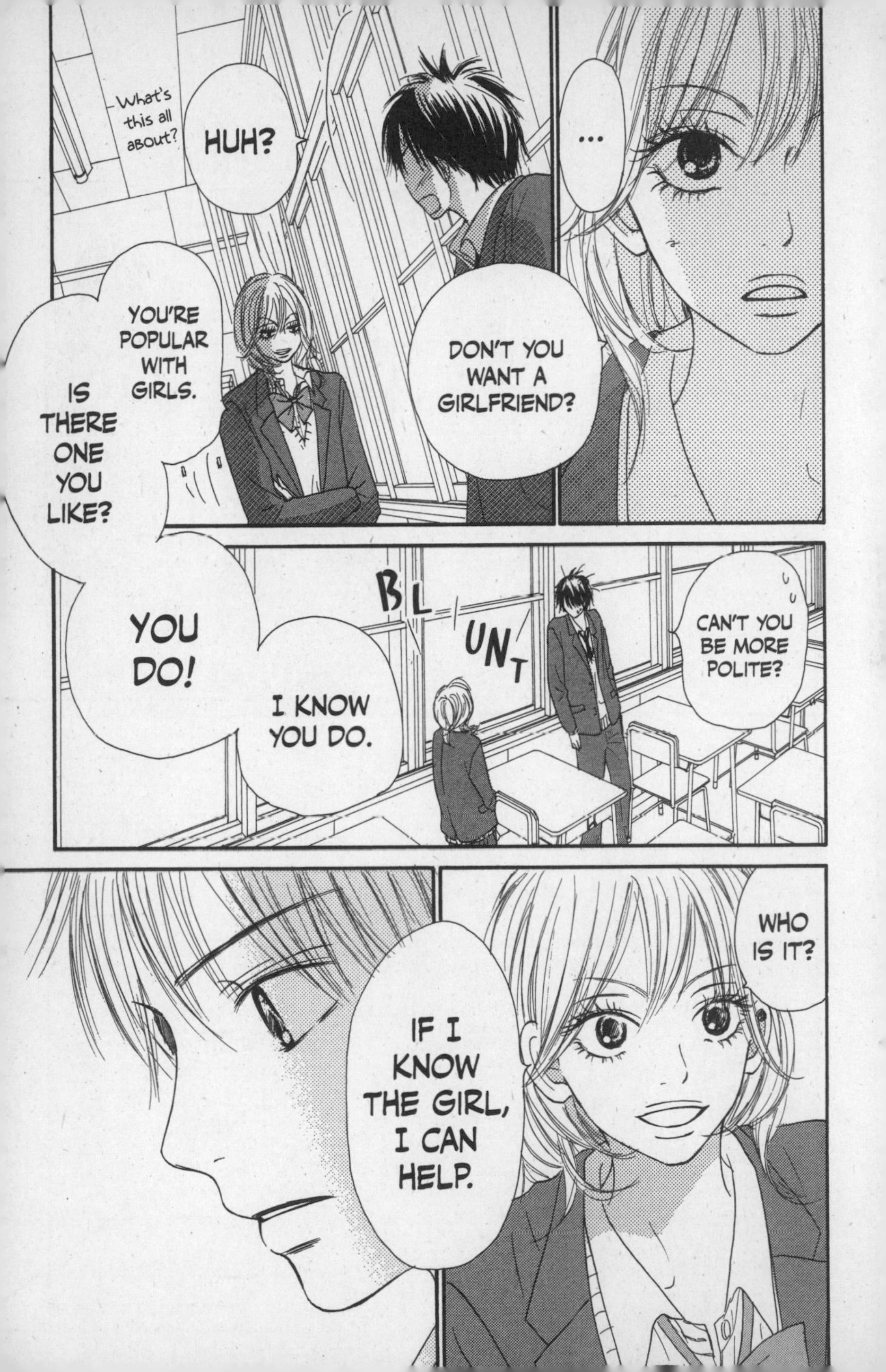
...
HUH?
What's this all about?
DON'T YOU WANT A GIRLFRIEND?
YOU'RE POPULAR WITH GIRLS.
IS THERE ONE YOU LIKE?
CAN'T YOU BE MORE POLITE?
BLUNT
YOU DO!
I KNOW YOU DO.
WHO IS IT?
IF I KNOW THE GIRL, I CAN HELP.

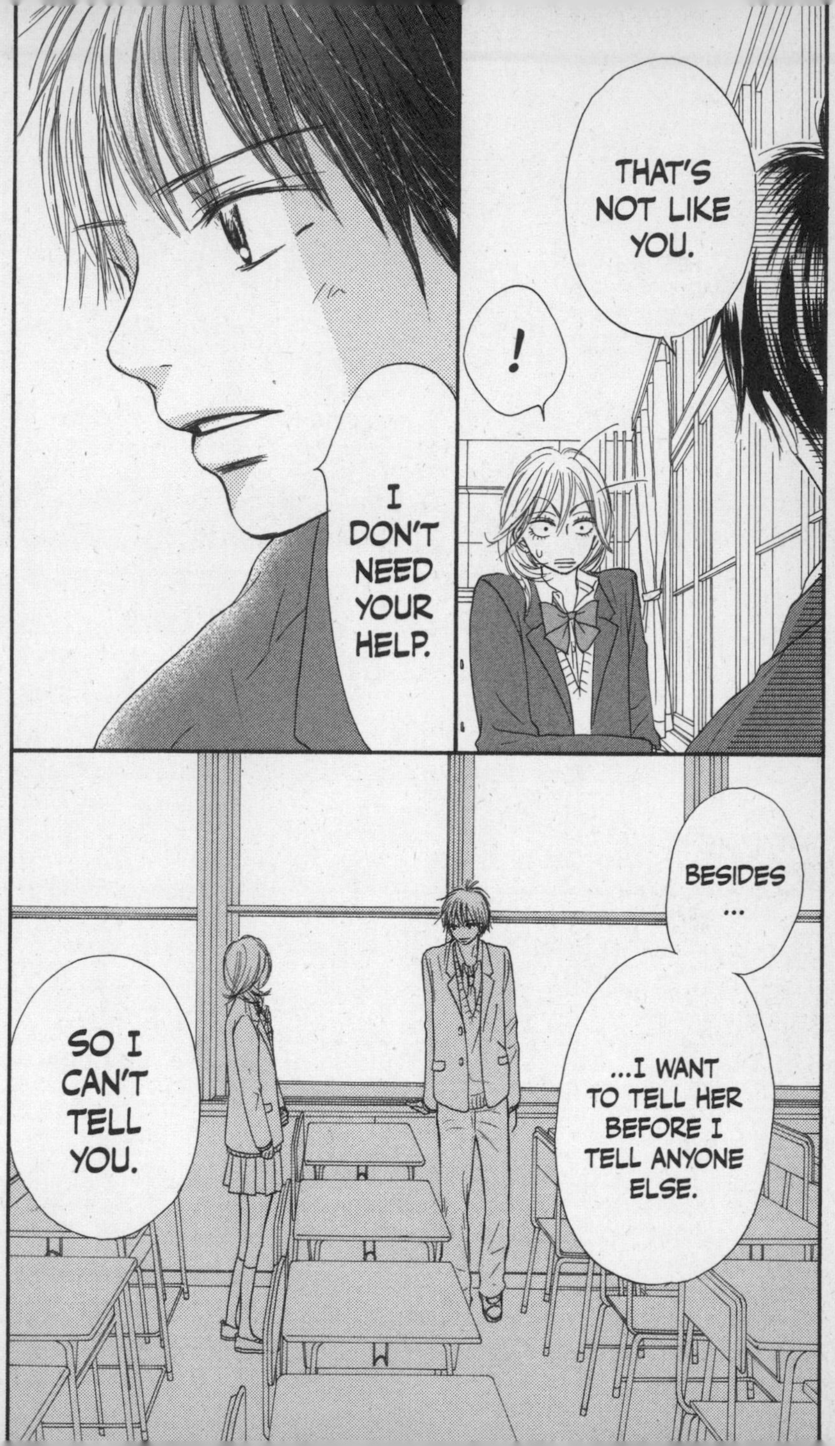
THAT'S NOT LIKE YOU.
!
I DON'T NEED YOUR HELP.
BESIDES ...
...I WANT TO TELL HER BEFORE I TELL ANYONE ELSE.
SO I CAN'T TELL YOU.

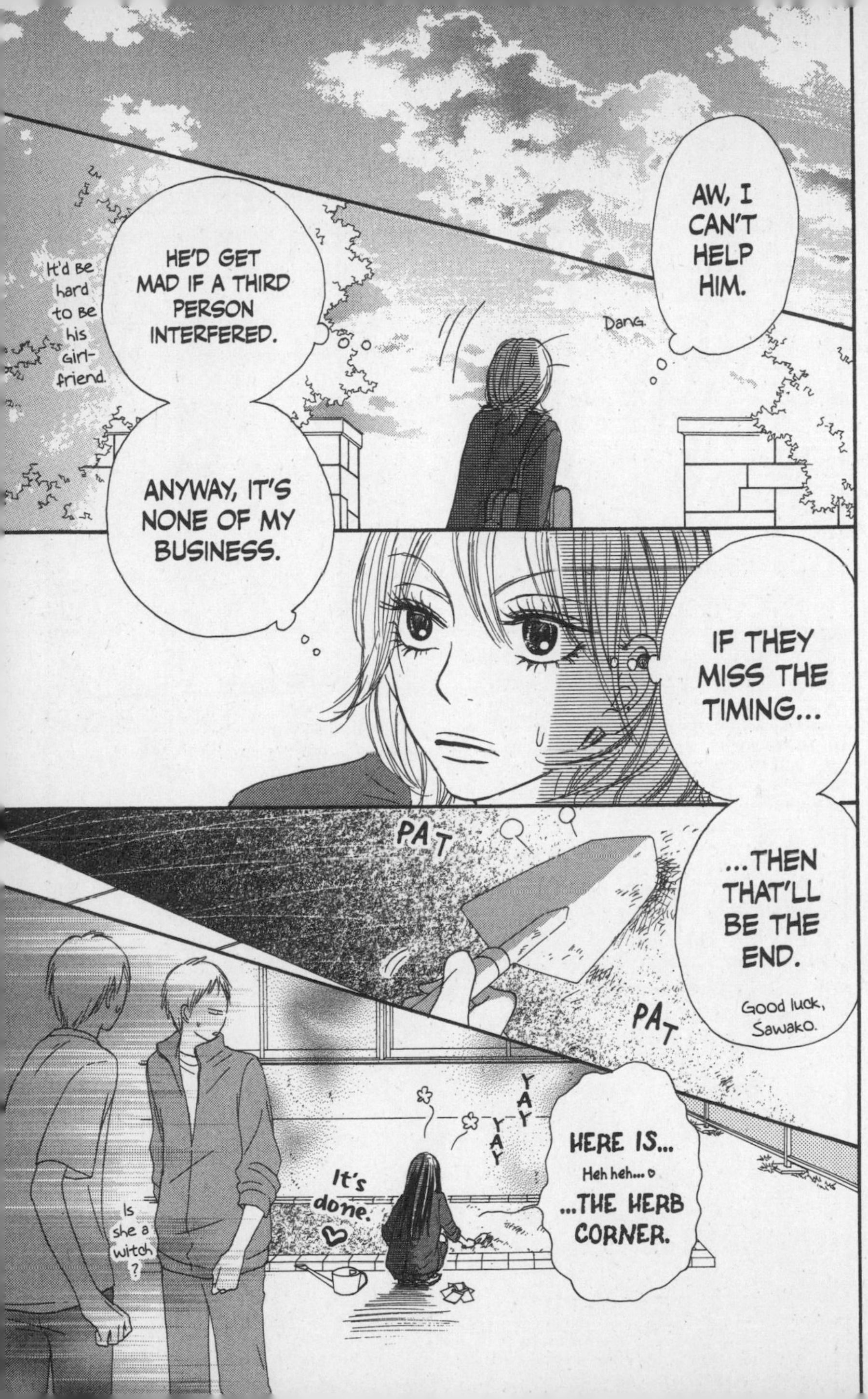
AW, I CAN'T HELP HIM.
Dang.
HE'D GET MAD IF A THIRD PERSON INTERFERED.
It'd be hard to be his girl-friend.
ANYWAY, IT'S NONE OF MY BUSINESS.
IF THEY MISS THE TIMING...
...THEN THAT'LL BE THE END.
Good luck, Sawako.
PAT
PAT
HERE IS...
Heh heh...
...THE HERB CORNER.
YAY
YAY
It's done.
Is she a witch?

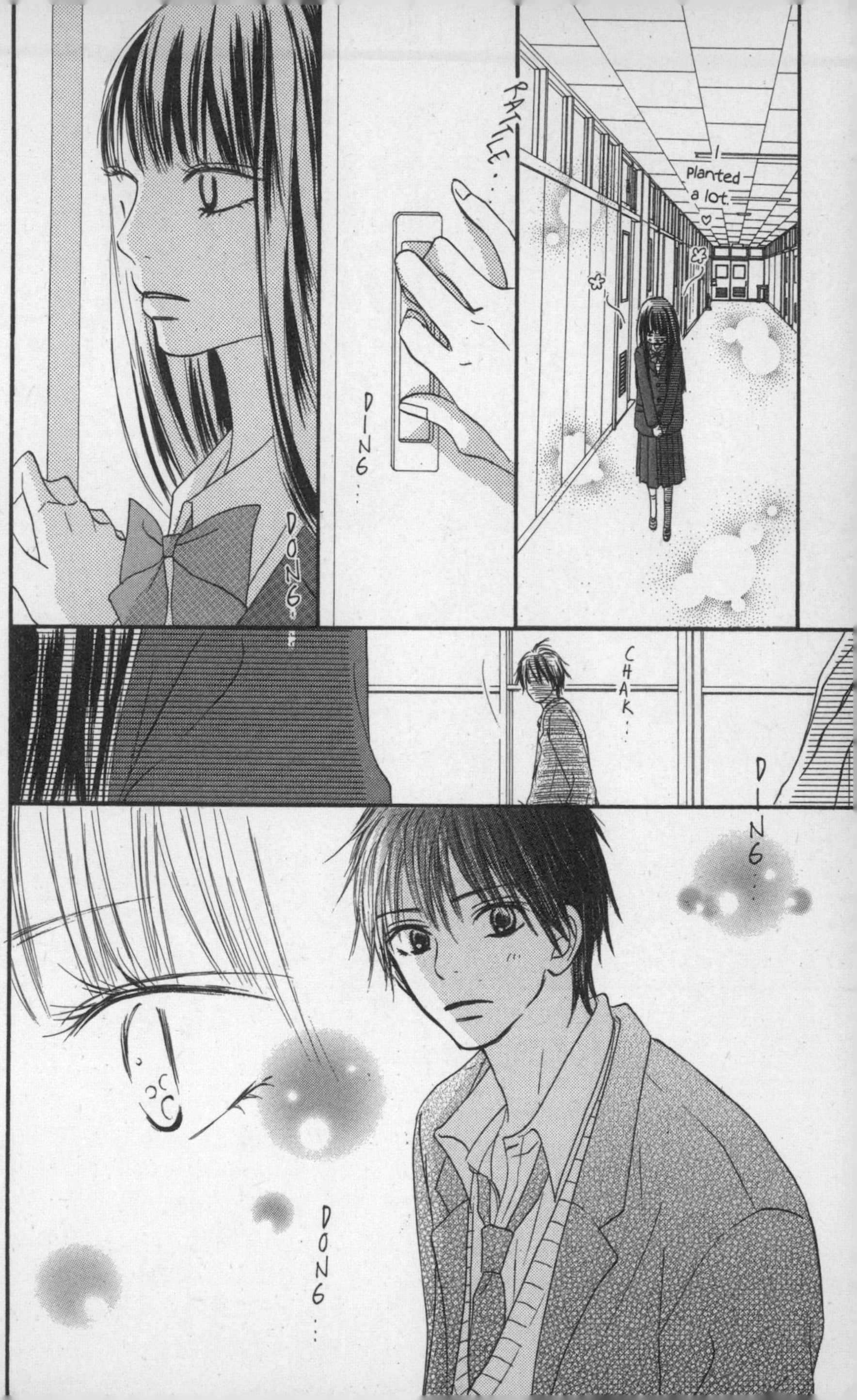
I planted a lot.
RATTLE...
DING...
DONG...
CHAK...
DING...
DONG...

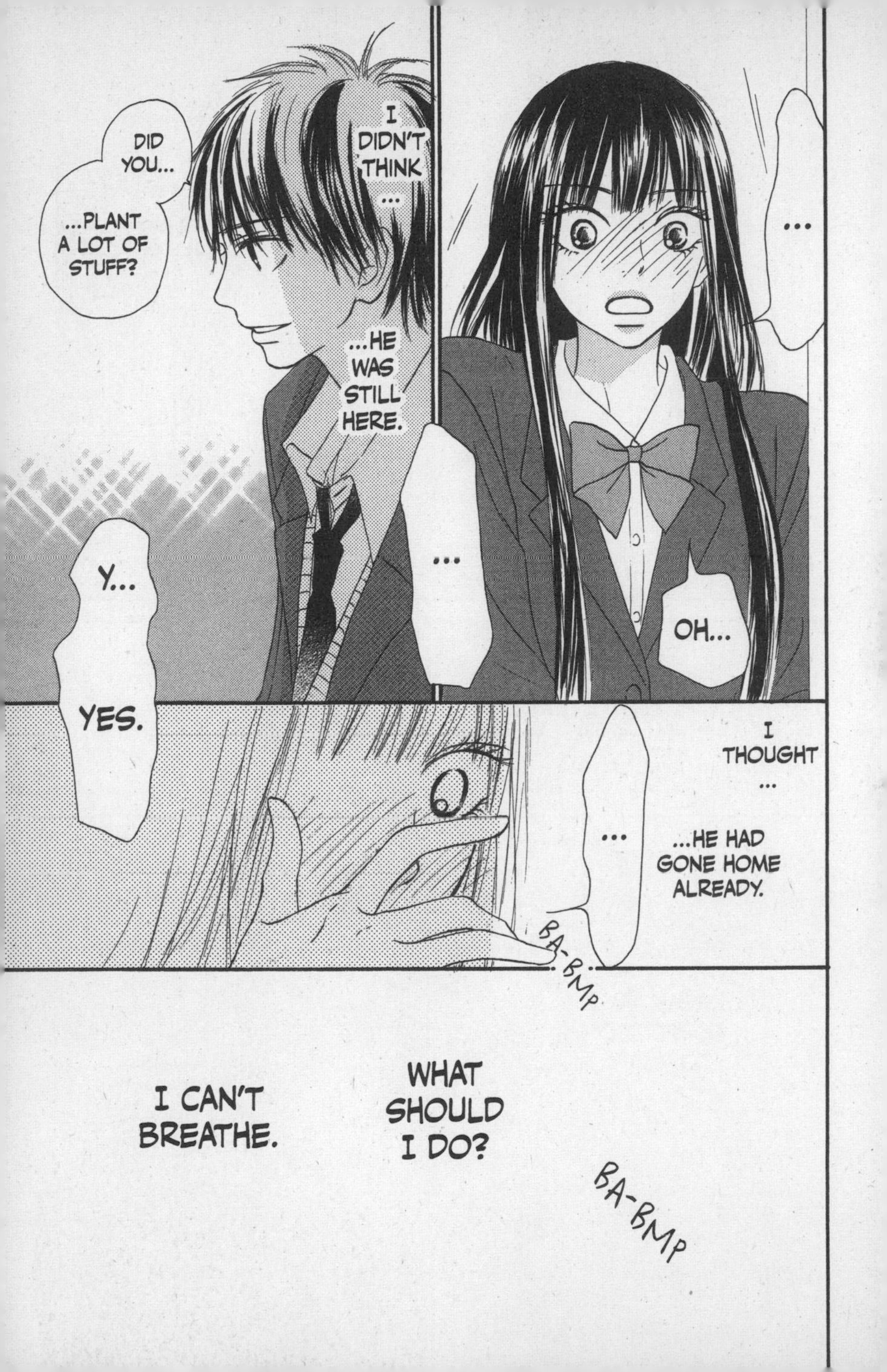
...
OH...
...
I DIDN'T THINK ...
...HE WAS STILL HERE.
DID YOU...
...PLANT A LOT OF STUFF?
Y...
I THOUGHT ...
...HE HAD GONE HOME ALREADY.
...
BA-BMP
YES.
WHAT SHOULD I DO?
I CAN'T BREATHE.
BA-BMP

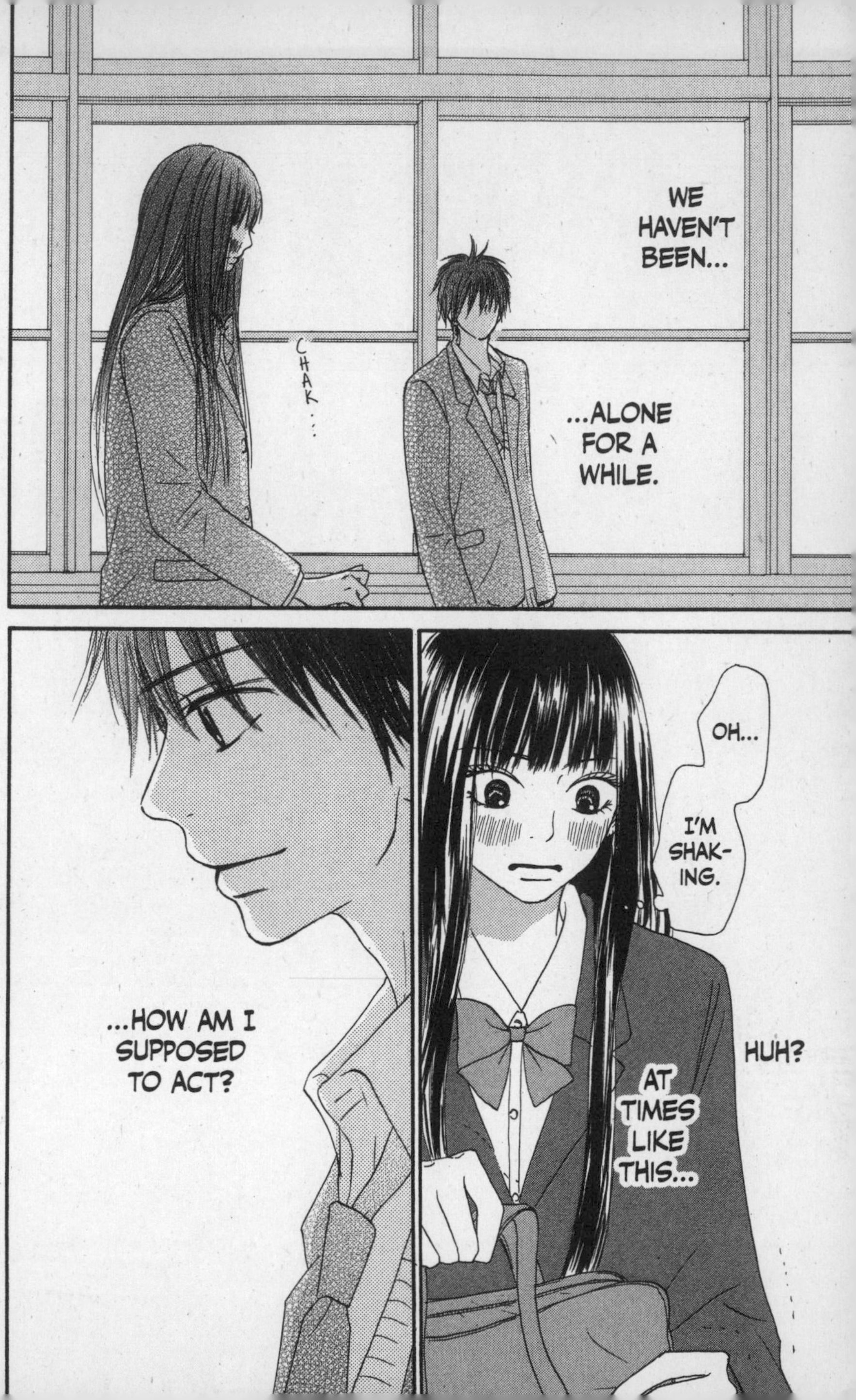
WE HAVEN'T BEEN...
...ALONE FOR A WHILE.
CHAK...
OH...
I'M SHAK-ING.
HUH?
AT TIMES LIKE THIS...
...HOW AM I SUPPOSED TO ACT?

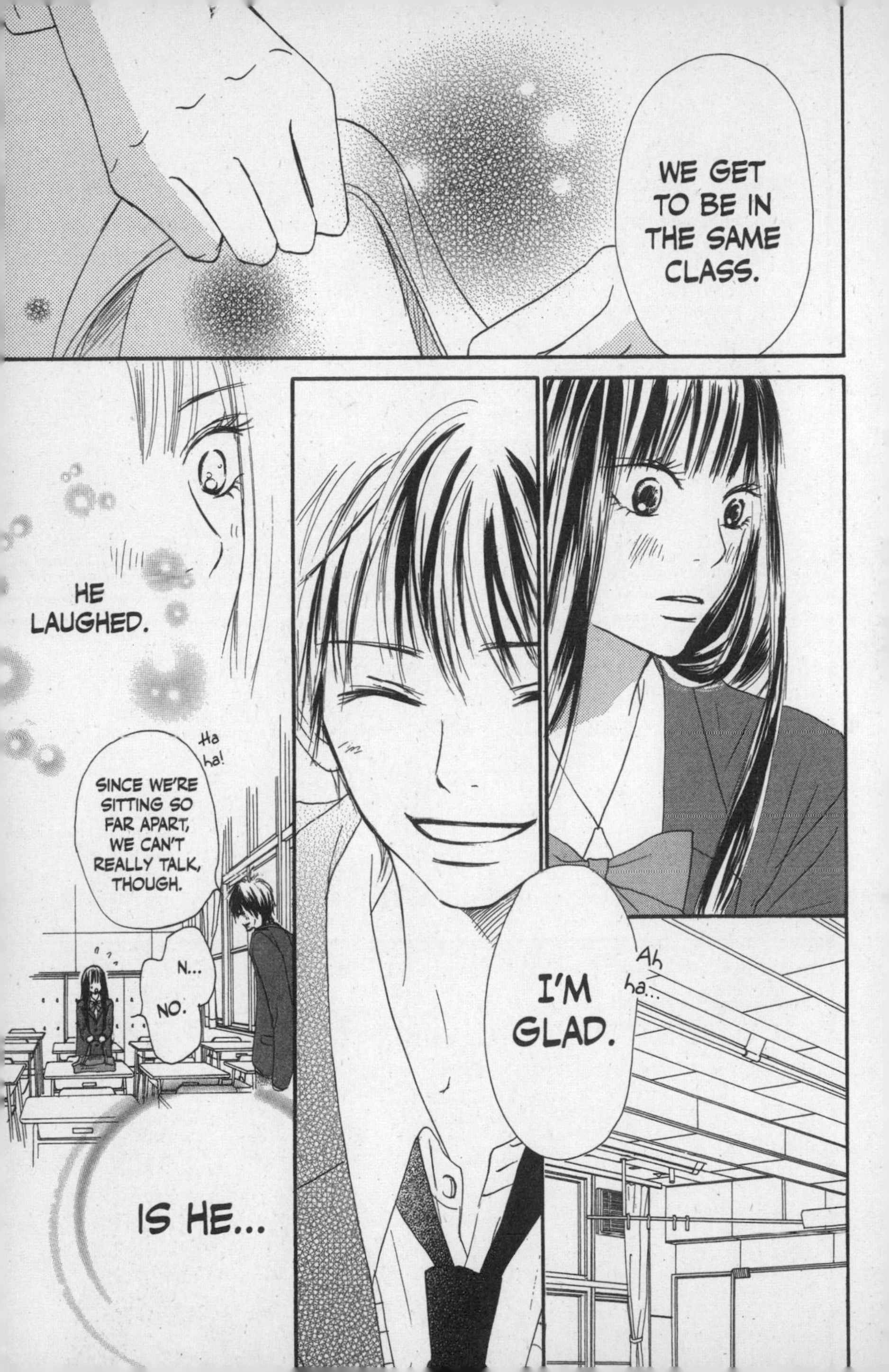
WE GET TO BE IN THE SAME CLASS.
Ah ha...
I'M GLAD.
HE LAUGHED.
Ha ha!
SINCE WE'RE SITTING SO FAR APART, WE CAN'T REALLY TALK, THOUGH.
N... NO.
IS HE...

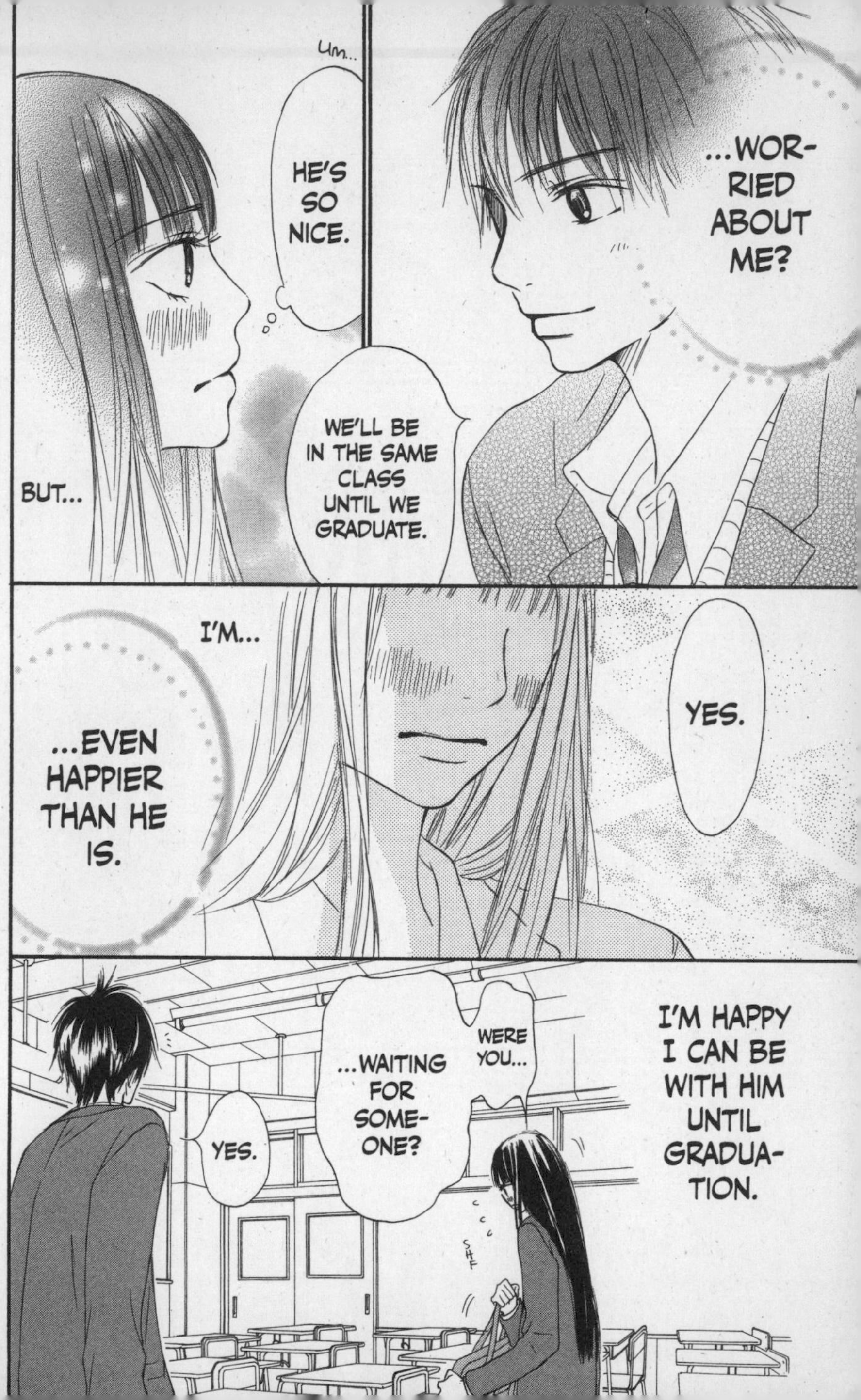
...WORRIED ABOUT ME?
WE'LL BE IN THE SAME CLASS UNTIL WE GRADUATE.
Um...
HE'S SO NICE.
BUT...
YES.
I'M...
...EVEN HAPPIER THAN HE IS.
I'M HAPPY I CAN BE WITH HIM UNTIL GRADUATION.
WERE YOU...
...WAITING FOR SOMEONE?
YES.
SHF

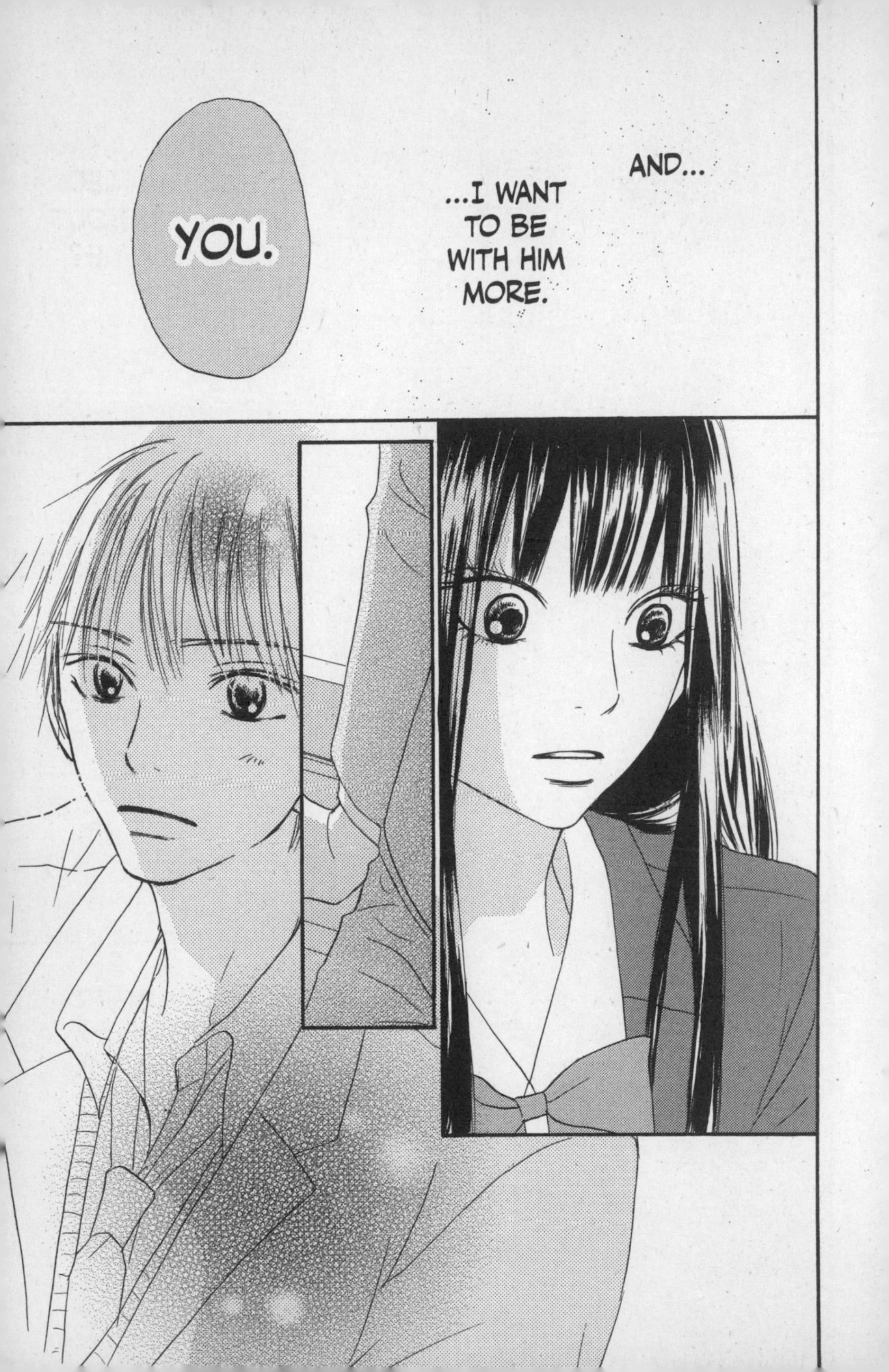
AND...
...I WANT TO BE WITH HIM MORE.
YOU.

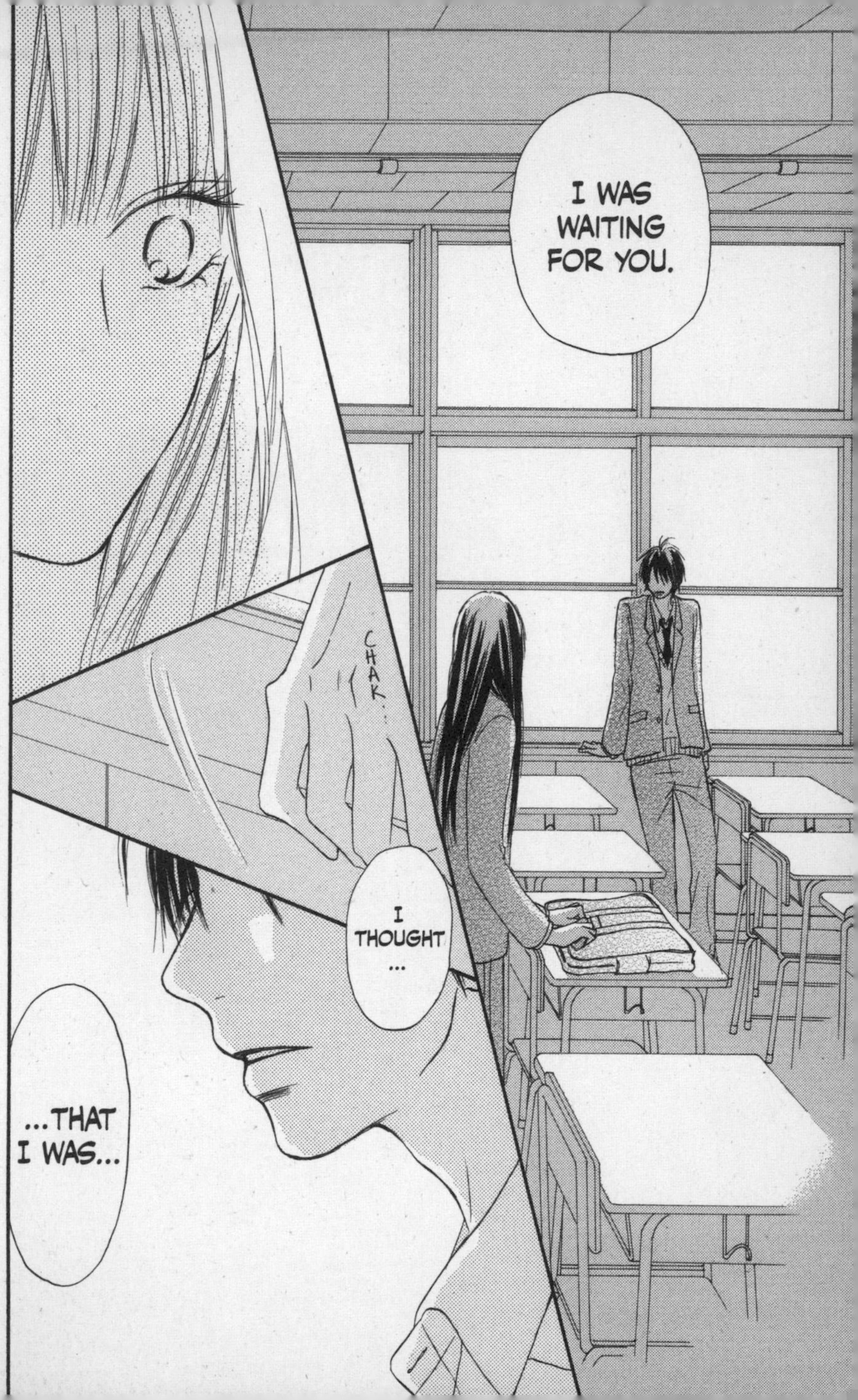
I WAS WAITING FOR YOU.
CHAK...
I THOUGHT...
...THAT I WAS...

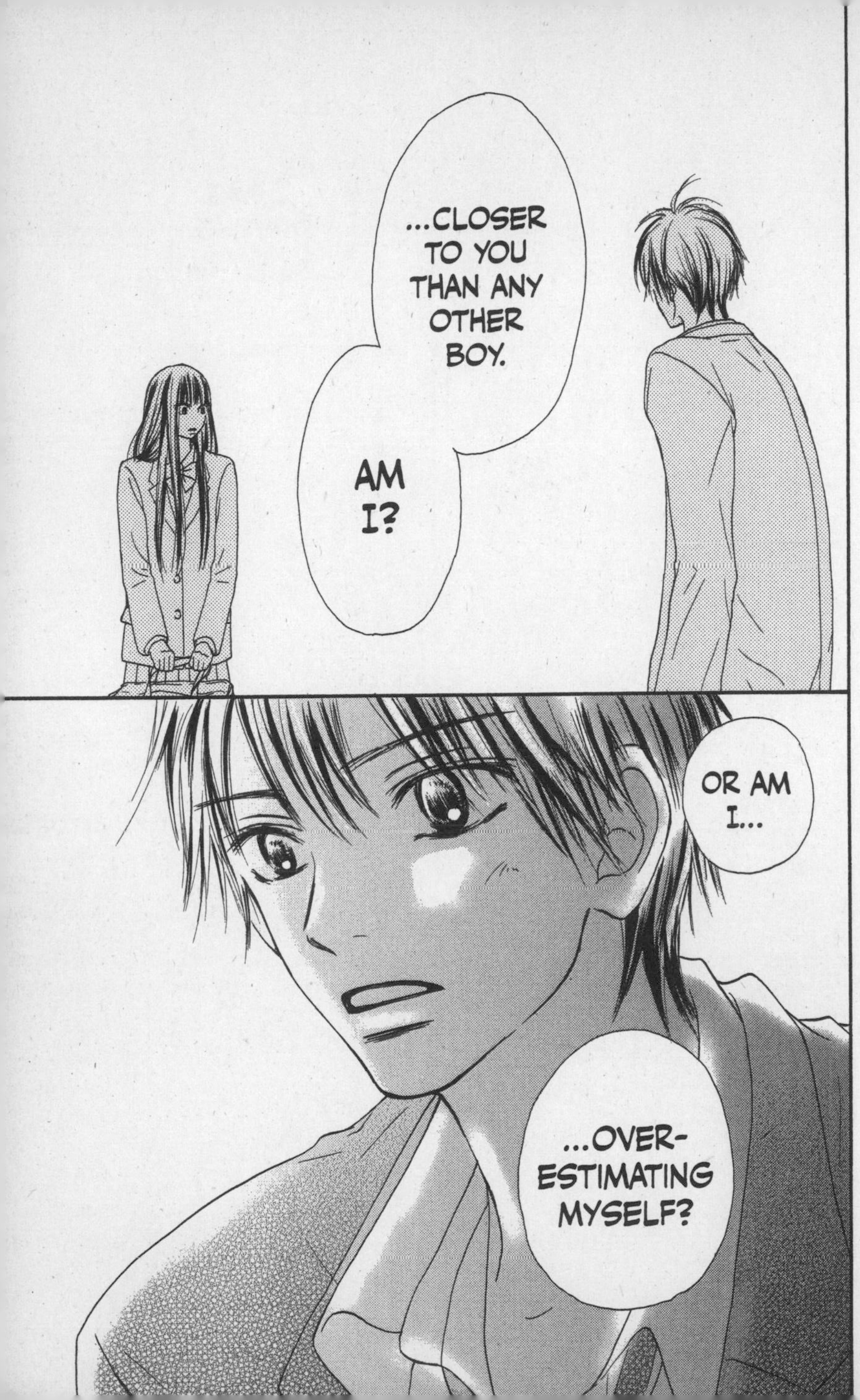
...CLOSER TO YOU THAN ANY OTHER BOY.
AM I?
OR AM I...
...OVER-ESTIMATING MYSELF?

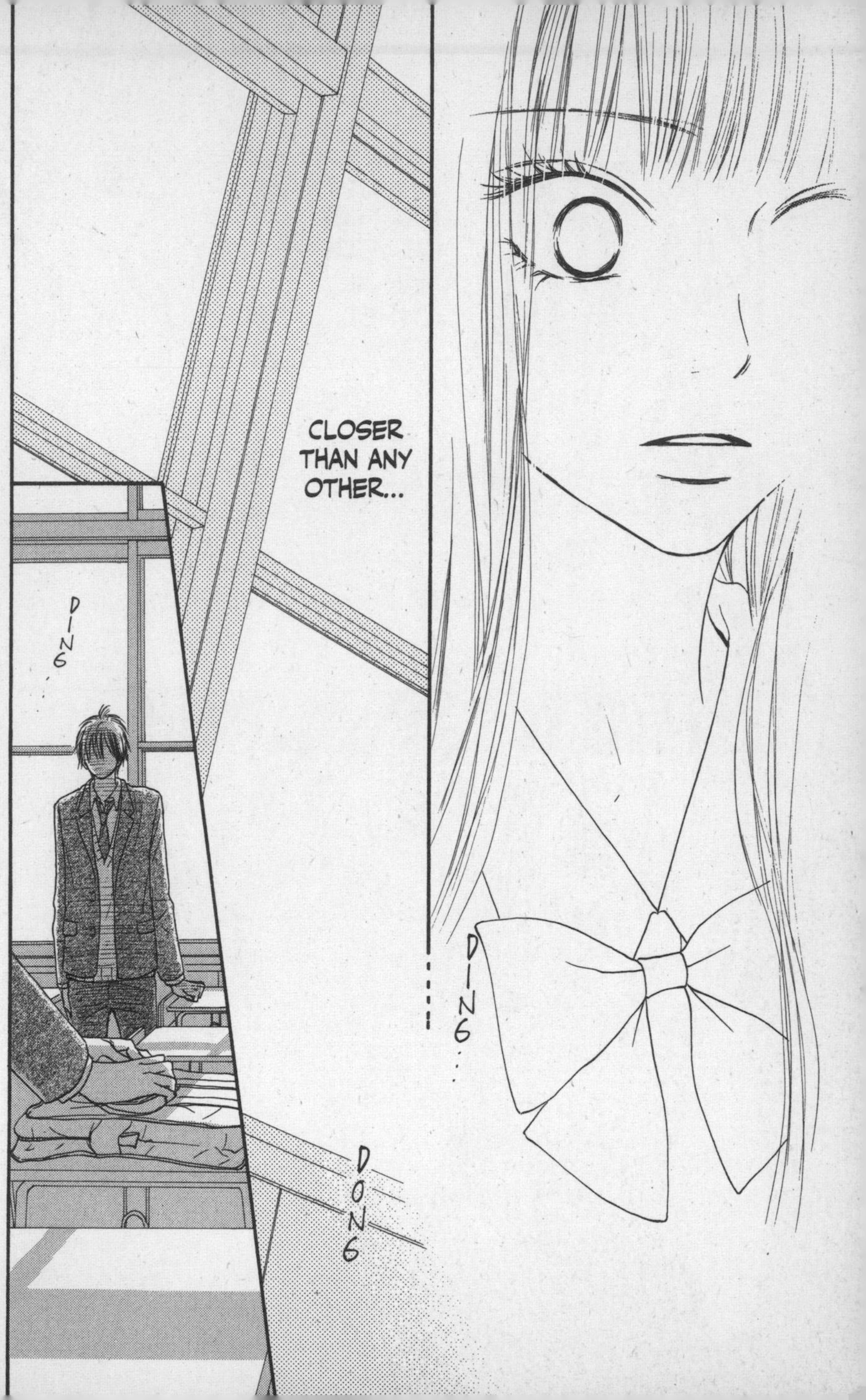

DING..
CLOSER THAN ANY OTHER...
DING..
DONG

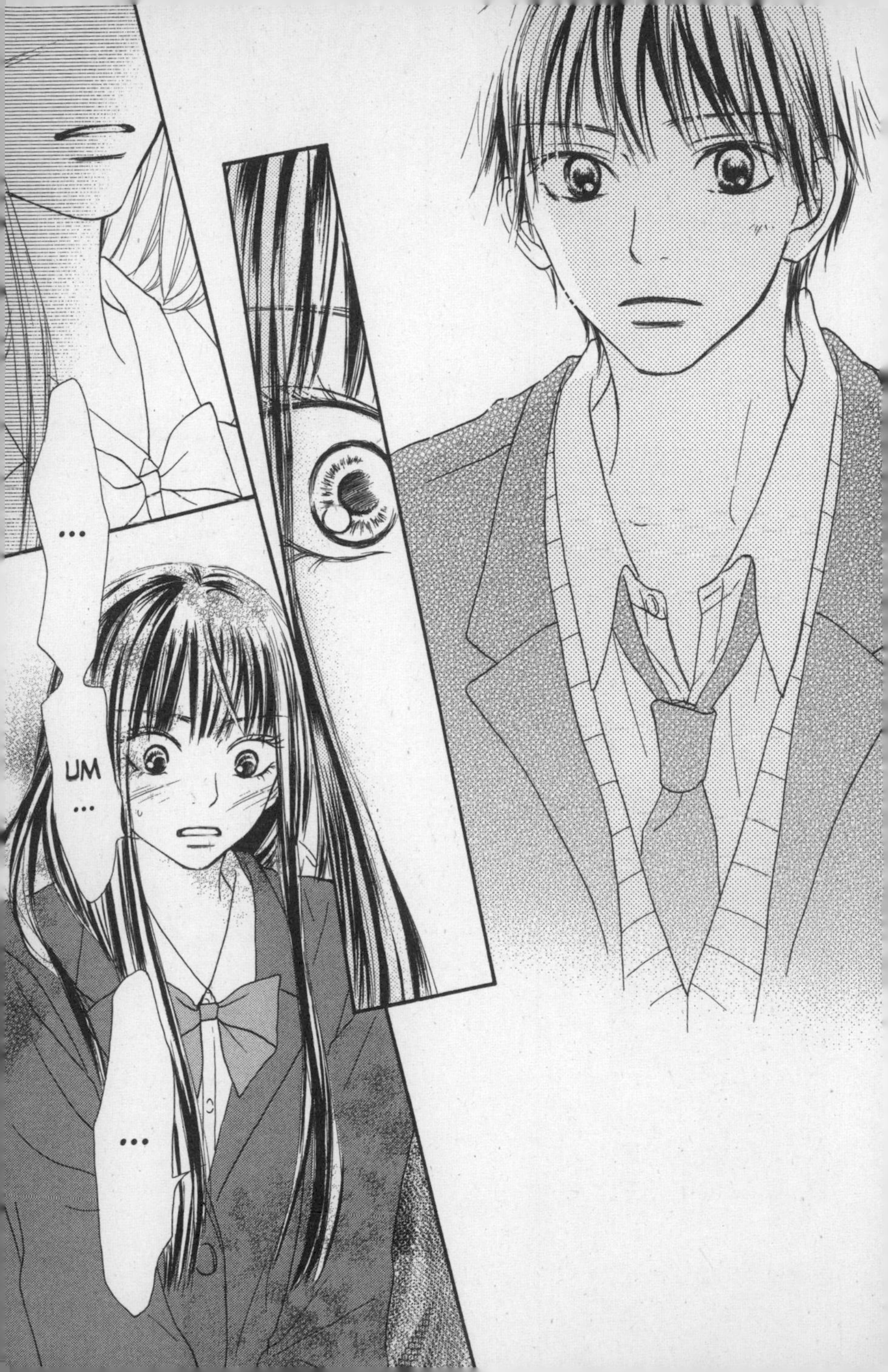
...
UM ...
...

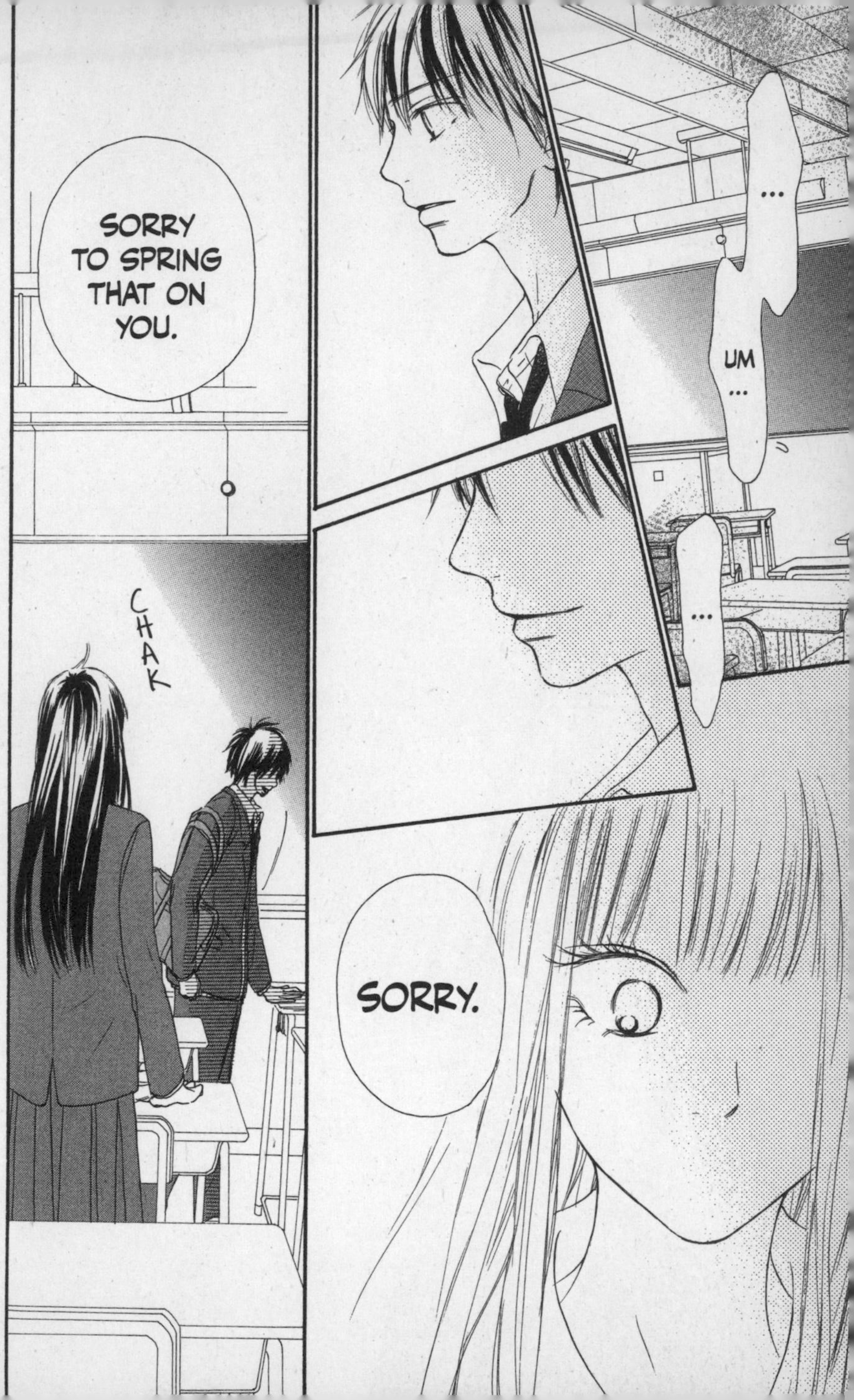
...
UM ...
...
SORRY.
SORRY TO SPRING THAT ON YOU.
CHAK

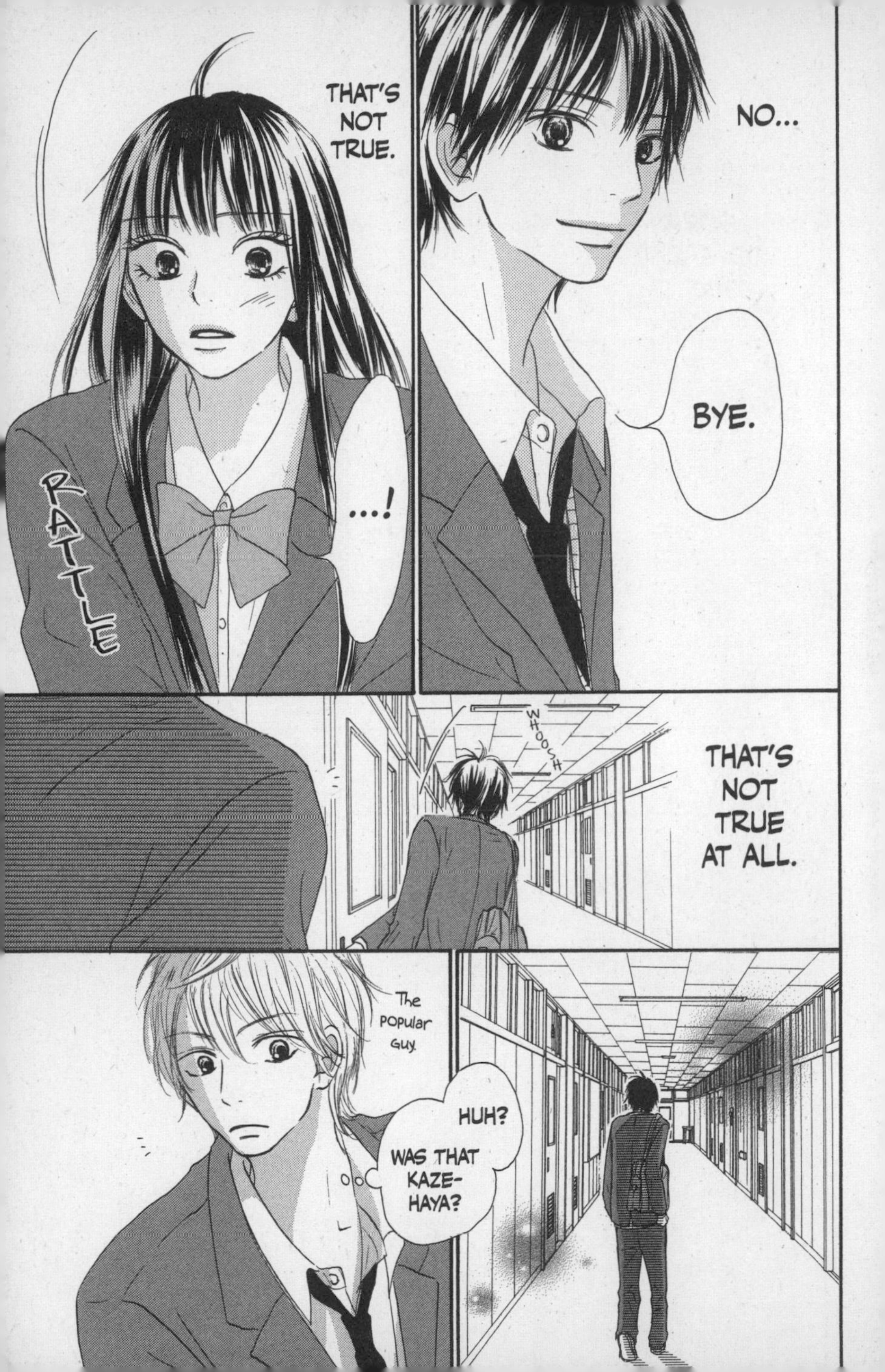
NO...
BYE.
THAT'S NOT TRUE.
...!
RATTLE
THAT'S NOT TRUE AT ALL.
WHOOSH
HUH?
WAS THAT KAZE-HAYA?
The popular guy.

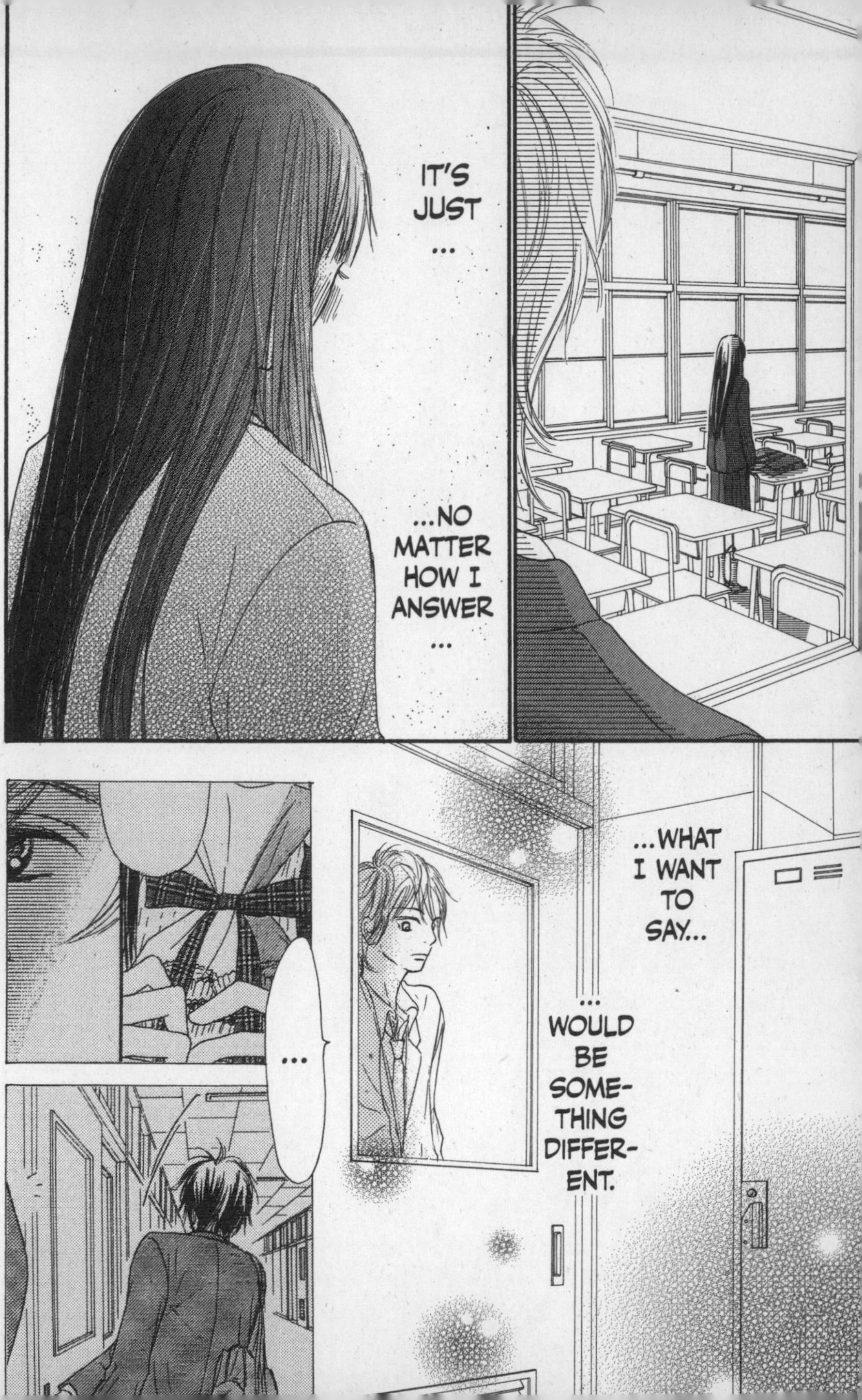
IT'S JUST ...
...NO MATTER HOW I ANSWER ...
...WHAT I WANT TO SAY...
...WOULD BE SOME-THING DIFFER-ENT.
...

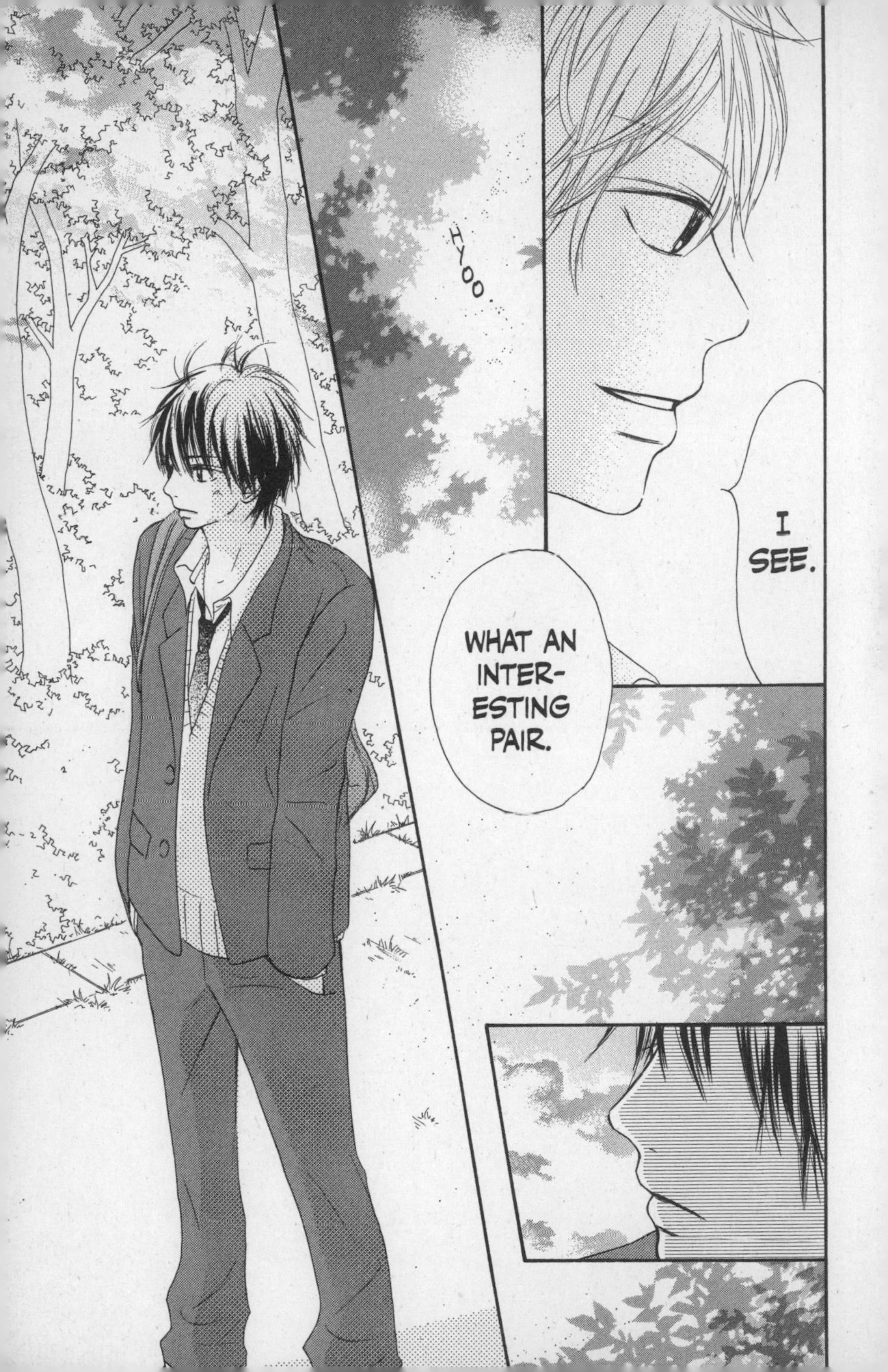
I SEE.
WHAT AN INTER-ESTING PAIR.
HYOO...

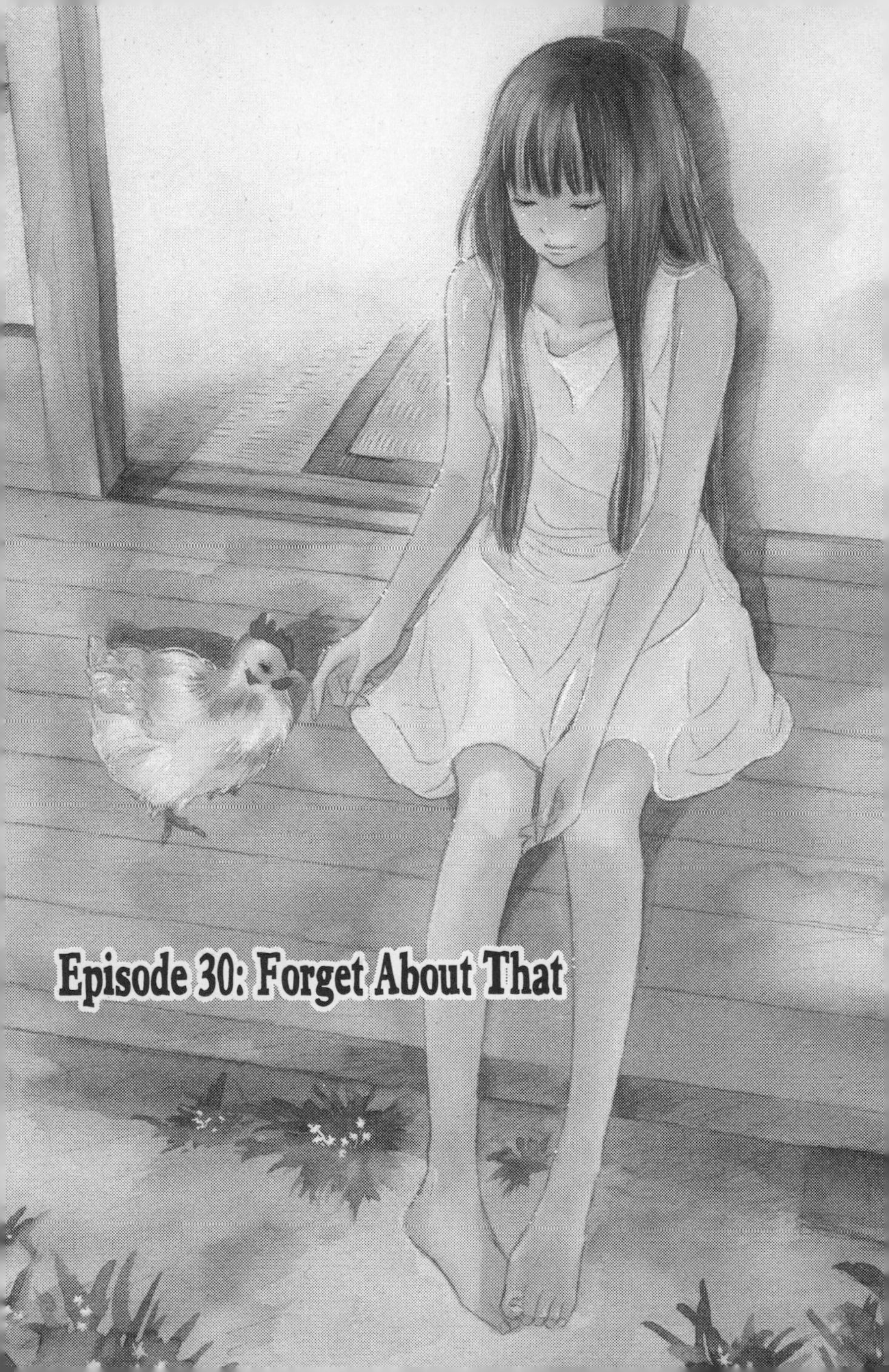
Episode 30: Forget About That

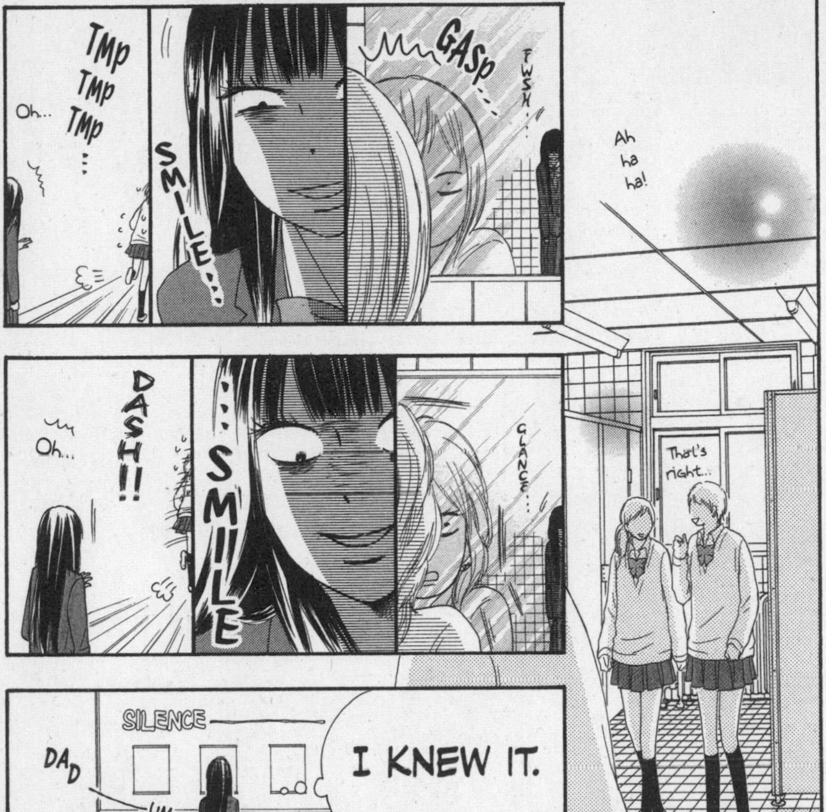
Ah ha ha!
That's right...
GASp...
FWSH...
SMILE...
TMp TMp TMp...
Oh...
GLANCE...
SMILE
DASH!!
Oh...
I KNEW IT.
SILENCE
DAD
UM...

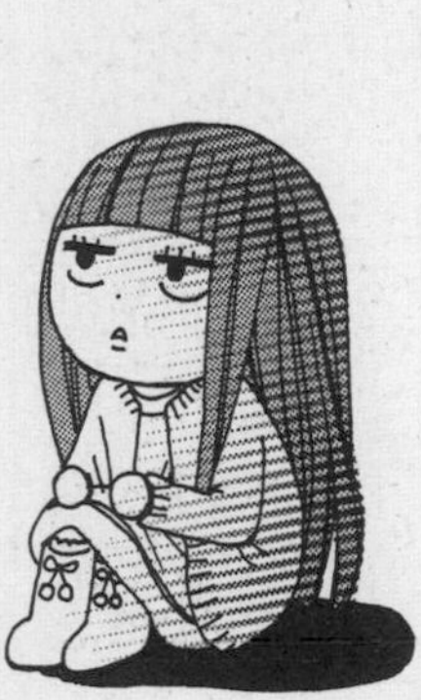

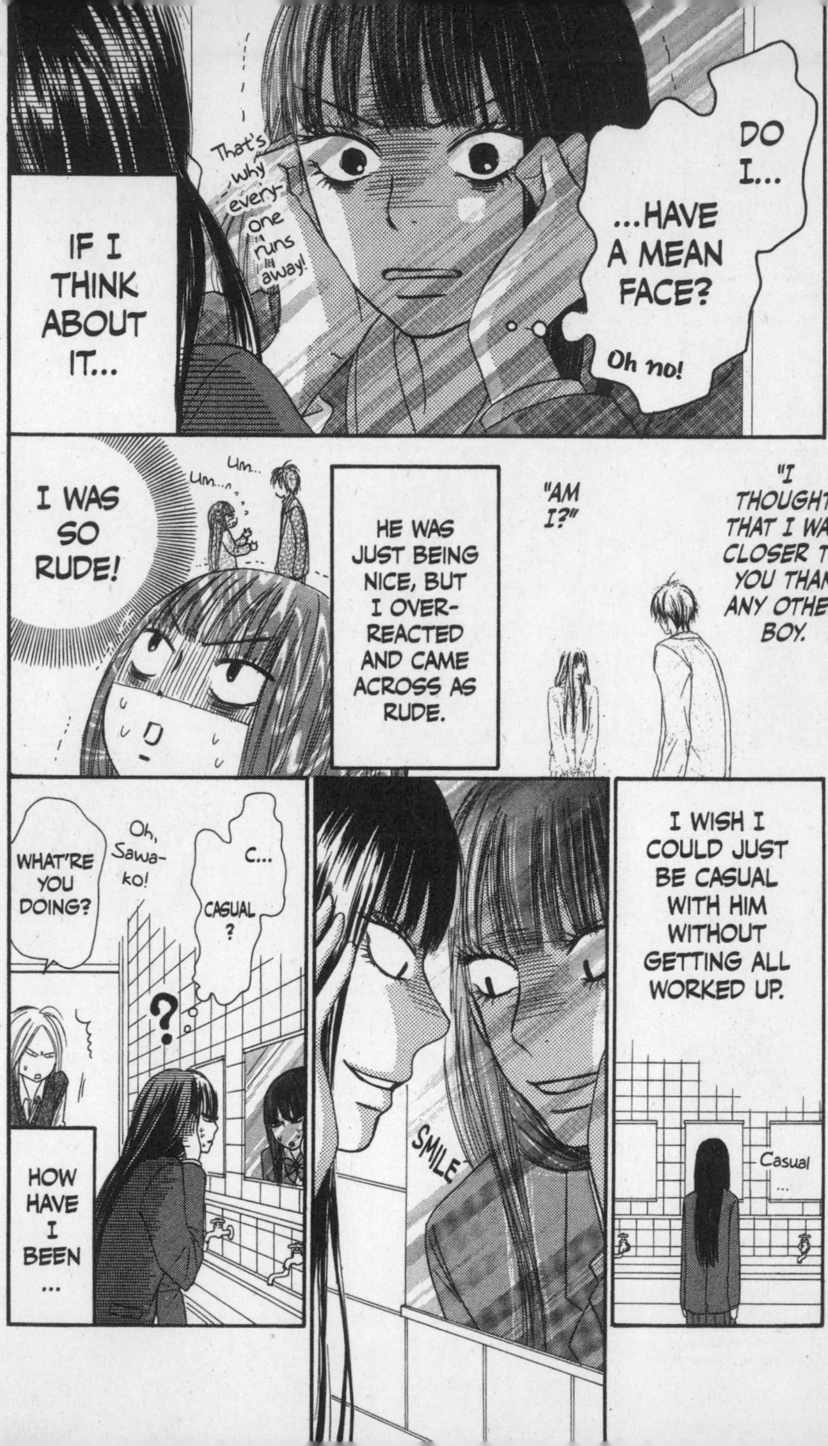
DO I...
...HAVE A MEAN FACE?
That's why every-one runs away!
Oh no!
IF I THINK ABOUT IT...
"I THOUGHT THAT I WAS CLOSER TO YOU THAN ANY OTHER BOY.
"AM I?"
HE WAS JUST BEING NICE, BUT I OVER-REACTED AND CAME ACROSS AS RUDE.
Um...
Um...
I WAS SO RUDE!
I WISH I COULD JUST BE CASUAL WITH HIM WITHOUT GETTING ALL WORKED UP.
Casual ...
SMILE
C...
CASUAL ?
Oh, Sawa-ko!
WHAT'RE YOU DOING?
?
HOW HAVE I BEEN ...

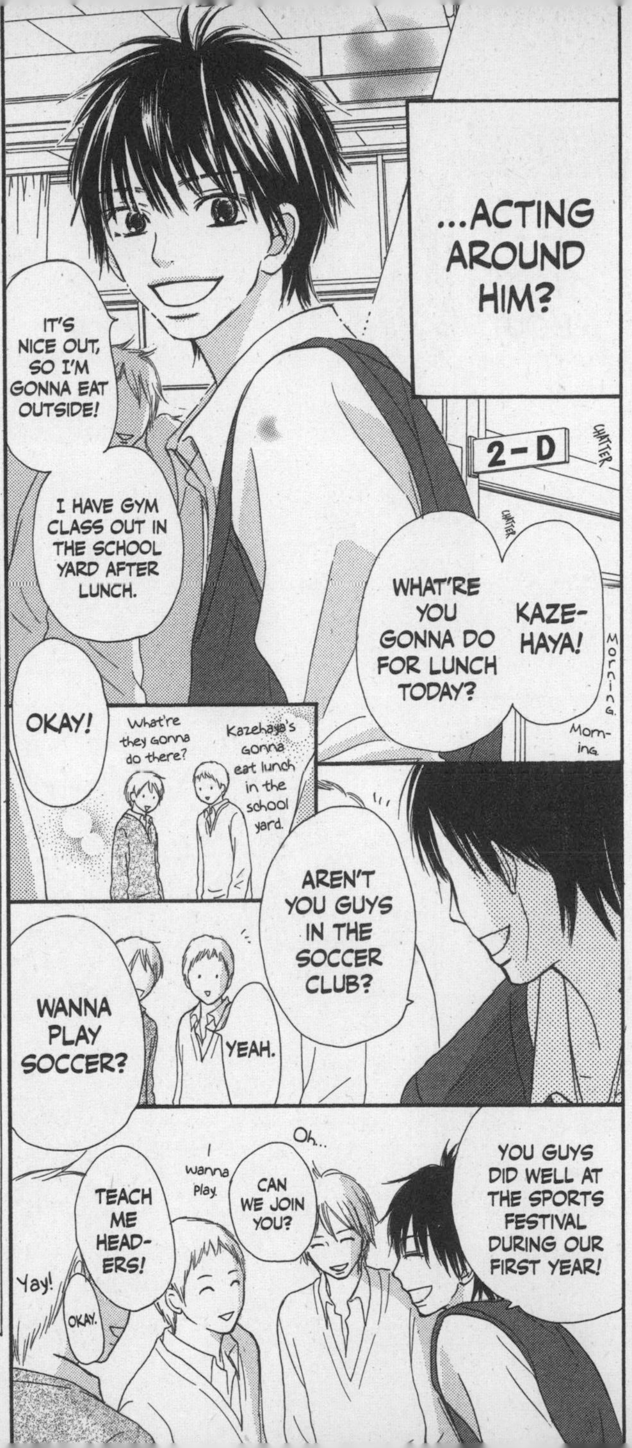
...ACTING AROUND HIM?
2-D
CHATTER
CHATTER
Morning.
Morning.
KAZEHAYA!
WHAT'RE YOU GONNA DO FOR LUNCH TODAY?
IT'S NICE OUT, SO I'M GONNA EAT OUTSIDE!
I HAVE GYM CLASS OUT IN THE SCHOOL YARD AFTER LUNCH.
OKAY!
Kazehaya's gonna eat lunch in the school yard.
What're they gonna do there?
AREN'T YOU GUYS IN THE SOCCER CLUB?
YEAH.
WANNA PLAY SOCCER?
YOU GUYS DID WELL AT THE SPORTS FESTIVAL DURING OUR FIRST YEAR!
Oh...
CAN WE JOIN YOU?
I wanna play.
TEACH ME HEADERS!
Yay!
OKAY.

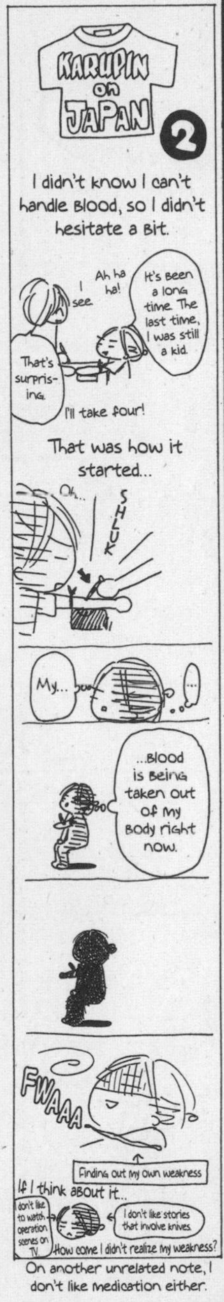
KARUPIN on JAPAN
2
I didn't know I can't handle blood, so I didn't hesitate a bit.
It's been a long time. The last time, I was still a kid.
Ah ha ha!
I see.
That's surprising.
I'll take four!
That was how it started...
Oh...
SHLUK
My...
...
...Blood is being taken out of my body right now.
FWAAA
Finding out my own weakness
If I think about it...
I don't like to watch operation scenes on TV.
I don't like stories that involve knives.
How come I didn't realize my weakness?
On another unrelated note, I don't like medication either.

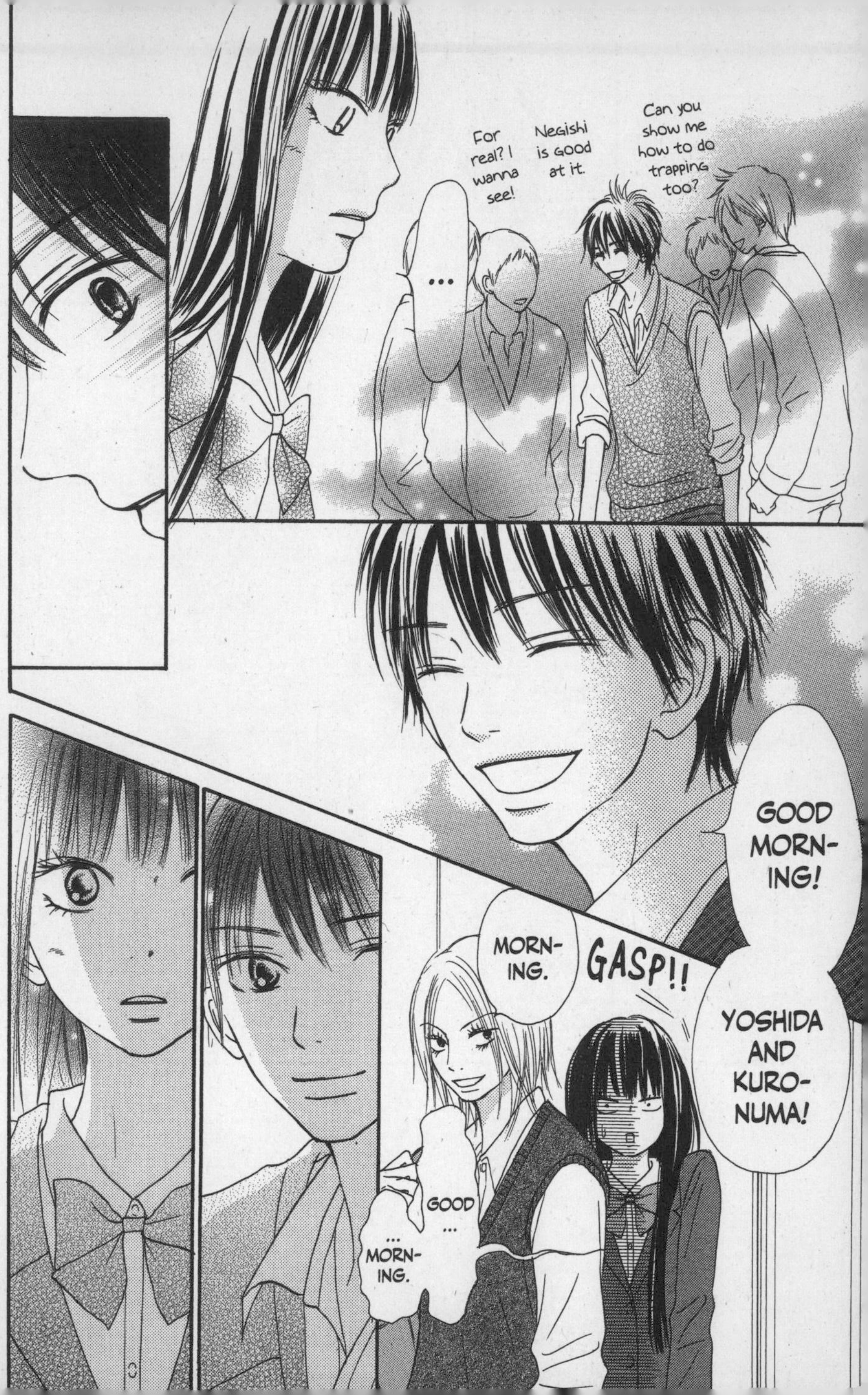
Can you show me how to do trapping too?
Negishi is good at it.
For real? I wanna see!
...
GOOD MORN-ING!
YOSHIDA AND KURO-NUMA!
GASP!!
MORN-ING.
GOOD ...
... MORN-ING.

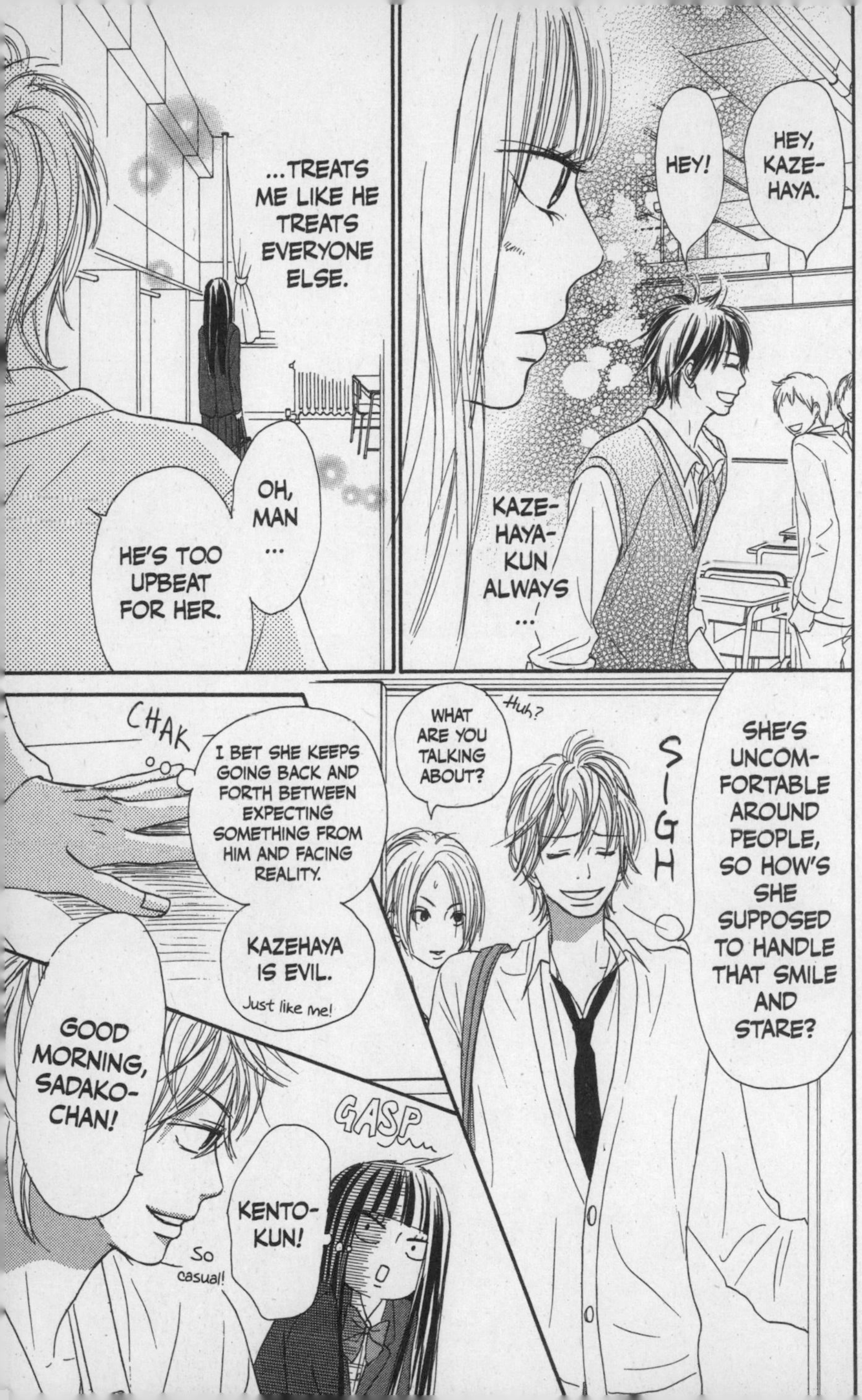
HEY, KAZE-HAYA.
HEY!
KAZE-HAYA-KUN ALWAYS...
...TREATS ME LIKE HE TREATS EVERYONE ELSE.
OH, MAN...
HE'S TOO UPBEAT FOR HER.
SHE'S UNCOMFORTABLE AROUND PEOPLE, SO HOW'S SHE SUPPOSED TO HANDLE THAT SMILE AND STARE?
SIGH
Huh?
WHAT ARE YOU TALKING ABOUT?
I BET SHE KEEPS GOING BACK AND FORTH BETWEEN EXPECTING SOMETHING FROM HIM AND FACING REALITY.
KAZEHAYA IS EVIL.
Just like me!
CHAK
GASP
KENTO-KUN!
GOOD MORNING, SADAKO-CHAN!
So casual!

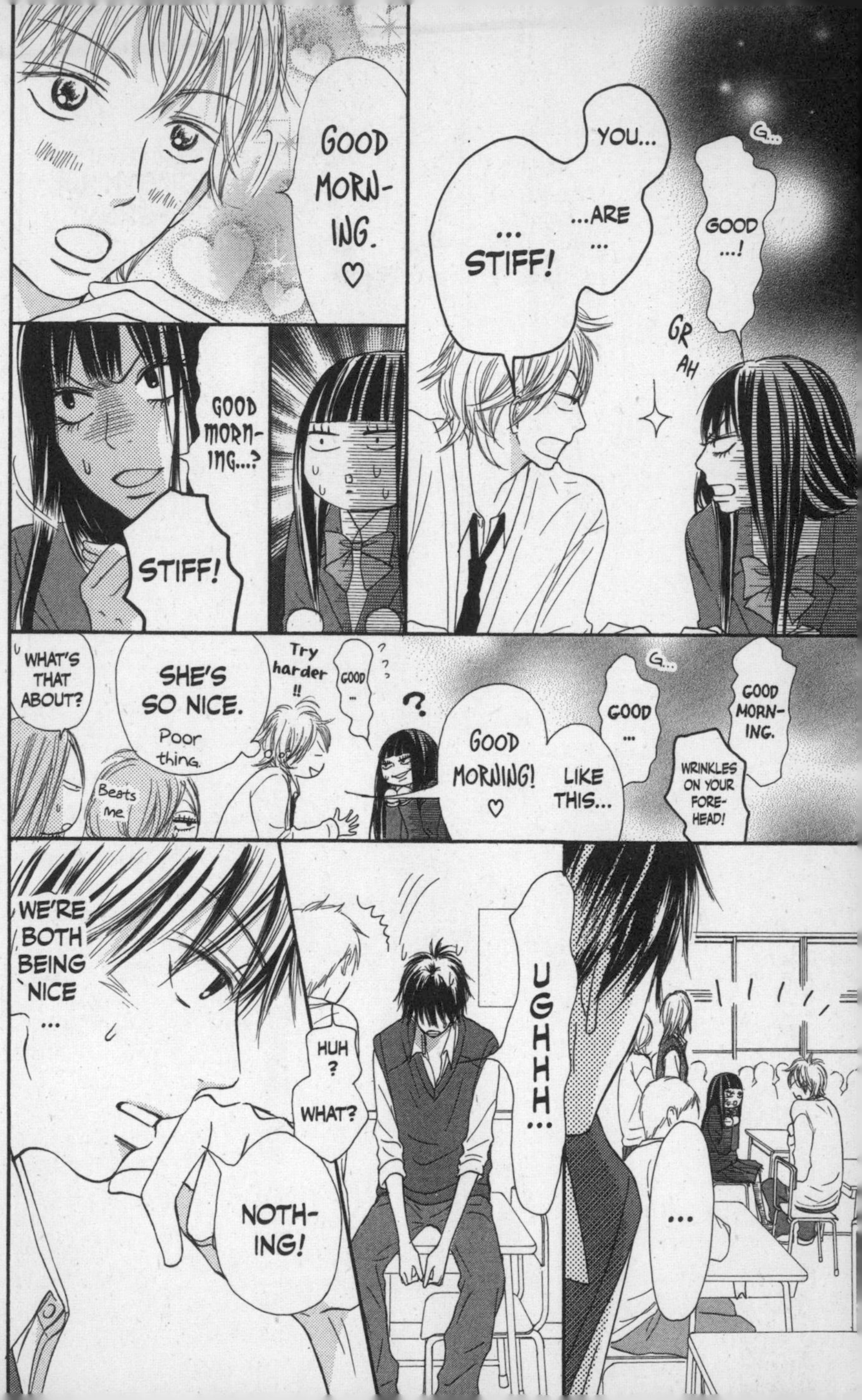
G...
GOOD ...!
YOU... ...ARE ... ... STIFF!
GRAH
GOOD MORNING. ♡
GOOD MORNING...?
STIFF!
G...
GOOD MORNING.
WRINKLES ON YOUR FOREHEAD!
GOOD ...
GOOD MORNING! ♡
LIKE THIS...
?
GOOD ...
Try harder!!
SHE'S SO NICE.
Poor thing.
WHAT'S THAT ABOUT?
Beats me
...
UGHHH...
HUH?
WHAT?
WE'RE BOTH BEING NICE ...
NOTHING!

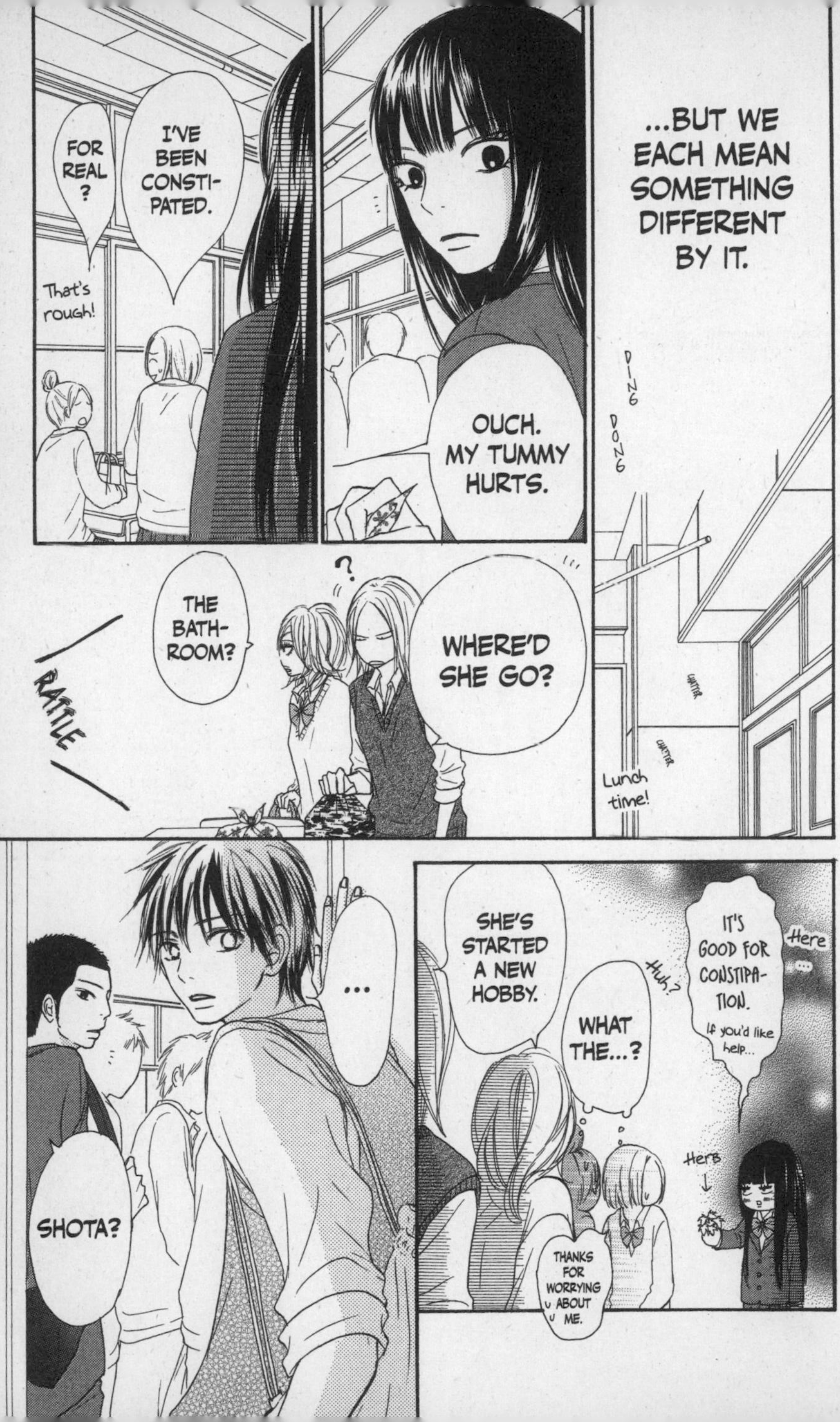
...BUT WE EACH MEAN SOMETHING DIFFERENT BY IT.
DING DONG
CHATTER
CHATTER
Lunch time!
OUCH. MY TUMMY HURTS.
I'VE BEEN CONSTIPATED.
FOR REAL?
That's rough!
WHERE'D SHE GO?
?
THE BATHROOM?
RATTLE
Here...
IT'S GOOD FOR CONSTIPATION.
If you'd like help...
Huh?
WHAT THE...?
SHE'S STARTED A NEW HOBBY.
Herb
THANKS FOR WORRYING ABOUT ME.
...
SHOTA?

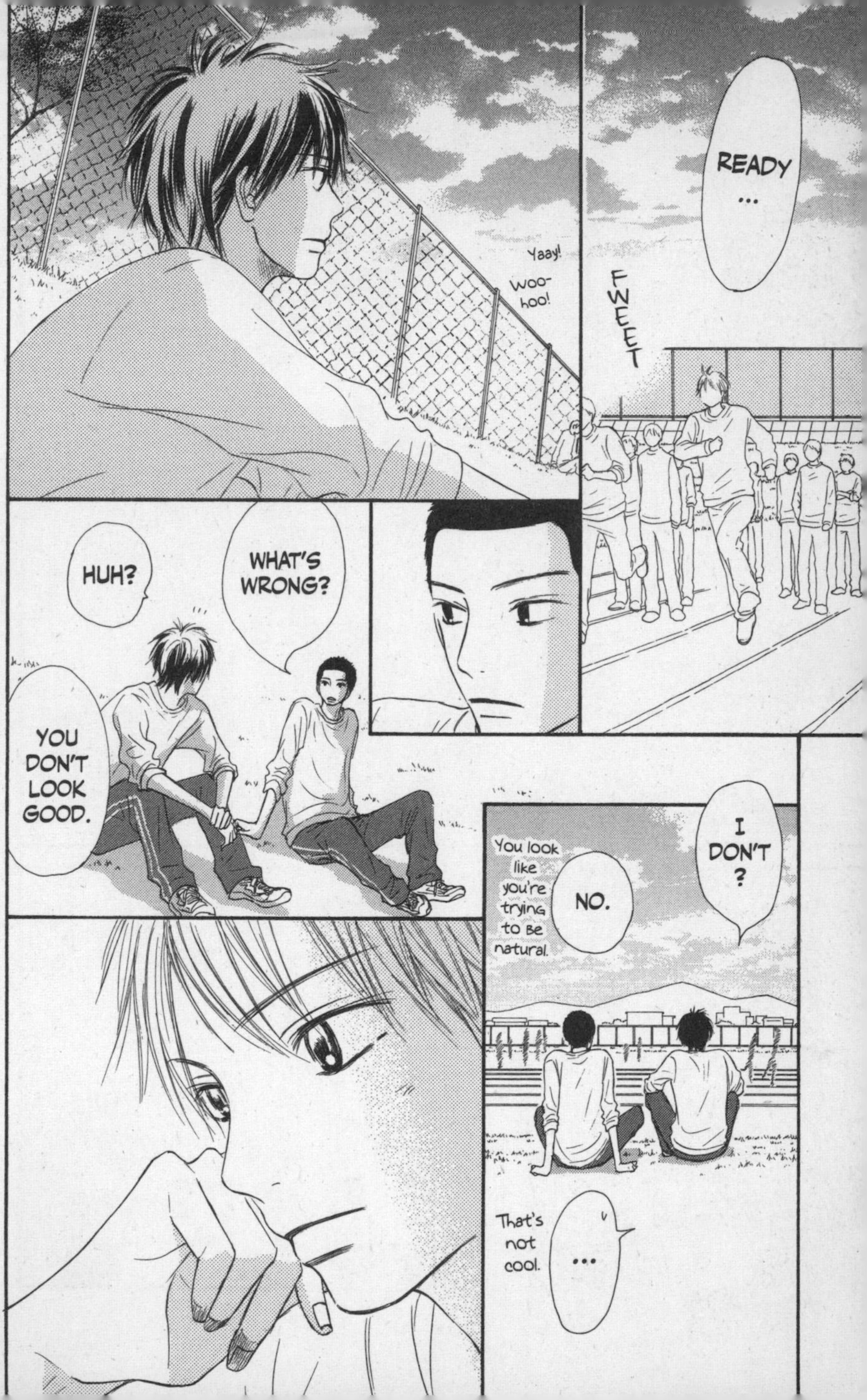
READY ...
FWEET
Yaay!
Woo-hoo!
WHAT'S WRONG?
HUH?
YOU DON'T LOOK GOOD.
I DON'T ?
NO.
You look like you're trying to be natural.
...
That's not cool.

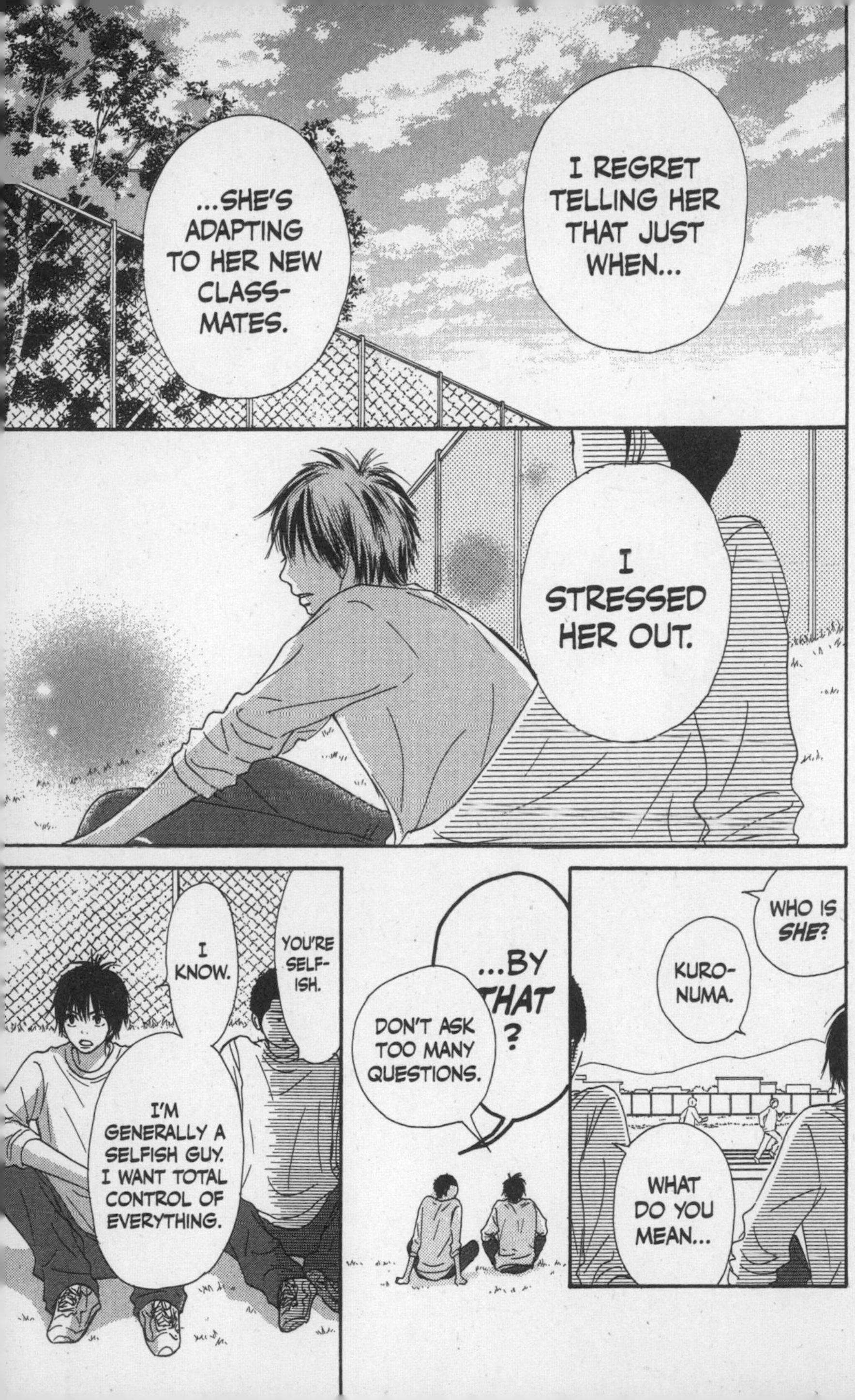
I REGRET TELLING HER THAT JUST WHEN...
...SHE'S ADAPTING TO HER NEW CLASS-MATES.
I STRESSED HER OUT.
WHO IS *SHE*?
KURO-NUMA.
WHAT DO YOU MEAN...
...BY *THAT*?
DON'T ASK TOO MANY QUESTIONS.
YOU'RE SELF-ISH.
I KNOW.
I'M GENERALLY A SELFISH GUY. I WANT TOTAL CONTROL OF EVERYTHING.

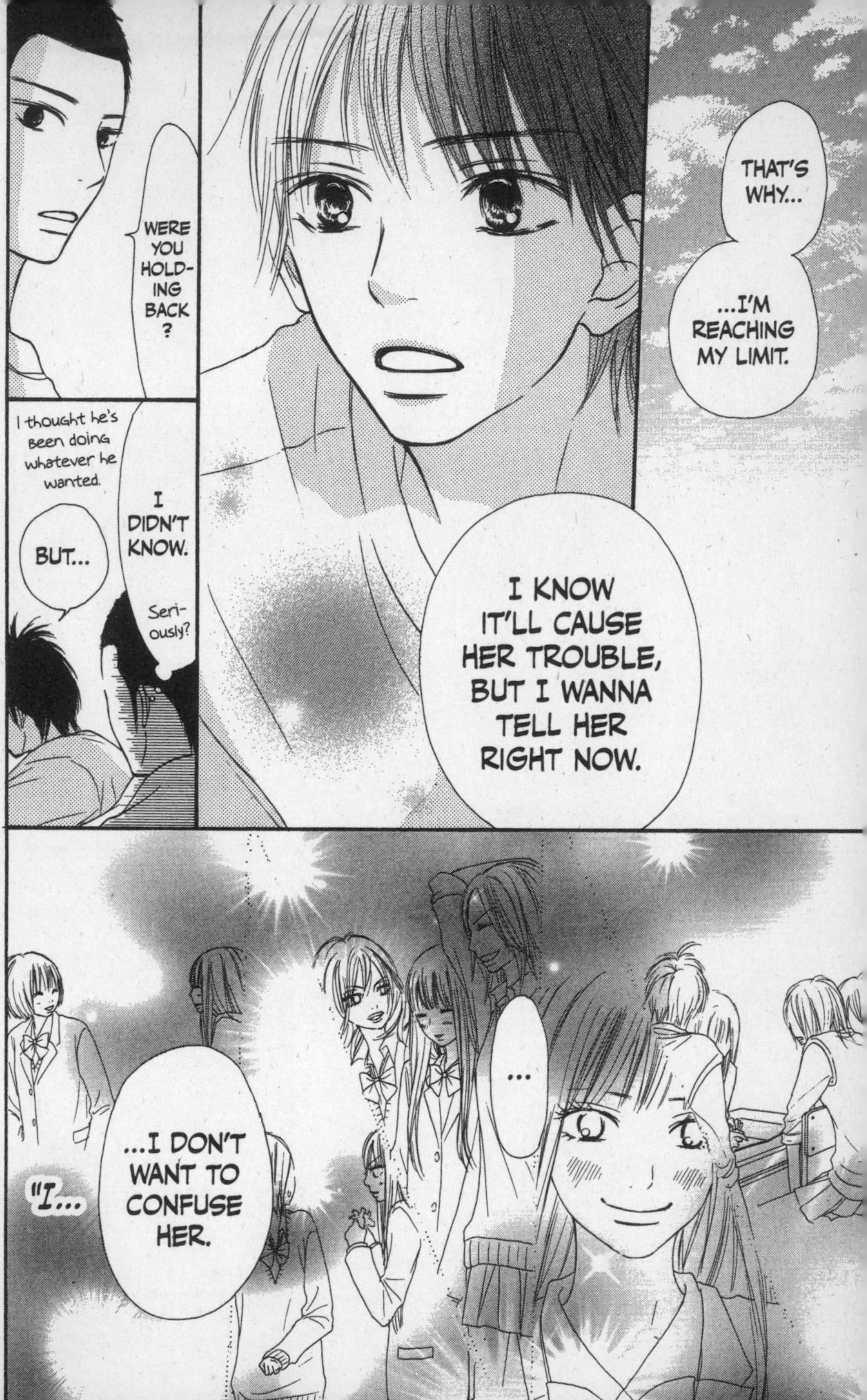
THAT'S WHY...
...I'M REACHING MY LIMIT.
I KNOW IT'LL CAUSE HER TROUBLE, BUT I WANNA TELL HER RIGHT NOW.
WERE YOU HOLDING-ING BACK?
I DIDN'T KNOW.
BUT...
I thought he's been doing whatever he wanted.
Seri-ously?
...
"I...
...I DON'T WANT TO CONFUSE HER.

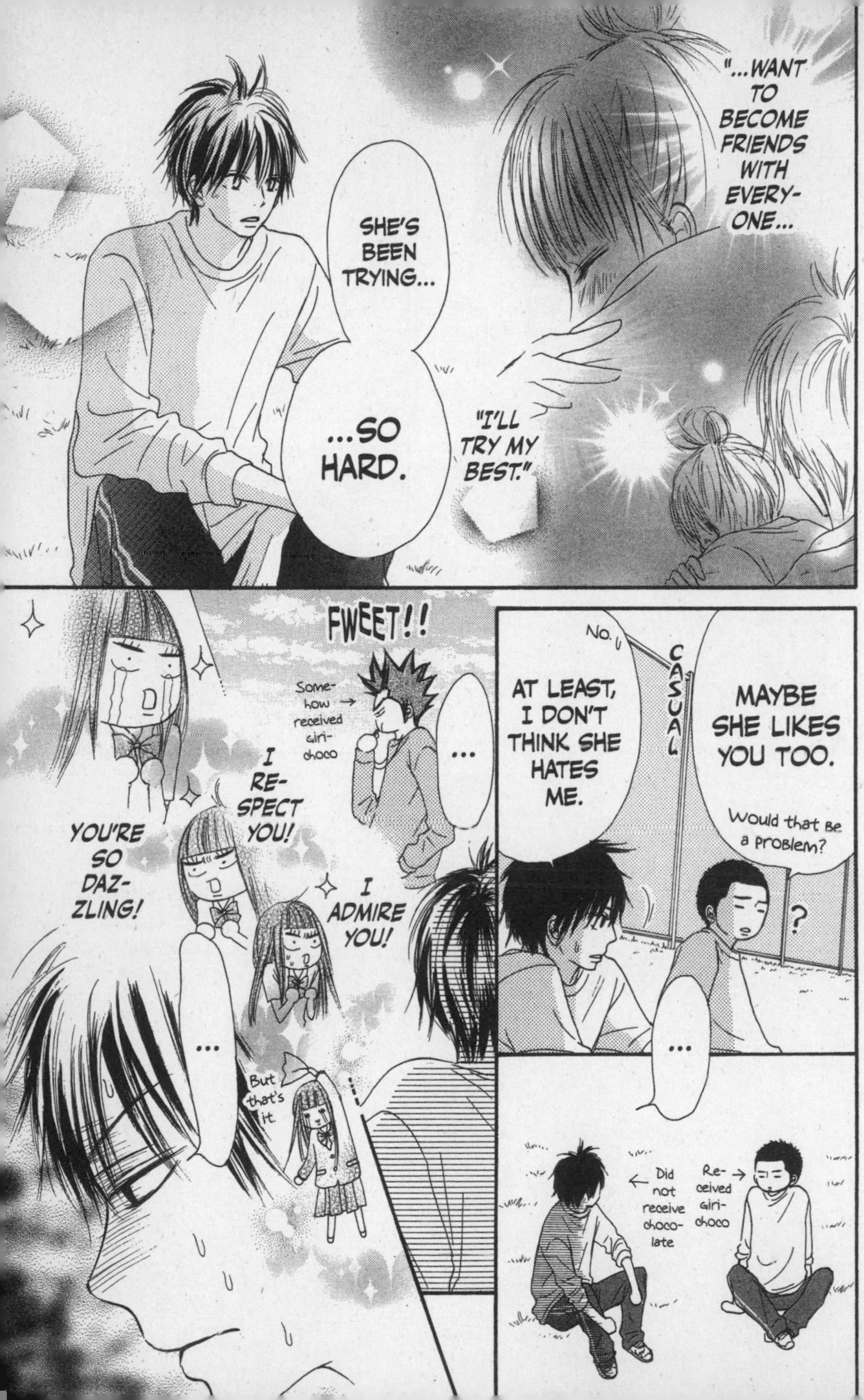
"...WANT TO BECOME FRIENDS WITH EVERY-ONE...
SHE'S BEEN TRYING...
...SO HARD.
"I'LL TRY MY BEST."
MAYBE SHE LIKES YOU TOO.
Would that be a problem?
CASUAL
No.
AT LEAST, I DON'T THINK SHE HATES ME.
?
...
Re-ceived giri-choco
Did not receive choco-late
FWEET!!
...
Some-how received giri-choco
I RE-SPECT YOU!
YOU'RE SO DAZ-ZLING!
I ADMIRE YOU!
...
But that's it.

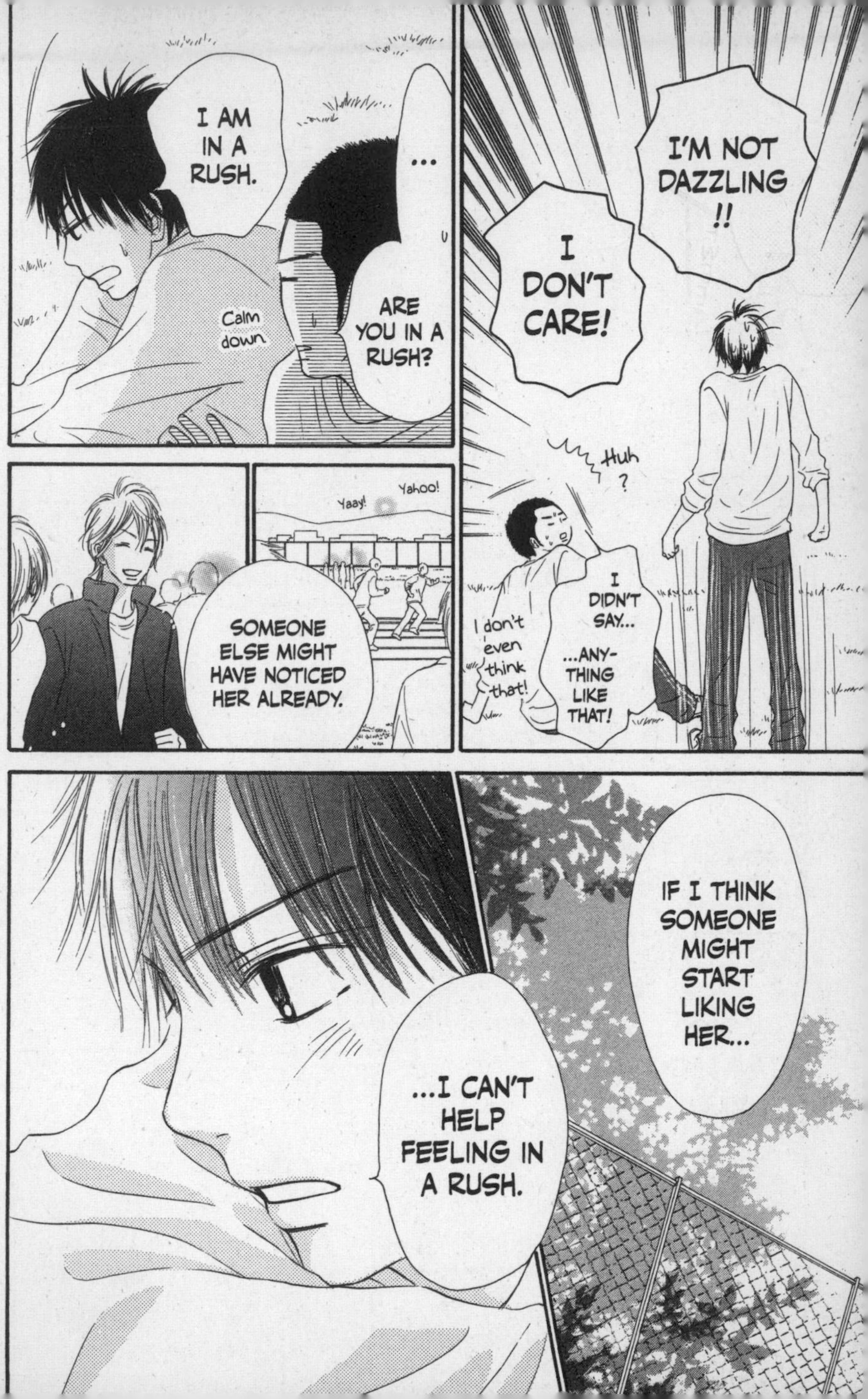
I'M NOT DAZZLING!!
I DON'T CARE!
Huh?
I DIDN'T SAY... ...ANY-THING LIKE THAT!
I don't even think that!
...
ARE YOU IN A RUSH?
I AM IN A RUSH.
Calm down
Yahoo!
Yaay!
SOMEONE ELSE MIGHT HAVE NOTICED HER ALREADY.
IF I THINK SOMEONE MIGHT START LIKING HER...
...I CAN'T HELP FEELING IN A RUSH.

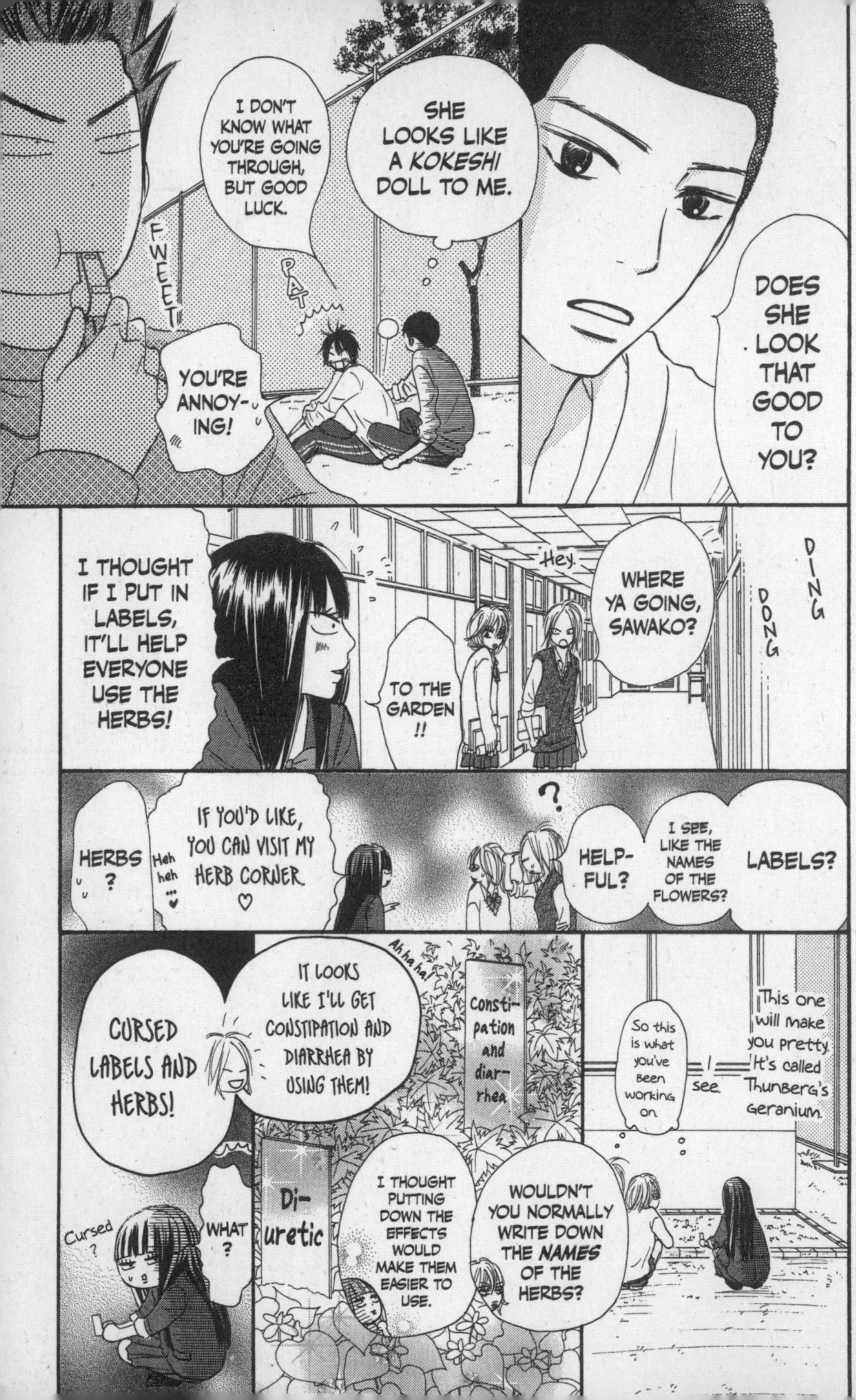
DOES SHE LOOK THAT GOOD TO YOU?
SHE LOOKS LIKE A KOKESHI DOLL TO ME.
I DON'T KNOW WHAT YOU'RE GOING THROUGH, BUT GOOD LUCK.
FWEET
PAT
YOU'RE ANNOY-ING!
DING DONG
WHERE YA GOING, SAWAKO?
Hey.
TO THE GARDEN!!
I THOUGHT IF I PUT IN LABELS, IT'LL HELP EVERYONE USE THE HERBS!
LABELS?
I SEE, LIKE THE NAMES OF THE FLOWERS?
HELP-FUL?
?
IF YOU'D LIKE, YOU CAN VISIT MY HERB CORNER. ♡
Heh heh ••• ♥
HERBS?
This one will make you pretty. It's called Thunberg's Geranium.
I see.
So this is what you've been working on.
Consti-pation and diar-rhea
Ah ha ha!
IT LOOKS LIKE I'LL GET CONSTIPATION AND DIARRHEA BY USING THEM!
CURSED LABELS AND HERBS!
WOULDN'T YOU NORMALLY WRITE DOWN THE NAMES OF THE HERBS?
I THOUGHT PUTTING DOWN THE EFFECTS WOULD MAKE THEM EASIER TO USE.
Di-uretic
WHAT?
Cursed?

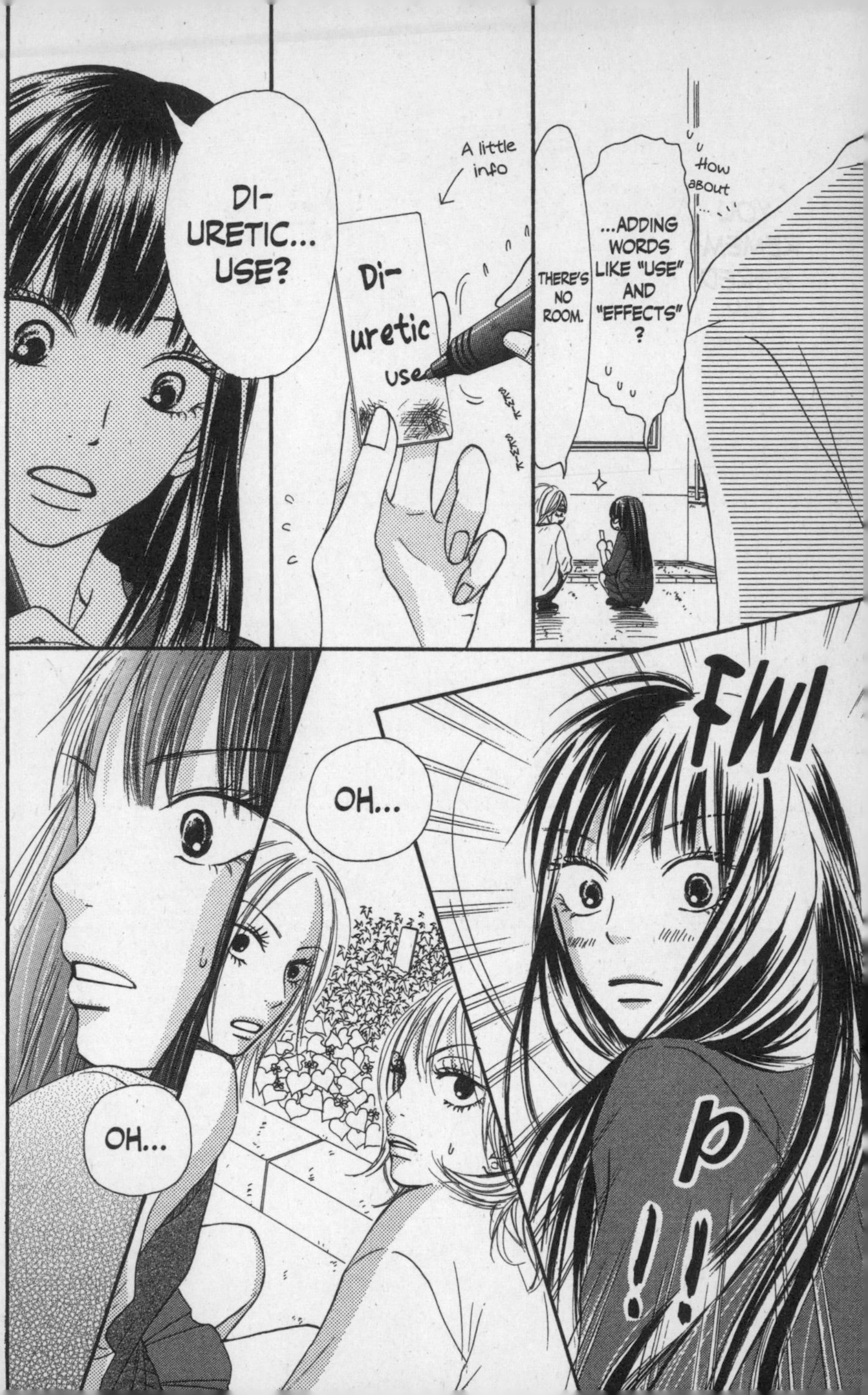
How about...
...ADDING WORDS LIKE "USE" AND "EFFECTS"?
THERE'S NO ROOM.
A little info
Di-uretic use
DI-URETIC... USE?
FWI
p!!
OH...
OH...

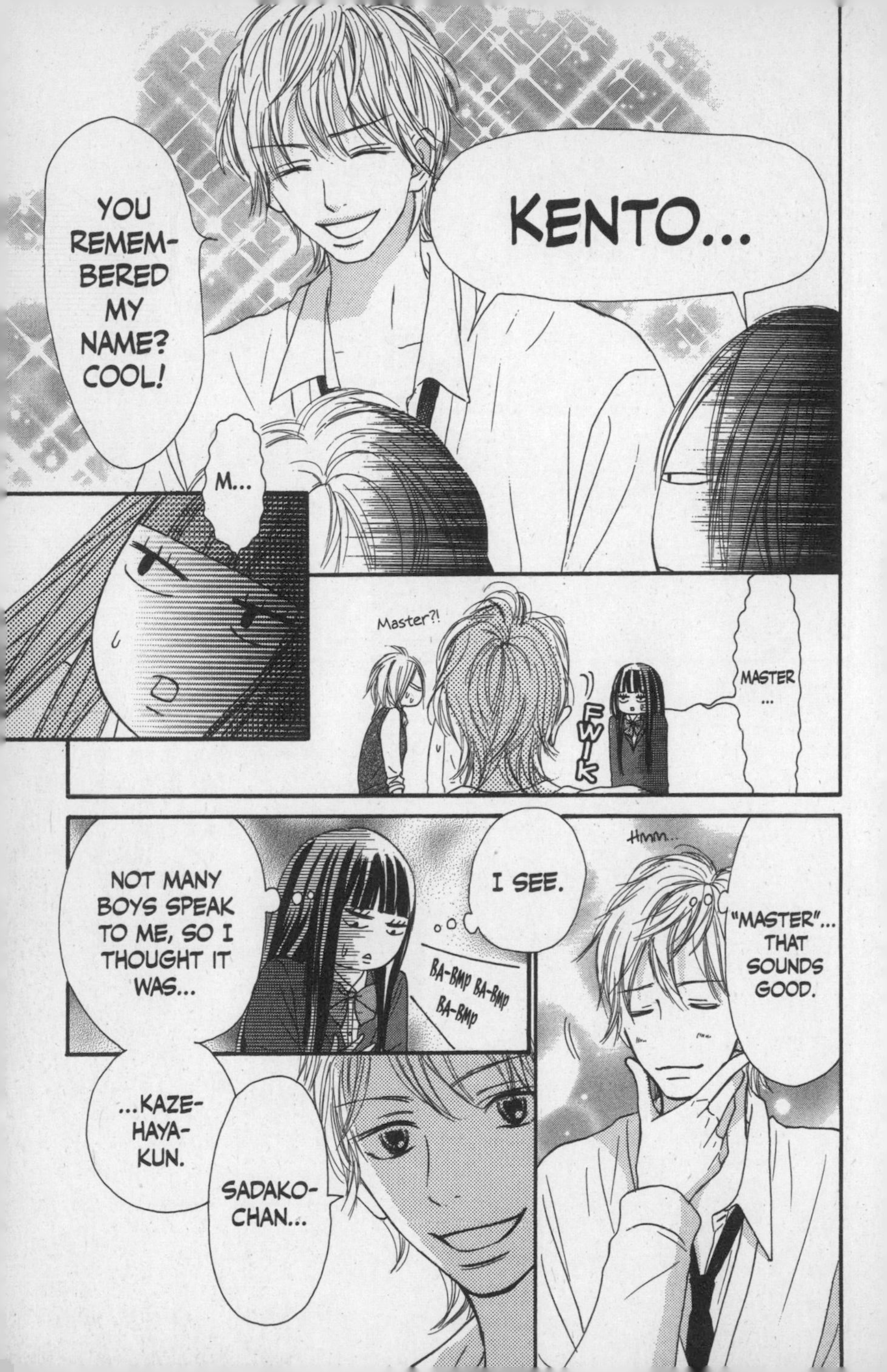
KENTO...
YOU REMEMBERED MY NAME? COOL!
M...
MASTER ...
FWIK
Master?!
Hmm...
"MASTER"... THAT SOUNDS GOOD.
I SEE.
BA-BMP BA-BMP BA-BMP
NOT MANY BOYS SPEAK TO ME, SO I THOUGHT IT WAS...
...KAZE-HAYA-KUN.
SADAKO-CHAN...

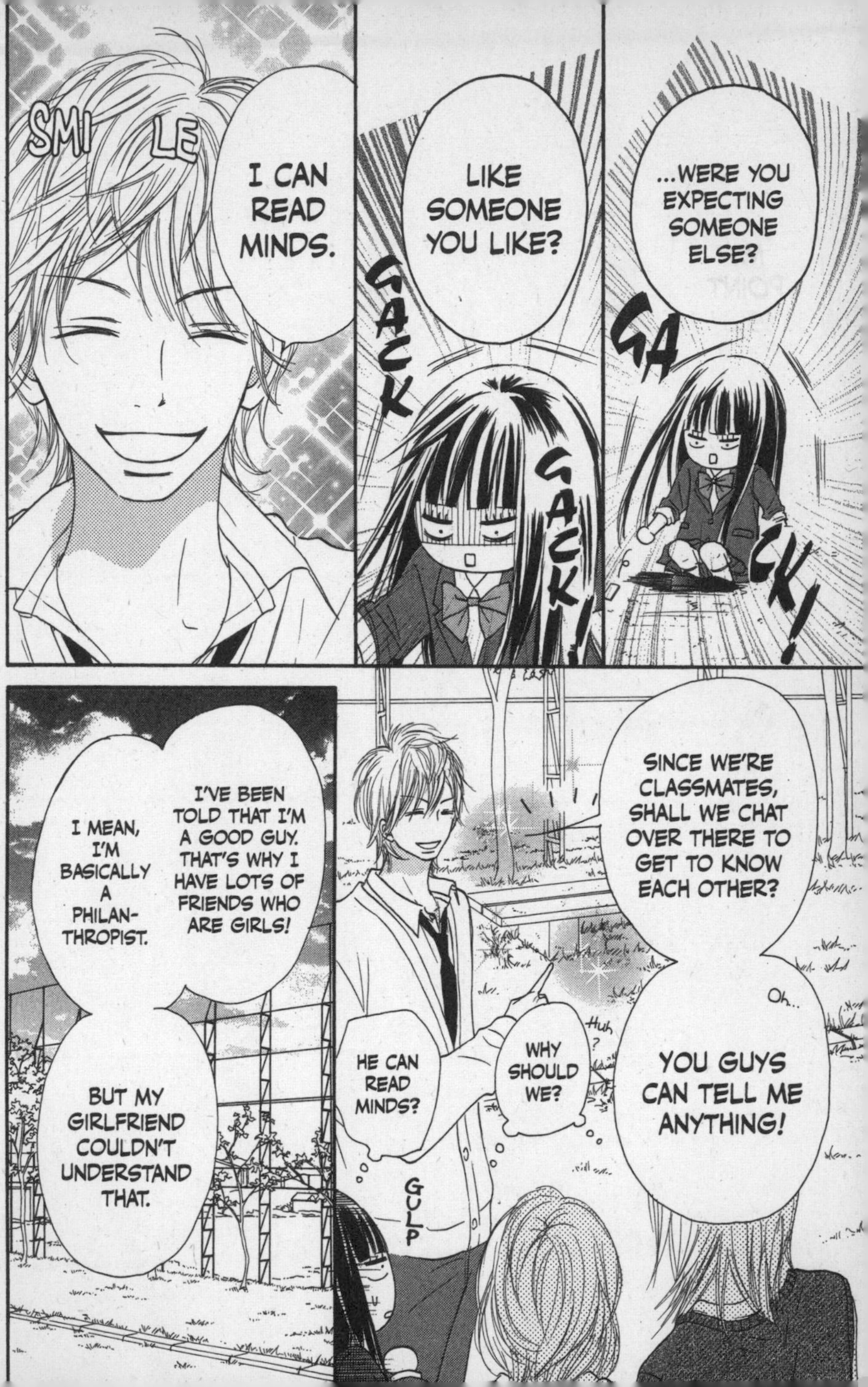
...WERE YOU EXPECTING SOMEONE ELSE?
GACK!
LIKE SOMEONE YOU LIKE?
GACK
GACK!
SMILE
I CAN READ MINDS.
SINCE WE'RE CLASSMATES, SHALL WE CHAT OVER THERE TO GET TO KNOW EACH OTHER?
Oh...
YOU GUYS CAN TELL ME ANYTHING!
Huh?
WHY SHOULD WE?
HE CAN READ MINDS?
GULP
I'VE BEEN TOLD THAT I'M A GOOD GUY. THAT'S WHY I HAVE LOTS OF FRIENDS WHO ARE GIRLS!
I MEAN, I'M BASICALLY A PHILANTHROPIST.
BUT MY GIRLFRIEND COULDN'T UNDERSTAND THAT.

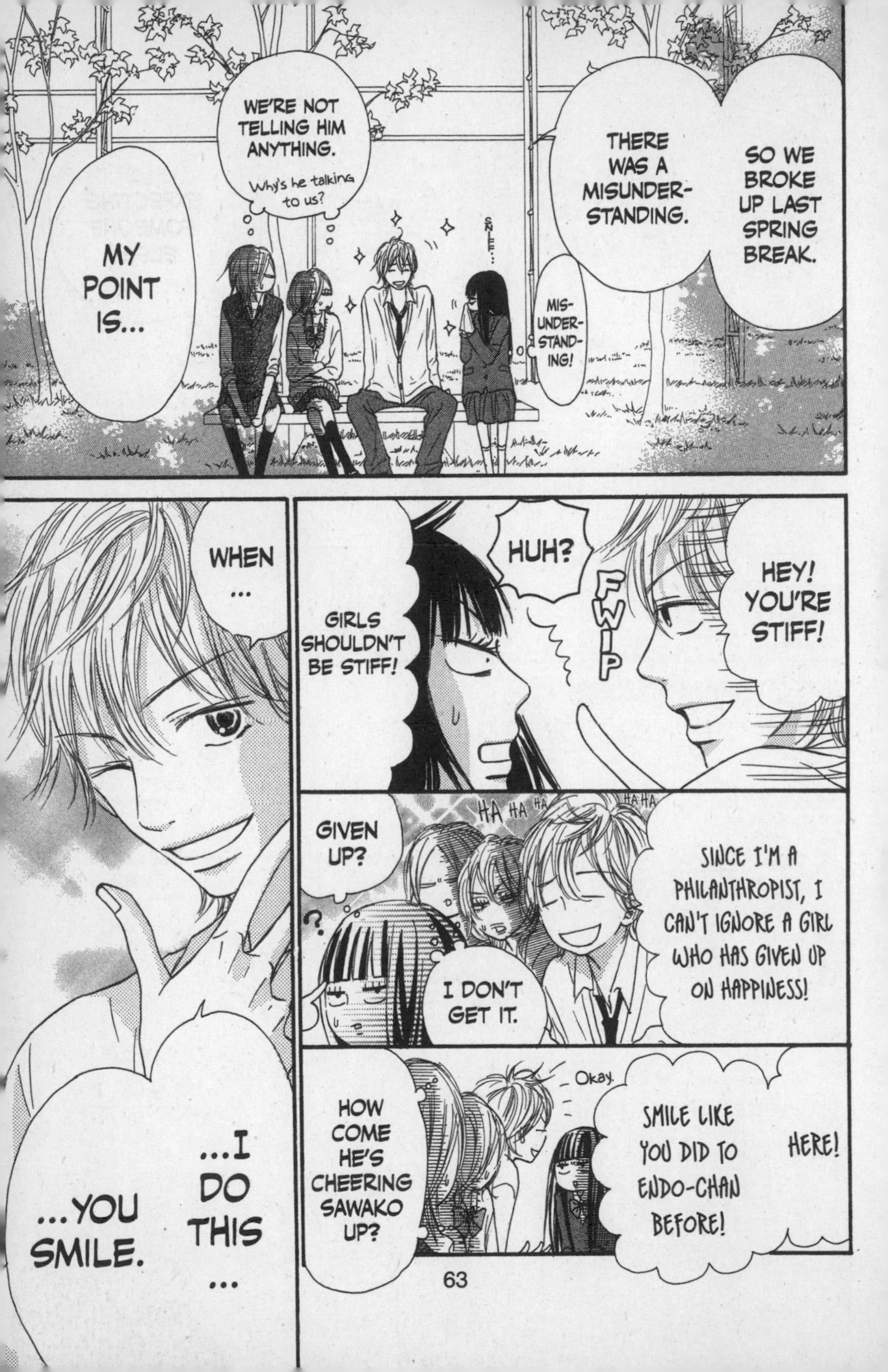
SO WE BROKE UP LAST SPRING BREAK.
THERE WAS A MISUNDER-STANDING.
MIS-UNDER-STAND-ING!
SNIFF...
WE'RE NOT TELLING HIM ANYTHING.
Why's he talking to us?
MY POINT IS...
HEY! YOU'RE STIFF!
FWIP
HUH?
GIRLS SHOULDN'T BE STIFF!
SINCE I'M A PHILANTHROPIST, I CAN'T IGNORE A GIRL WHO HAS GIVEN UP ON HAPPINESS!
HA HA
HA HA HA
GIVEN UP?
I DON'T GET IT.
SMILE LIKE YOU DID TO ENDO-CHAN BEFORE!
HERE!
Okay.
HOW COME HE'S CHEERING SAWAKO UP?
WHEN ...
...I DO THIS ...
...YOU SMILE.

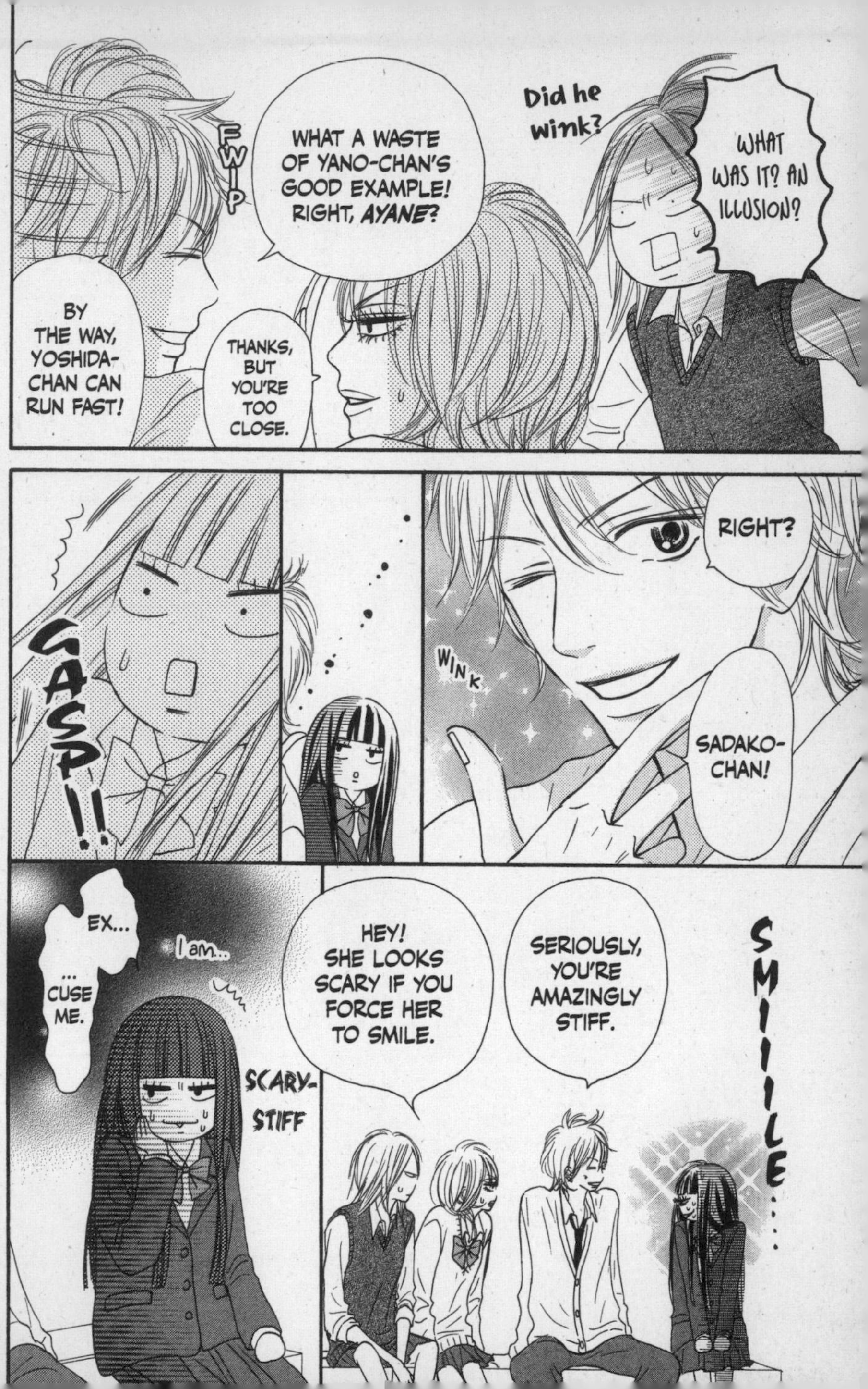
WHAT WAS IT? AN ILLUSION?
Did he wink?
WHAT A WASTE OF YANO-CHAN'S GOOD EXAMPLE! RIGHT, *AYANE*?
FWIP
THANKS, BUT YOU'RE TOO CLOSE.
BY THE WAY, YOSHIDA-CHAN CAN RUN FAST!
RIGHT?
WINK
SADAKO-CHAN!
GASP!!
SMIIILE...
SERIOUSLY, YOU'RE AMAZINGLY STIFF.
HEY! SHE LOOKS SCARY IF YOU FORCE HER TO SMILE.
I am...
EX... ...CUSE ME.
SCARY-STIFF

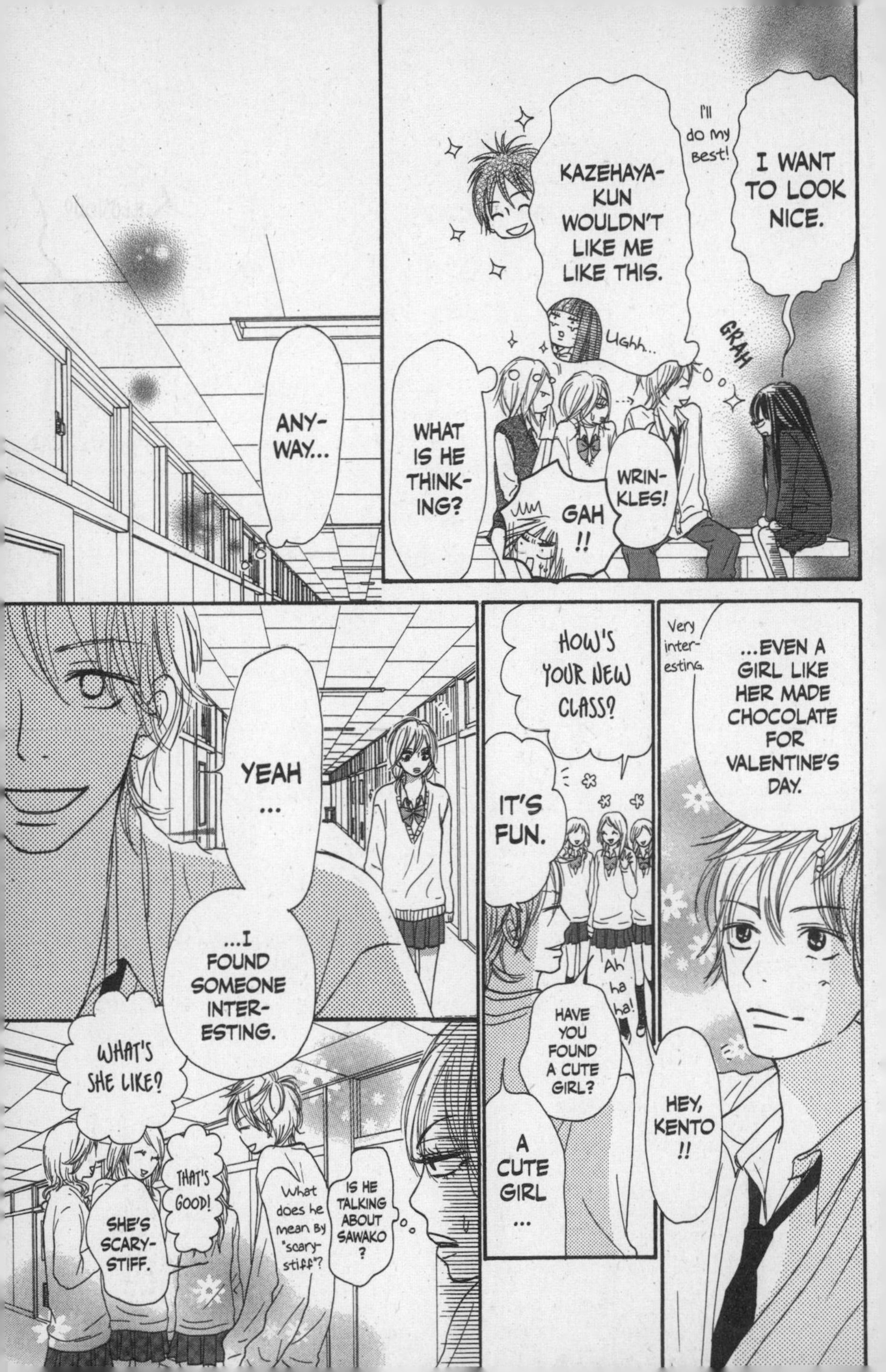
I WANT TO LOOK NICE.
I'll do my best!
KAZEHAYA-KUN WOULDN'T LIKE ME LIKE THIS.
GRAH
Ughh...
WRIN-KLES!
GAH !!
WHAT IS HE THINKING?
ANY-WAY...
...EVEN A GIRL LIKE HER MADE CHOCOLATE FOR VALENTINE'S DAY.
Very inter-esting.
HEY, KENTO !!
HOW'S YOUR NEW CLASS?
IT'S FUN.
Ah ha ha!
HAVE YOU FOUND A CUTE GIRL?
A CUTE GIRL ...
YEAH ...
...I FOUND SOMEONE INTER-ESTING.
WHAT'S SHE LIKE?
THAT'S GOOD!
SHE'S SCARY-STIFF.
IS HE TALKING ABOUT SAWAKO ?
What does he mean by "scary-stiff"?

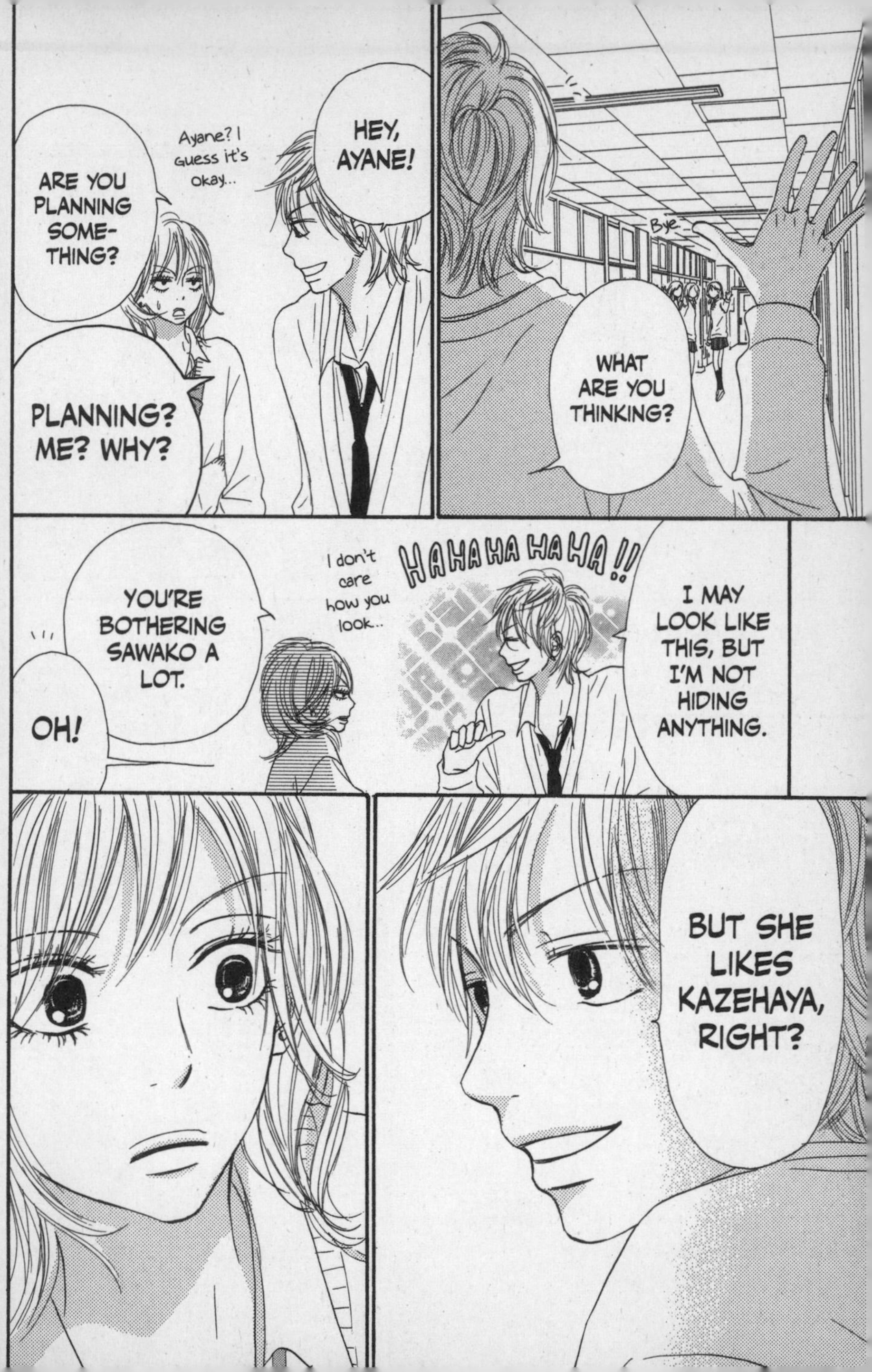
Bye
WHAT ARE YOU THINKING?
HEY, AYANE!
Ayane? I guess it's okay...
ARE YOU PLANNING SOME-THING?
PLANNING? ME? WHY?
I MAY LOOK LIKE THIS, BUT I'M NOT HIDING ANYTHING.
HAHAHA HAHA!!
I don't care how you look..
YOU'RE BOTHERING SAWAKO A LOT.
OH!
BUT SHE LIKES KAZEHAYA, RIGHT?

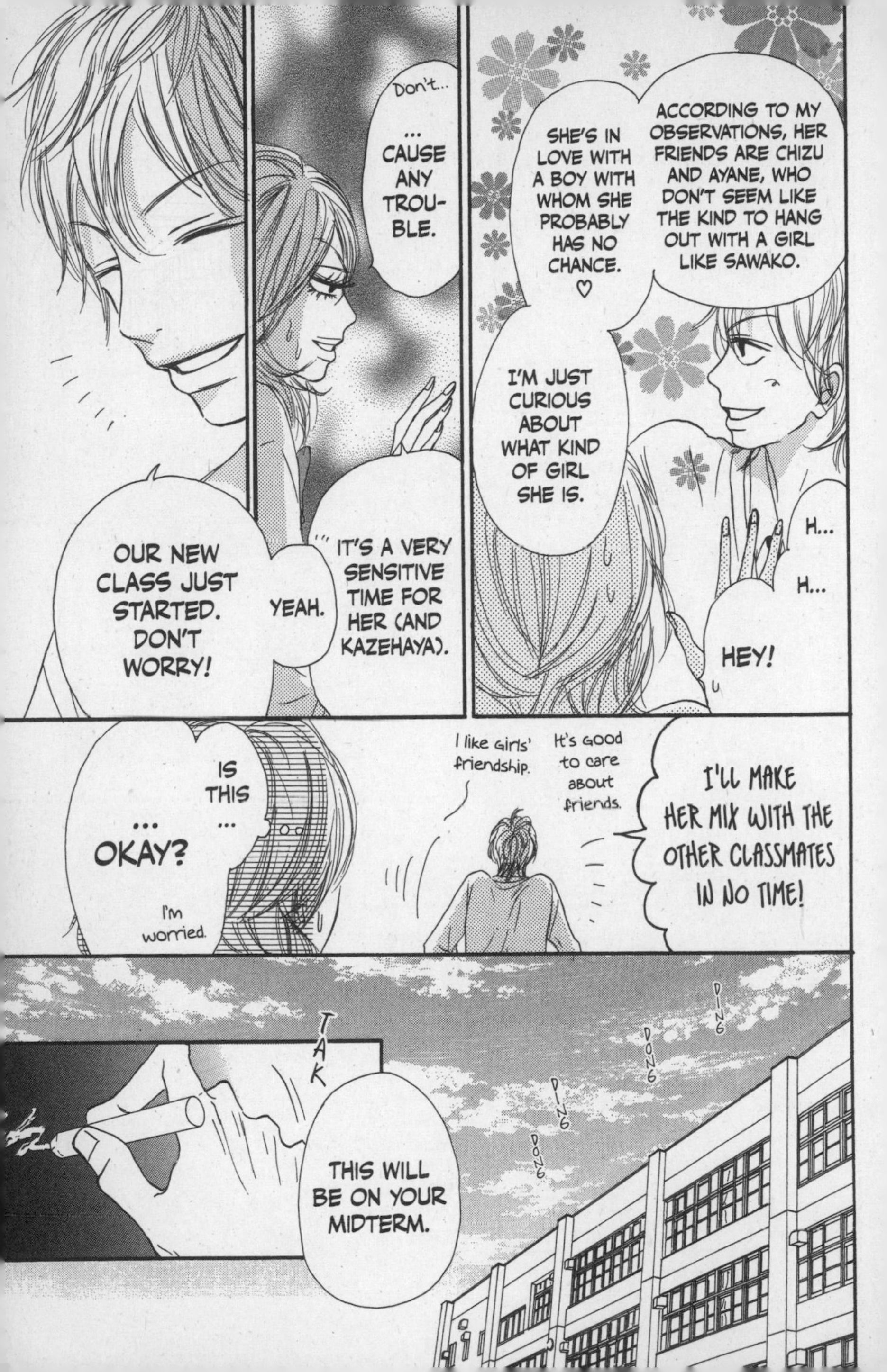
ACCORDING TO MY OBSERVATIONS, HER FRIENDS ARE CHIZU AND AYANE, WHO DON'T SEEM LIKE THE KIND TO HANG OUT WITH A GIRL LIKE SAWAKO.
SHE'S IN LOVE WITH A BOY WITH WHOM SHE PROBABLY HAS NO CHANCE. ♡
I'M JUST CURIOUS ABOUT WHAT KIND OF GIRL SHE IS.
H... H...
HEY!
Don't...
...CAUSE ANY TROU-BLE.
IT'S A VERY SENSITIVE TIME FOR HER (AND KAZEHAYA).
YEAH.
OUR NEW CLASS JUST STARTED. DON'T WORRY!
I'LL MAKE HER MIX WITH THE OTHER CLASSMATES IN NO TIME!
It's good to care about friends.
I like girls' friendship.
IS THIS... ...OKAY?
I'm worried.
DING DONG DING DONG
TAK
THIS WILL BE ON YOUR MIDTERM.

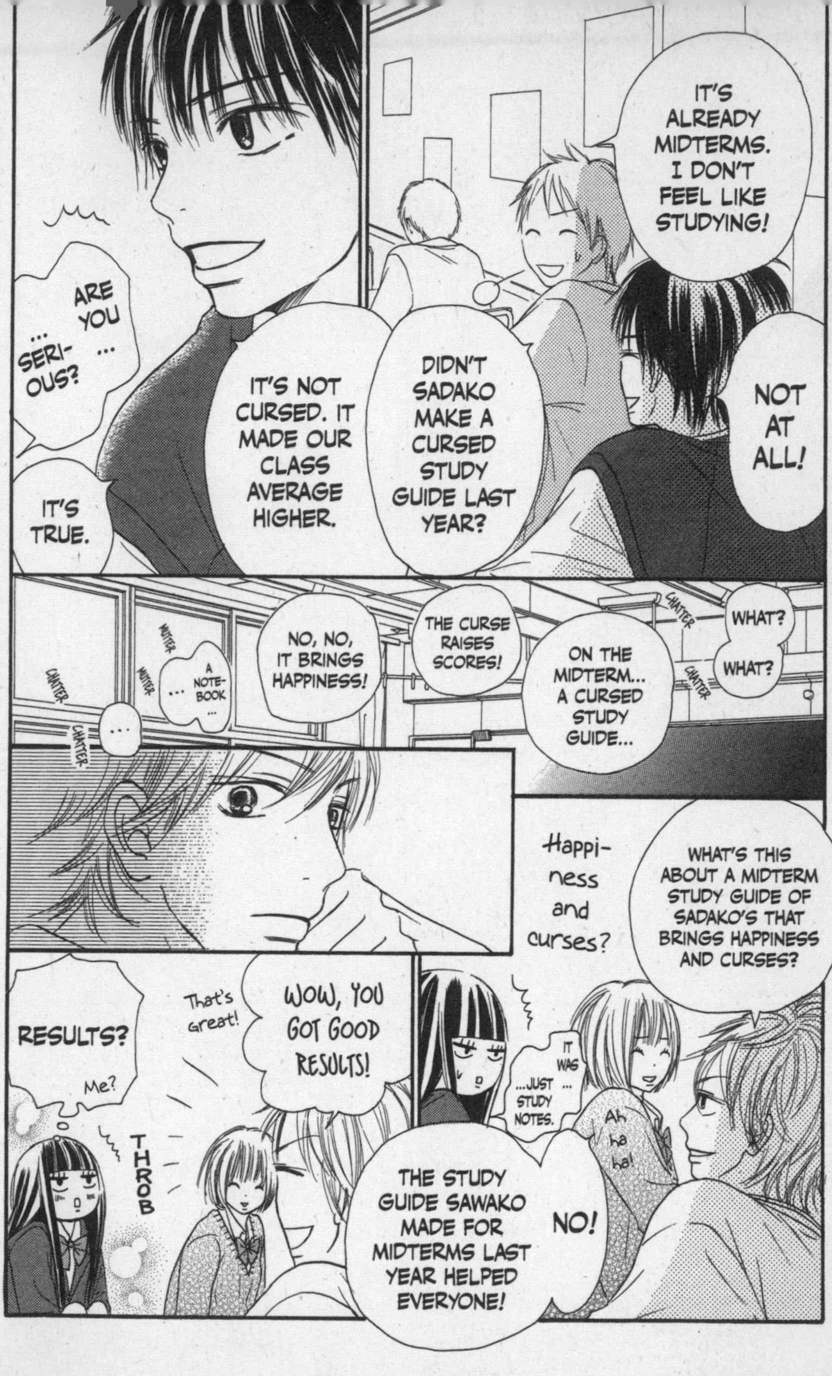
IT'S ALREADY MIDTERMS. I DON'T FEEL LIKE STUDYING!
NOT AT ALL!
DIDN'T SADAKO MAKE A CURSED STUDY GUIDE LAST YEAR?
IT'S NOT CURSED. IT MADE OUR CLASS AVERAGE HIGHER.
...ARE YOU ... SERIOUS?
IT'S TRUE.
WHAT?
WHAT?
CHATTER
CHATTER
ON THE MIDTERM... A CURSED STUDY GUIDE...
THE CURSE RAISES SCORES!
NO, NO, IT BRINGS HAPPINESS!
MUTTER
MUTTER
... A NOTEBOOK ...
...
CHATTER
CHATTER
WHAT'S THIS ABOUT A MIDTERM STUDY GUIDE OF SADAKO'S THAT BRINGS HAPPINESS AND CURSES?
Happiness and curses?
THE STUDY GUIDE SAWAKO MADE FOR MIDTERMS LAST YEAR HELPED EVERYONE!
NO!
IT WAS ... ...JUST STUDY NOTES.
Ah ha ha!
WOW, YOU GOT GOOD RESULTS!
That's great!
RESULTS?
Me?
THROB

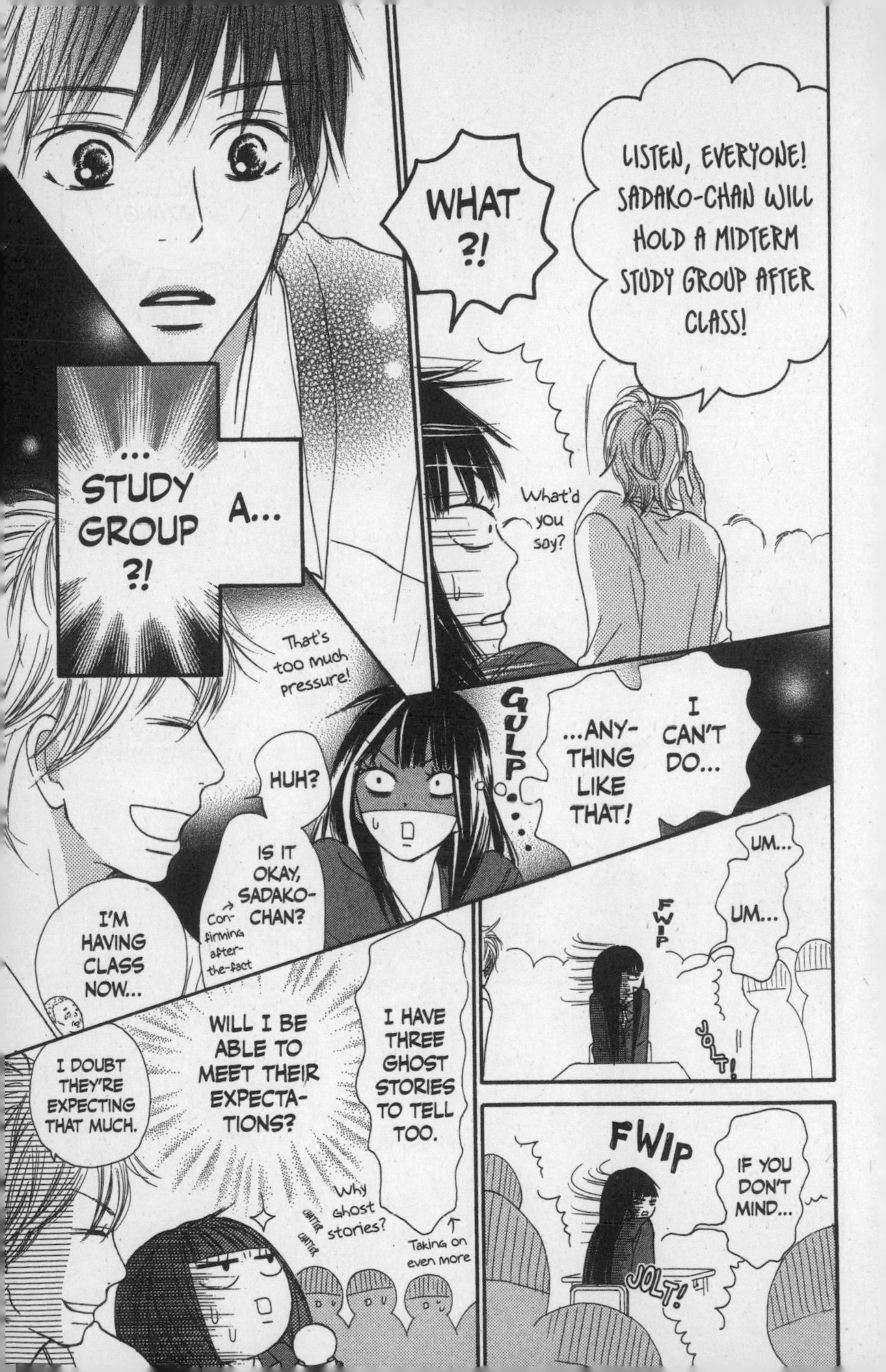
LISTEN, EVERYONE! SADAKO-CHAN WILL HOLD A MIDTERM STUDY GROUP AFTER CLASS!
What'd you say?
WHAT ?!
A...
... STUDY GROUP ?!
I CAN'T DO...
...ANYTHING LIKE THAT!
GULP...
That's too much pressure!
HUH?
IS IT OKAY, SADAKO-CHAN?
Confirming after-the-fact
I'M HAVING CLASS NOW...
UM...
UM...
FWIP
JOLT!
IF YOU DON'T MIND...
FWIP
JOLT!
I HAVE THREE GHOST STORIES TO TELL TOO.
Taking on even more
WILL I BE ABLE TO MEET THEIR EXPECTATIONS?
Why ghost stories?
CHATTER CHATTER
I DOUBT THEY'RE EXPECTING THAT MUCH.

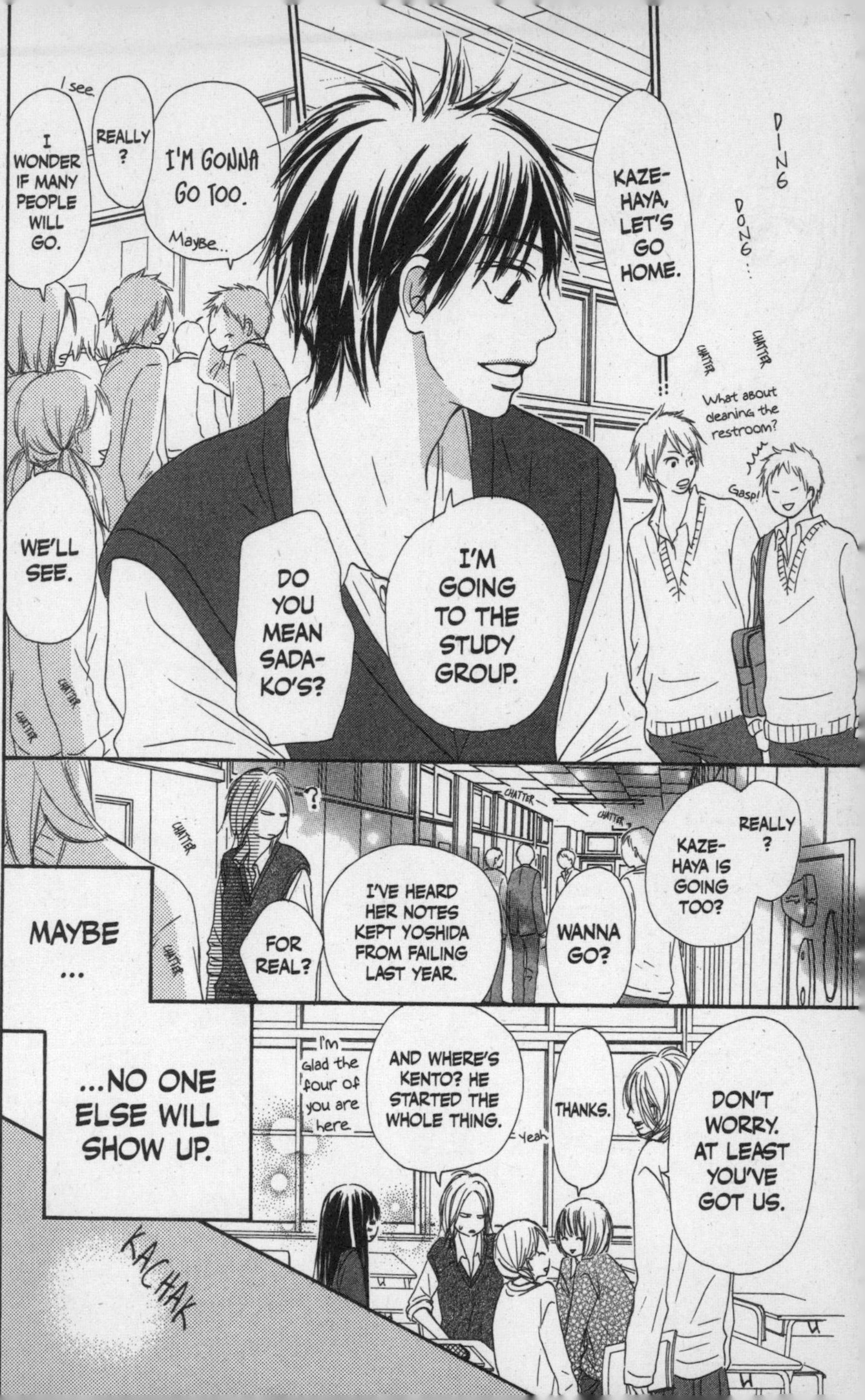
DING DONG...
KAZE-HAYA, LET'S GO HOME.
CHATTER CHATTER
What about cleaning the restroom?
Gasp!
I'M GOING TO THE STUDY GROUP.
DO YOU MEAN SADA-KO'S?
I'M GONNA GO TOO.
Maybe...
REALLY?
I see.
I WONDER IF MANY PEOPLE WILL GO.
WE'LL SEE.
CHATTER CHATTER
CHATTER
REALLY? KAZE-HAYA IS GOING TOO?
WANNA GO?
I'VE HEARD HER NOTES KEPT YOSHIDA FROM FAILING LAST YEAR.
FOR REAL?
CHATTER CHATTER
MAYBE...
DON'T WORRY. AT LEAST YOU'VE GOT US.
THANKS.
Yeah
AND WHERE'S KENTO? HE STARTED THE WHOLE THING.
I'm glad the four of you are here.
...NO ONE ELSE WILL SHOW UP.
KACHAK

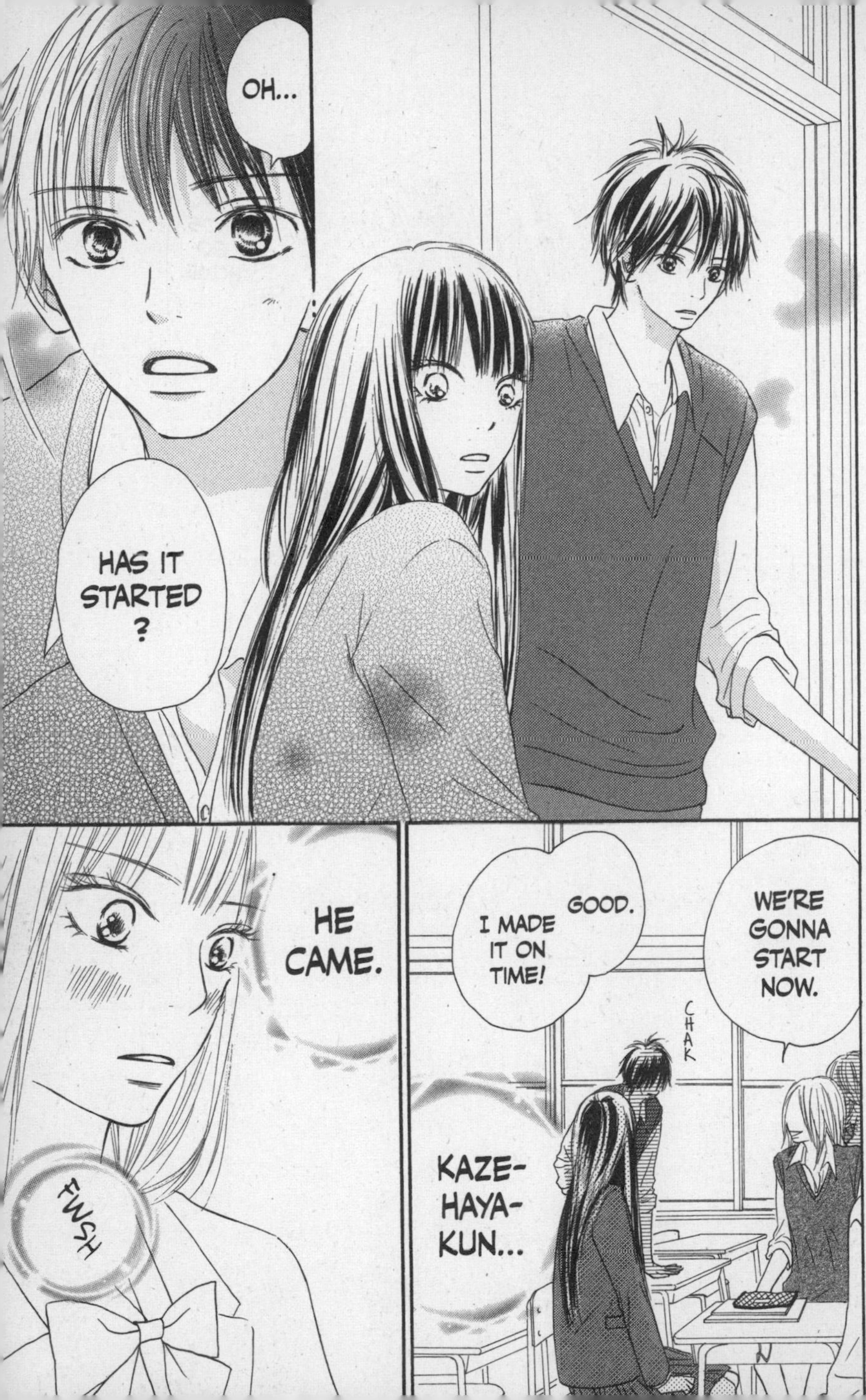
OH...
HAS IT STARTED?
WE'RE GONNA START NOW.
GOOD. I MADE IT ON TIME!
CHAK
KAZE-HAYA-KUN...
HE CAME.
FWSH

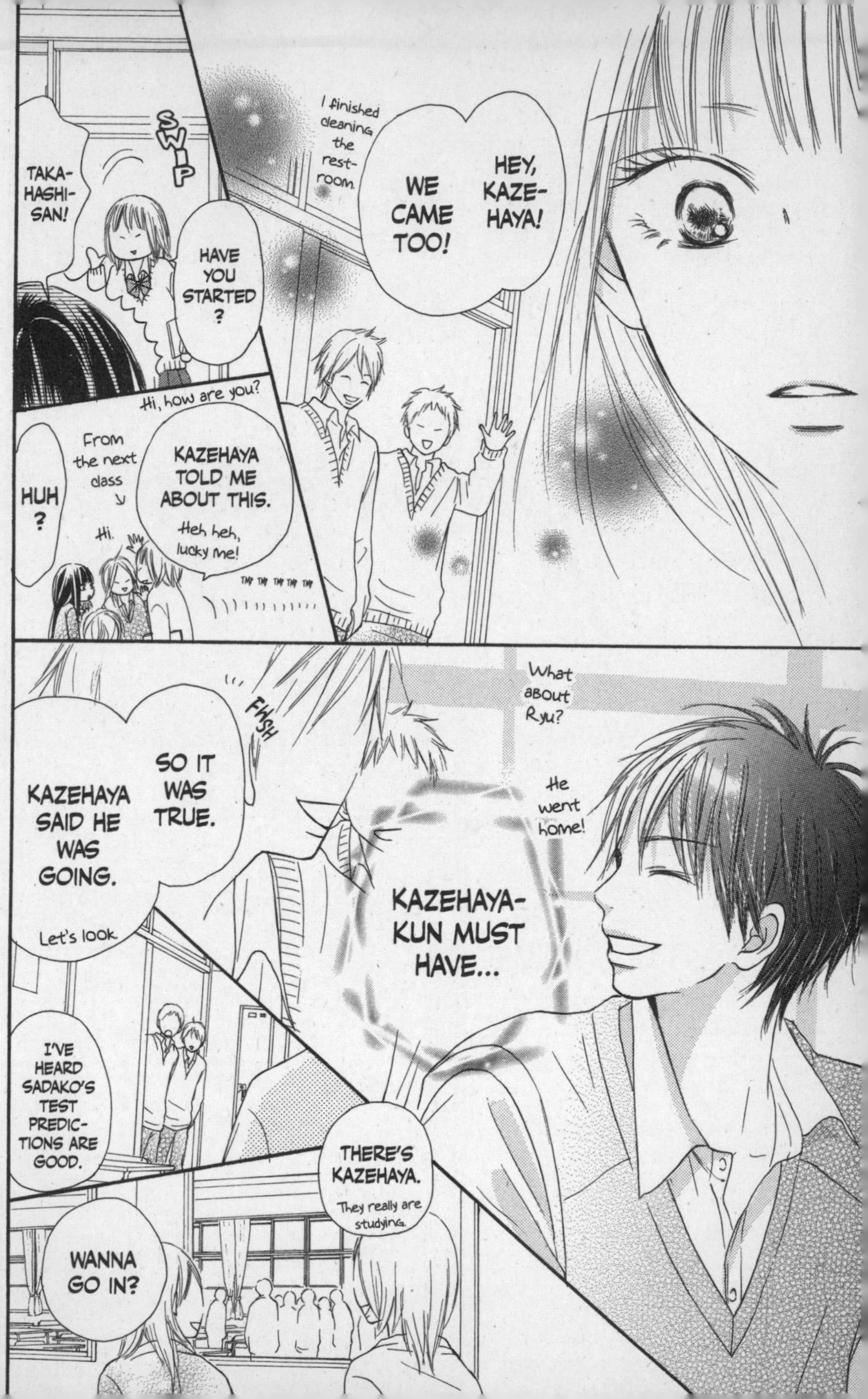
HEY, KAZE-HAYA!
WE CAME TOO!
I finished cleaning the rest-room.
TAKA-HASHI-SAN!
SWIP
HAVE YOU STARTED?
Hi, how are you?
KAZEHAYA TOLD ME ABOUT THIS.
Heh heh, lucky me!
From the next class
HUH?
Hi.
TMP TMP TMP TMP TMP
What about Ryu?
He went home!
KAZEHAYA-KUN MUST HAVE...
FWSH
SO IT WAS TRUE.
KAZEHAYA SAID HE WAS GOING.
Let's look.
THERE'S KAZEHAYA.
They really are studying.
I'VE HEARD SADAKO'S TEST PREDIC-TIONS ARE GOOD.
WANNA GO IN?

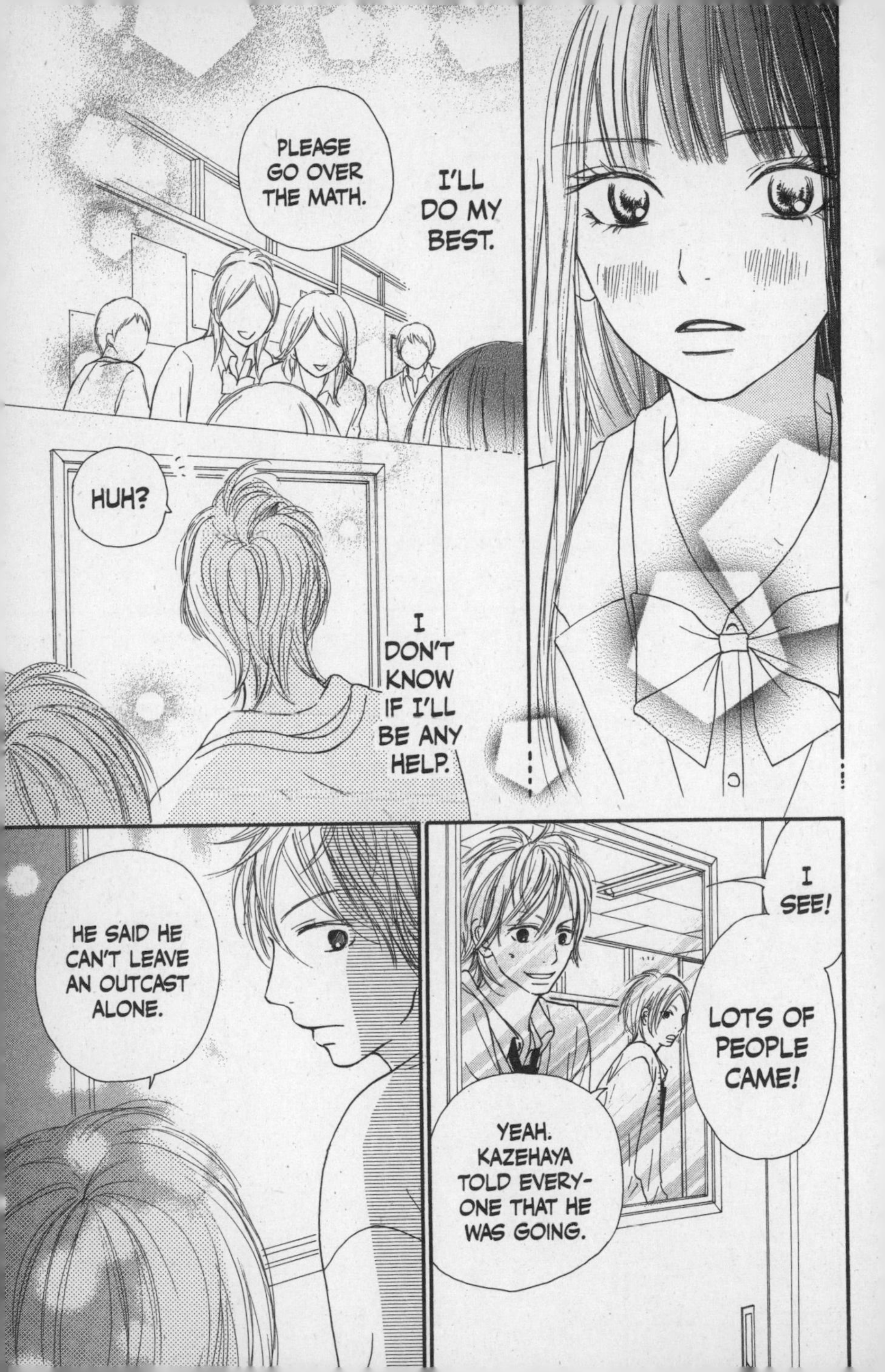
PLEASE GO OVER THE MATH.
I'LL DO MY BEST.
HUH?
I DON'T KNOW IF I'LL BE ANY HELP.
I SEE!
LOTS OF PEOPLE CAME!
YEAH. KAZEHAYA TOLD EVERY-ONE THAT HE WAS GOING.
HE SAID HE CAN'T LEAVE AN OUTCAST ALONE.

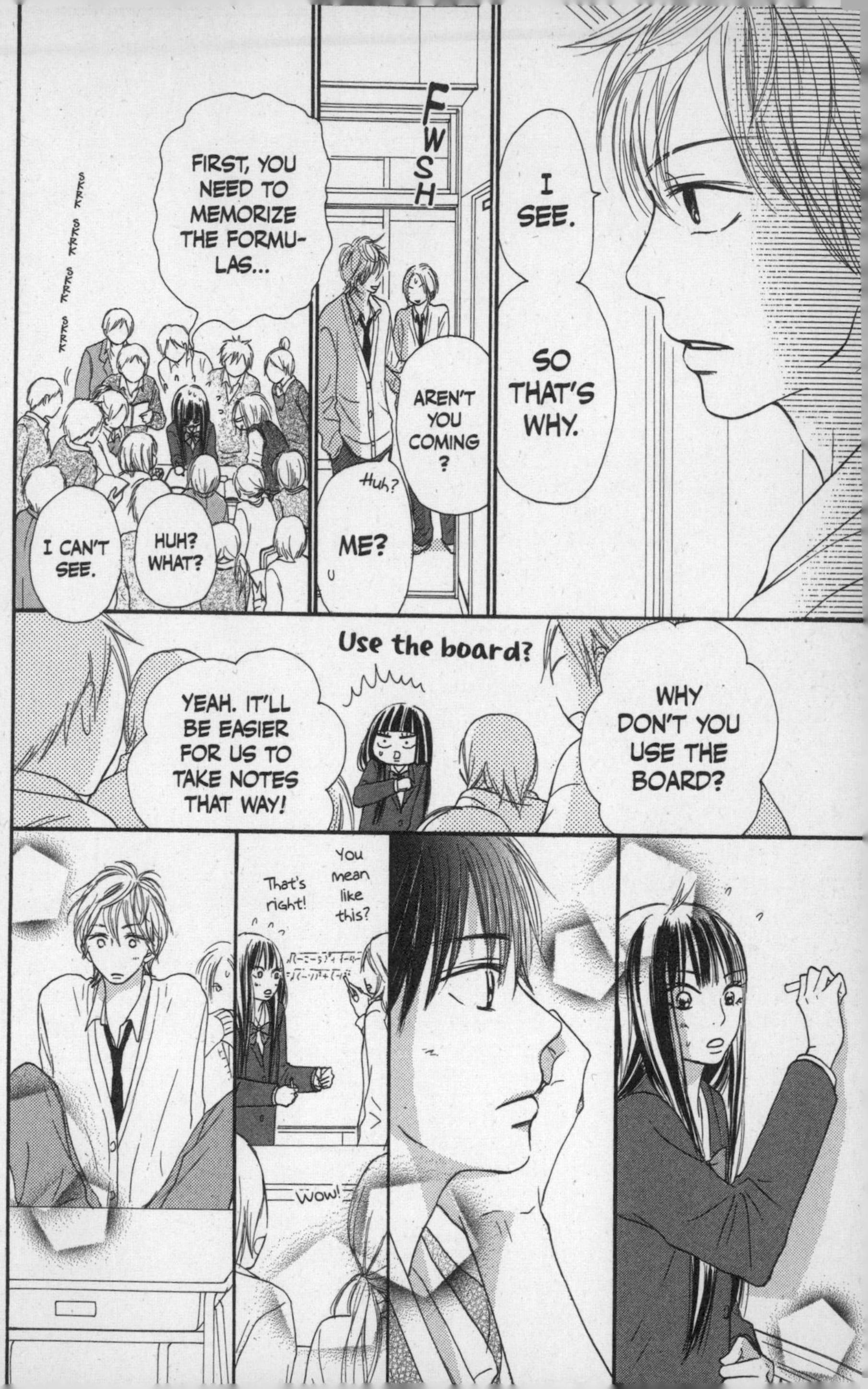
I SEE.
SO THAT'S WHY.
FWSH
AREN'T YOU COMING?
Huh?
ME?
FIRST, YOU NEED TO MEMORIZE THE FORMU-LAS...
SKRK SKRK SKRK SKRK
HUH? WHAT?
I CAN'T SEE.
WHY DON'T YOU USE THE BOARD?
Use the board?
YEAH. IT'LL BE EASIER FOR US TO TAKE NOTES THAT WAY!
You mean like this?
That's right!
WOW!

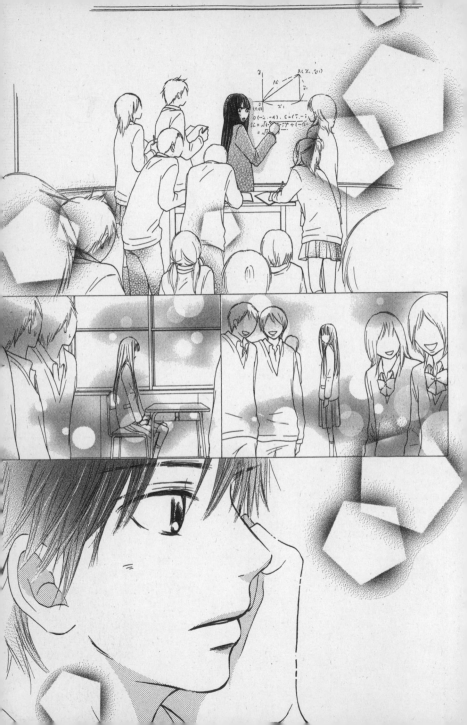

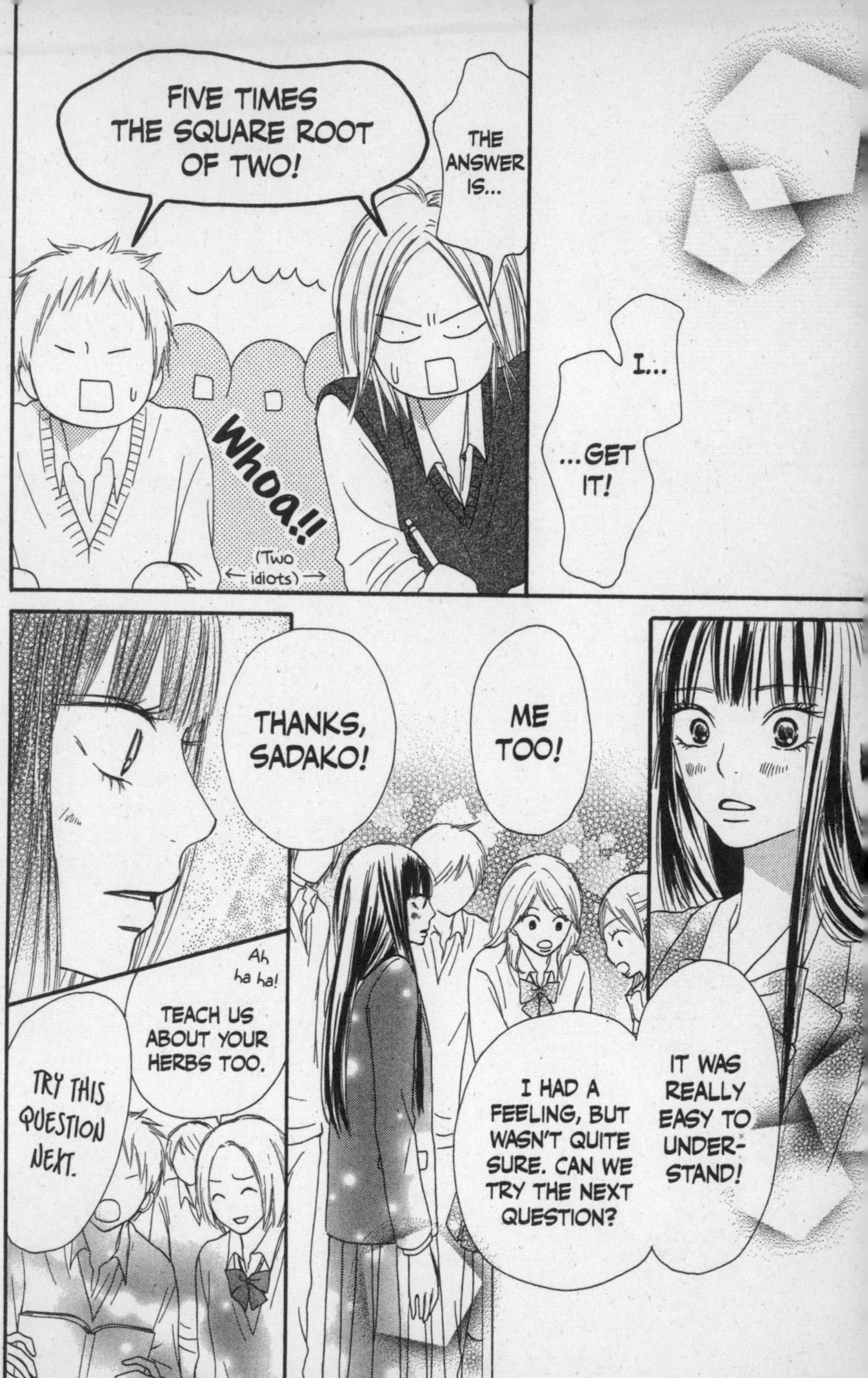
I...
...GET IT!
THE ANSWER IS...
FIVE TIMES THE SQUARE ROOT OF TWO!
Whoa!!
(Two idiots)
IT WAS REALLY EASY TO UNDER-STAND!
I HAD A FEELING, BUT WASN'T QUITE SURE. CAN WE TRY THE NEXT QUESTION?
ME TOO!
THANKS, SADAKO!
Ah ha ha!
TEACH US ABOUT YOUR HERBS TOO.
TRY THIS QUESTION NEXT.

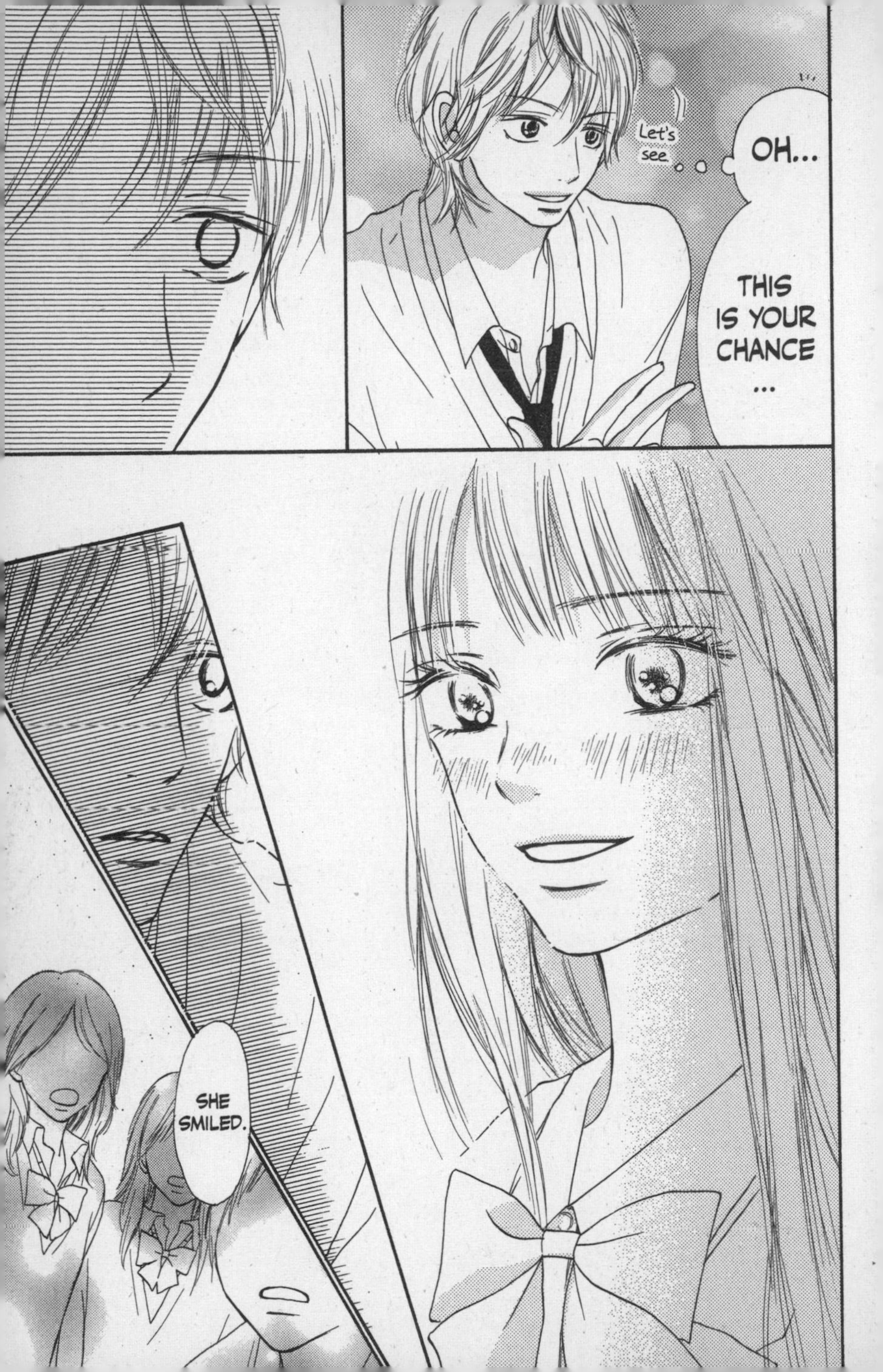
Let's see
OH...
THIS IS YOUR CHANCE ...
SHE SMILED.

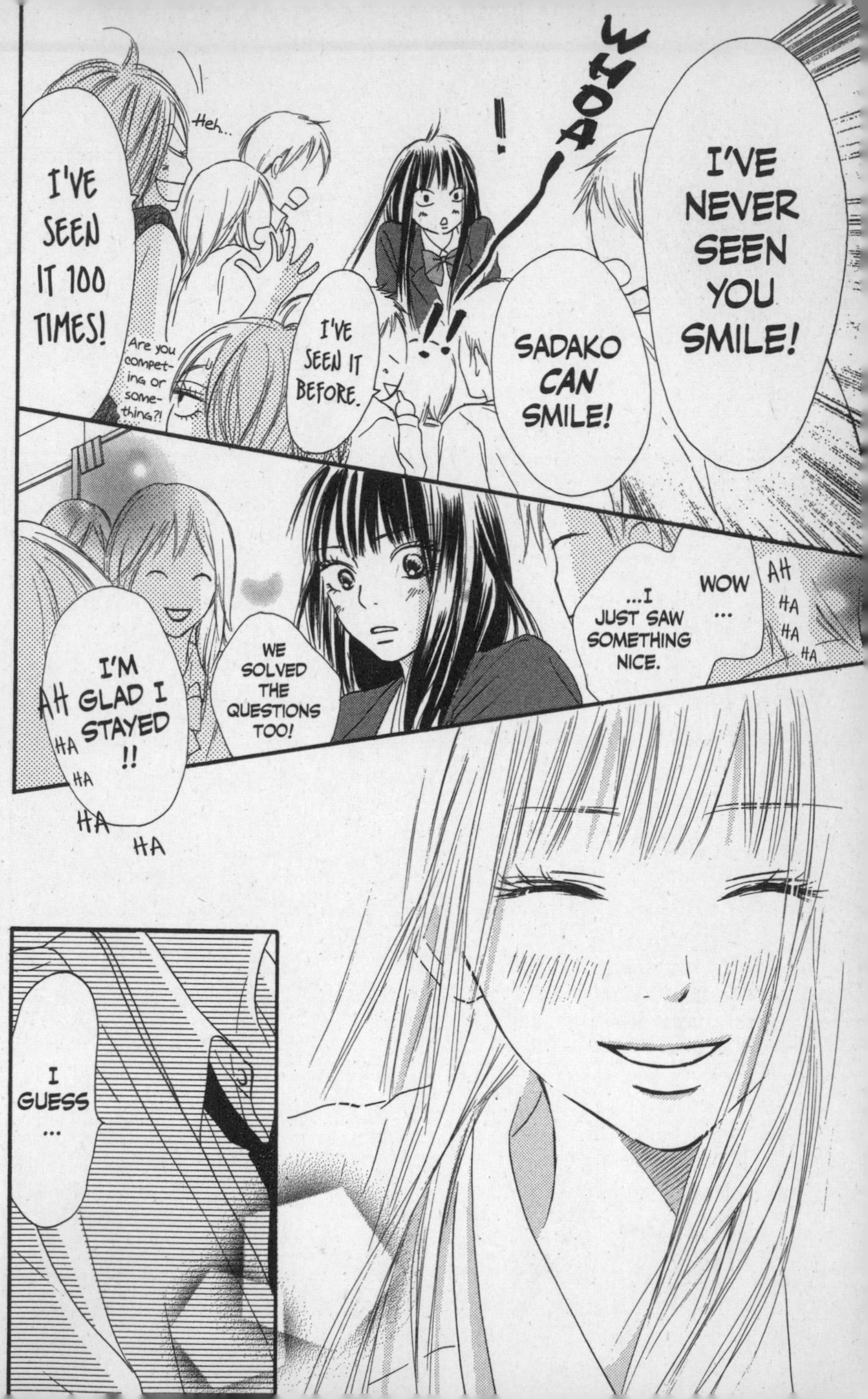
WHOA!
I'VE NEVER SEEN YOU SMILE!
!
SADAKO CAN SMILE!
!!
I'VE SEEN IT BEFORE.
Heh...
I'VE SEEN IT 100 TIMES!
Are you competing or something?!
AH HA HA HA
WOW ...
...I JUST SAW SOMETHING NICE.
WE SOLVED THE QUESTIONS TOO!
I'M GLAD I STAYED !!
AH HA HA HA HA
I GUESS ...

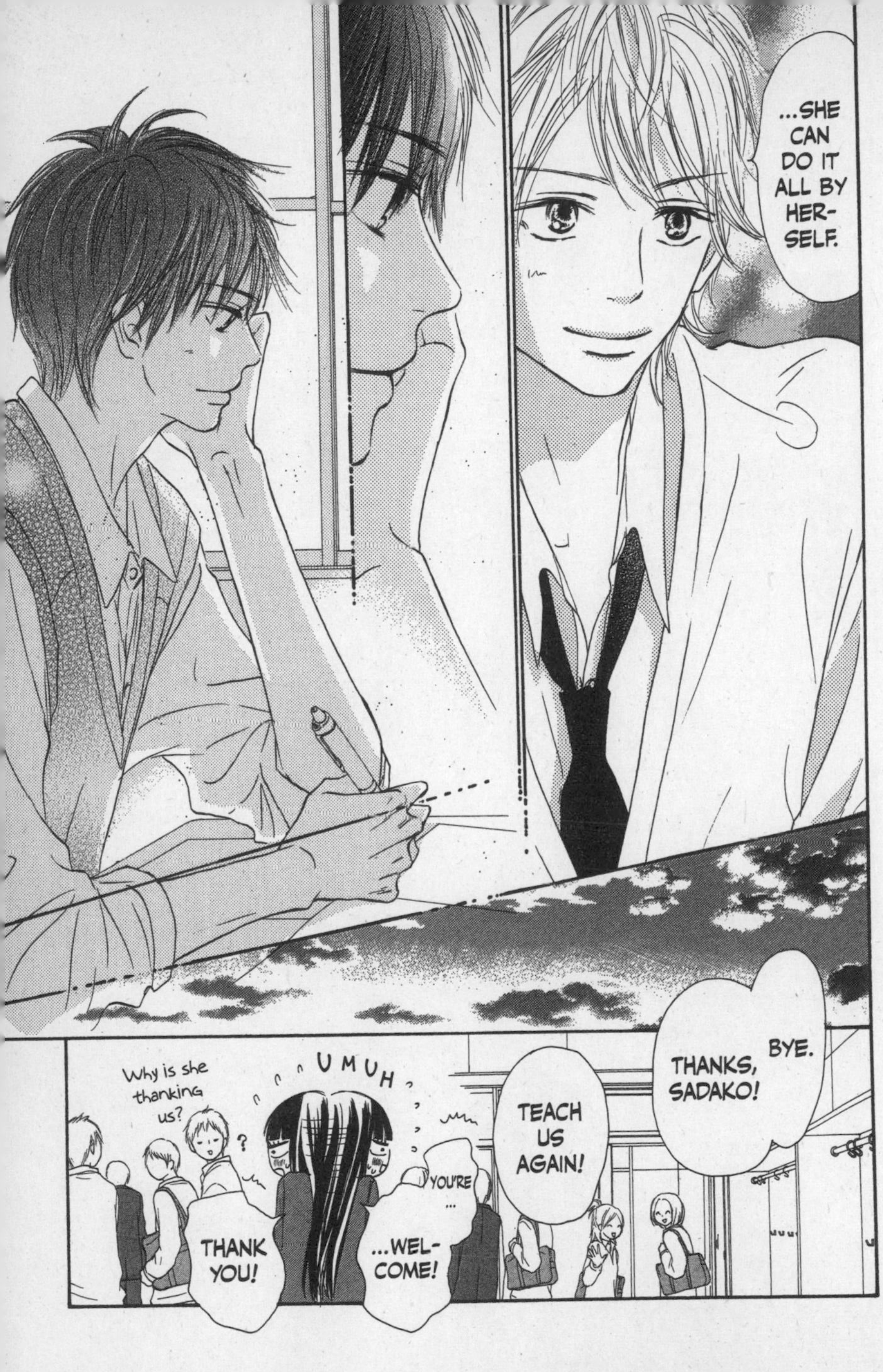
...SHE CAN DO IT ALL BY HER-SELF.
BYE.
THANKS, SADAKO!
TEACH US AGAIN!
YOU'RE ...
...WEL-COME!
UMUH
THANK YOU!
Why is she thanking us?

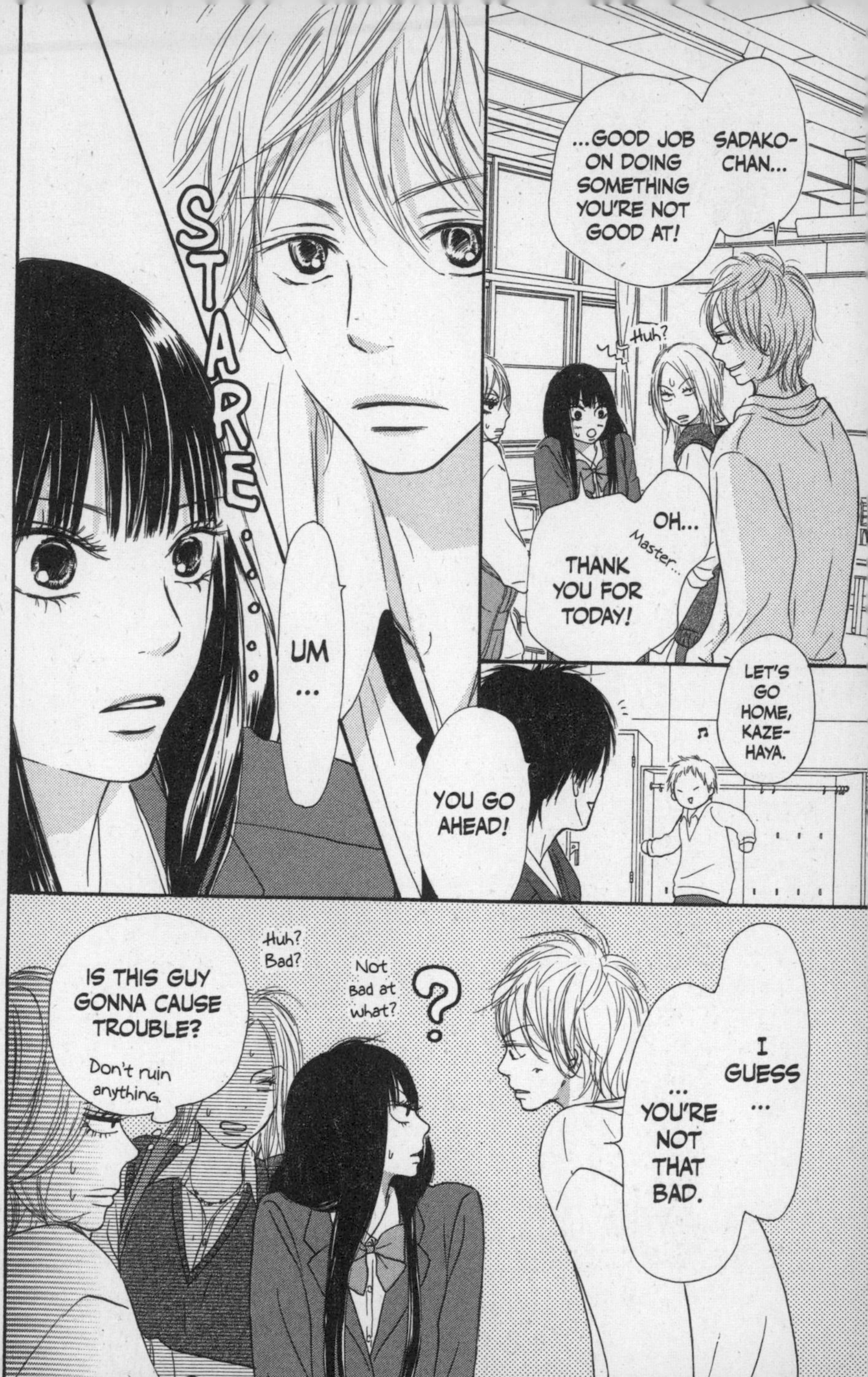
SADAKO-CHAN...
...GOOD JOB ON DOING SOMETHING YOU'RE NOT GOOD AT!
Huh?
OH...
Master...
THANK YOU FOR TODAY!
LET'S GO HOME, KAZE-HAYA.
YOU GO AHEAD!
STARE
UM...
I GUESS...
...YOU'RE NOT THAT BAD.
?
Not bad at what?
Huh? Bad?
IS THIS GUY GONNA CAUSE TROUBLE?
Don't ruin anything.

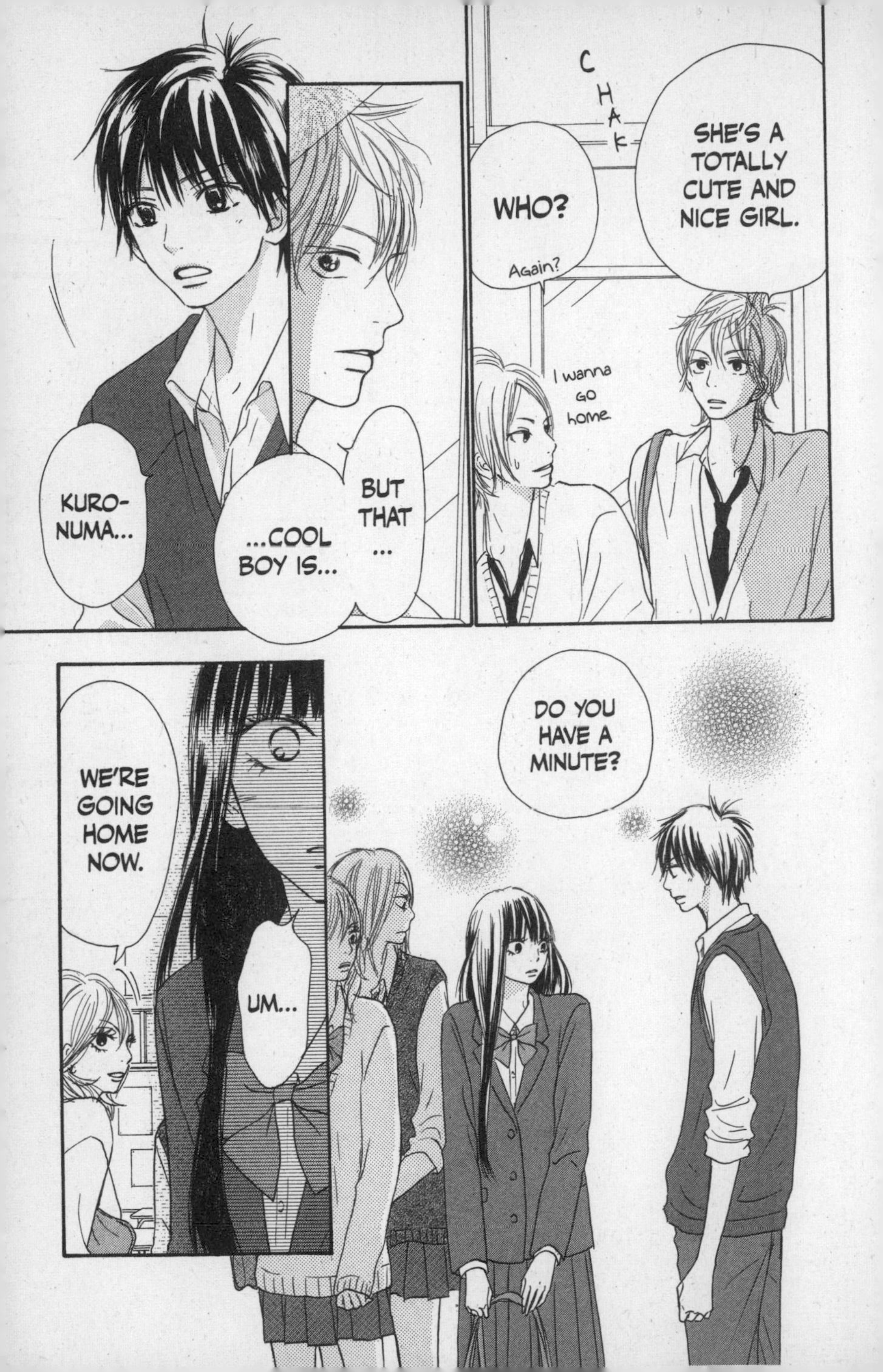
SHE'S A TOTALLY CUTE AND NICE GIRL.
CHAK
WHO?
Again?
I wanna go home.
BUT THAT...
...COOL BOY IS...
KURO-NUMA...
DO YOU HAVE A MINUTE?
WE'RE GOING HOME NOW.
UM...

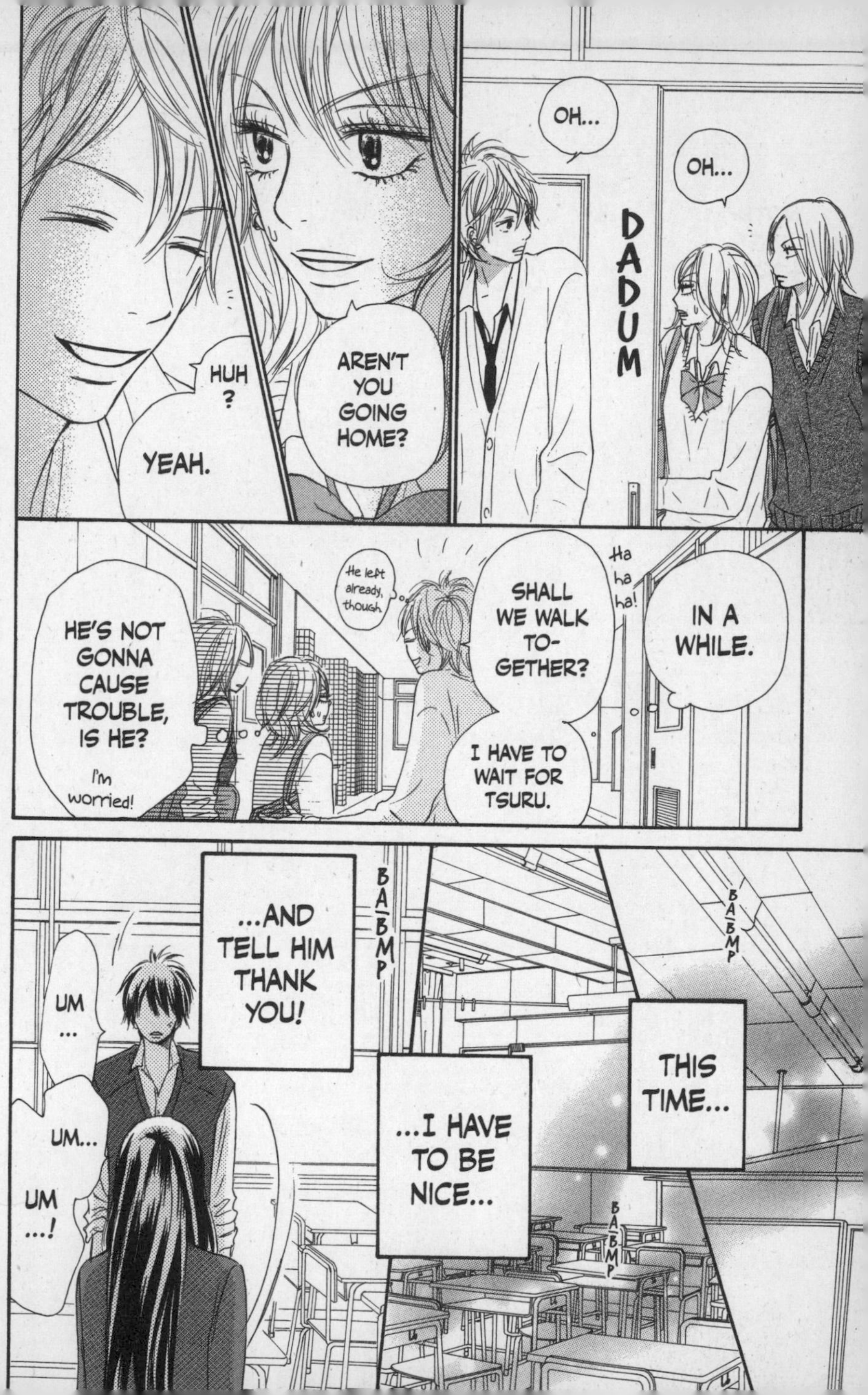
OH...
OH...
DADUM
AREN'T YOU GOING HOME?
HUH?
YEAH.
IN A WHILE.
Ha ha ha!
SHALL WE WALK TO-GETHER?
I HAVE TO WAIT FOR TSURU.
He left already, though.
HE'S NOT GONNA CAUSE TROUBLE, IS HE?
I'm worried!
BA-BMP
THIS TIME...
BA-BMP
...I HAVE TO BE NICE...
BA-BMP
...AND TELL HIM THANK YOU!
UM...
UM...
UM...!

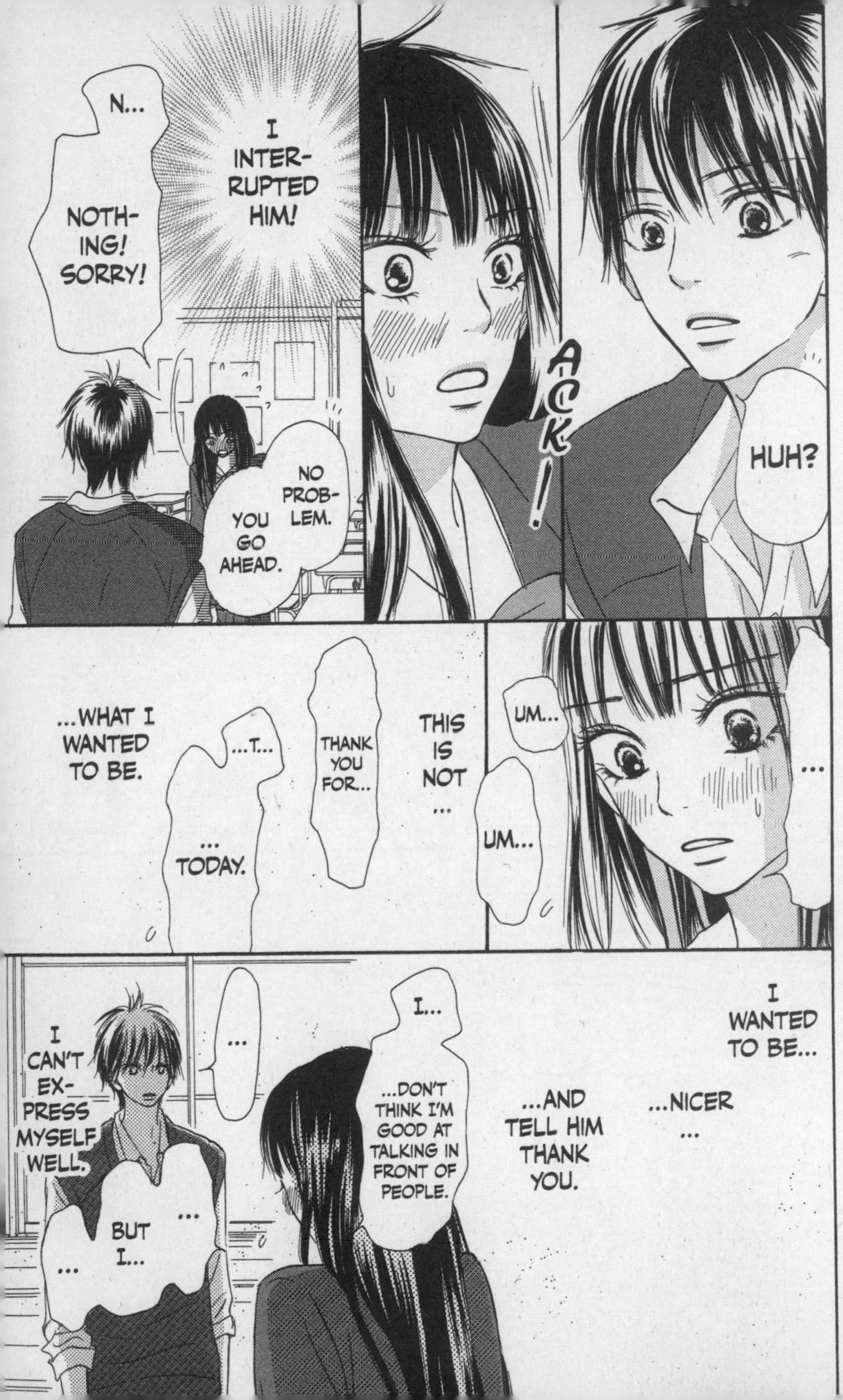
HUH?
ACK!
I INTERRUPTED HIM!
N... NOTHING! SORRY!
NO PROBLEM. YOU GO AHEAD.
...
UM...
UM...
THIS IS NOT ...
THANK YOU FOR...
...T... ...TODAY.
...WHAT I WANTED TO BE.
I WANTED TO BE...
...NICER ...
...AND TELL HIM THANK YOU.
I...
...DON'T THINK I'M GOOD AT TALKING IN FRONT OF PEOPLE.
...
I CAN'T EXPRESS MYSELF WELL.
... BUT I... ...

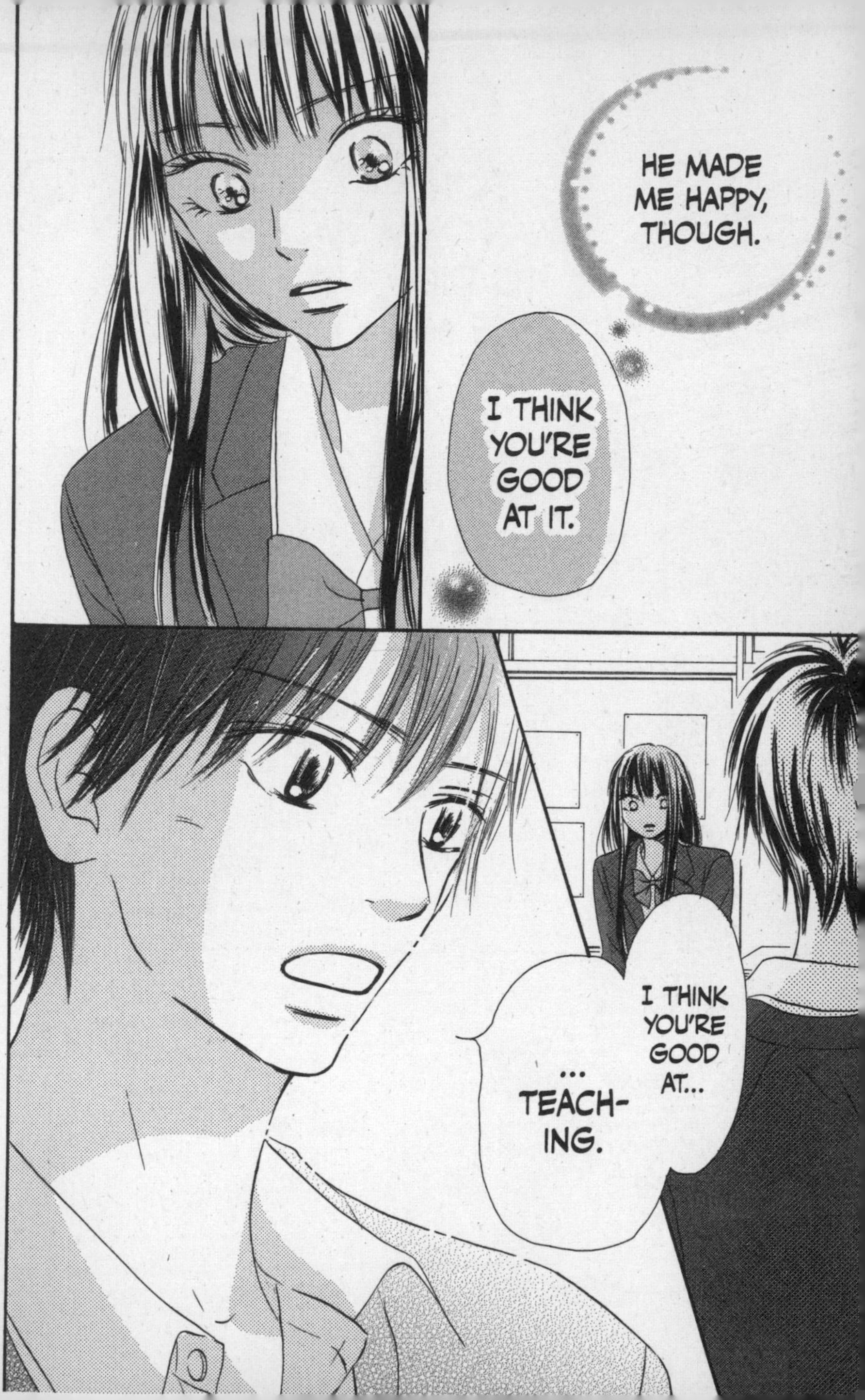
HE MADE ME HAPPY, THOUGH.
I THINK YOU'RE GOOD AT IT.
I THINK YOU'RE GOOD AT...
...TEACHING.

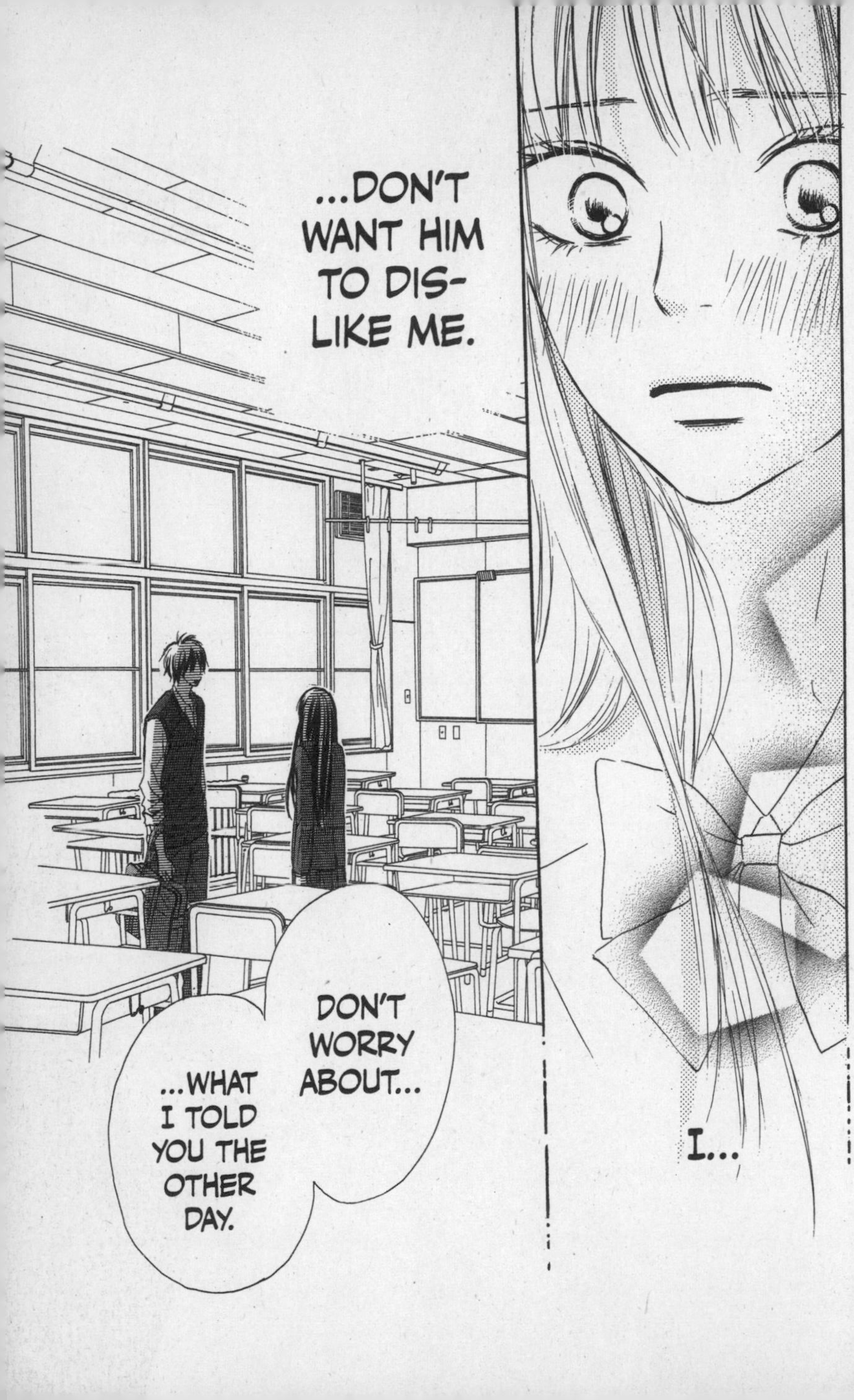
I...
...DON'T WANT HIM TO DIS-LIKE ME.
DON'T WORRY ABOUT...
...WHAT I TOLD YOU THE OTHER DAY.

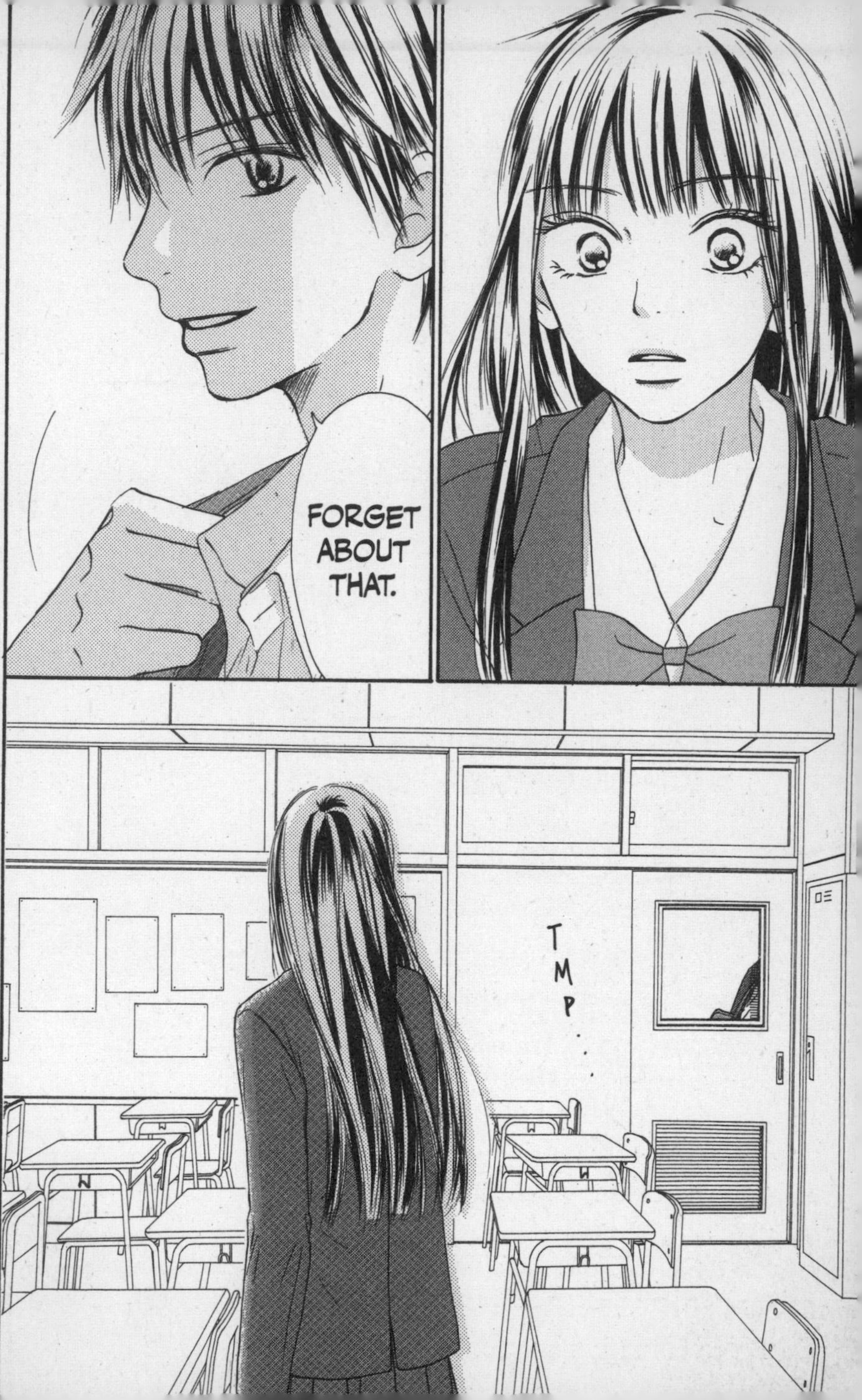
FORGET ABOUT THAT.
TMP . . .

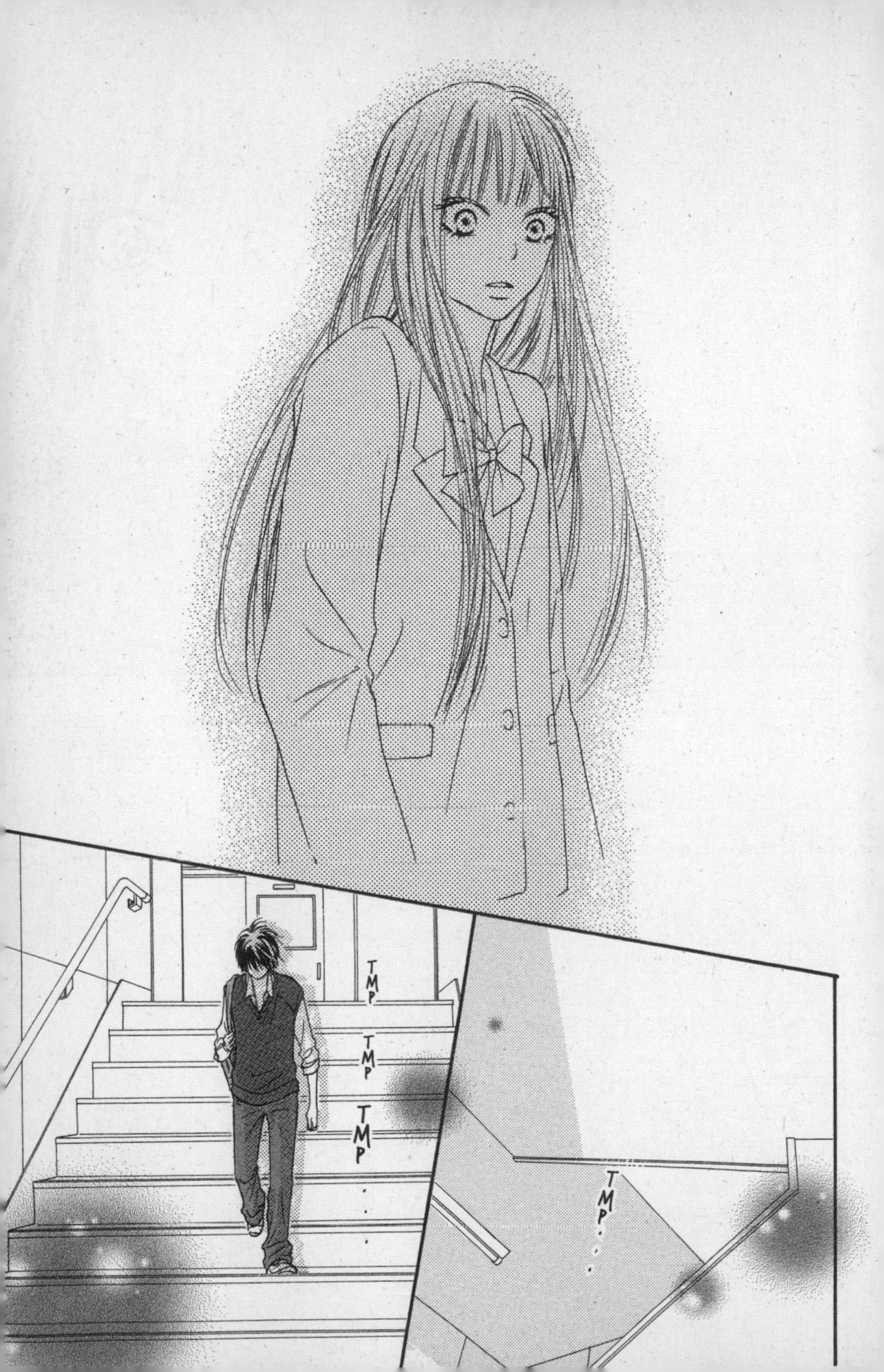
TMP...
TMP
TMP
TMP
. . .

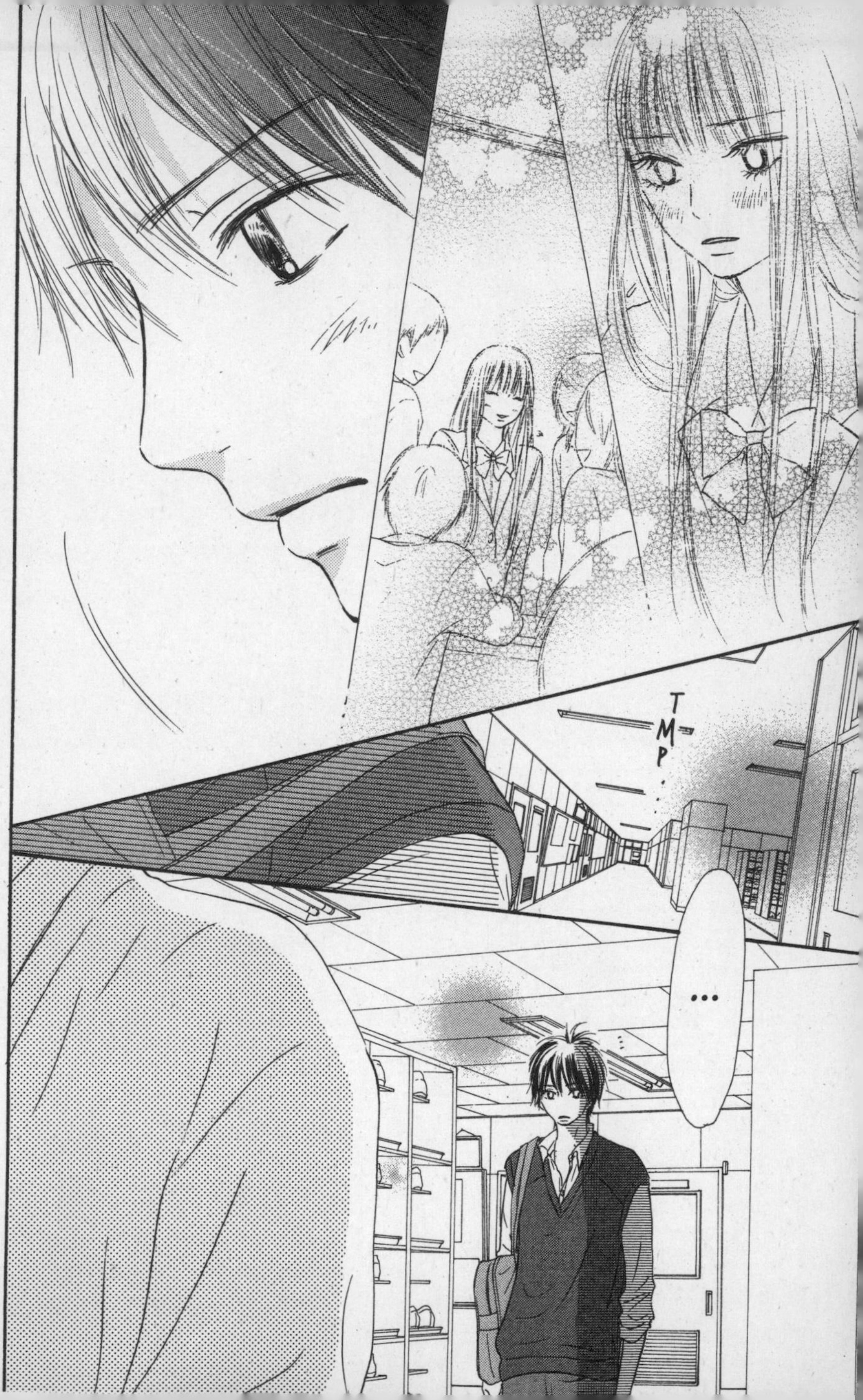
TMP . .
...

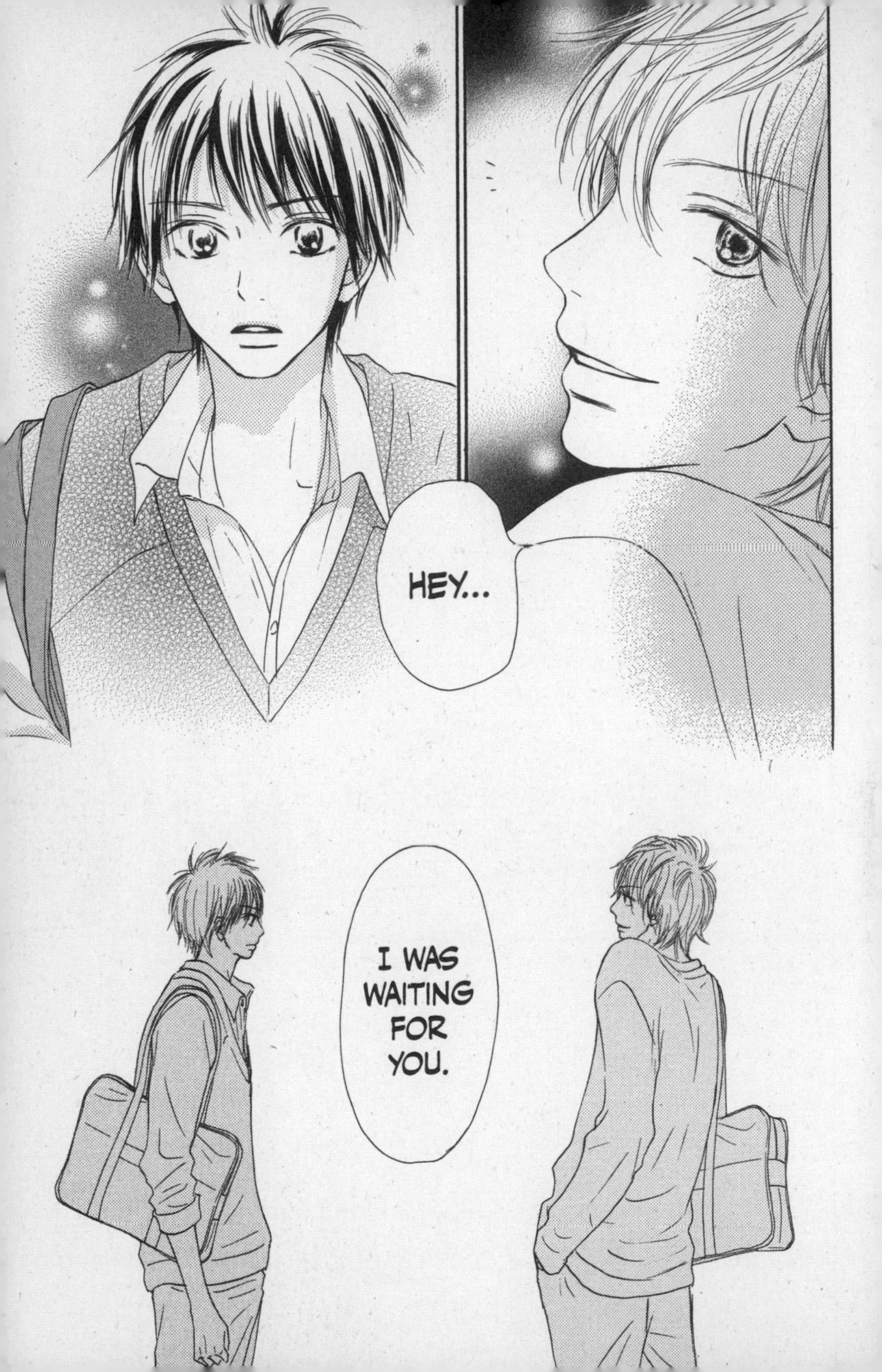
HEY...
I WAS WAITING FOR YOU.

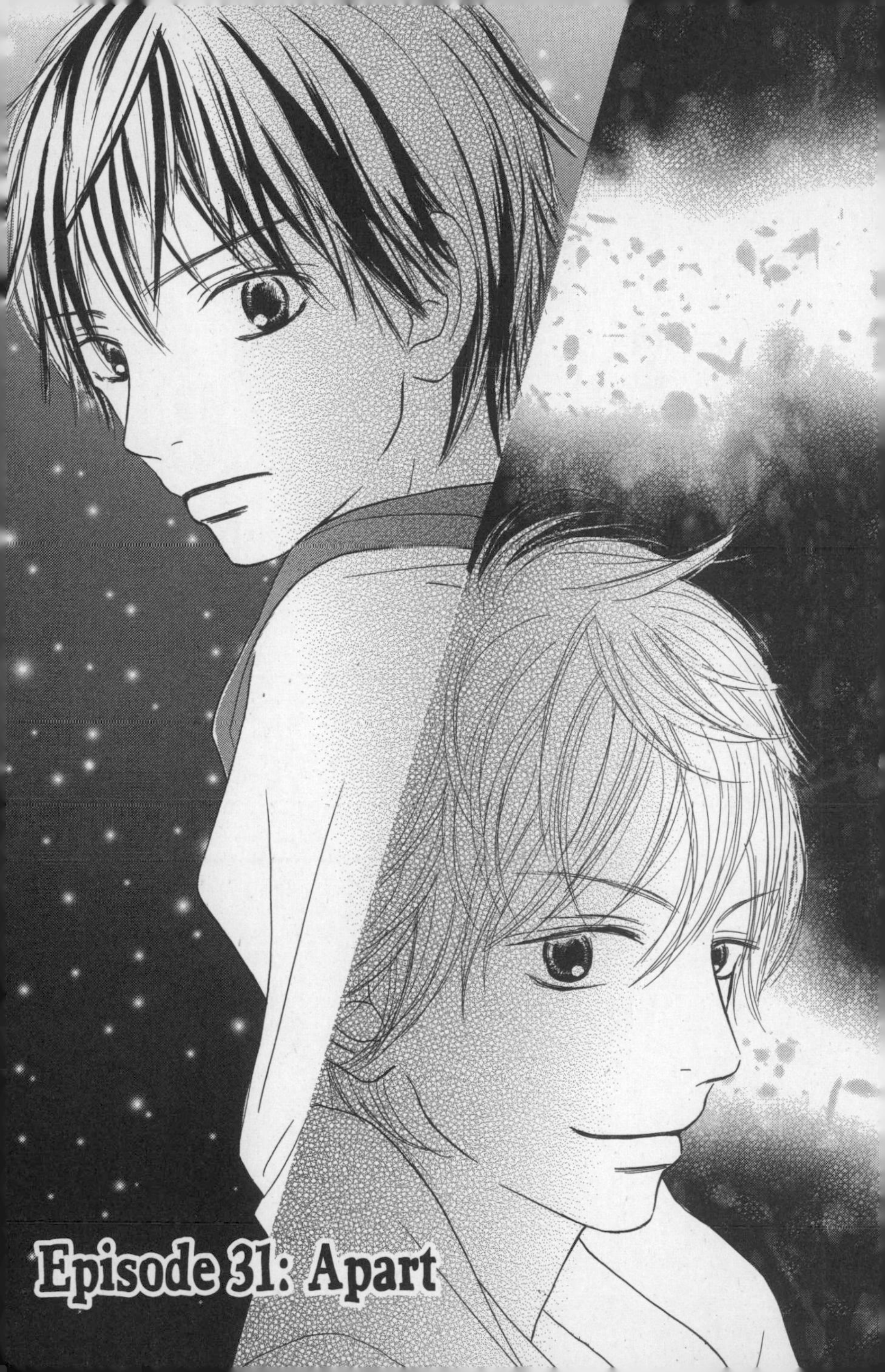
Episode 31: Apart

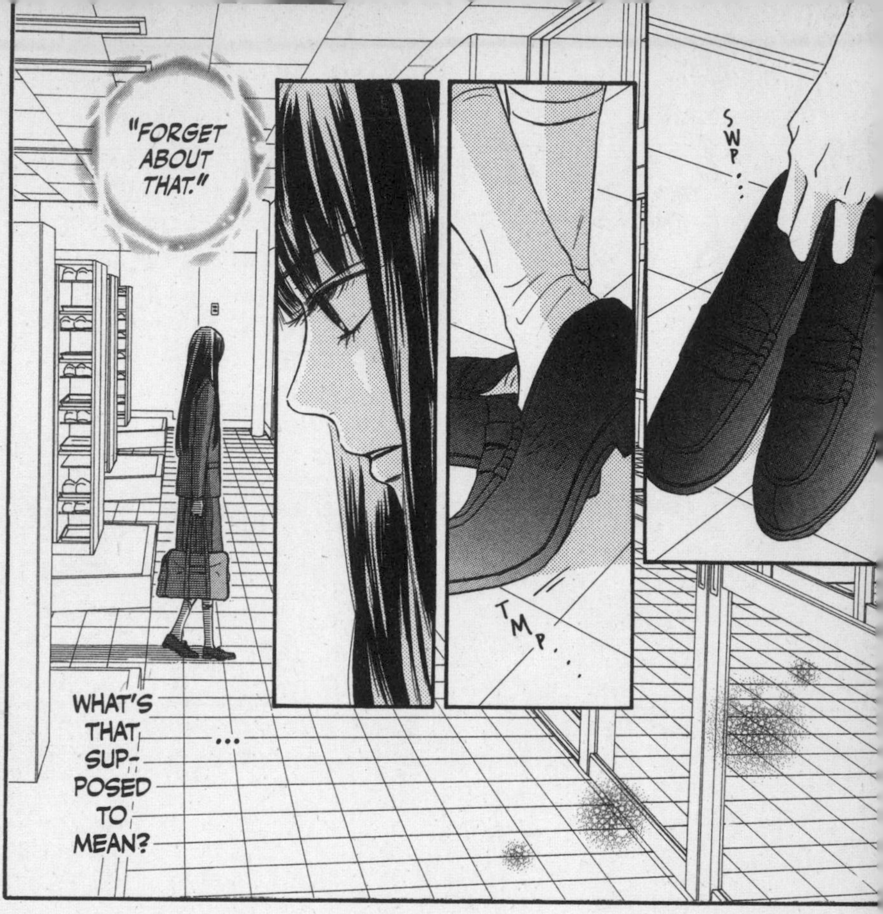
SWP...
TMP...
"FORGET ABOUT THAT."
...
WHAT'S THAT SUP-POSED TO MEAN?

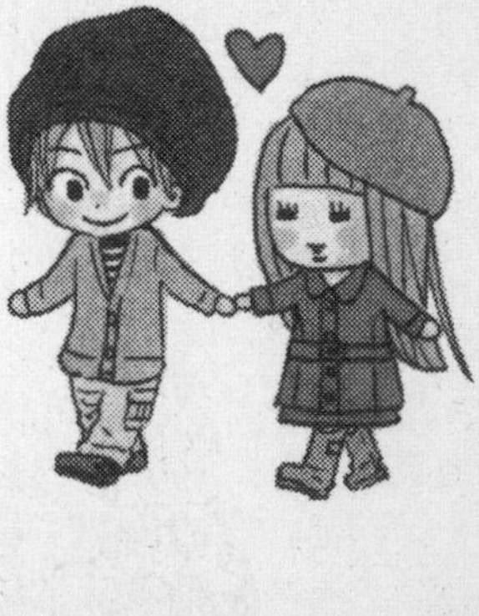

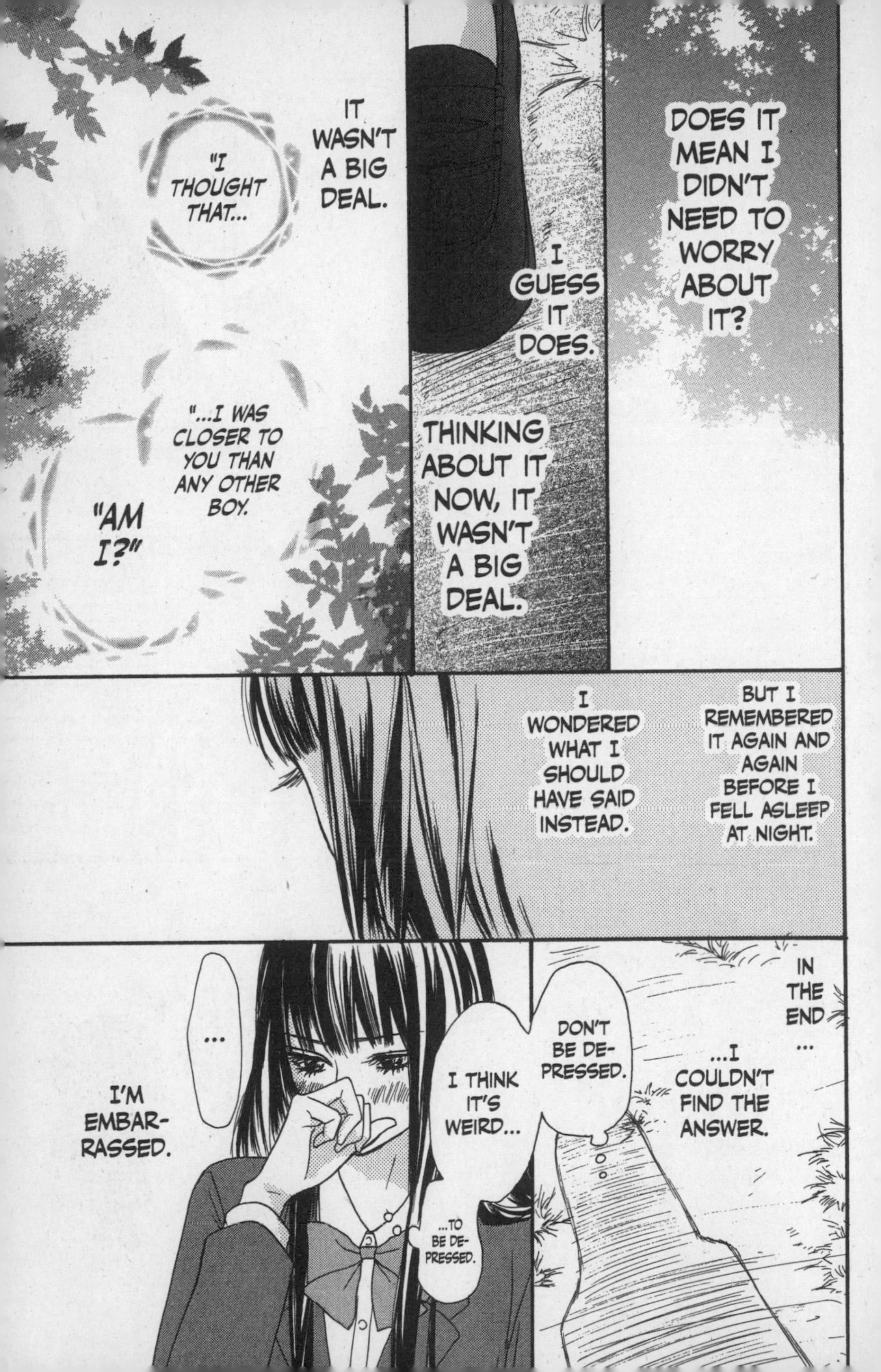
DOES IT MEAN I DIDN'T NEED TO WORRY ABOUT IT?
I GUESS IT DOES.
THINKING ABOUT IT NOW, IT WASN'T A BIG DEAL.
IT WASN'T A BIG DEAL.
"I THOUGHT THAT...
"...I WAS CLOSER TO YOU THAN ANY OTHER BOY.
"AM I?"
BUT I REMEMBERED IT AGAIN AND AGAIN BEFORE I FELL ASLEEP AT NIGHT.
I WONDERED WHAT I SHOULD HAVE SAID INSTEAD.
IN THE END...
...I COULDN'T FIND THE ANSWER.
DON'T BE DE-PRESSED.
I THINK IT'S WEIRD...
...TO BE DE-PRESSED.
...
I'M EMBAR-RASSED.

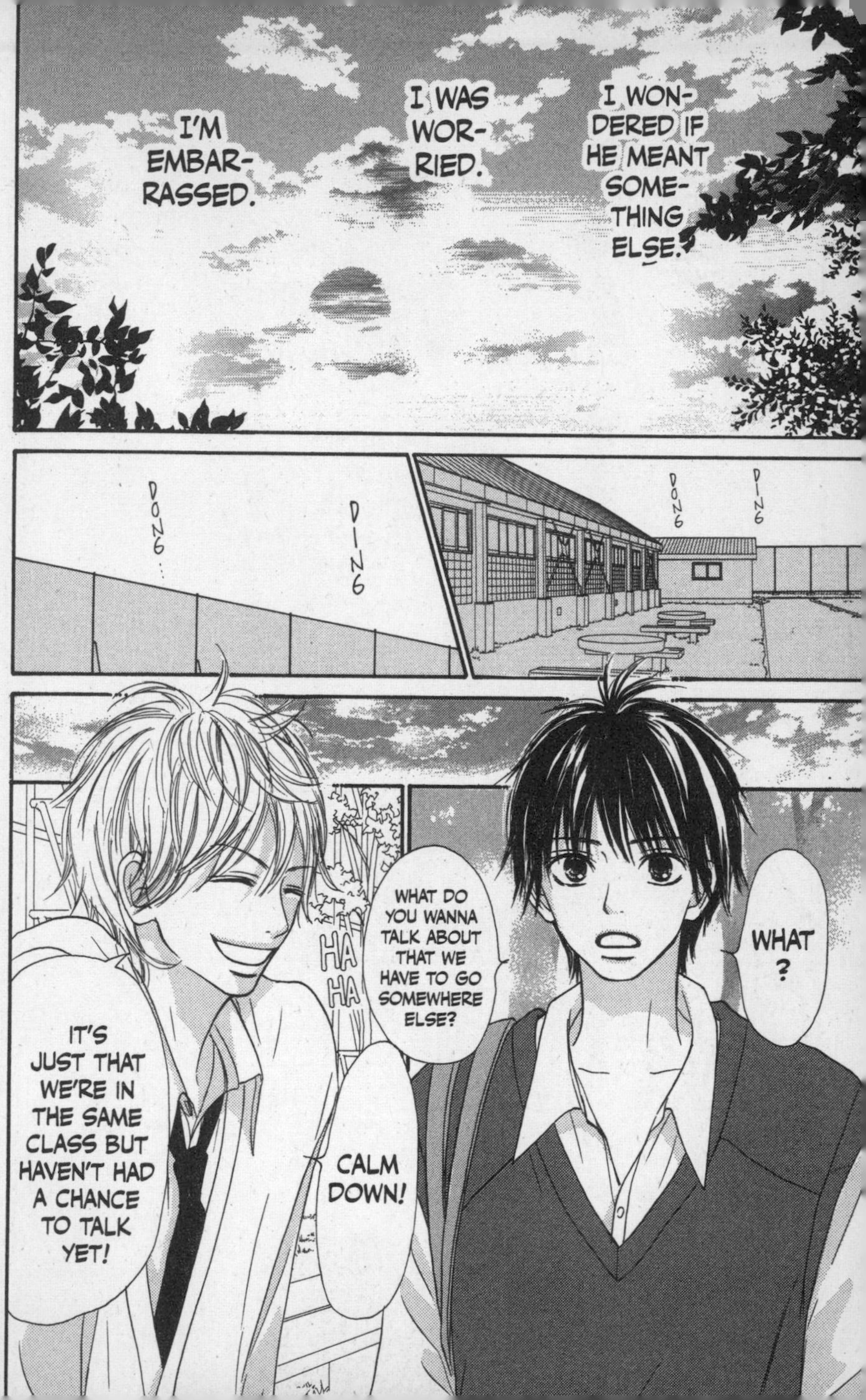
I WONDERED IF HE MEANT SOMETHING ELSE.
I WAS WORRIED.
I'M EMBARRASSED.
DING
DONG
DING
DONG...
WHAT?
WHAT DO YOU WANNA TALK ABOUT THAT WE HAVE TO GO SOMEWHERE ELSE?
HA HA
CALM DOWN!
IT'S JUST THAT WE'RE IN THE SAME CLASS BUT HAVEN'T HAD A CHANCE TO TALK YET!

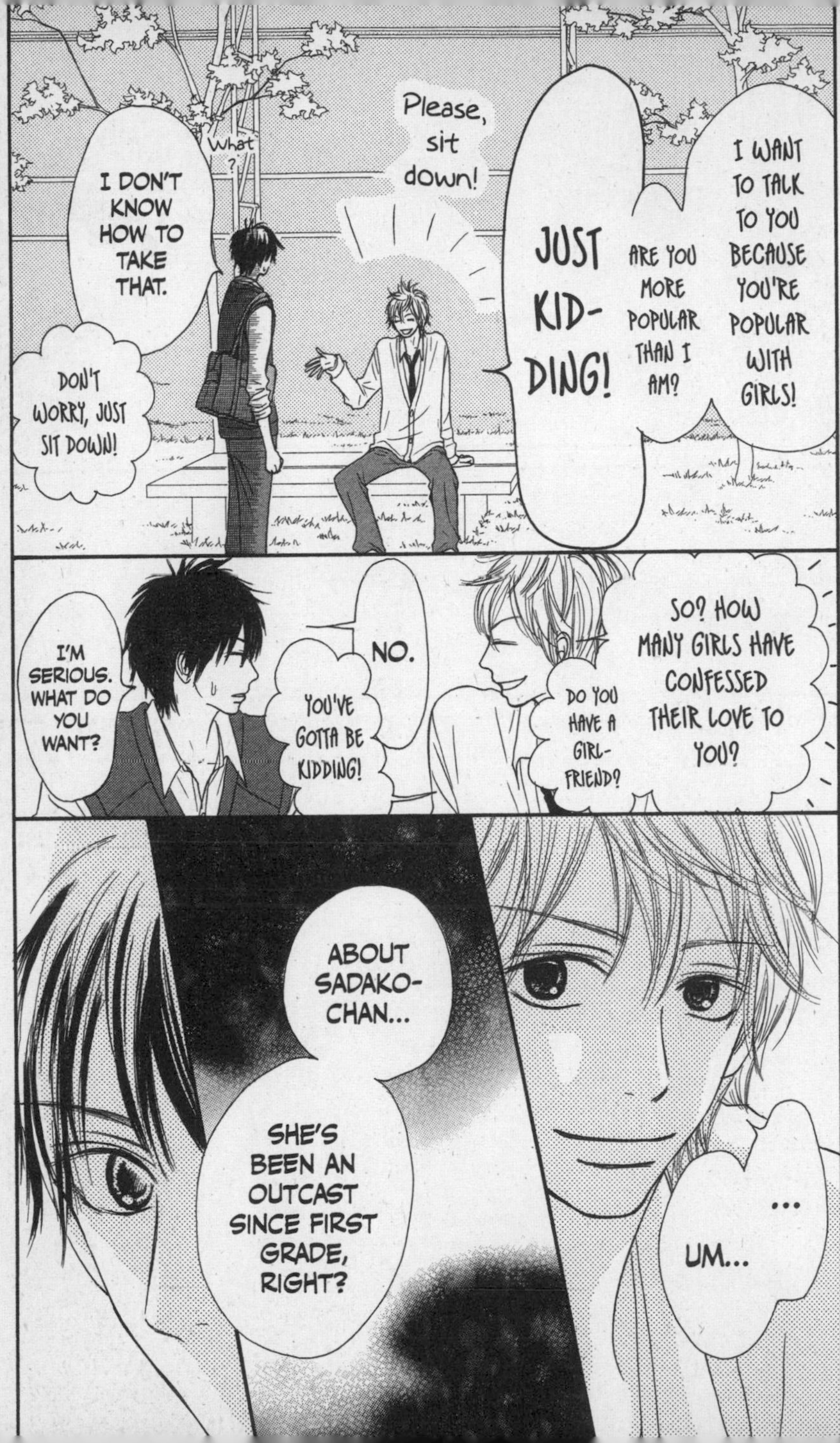
I WANT TO TALK TO YOU BECAUSE YOU'RE POPULAR WITH GIRLS!
ARE YOU MORE POPULAR THAN I AM?
JUST KIDDING!
Please, sit down!
What?
I DON'T KNOW HOW TO TAKE THAT.
DON'T WORRY, JUST SIT DOWN!
SO? HOW MANY GIRLS HAVE CONFESSED THEIR LOVE TO YOU?
DO YOU HAVE A GIRLFRIEND?
NO.
YOU'VE GOTTA BE KIDDING!
I'M SERIOUS. WHAT DO YOU WANT?
ABOUT SADAKO-CHAN...
SHE'S BEEN AN OUTCAST SINCE FIRST GRADE, RIGHT?
...
UM...

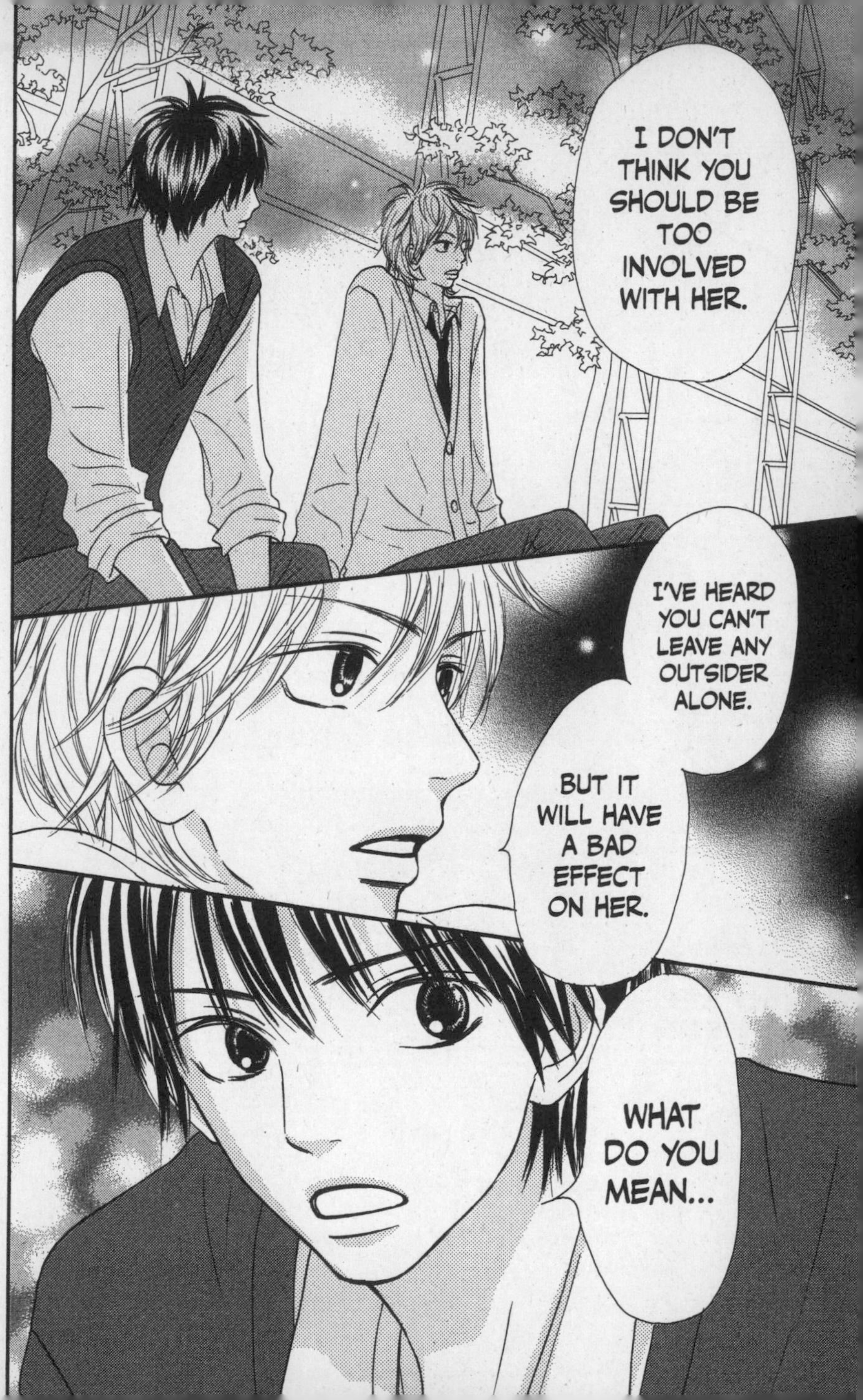
I DON'T THINK YOU SHOULD BE TOO INVOLVED WITH HER.
I'VE HEARD YOU CAN'T LEAVE ANY OUTSIDER ALONE.
BUT IT WILL HAVE A BAD EFFECT ON HER.
WHAT DO YOU MEAN...

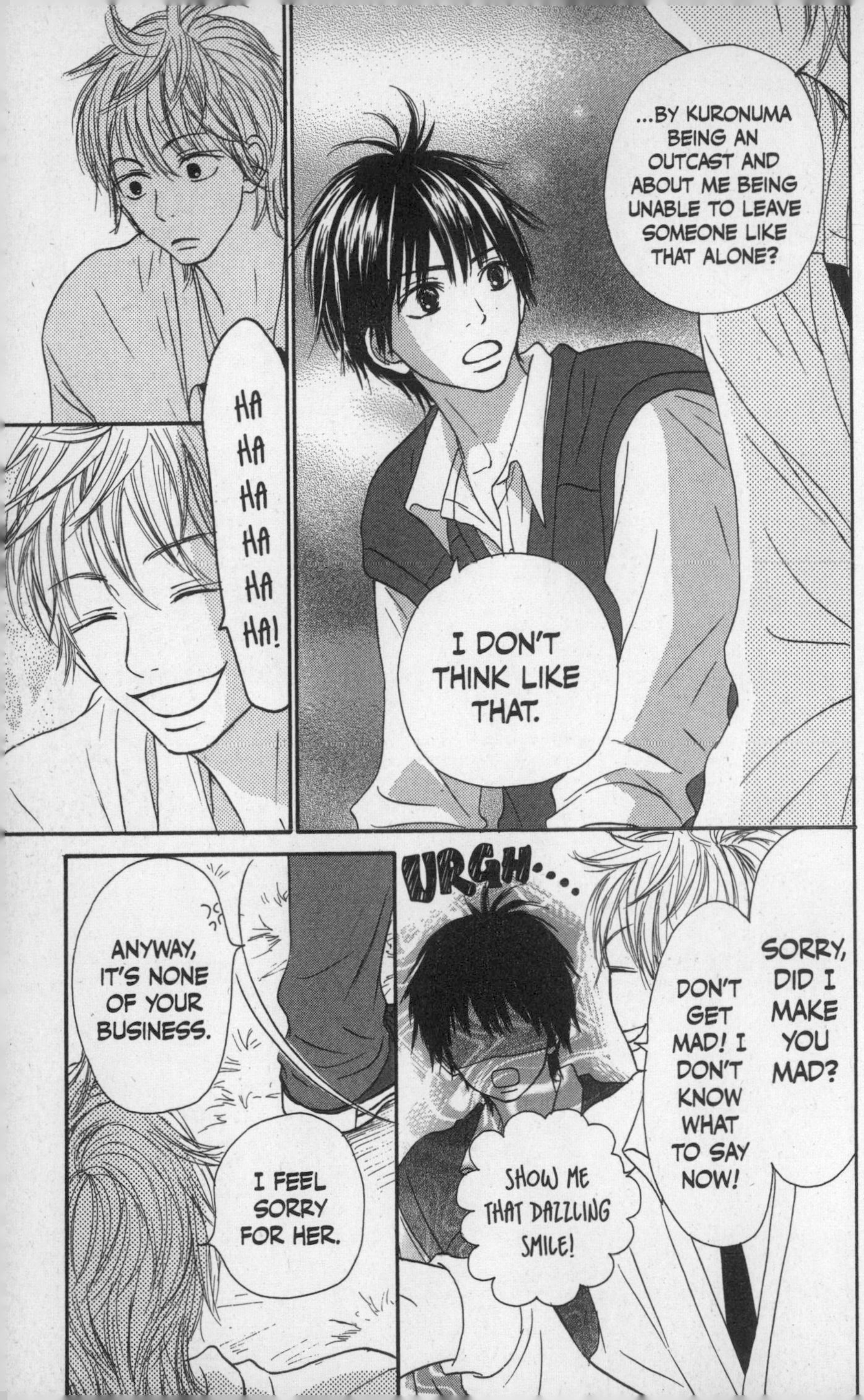
...BY KURONUMA BEING AN OUTCAST AND ABOUT ME BEING UNABLE TO LEAVE SOMEONE LIKE THAT ALONE?
I DON'T THINK LIKE THAT.
HA HA HA HA HA HA!
SORRY, DID I MAKE YOU MAD?
DON'T GET MAD! I DON'T KNOW WHAT TO SAY NOW!
URGH...
SHOW ME THAT DAZZLING SMILE!
ANYWAY, IT'S NONE OF YOUR BUSINESS.
I FEEL SORRY FOR HER.

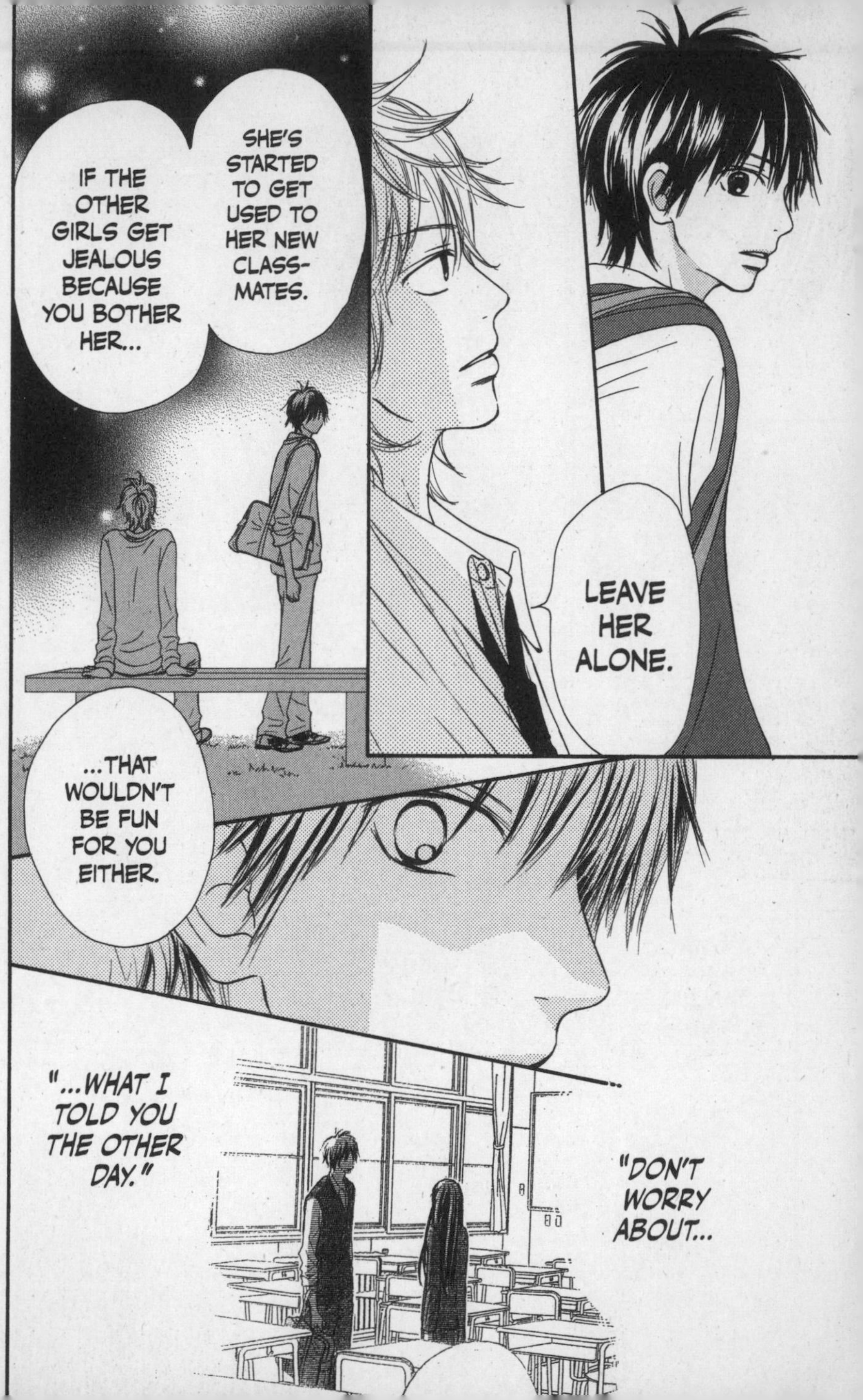
LEAVE HER ALONE.
SHE'S STARTED TO GET USED TO HER NEW CLASS-MATES.
IF THE OTHER GIRLS GET JEALOUS BECAUSE YOU BOTHER HER...
...THAT WOULDN'T BE FUN FOR YOU EITHER.
"DON'T WORRY ABOUT...
"...WHAT I TOLD YOU THE OTHER DAY."

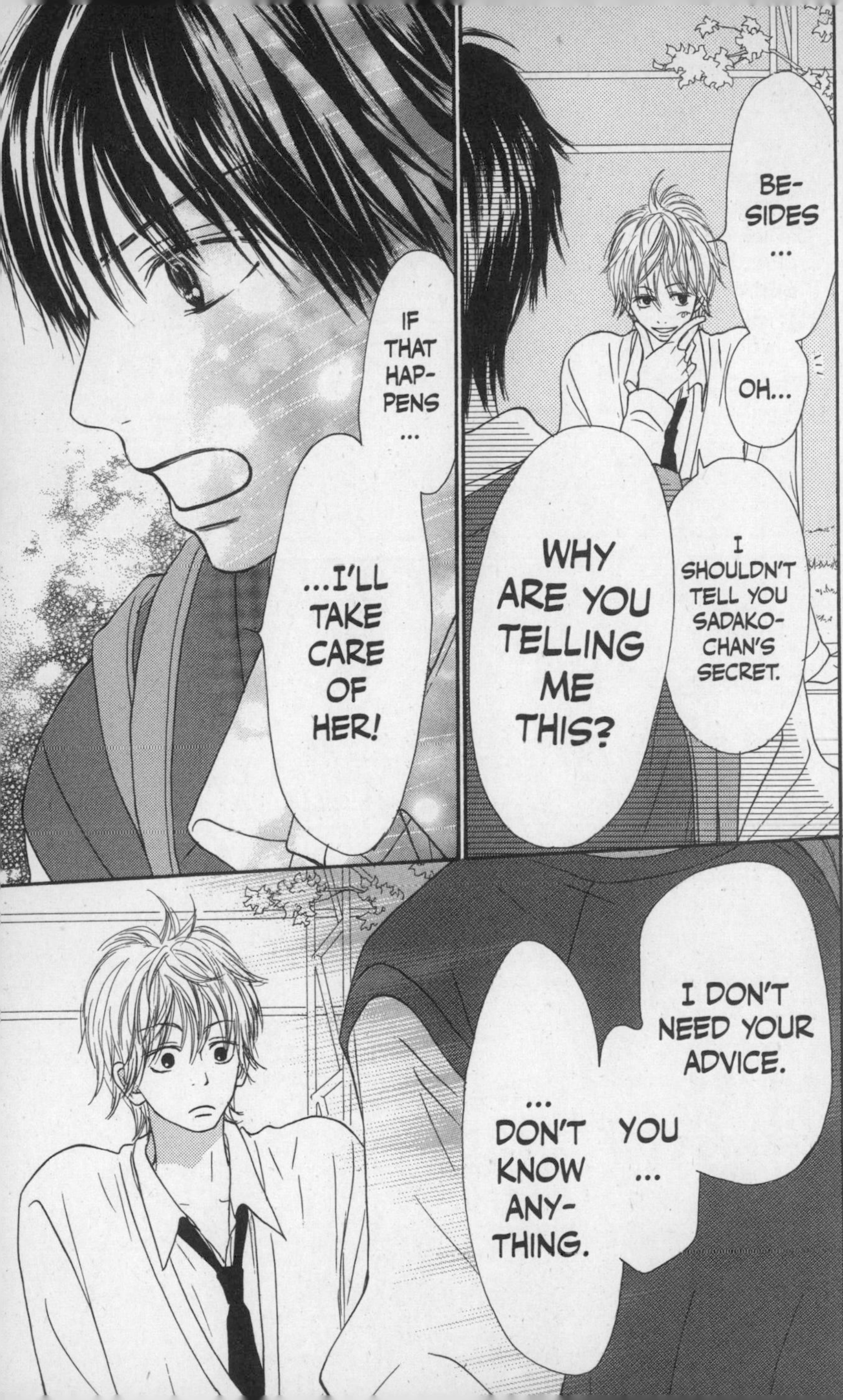
BE-
SIDES
...
OH...
I SHOULDN'T TELL YOU SADAKO-CHAN'S SECRET.
WHY ARE YOU TELLING ME THIS?
IF THAT HAP-
PENS
...
...I'LL TAKE CARE OF HER!
I DON'T NEED YOUR ADVICE.
YOU
...
...
DON'T KNOW ANY-
THING.

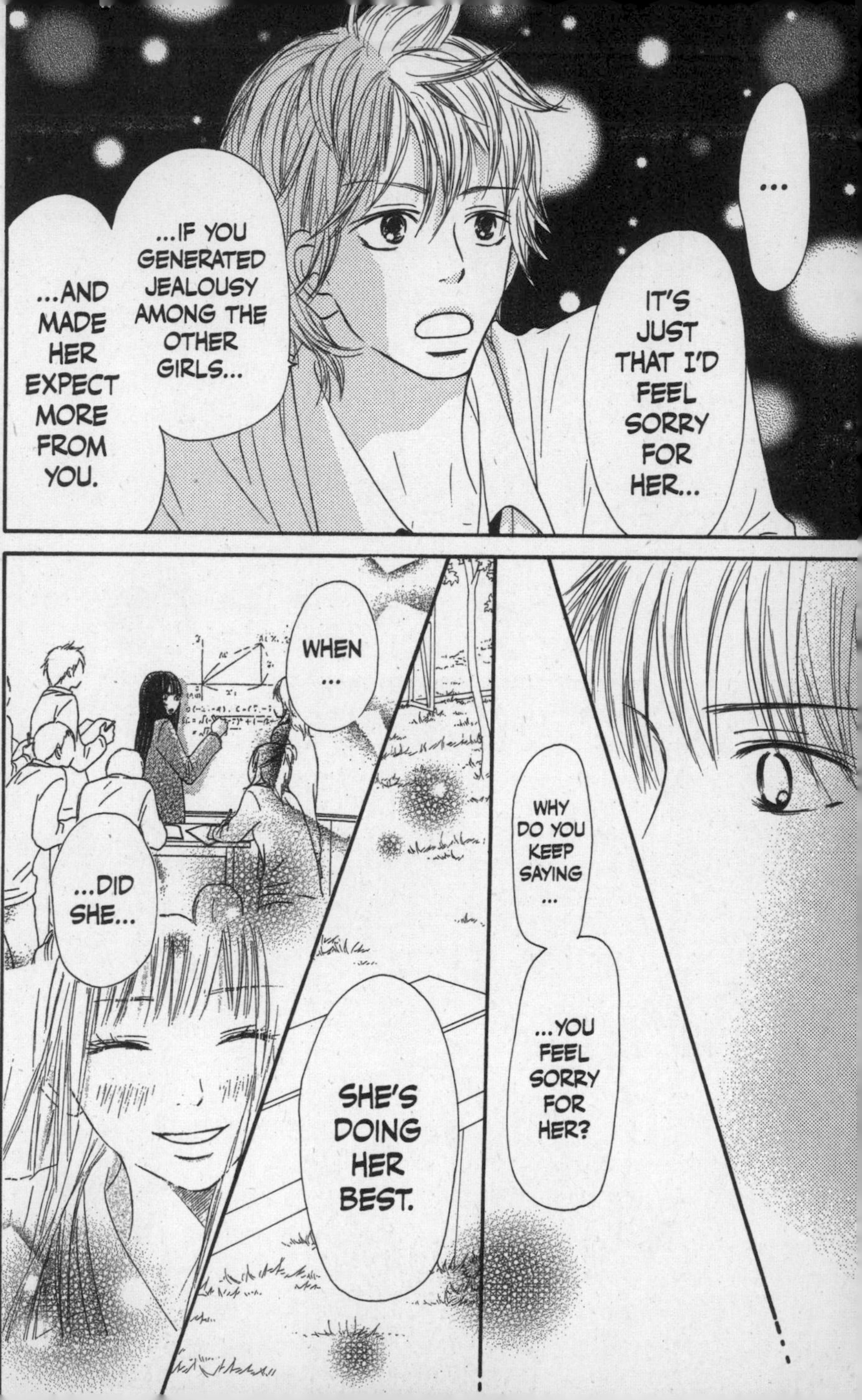
...
IT'S JUST THAT I'D FEEL SORRY FOR HER...
...IF YOU GENERATED JEALOUSY AMONG THE OTHER GIRLS...
...AND MADE HER EXPECT MORE FROM YOU.
WHY DO YOU KEEP SAYING...
...YOU FEEL SORRY FOR HER?
WHEN...
...DID SHE...
SHE'S DOING HER BEST.

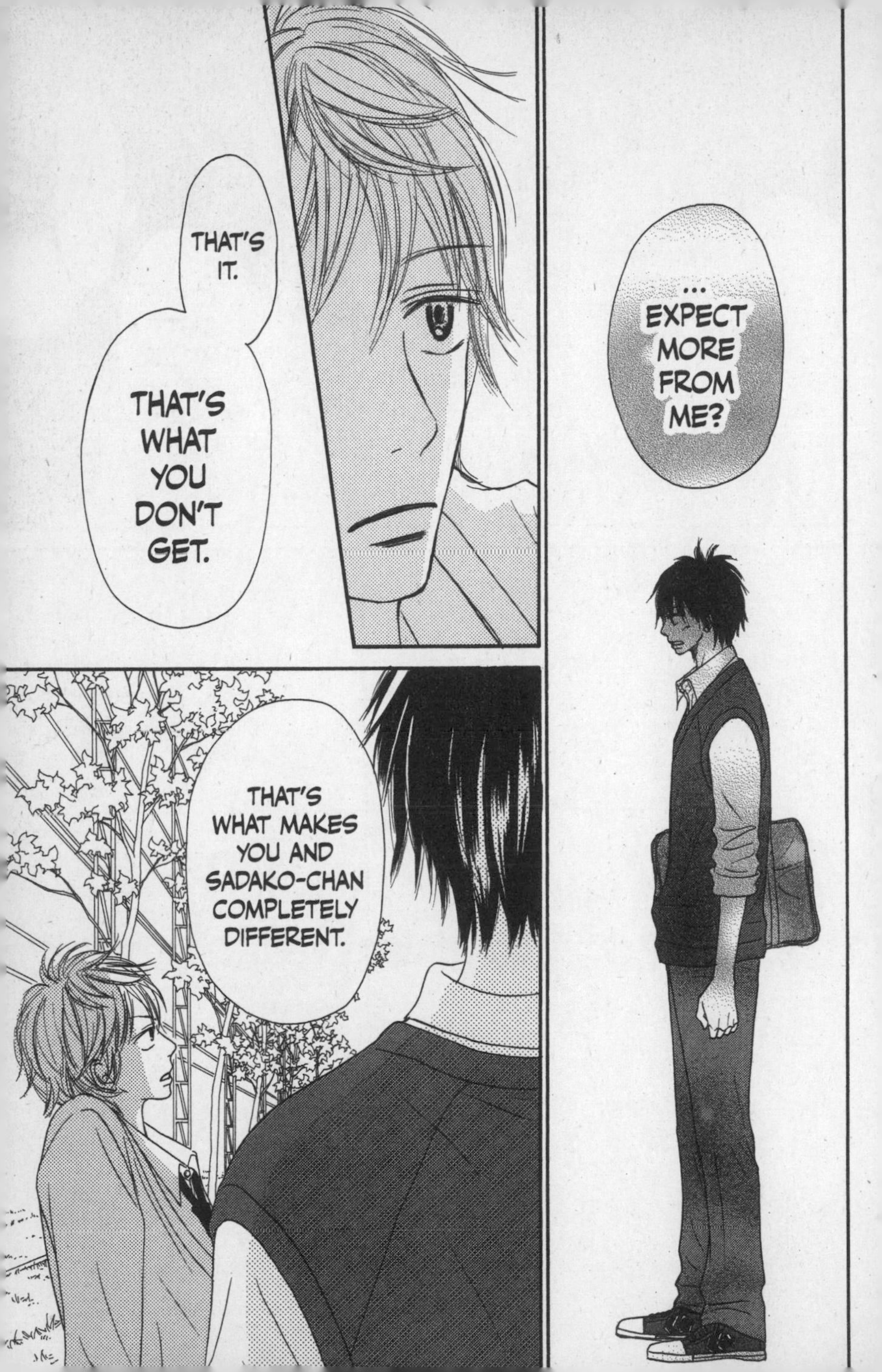
...EXPECT MORE FROM ME?
THAT'S IT.
THAT'S WHAT YOU DON'T GET.
THAT'S WHAT MAKES YOU AND SADAKO-CHAN COMPLETELY DIFFERENT.

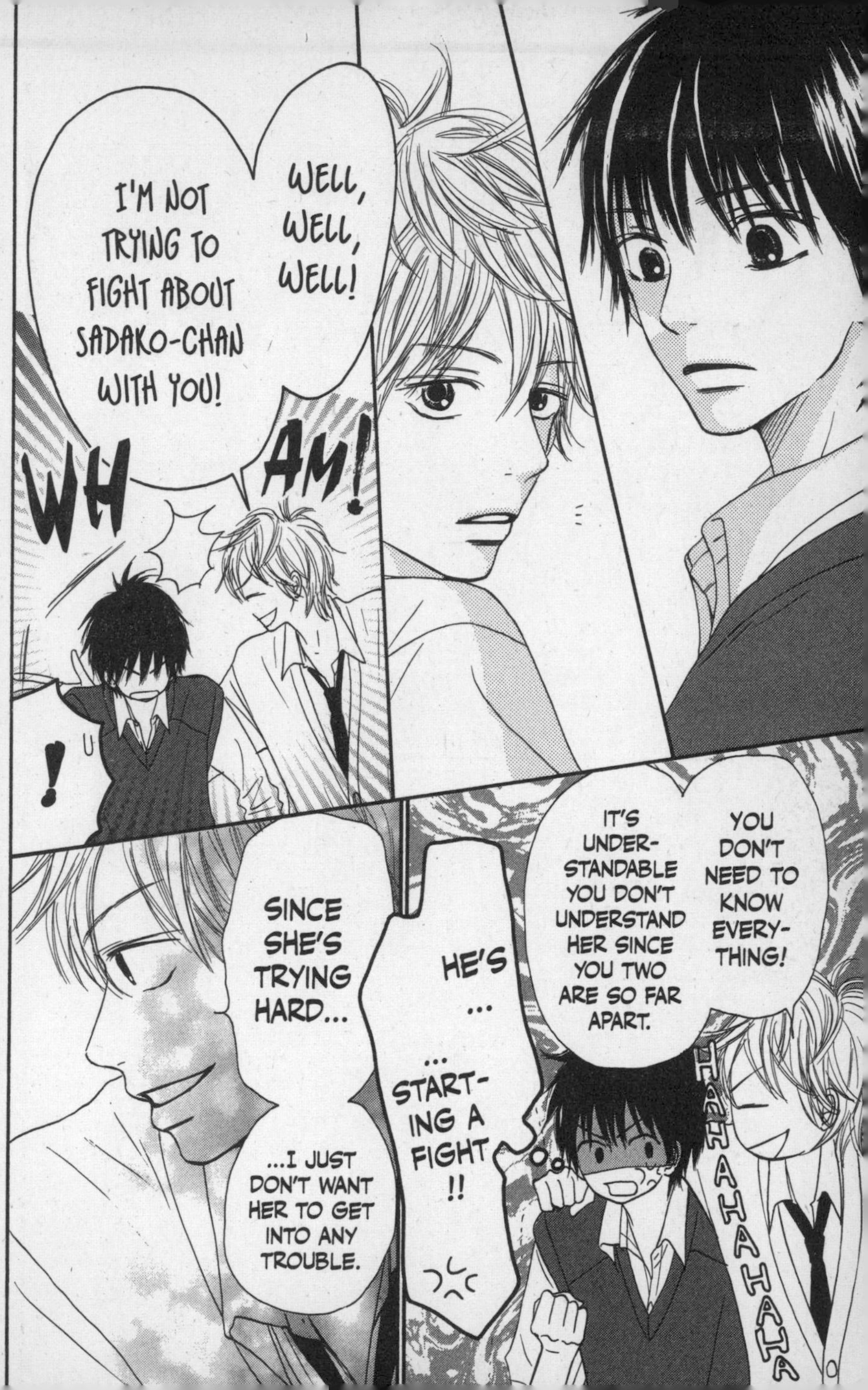
WELL, WELL, WELL!
I'M NOT TRYING TO FIGHT ABOUT SADAKO-CHAN WITH YOU!
WHAM!
YOU DON'T NEED TO KNOW EVERYTHING!
IT'S UNDER-STANDABLE YOU DON'T UNDERSTAND HER SINCE YOU TWO ARE SO FAR APART.
HAHAHAHAHAHAHAHA
HE'S ...
... START-ING A FIGHT !!
SINCE SHE'S TRYING HARD...
...I JUST DON'T WANT HER TO GET INTO ANY TROUBLE.

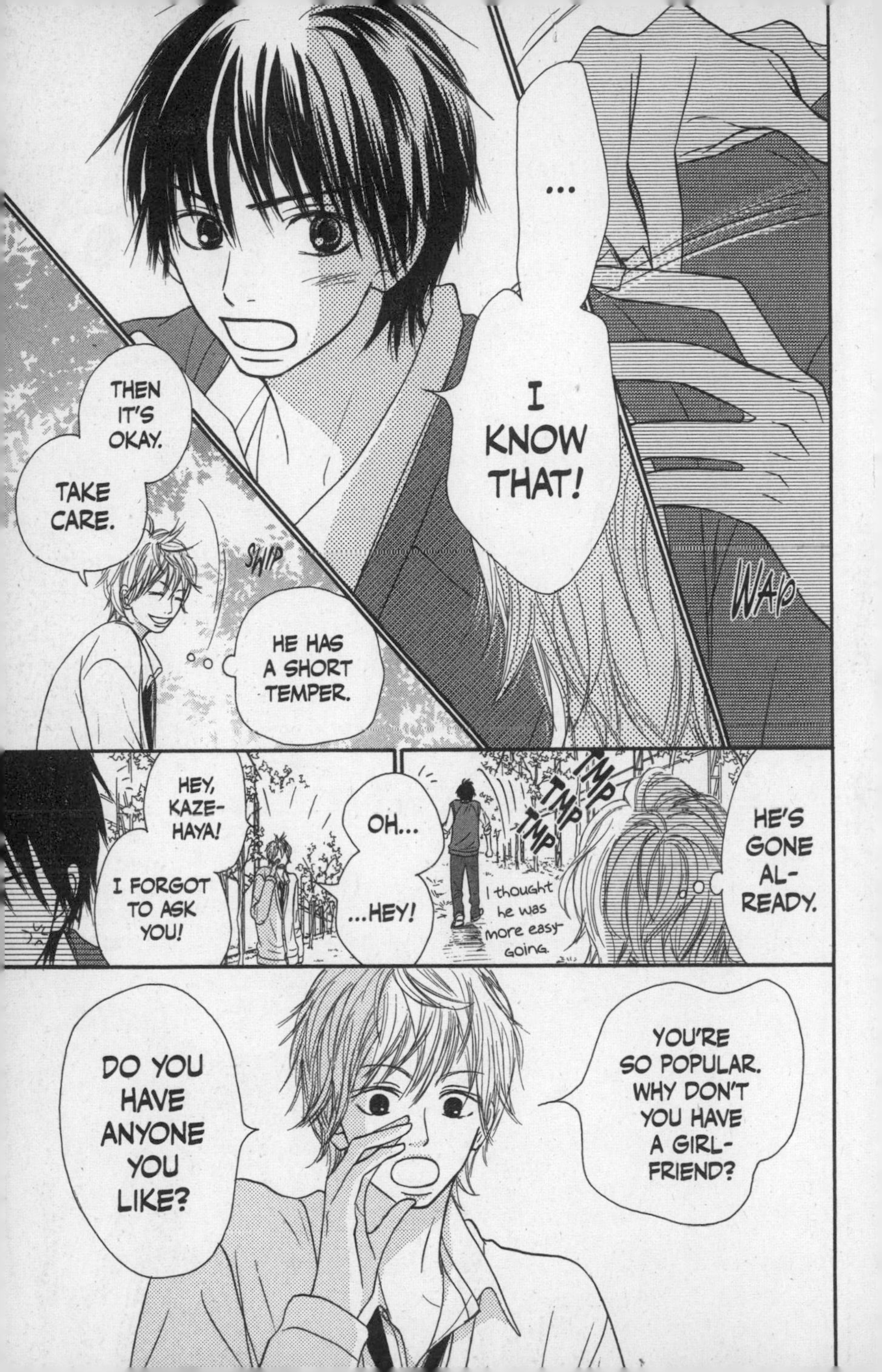
...
I KNOW THAT!
WAP
THEN IT'S OKAY.
TAKE CARE.
SWIP
HE HAS A SHORT TEMPER.
TMP TMP TMP
HE'S GONE AL-READY.
I thought he was more easy-going.
OH...
...HEY!
HEY, KAZE-HAYA!
I FORGOT TO ASK YOU!
YOU'RE SO POPULAR. WHY DON'T YOU HAVE A GIRL-FRIEND?
DO YOU HAVE ANYONE YOU LIKE?

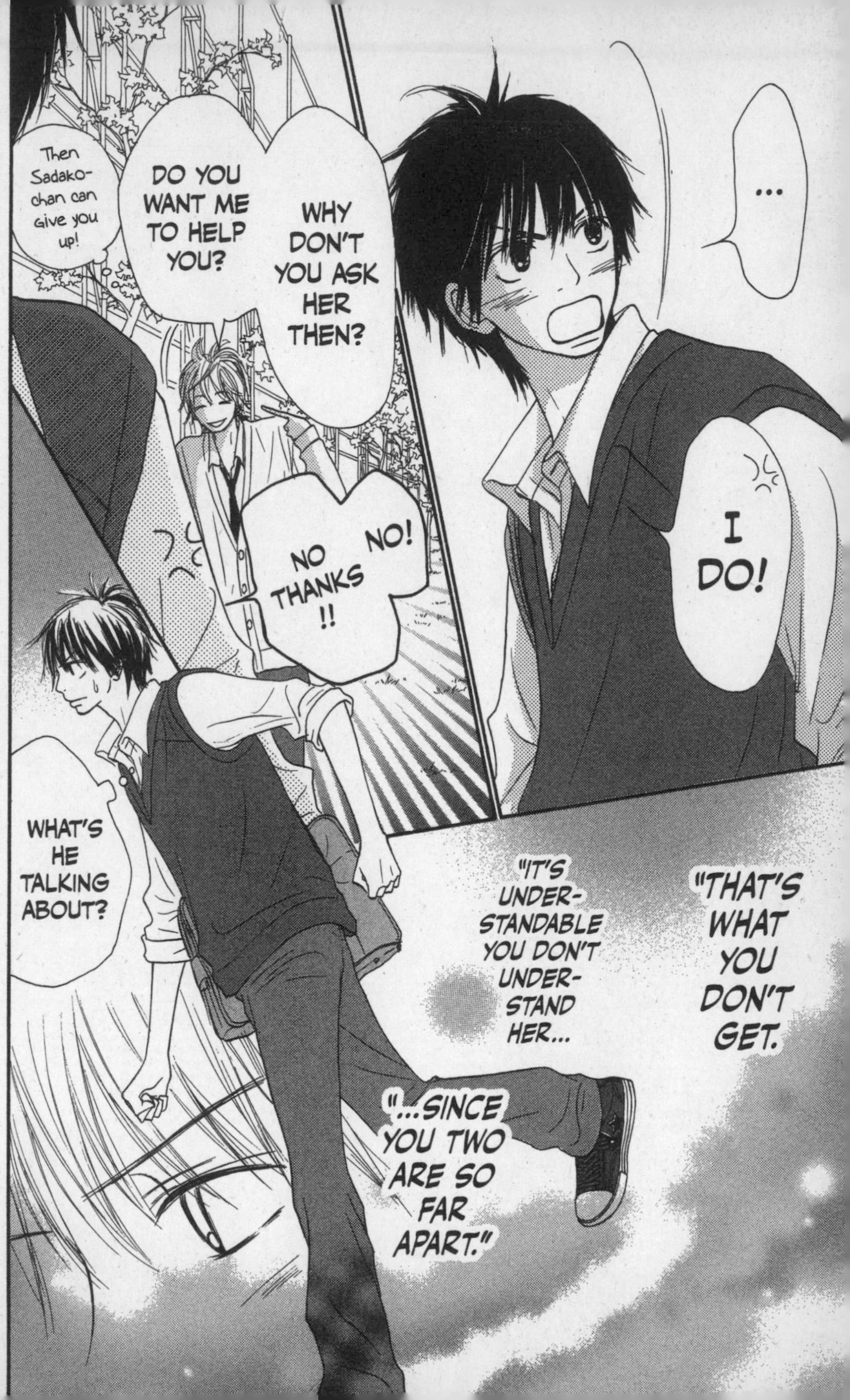
...
I DO!
WHY DON'T YOU ASK HER THEN?
DO YOU WANT ME TO HELP YOU?
Then Sadako-chan can give you up!
NO THANKS NO!!
"THAT'S WHAT YOU DON'T GET.
"IT'S UNDER-STANDABLE YOU DON'T UNDER-STAND HER...
"...SINCE YOU TWO ARE SO FAR APART."
WHAT'S HE TALKING ABOUT?

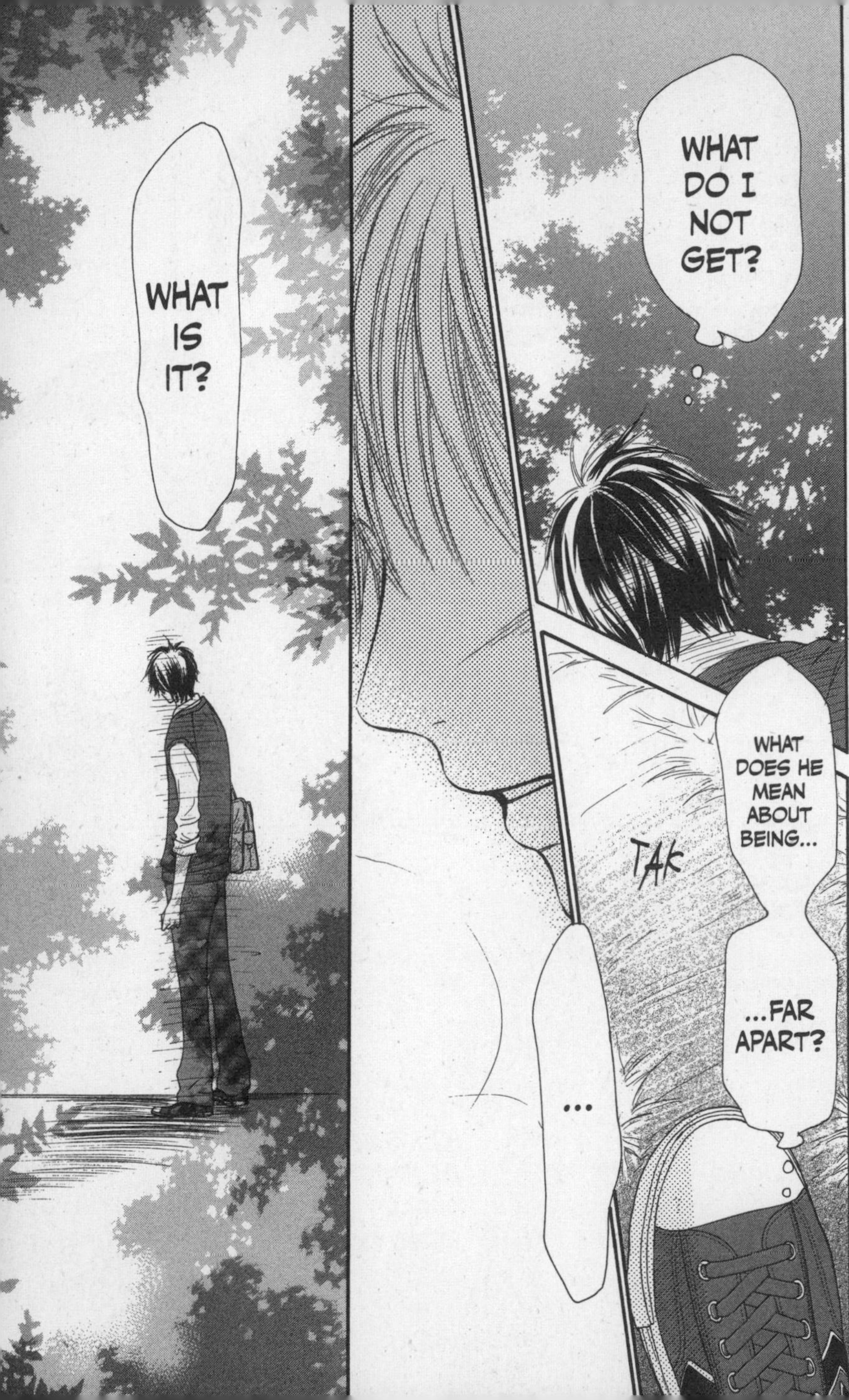
WHAT DO I NOT GET?
WHAT DOES HE MEAN ABOUT BEING...
TAK
...FAR APART?
...
WHAT IS IT?

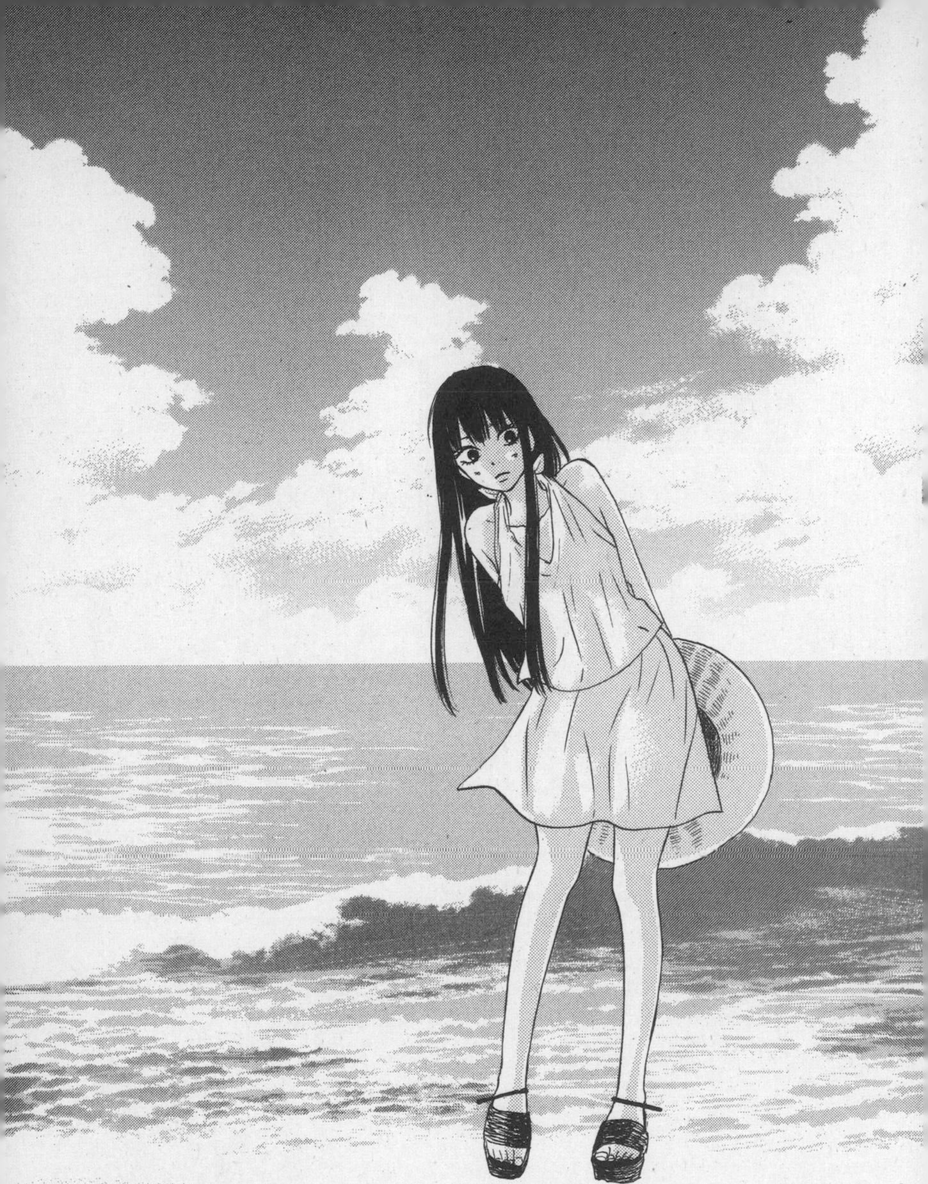

Episode 32: You Don't Understand Her

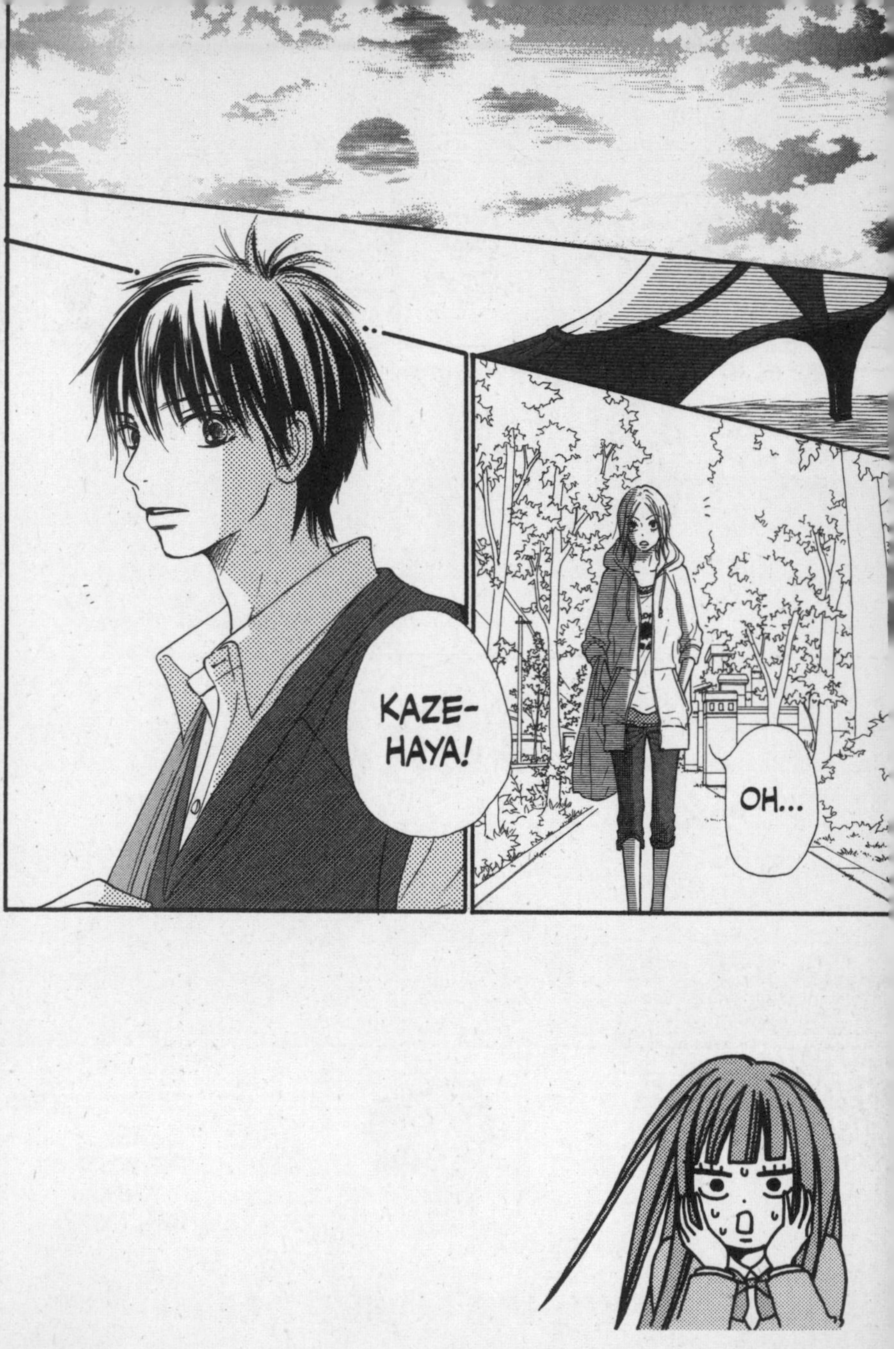
OH...
KAZE-HAYA!

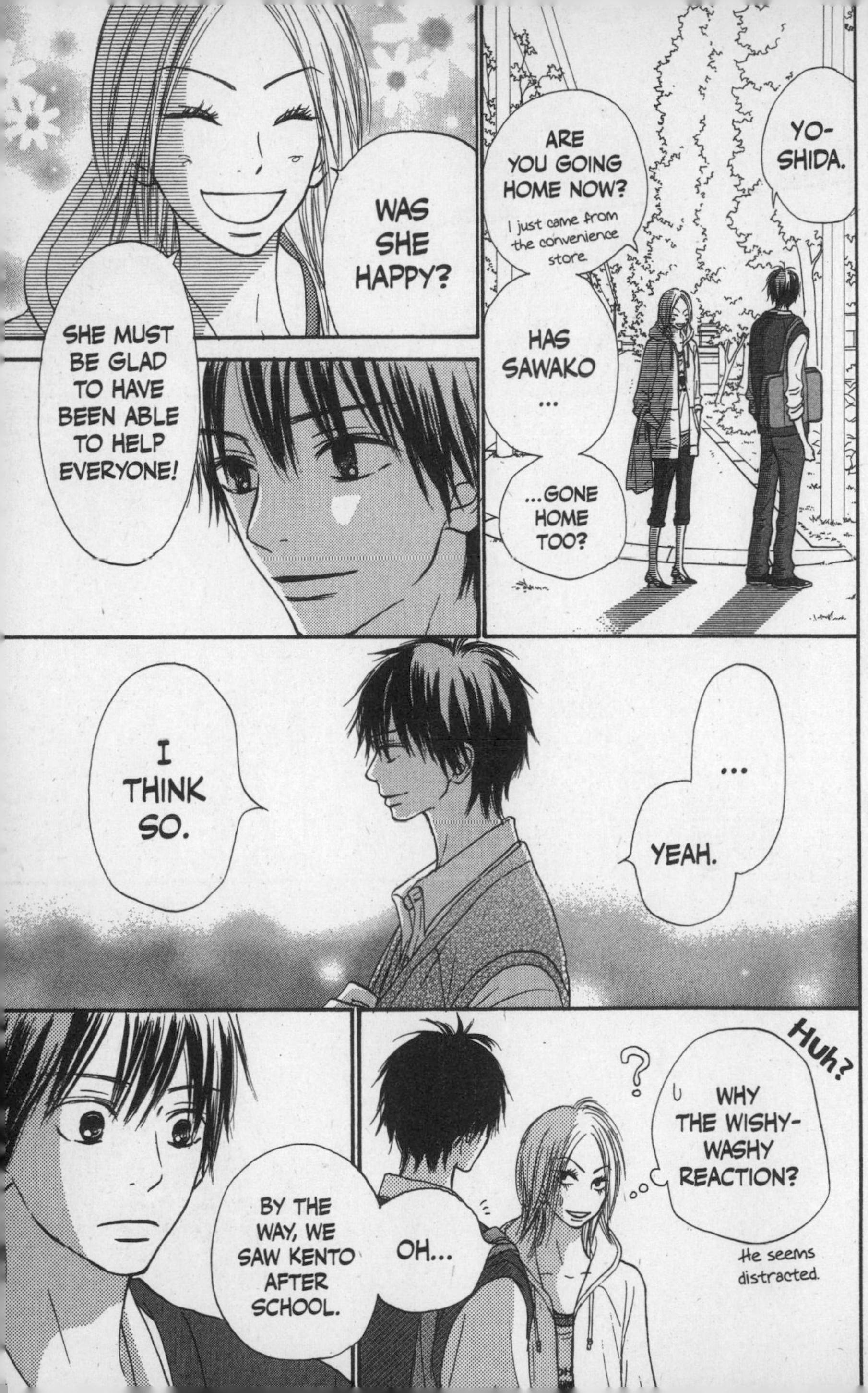

YO-SHIDA.
ARE YOU GOING HOME NOW?
I just came from the convenience store.
HAS SAWAKO ...
...GONE HOME TOO?
WAS SHE HAPPY?
SHE MUST BE GLAD TO HAVE BEEN ABLE TO HELP EVERYONE!
...
YEAH.
I THINK SO.
Huh?
WHY THE WISHY-WASHY REACTION?
He seems distracted.
OH...
BY THE WAY, WE SAW KENTO AFTER SCHOOL.

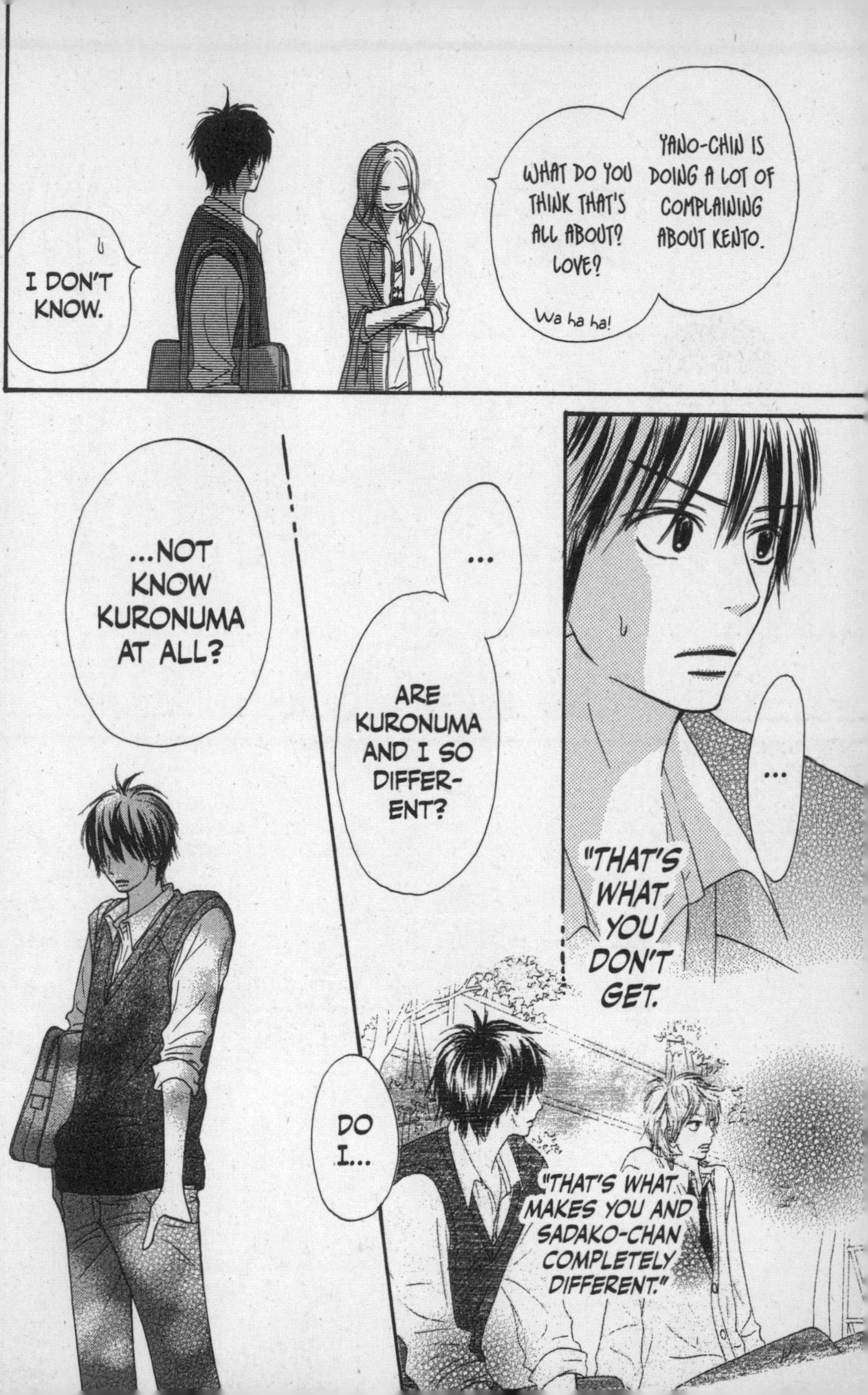
YANO-CHIN IS DOING A LOT OF COMPLAINING ABOUT KENTO.
WHAT DO YOU THINK THAT'S ALL ABOUT? LOVE?
Wa ha ha!
I DON'T KNOW.
...
"THAT'S WHAT YOU DON'T GET.
"THAT'S WHAT MAKES YOU AND SADAKO-CHAN COMPLETELY DIFFERENT."
...
ARE KURONUMA AND I SO DIFFER-ENT?
DO I...
...NOT KNOW KURONUMA AT ALL?

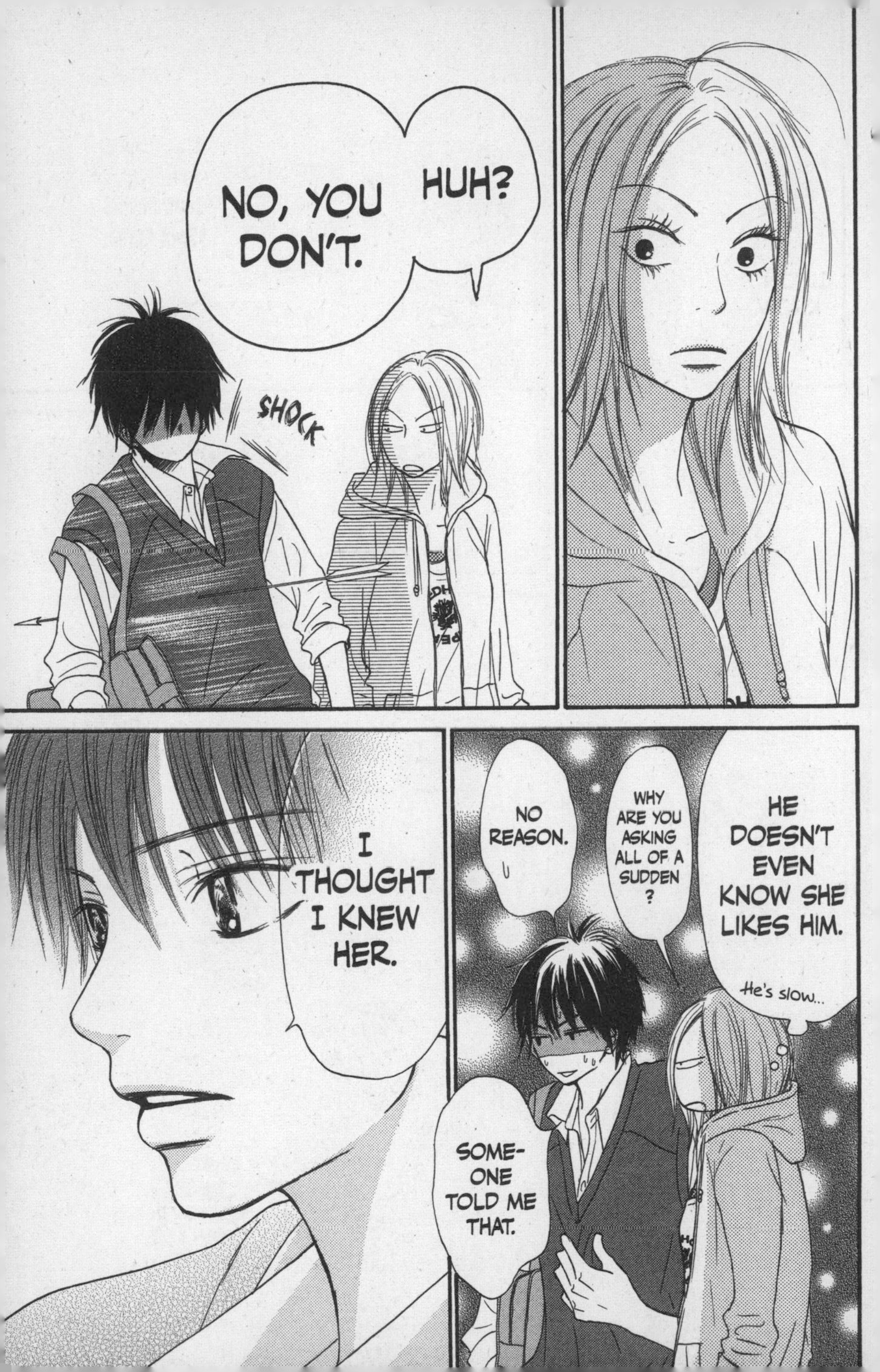
HUH?
NO, YOU DON'T.
SHOCK
HE DOESN'T EVEN KNOW SHE LIKES HIM.
WHY ARE YOU ASKING ALL OF A SUDDEN?
NO REASON.
He's slow...
SOME-ONE TOLD ME THAT.
I THOUGHT I KNEW HER.

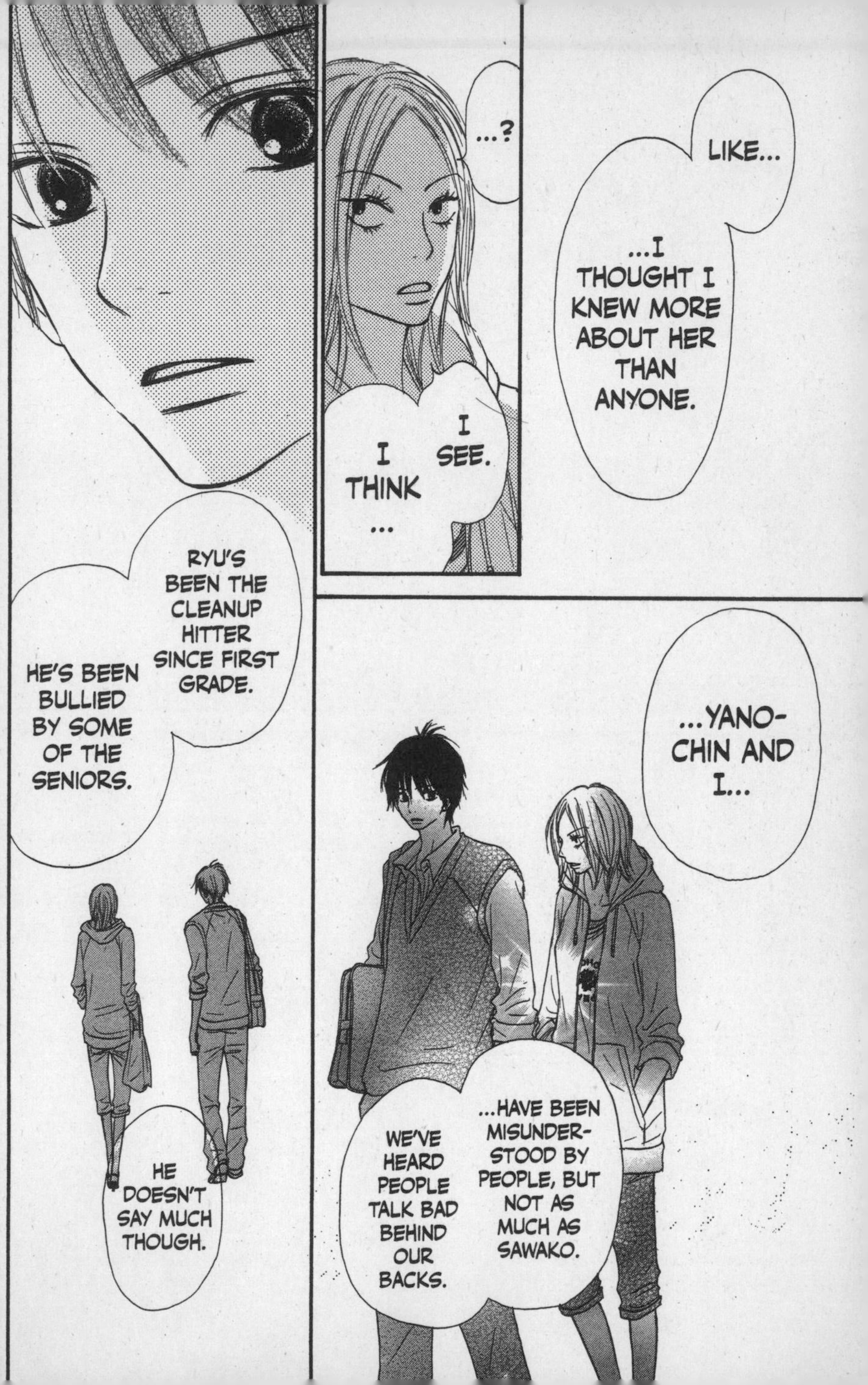

LIKE...
...?
...I THOUGHT I KNEW MORE ABOUT HER THAN ANYONE.
I SEE.
I THINK...
...YANO-CHIN AND I...
...HAVE BEEN MISUNDERSTOOD BY PEOPLE, BUT NOT AS MUCH AS SAWAKO.
WE'VE HEARD PEOPLE TALK BAD BEHIND OUR BACKS.
RYU'S BEEN THE CLEANUP HITTER SINCE FIRST GRADE.
HE'S BEEN BULLIED BY SOME OF THE SENIORS.
HE DOESN'T SAY MUCH THOUGH.

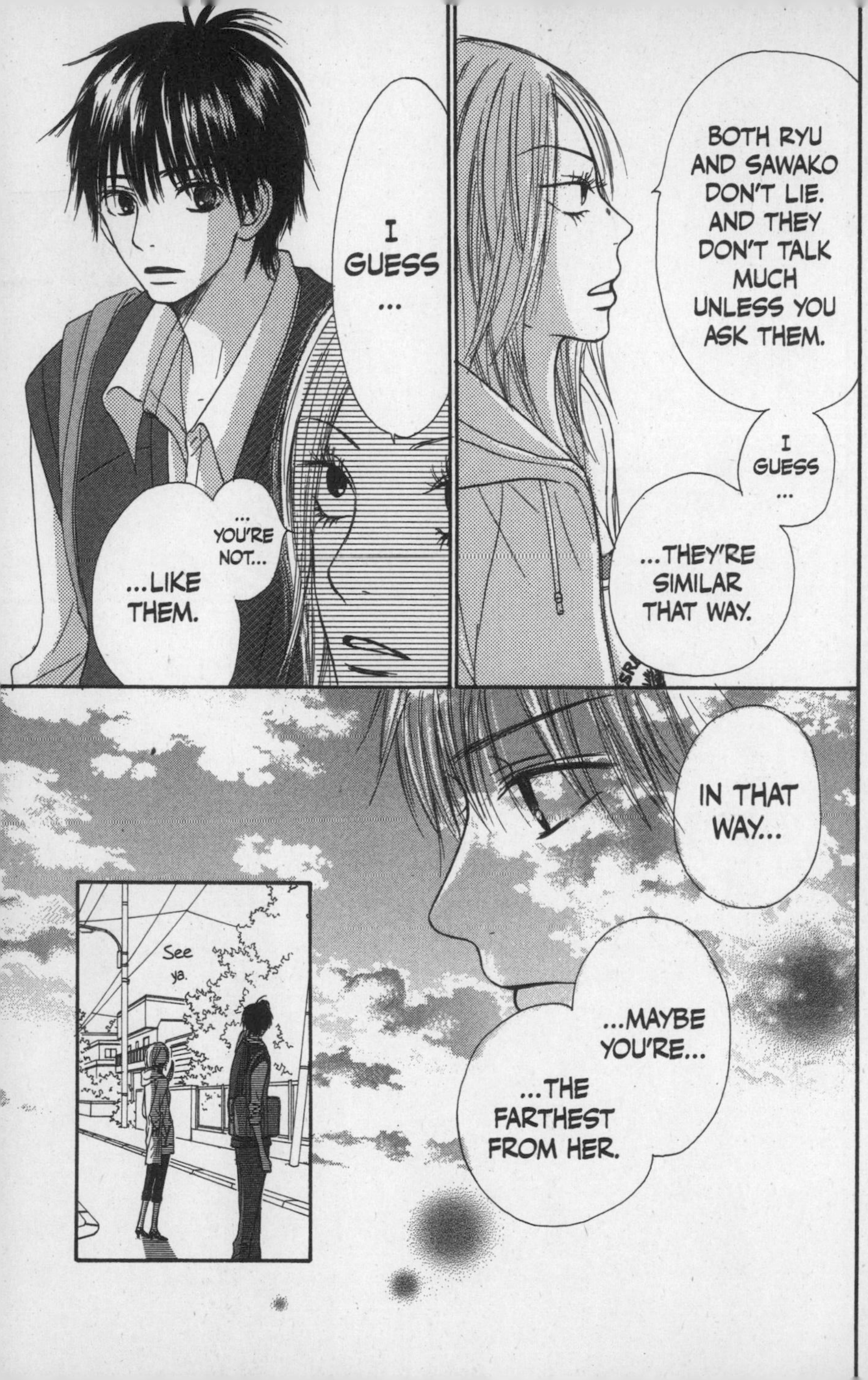
BOTH RYU AND SAWAKO DON'T LIE. AND THEY DON'T TALK MUCH UNLESS YOU ASK THEM.
I GUESS ...
...THEY'RE SIMILAR THAT WAY.
I GUESS ...
... YOU'RE NOT...
...LIKE THEM.
IN THAT WAY...
...MAYBE YOU'RE...
...THE FARTHEST FROM HER.
See ya.

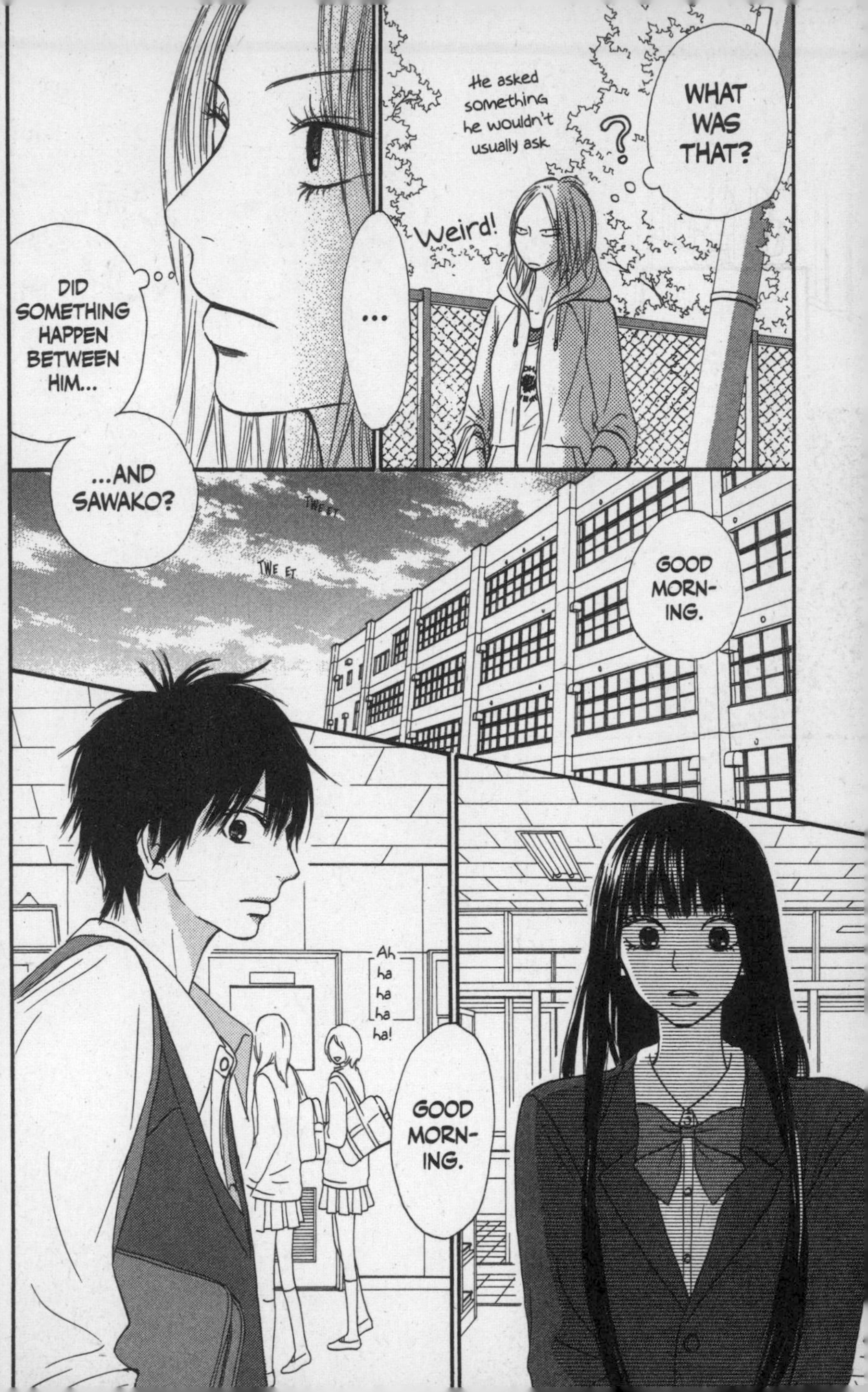
WHAT WAS THAT?
He asked something he wouldn't usually ask.
Weird!
...
DID SOMETHING HAPPEN BETWEEN HIM...
...AND SAWAKO?
TWEET
TWE ET
GOOD MORNING.
Ah ha ha ha ha!
GOOD MORNING.

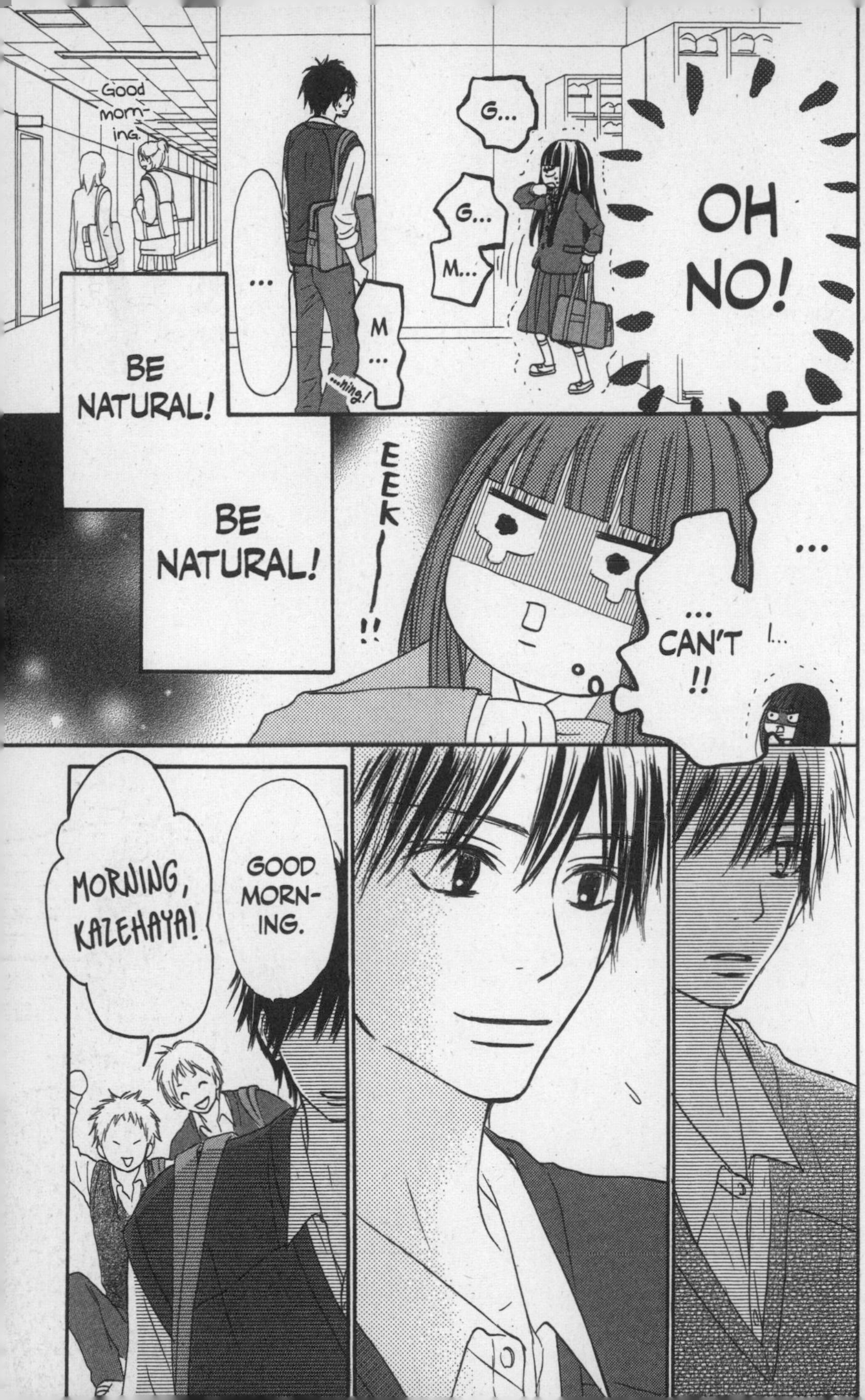
OH NO!
G...
G... M...
M ... ...ning!
...
Good morn-ing.
BE NATURAL!
BE NATURAL!
...
I...
... CAN'T !!
EEK——!!
GOOD MORN-ING.
MORNING, KAZEHAYA!

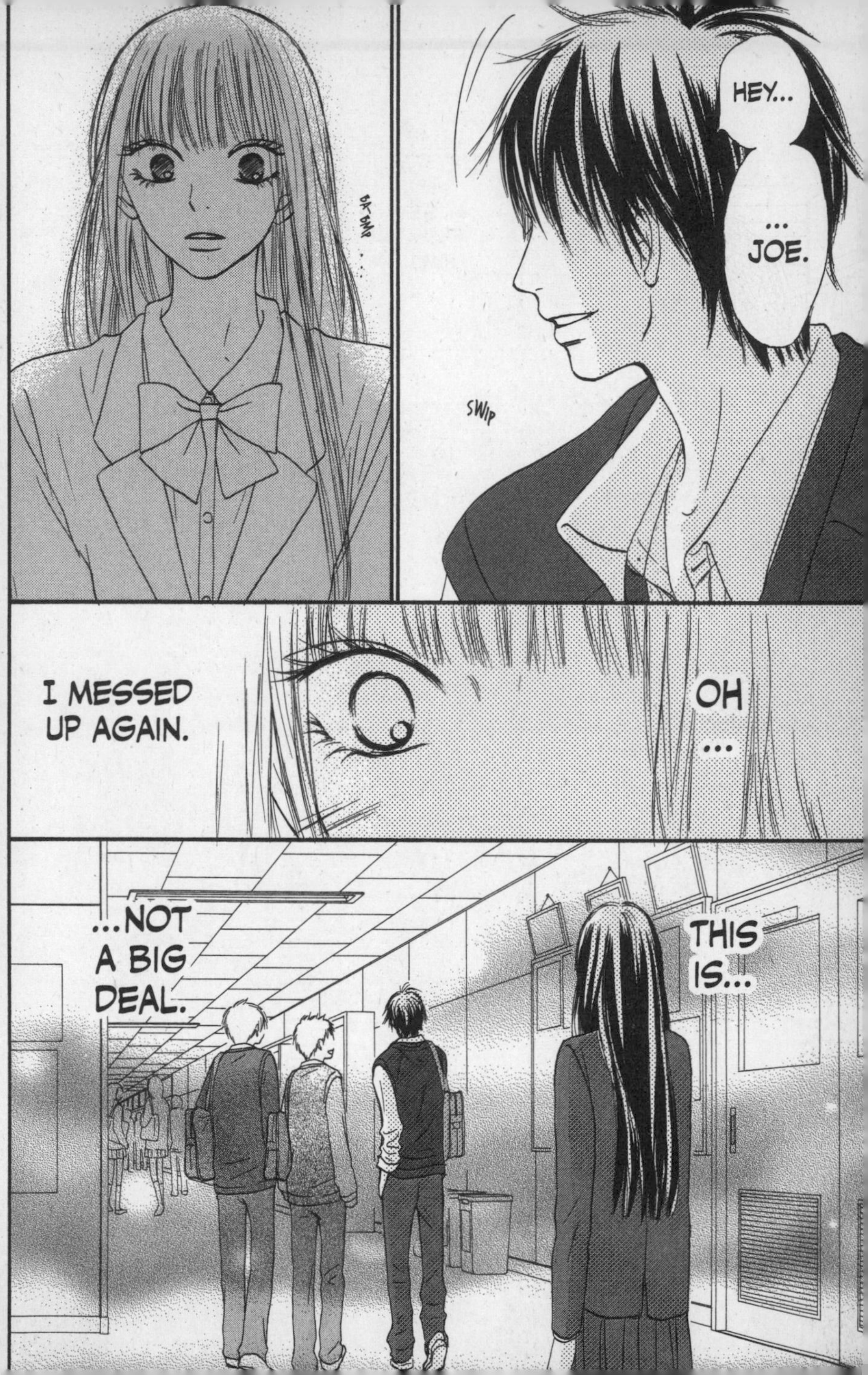
HEY...
...JOE.
SWIP
BA-DMP...
OH...
I MESSED UP AGAIN.
THIS IS...
...NOT A BIG DEAL.

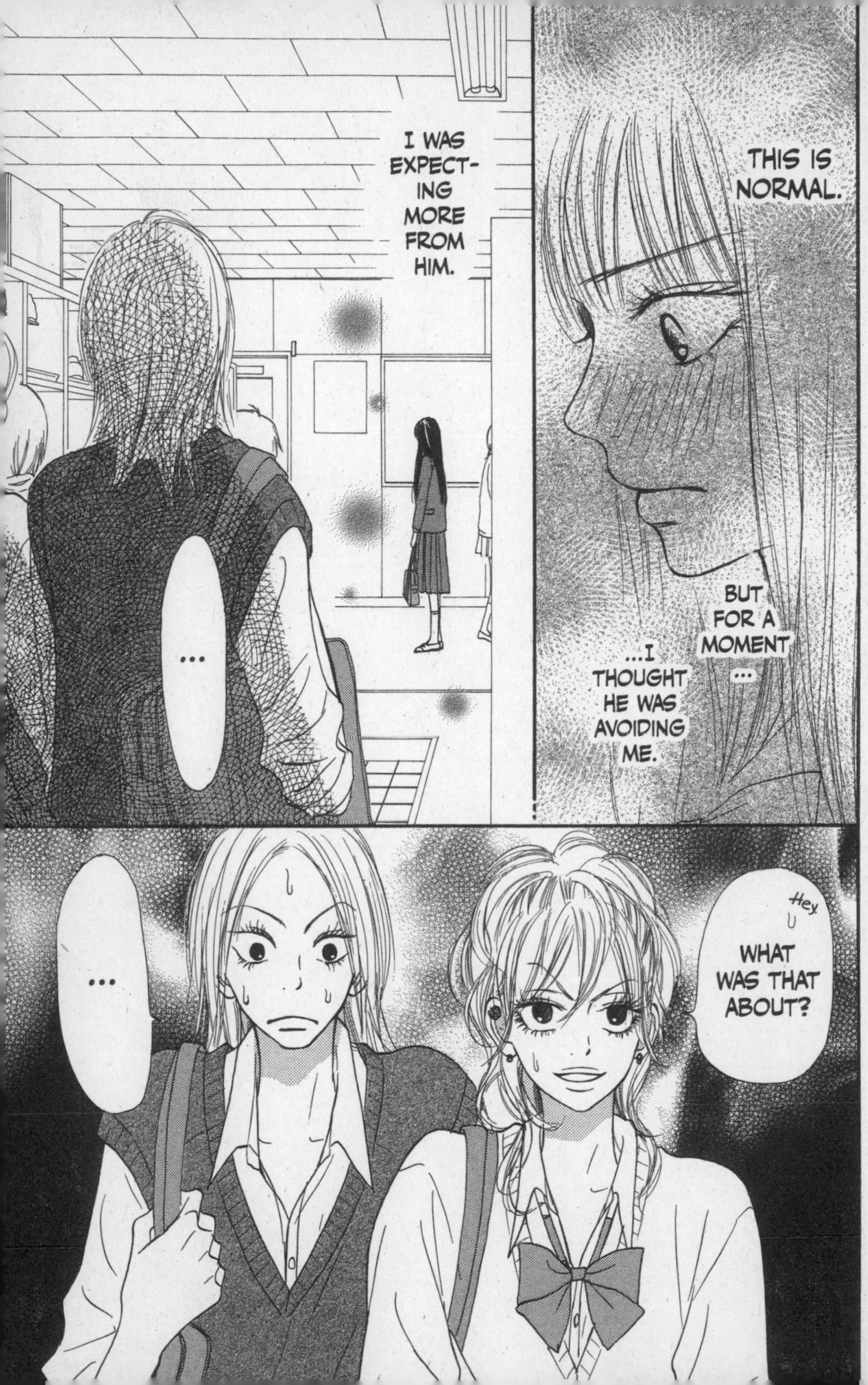
THIS IS NORMAL.
BUT FOR A MOMENT...
...I THOUGHT HE WAS AVOIDING ME.
I WAS EXPECTING MORE FROM HIM.
...
Hey.
WHAT WAS THAT ABOUT?
...

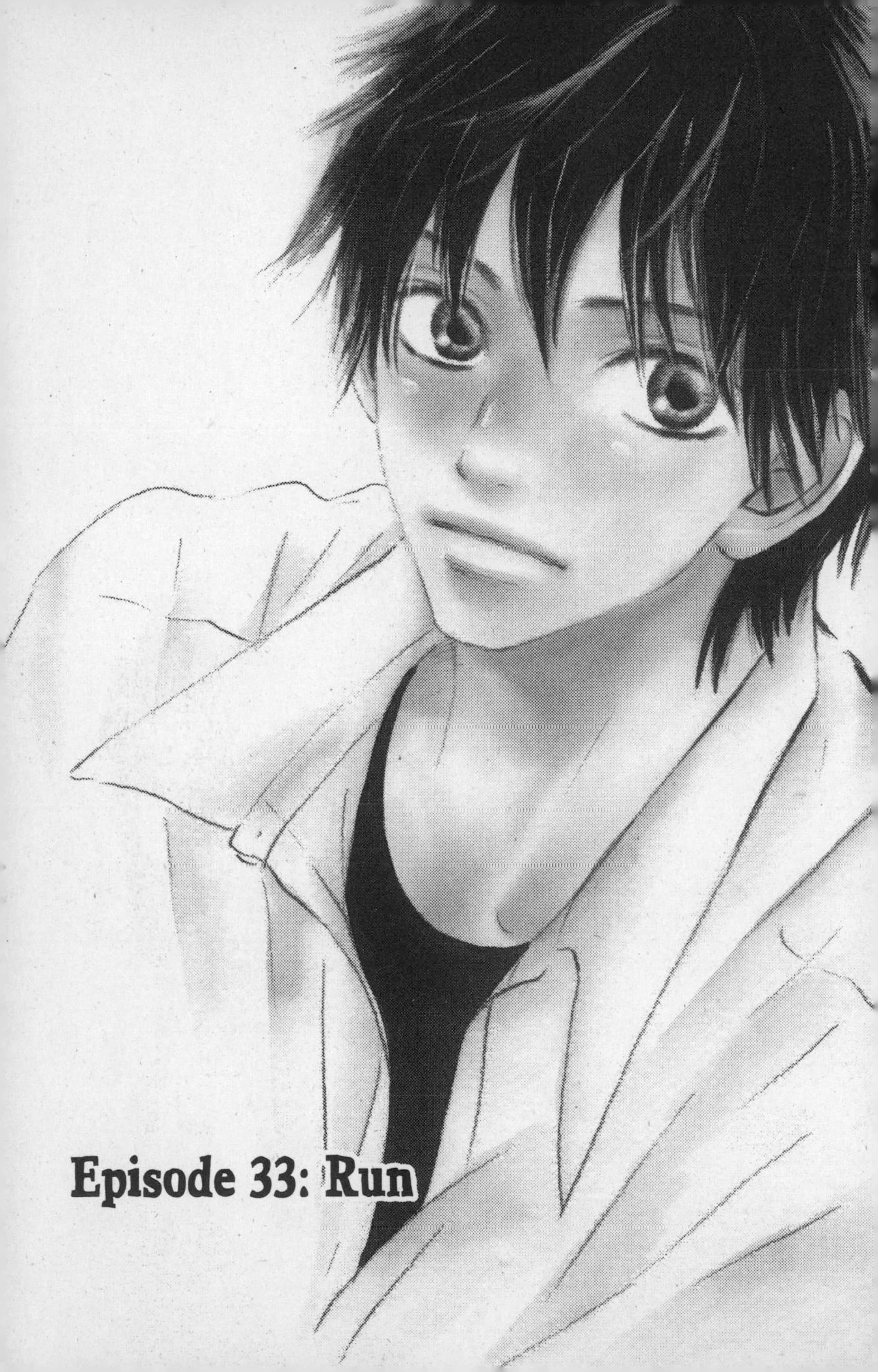

Episode 33: Run

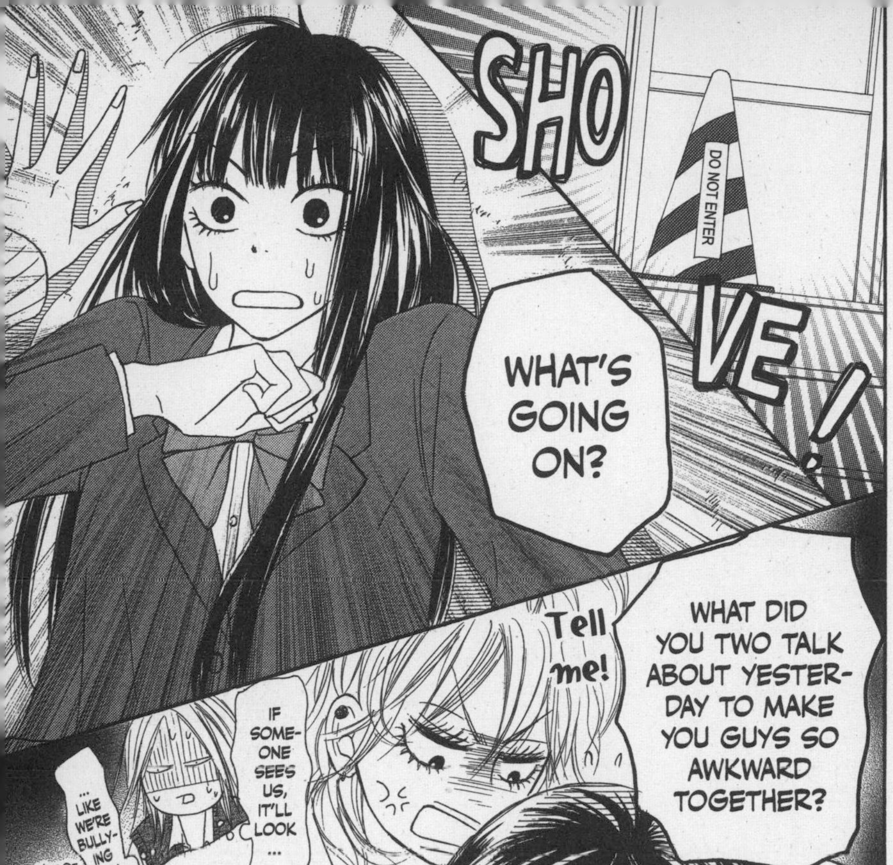
SHOVE!
DO NOT ENTER
WHAT'S GOING ON?
WHAT DID YOU TWO TALK ABOUT YESTER-DAY TO MAKE YOU GUYS SO AWKWARD TOGETHER?
Tell me!
IF SOME-ONE SEES US, IT'LL LOOK ...
... LIKE WE'RE BULLY-ING HER!
Yano-chin..

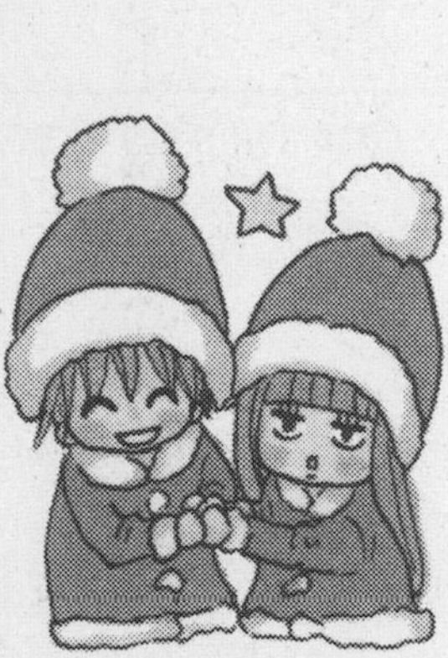

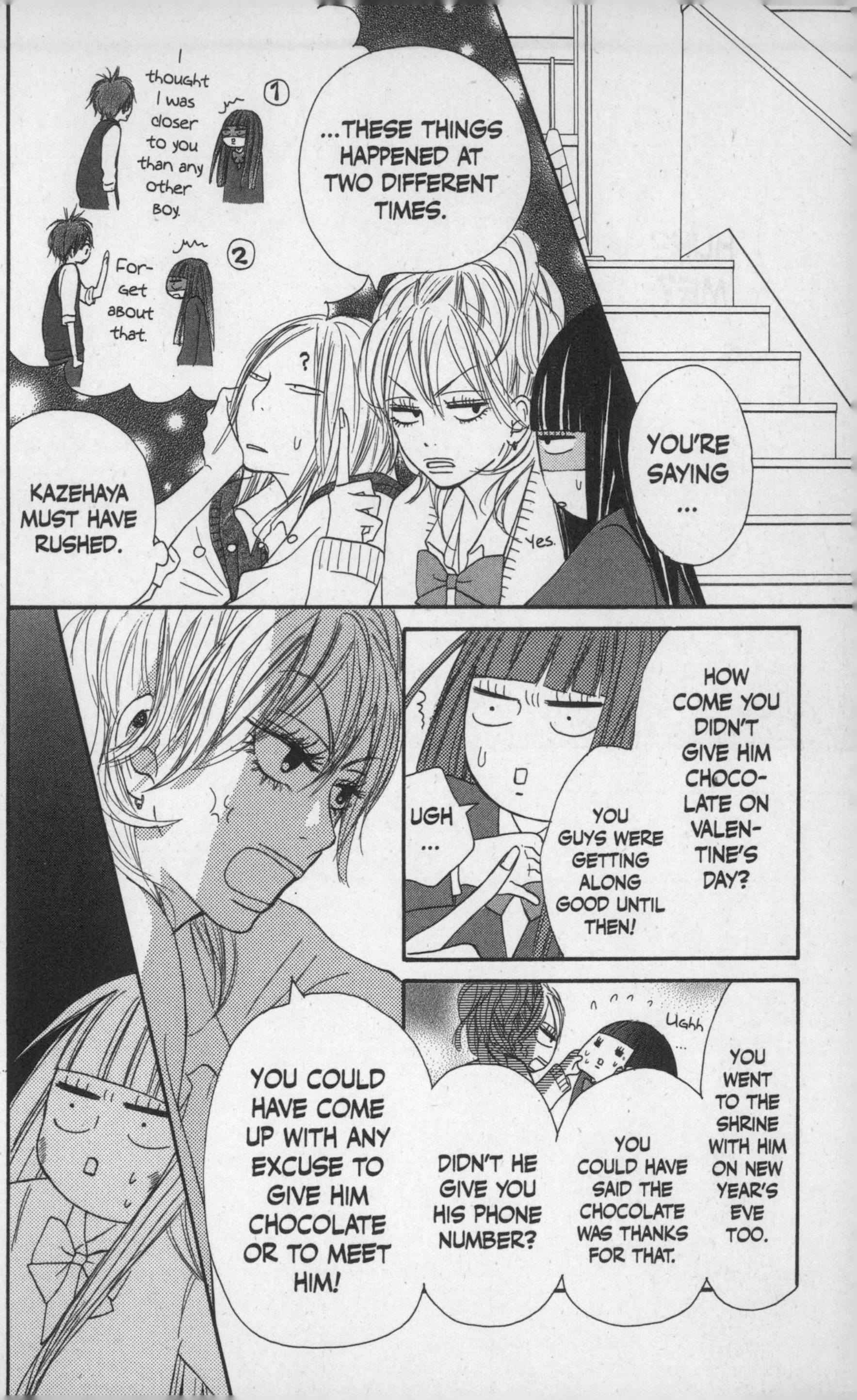
YOU'RE SAYING ...
...THESE THINGS HAPPENED AT TWO DIFFERENT TIMES.
1
I thought I was closer to you than any other boy.
2
For-get about that.
Yes.
KAZEHAYA MUST HAVE RUSHED.
HOW COME YOU DIDN'T GIVE HIM CHOCO-LATE ON VALEN-TINE'S DAY?
YOU GUYS WERE GETTING ALONG GOOD UNTIL THEN!
UGH ...
Ughh ...
YOU WENT TO THE SHRINE WITH HIM ON NEW YEAR'S EVE TOO.
YOU COULD HAVE SAID THE CHOCOLATE WAS THANKS FOR THAT.
DIDN'T HE GIVE YOU HIS PHONE NUMBER?
YOU COULD HAVE COME UP WITH ANY EXCUSE TO GIVE HIM CHOCOLATE OR TO MEET HIM!

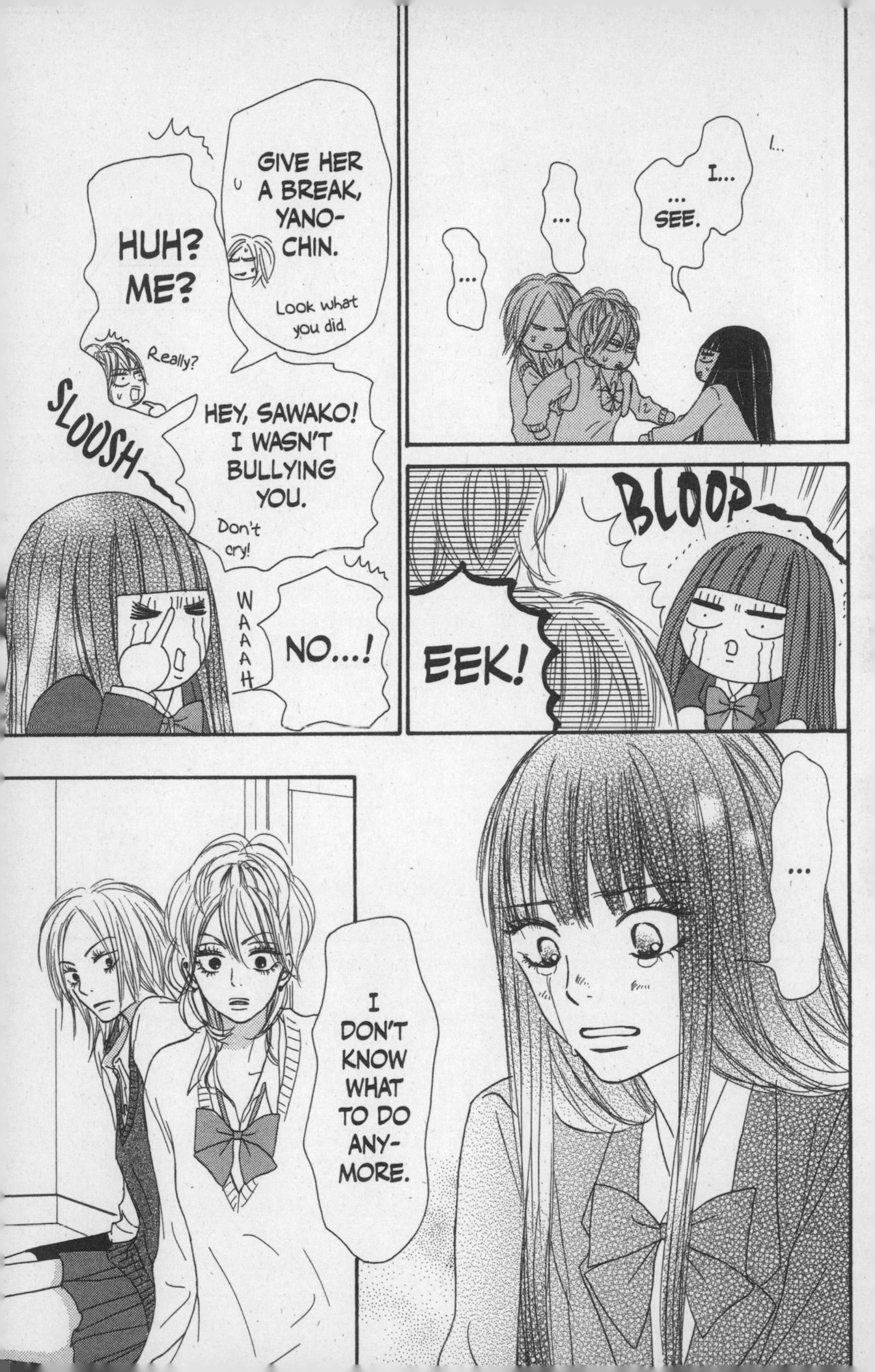

I...
I... ... SEE.
...
...
BLOOP
EEK!
GIVE HER A BREAK, YANO-CHIN.
Look what you did.
HUH? ME?
Really?
HEY, SAWAKO! I WASN'T BULLYING YOU.
Don't cry!
SLOOSH
WAAAAH
NO...!
...
I DON'T KNOW WHAT TO DO ANY-MORE.

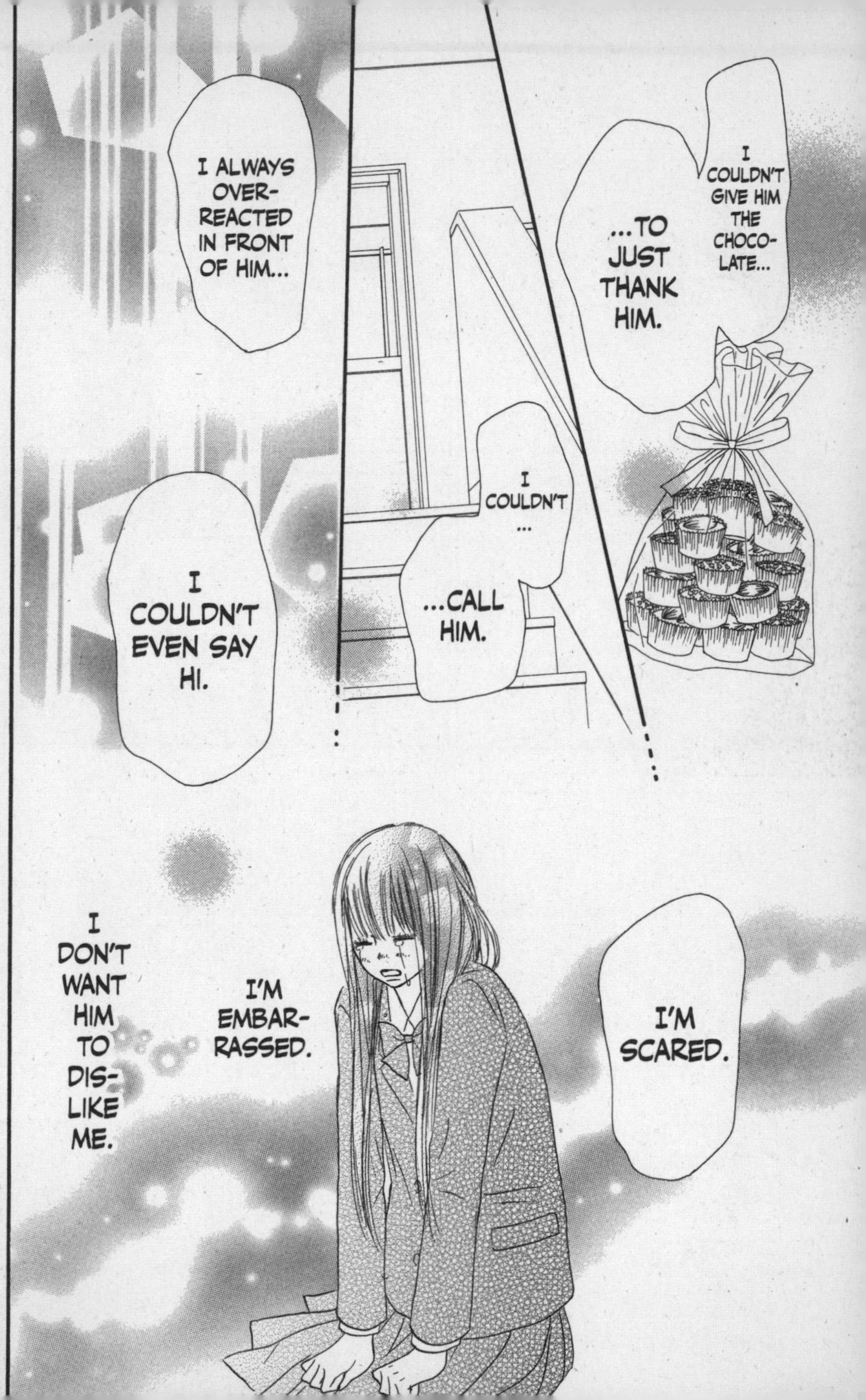
I COULDN'T GIVE HIM THE CHOCO-LATE...
...TO JUST THANK HIM.
I COULDN'T ...
...CALL HIM.
I ALWAYS OVER-REACTED IN FRONT OF HIM...
I COULDN'T EVEN SAY HI.
I'M SCARED.
I'M EMBAR-RASSED.
I DON'T WANT HIM TO DIS-LIKE ME.

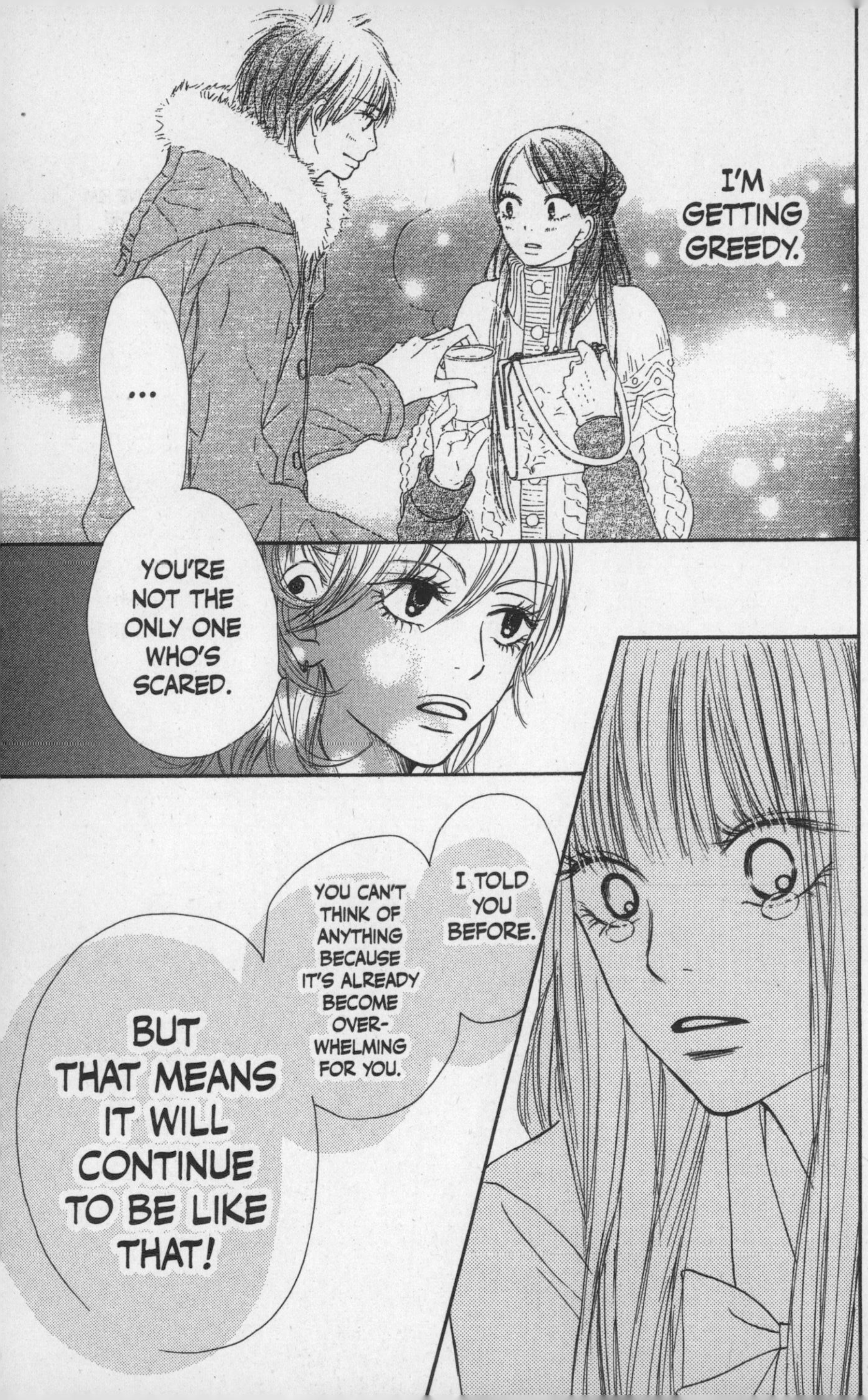
I'M GETTING GREEDY.
...
YOU'RE NOT THE ONLY ONE WHO'S SCARED.
I TOLD YOU BEFORE.
YOU CAN'T THINK OF ANYTHING BECAUSE IT'S ALREADY BECOME OVER-WHELMING FOR YOU.
BUT THAT MEANS IT WILL CONTINUE TO BE LIKE THAT!

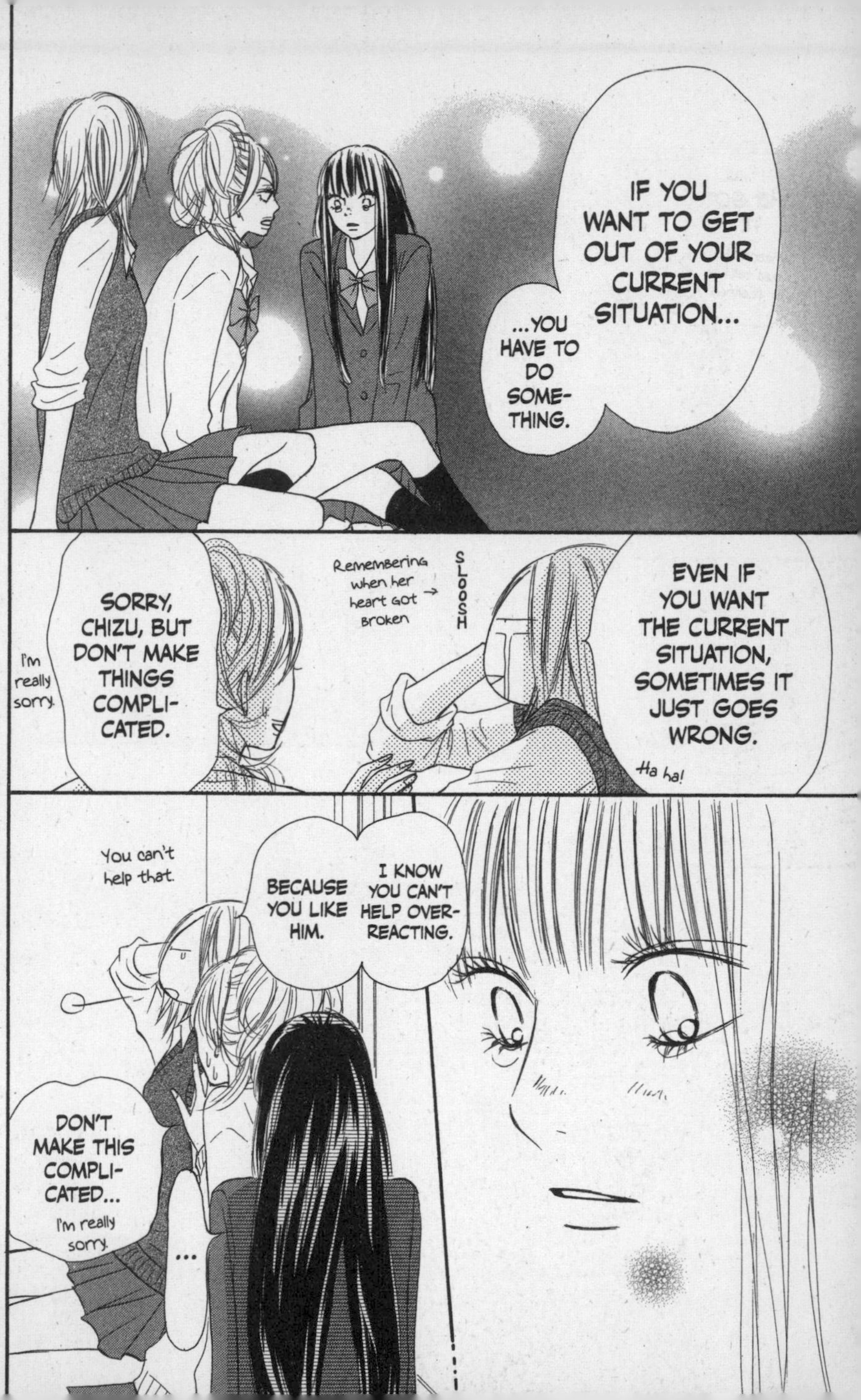
IF YOU WANT TO GET OUT OF YOUR CURRENT SITUATION...
...YOU HAVE TO DO SOME-THING.
EVEN IF YOU WANT THE CURRENT SITUATION, SOMETIMES IT JUST GOES WRONG.
Ha ha!
SLOOSH
Remembering when her heart got broken
SORRY, CHIZU, BUT DON'T MAKE THINGS COMPLI-CATED.
I'm really sorry.
I KNOW YOU CAN'T HELP OVER-REACTING.
BECAUSE YOU LIKE HIM.
You can't help that.
DON'T MAKE THIS COMPLI-CATED...
I'm really sorry.
...

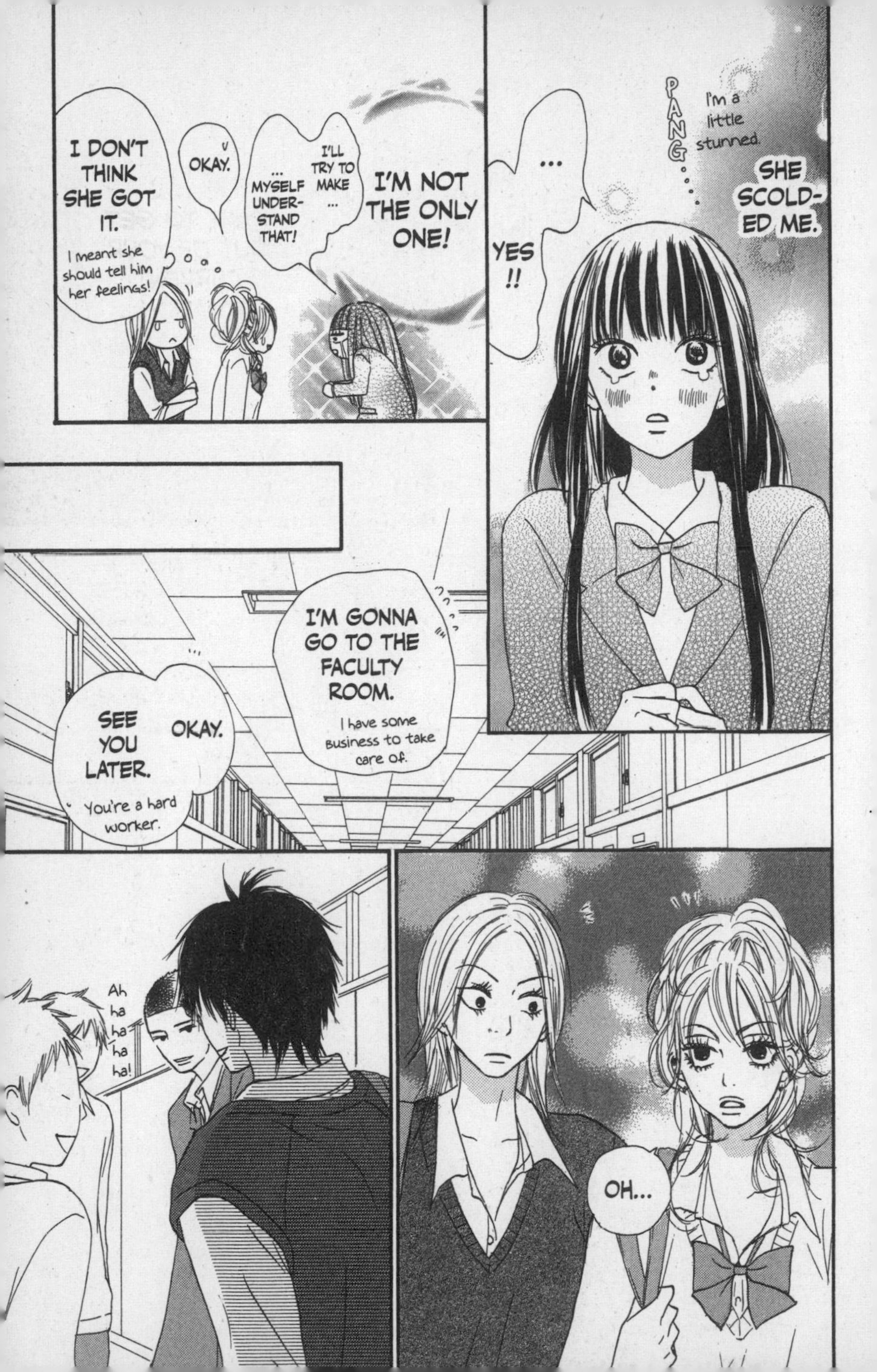
PANG...
I'm a little stunned.
SHE SCOLDED ME.
...
YES!!
I'M NOT THE ONLY ONE!
I'LL TRY TO MAKE ...
... MYSELF UNDERSTAND THAT!
OKAY.
I DON'T THINK SHE GOT IT.
I meant she should tell him her feelings!
I'M GONNA GO TO THE FACULTY ROOM.
I have some business to take care of.
OKAY.
SEE YOU LATER.
You're a hard worker.
OH...
Ah ha ha ha ha!

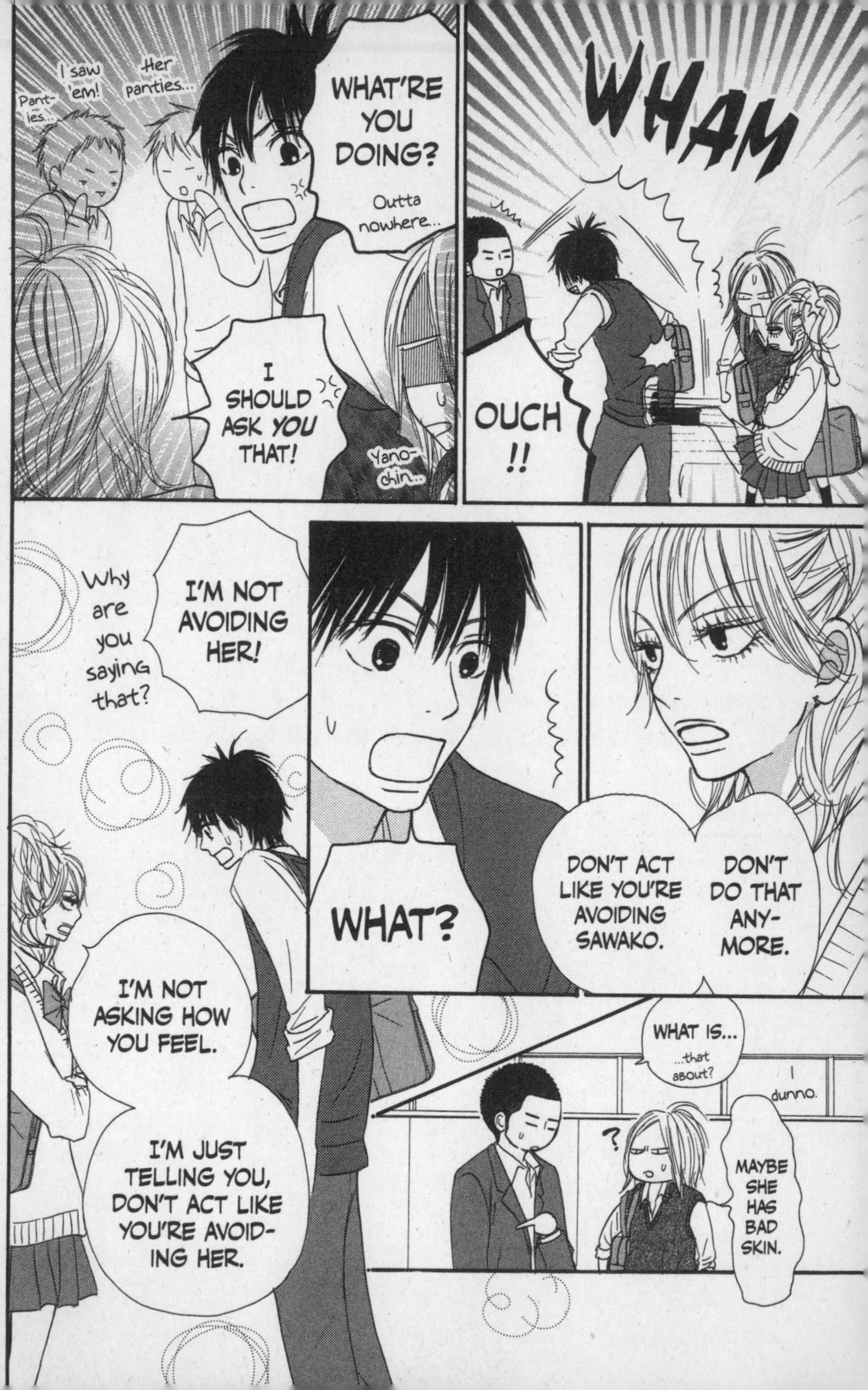
WHAM
OUCH !!
Pant-ies...
I saw 'em!
Her panties...
WHAT'RE YOU DOING?
Outta nowhere...
I SHOULD ASK YOU THAT!
Yano-chin...
DON'T DO THAT ANY-MORE.
DON'T ACT LIKE YOU'RE AVOIDING SAWAKO.
WHAT?
I'M NOT AVOIDING HER!
Why are you saying that?
I'M NOT ASKING HOW YOU FEEL.
I'M JUST TELLING YOU, DON'T ACT LIKE YOU'RE AVOID-ING HER.
WHAT IS...
...that about?
I dunno.
MAYBE SHE HAS BAD SKIN.

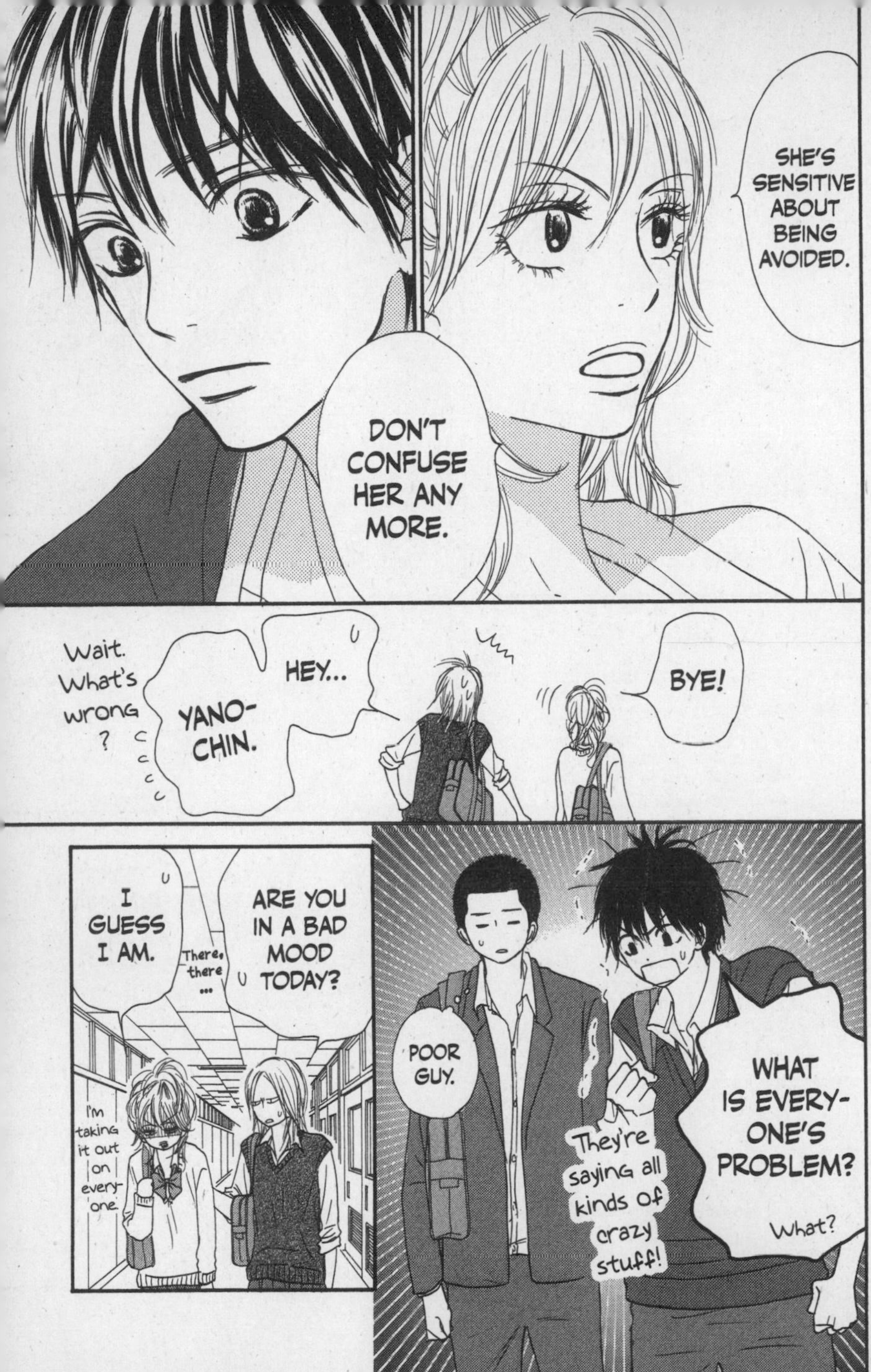
SHE'S SENSITIVE ABOUT BEING AVOIDED.
DON'T CONFUSE HER ANY MORE.
BYE!
HEY... YANO-CHIN.
Wait. What's wrong?
WHAT IS EVERY-ONE'S PROBLEM?
What?
They're saying all kinds of crazy stuff!
POOR GUY.
ARE YOU IN A BAD MOOD TODAY?
There, there ...
I GUESS I AM.
I'm taking it out on every-one.

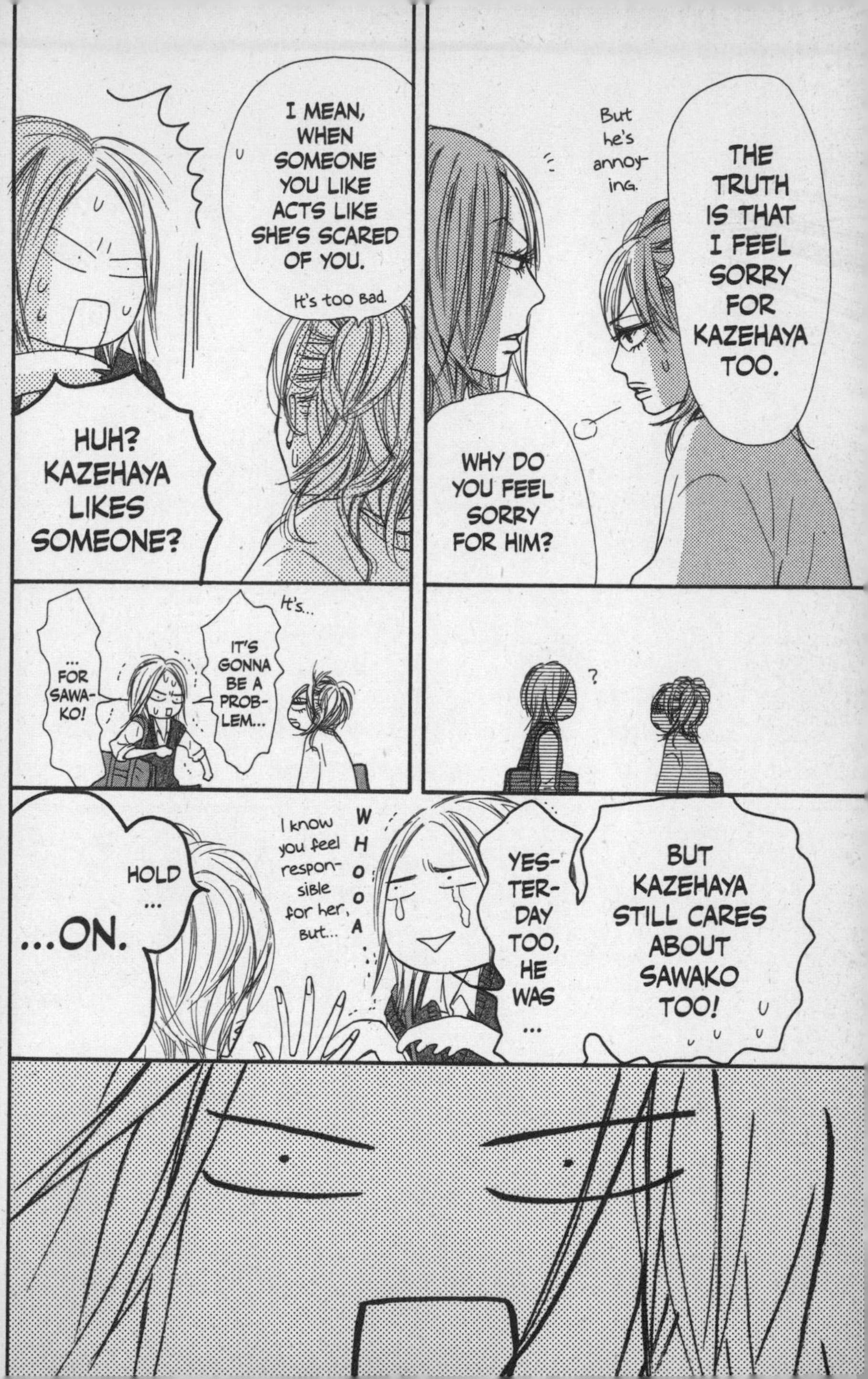
THE TRUTH IS THAT I FEEL SORRY FOR KAZEHAYA TOO.
But he's annoying.
WHY DO YOU FEEL SORRY FOR HIM?
I MEAN, WHEN SOMEONE YOU LIKE ACTS LIKE SHE'S SCARED OF YOU.
It's too bad.
HUH? KAZEHAYA LIKES SOMEONE?
?
It's...
IT'S GONNA BE A PROBLEM...
...FOR SAWAKO!
BUT KAZEHAYA STILL CARES ABOUT SAWAKO TOO!
YESTERDAY TOO, HE WAS ...
WHOOA
I know you feel responsible for her, but...
HOLD ...
...ON.

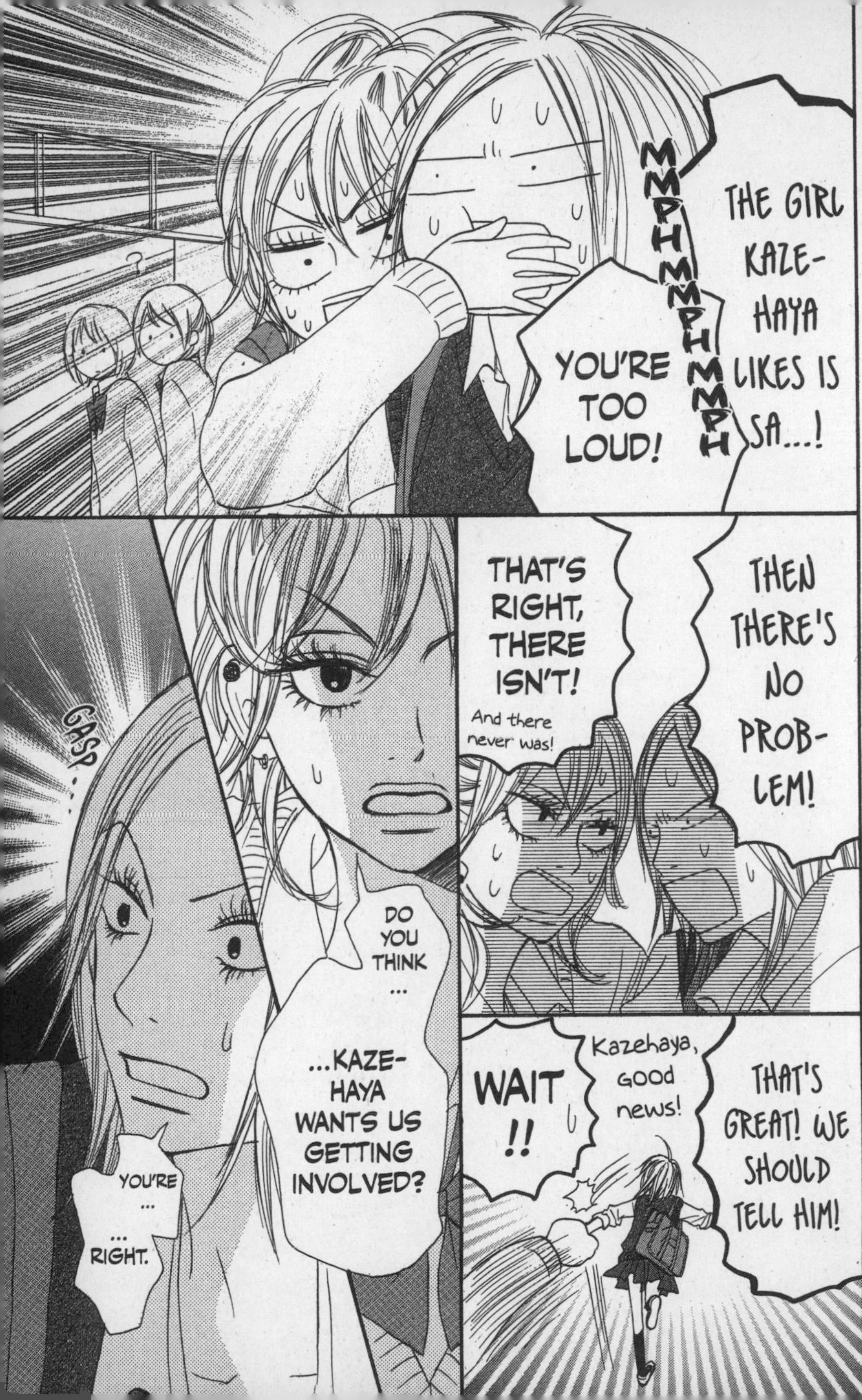
THE GIRL KAZE-HAYA LIKES IS SA...!
MMPH MMPH MMPH
YOU'RE TOO LOUD!
?
THEN THERE'S NO PROB-LEM!
THAT'S RIGHT, THERE ISN'T!
And there never was!
THAT'S GREAT! WE SHOULD TELL HIM!
Kazehaya, good news!
WAIT!!
DO YOU THINK ...
...KAZE-HAYA WANTS US GETTING INVOLVED?
GASP...
YOU'RE ...
... RIGHT.

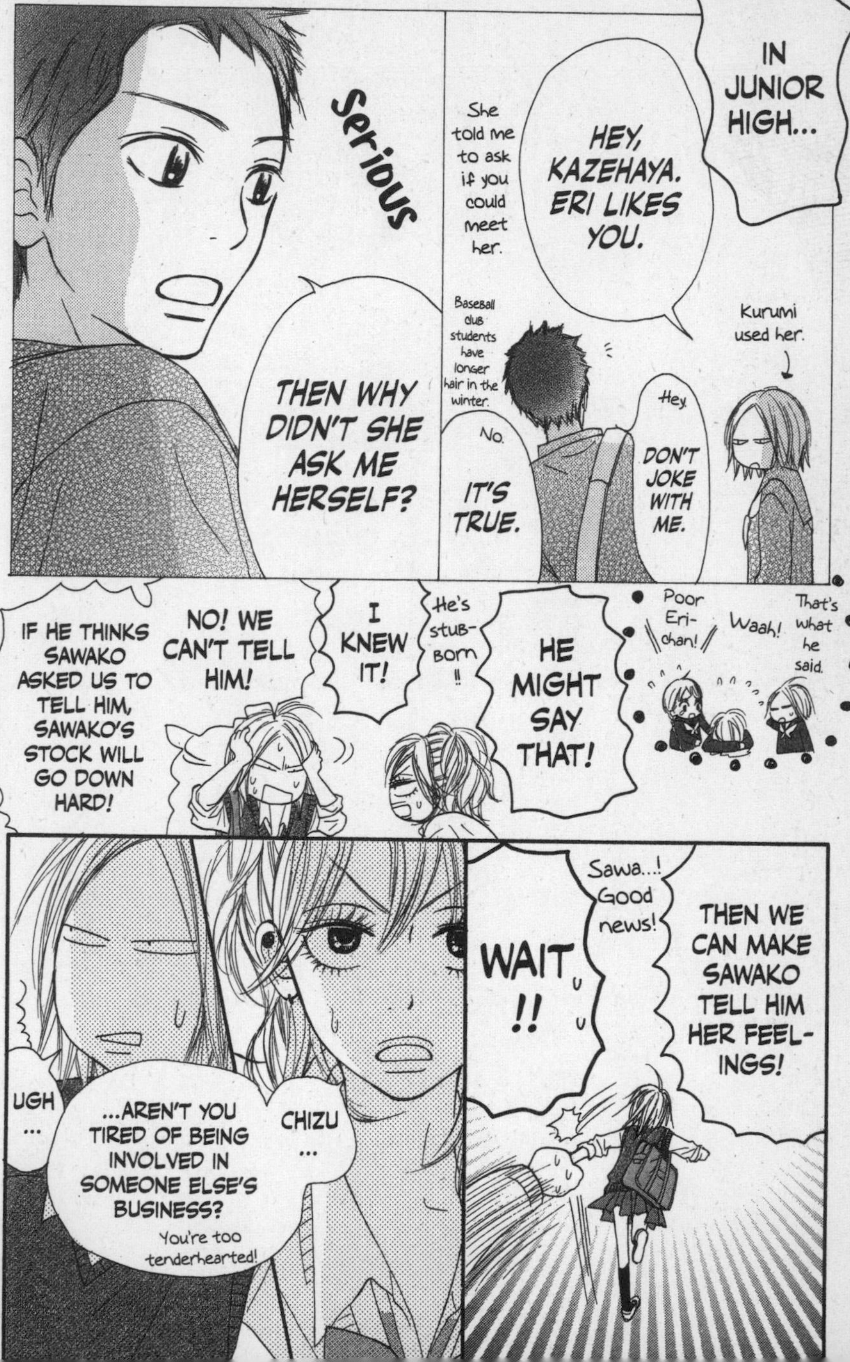
IN JUNIOR HIGH...
Kurumi used her.
HEY, KAZEHAYA. ERI LIKES YOU.
She told me to ask if you could meet her.
Hey.
DON'T JOKE WITH ME.
No.
IT'S TRUE.
Baseball club students have longer hair in the winter.
Serious
THEN WHY DIDN'T SHE ASK ME HERSELF?
That's what he said.
Waah!
Poor Eri-chan!
HE MIGHT SAY THAT!
He's stubborn!!
I KNEW IT!
NO! WE CAN'T TELL HIM!
IF HE THINKS SAWAKO ASKED US TO TELL HIM, SAWAKO'S STOCK WILL GO DOWN HARD!
THEN WE CAN MAKE SAWAKO TELL HIM HER FEELINGS!
Sawa...! Good news!
WAIT!!
CHIZU...
...AREN'T YOU TIRED OF BEING INVOLVED IN SOMEONE ELSE'S BUSINESS?
You're too tenderhearted!
UGH...

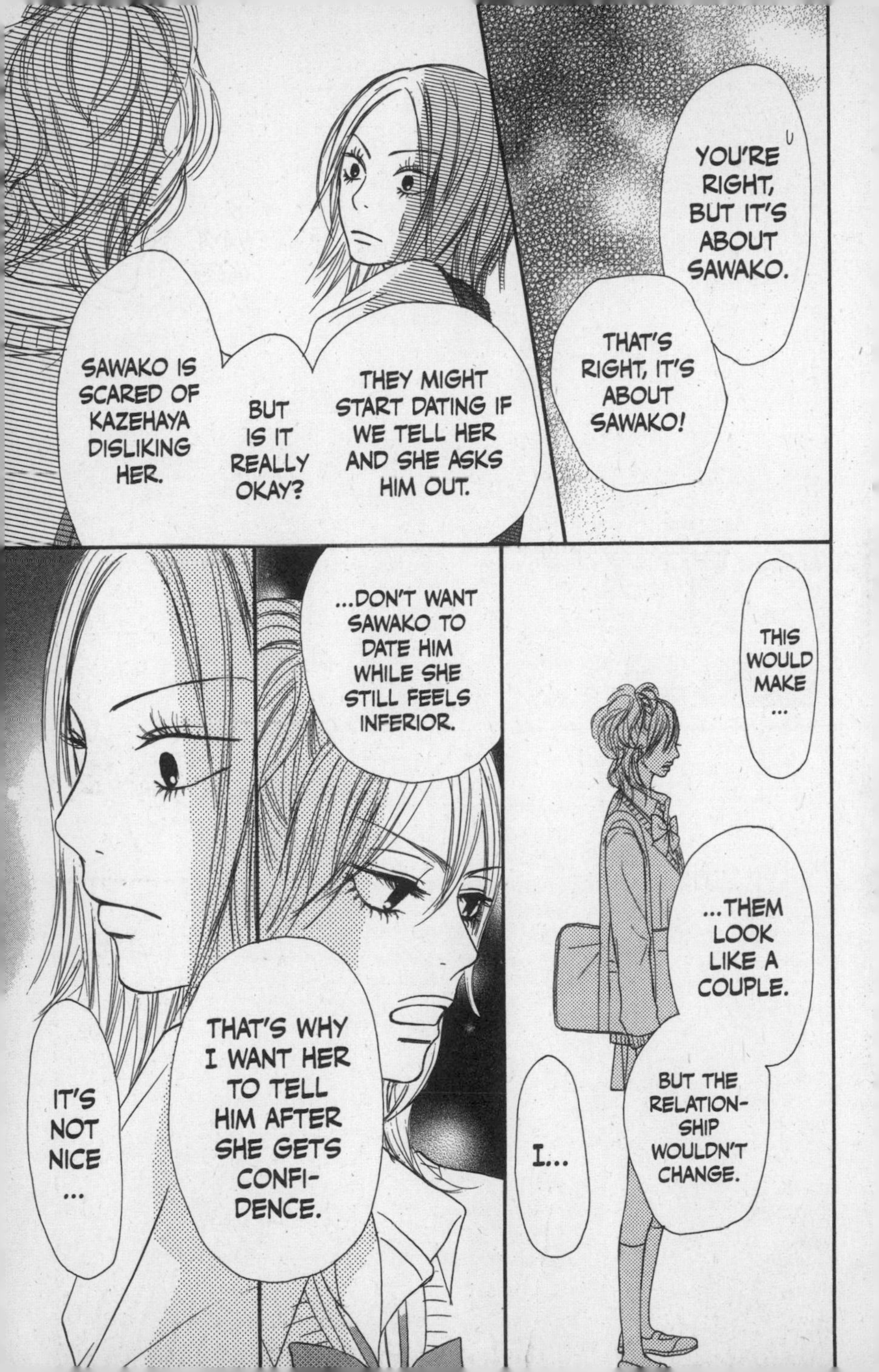
YOU'RE RIGHT, BUT IT'S ABOUT SAWAKO.
THAT'S RIGHT, IT'S ABOUT SAWAKO!
THEY MIGHT START DATING IF WE TELL HER AND SHE ASKS HIM OUT.
BUT IS IT REALLY OKAY?
SAWAKO IS SCARED OF KAZEHAYA DISLIKING HER.
THIS WOULD MAKE ...
...THEM LOOK LIKE A COUPLE.
BUT THE RELATION-SHIP WOULDN'T CHANGE.
I...
...DON'T WANT SAWAKO TO DATE HIM WHILE SHE STILL FEELS INFERIOR.
THAT'S WHY I WANT HER TO TELL HIM AFTER SHE GETS CONFI-DENCE.
IT'S NOT NICE ...

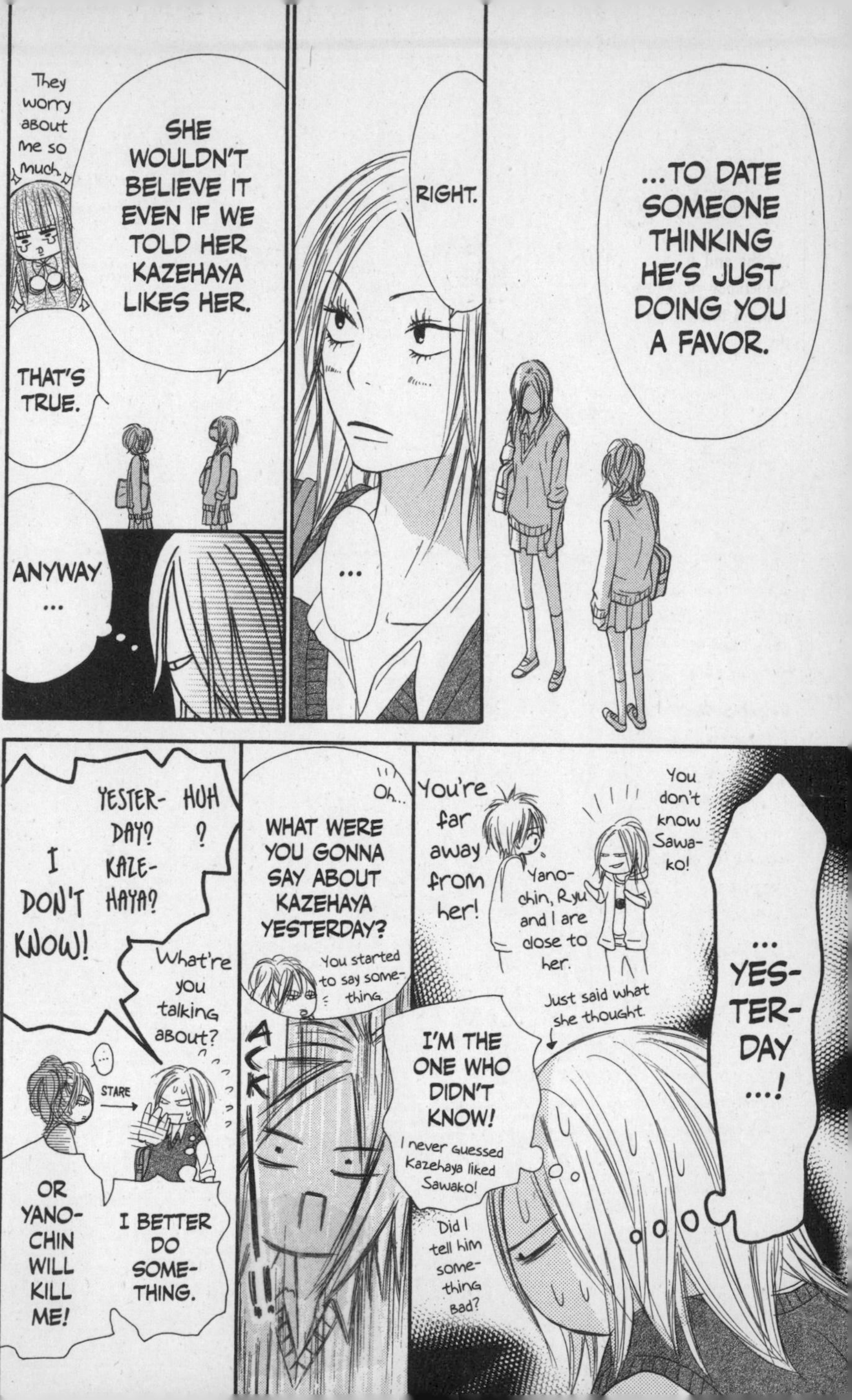
...TO DATE SOMEONE THINKING HE'S JUST DOING YOU A FAVOR.
RIGHT.
...
SHE WOULDN'T BELIEVE IT EVEN IF WE TOLD HER KAZEHAYA LIKES HER.
They worry about me so much.
THAT'S TRUE.
ANYWAY ...
You don't know Sawako!
Yano-chin, Ryu and I are close to her.
You're far away from her!
... YES-TER-DAY ...!
Just said what she thought.
I'M THE ONE WHO DIDN'T KNOW!
I never guessed Kazehaya liked Sawako!
Did I tell him something bad?
Oh..
WHAT WERE YOU GONNA SAY ABOUT KAZEHAYA YESTERDAY?
You started to say something.
ACK
HUH? YESTERDAY? KAZEHAYA?
I DON'T KNOW!
What're you talking about?
...
STARE
I BETTER DO SOMETHING.
OR YANO-CHIN WILL KILL ME!

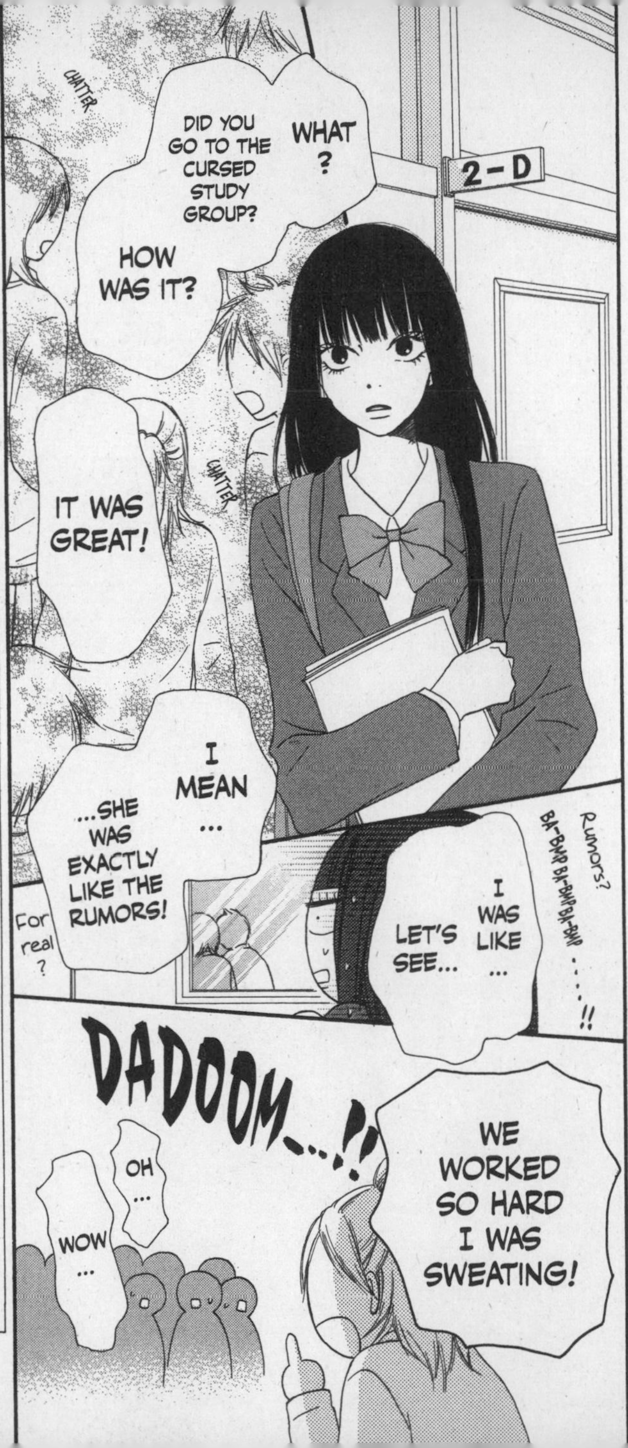
WHAT?
DID YOU GO TO THE CURSED STUDY GROUP?
HOW WAS IT?
CHATTER
2-D
IT WAS GREAT!
CHATTER
I MEAN...
...SHE WAS EXACTLY LIKE THE RUMORS!
For real?
Rumors?
BA-BMP BA-BMP BA-BMP ...!!
I WAS LIKE...
LET'S SEE...
WE WORKED SO HARD I WAS SWEATING!
DADOOM...!!
OH...
WOW...

KARUPIN on JAPAN 3

It's the end of September right now. Around this time of the year...

This year is almost over.

That's what I feel. When this graphic novel comes out, it will be November! Then it will be the end of the year for sure!

Goodbye, 2008! Or is it too early?

So many things happened this year. I was too busy. But so many good things happened. I will never forget this year.

Next year will be busy too. It could be busier than this year. Ha ha!

Volume 9 will come out next year (2009)! I'll be too busy, but I hope you'll keep reading!

The end of September 2008

Karuho Shiina

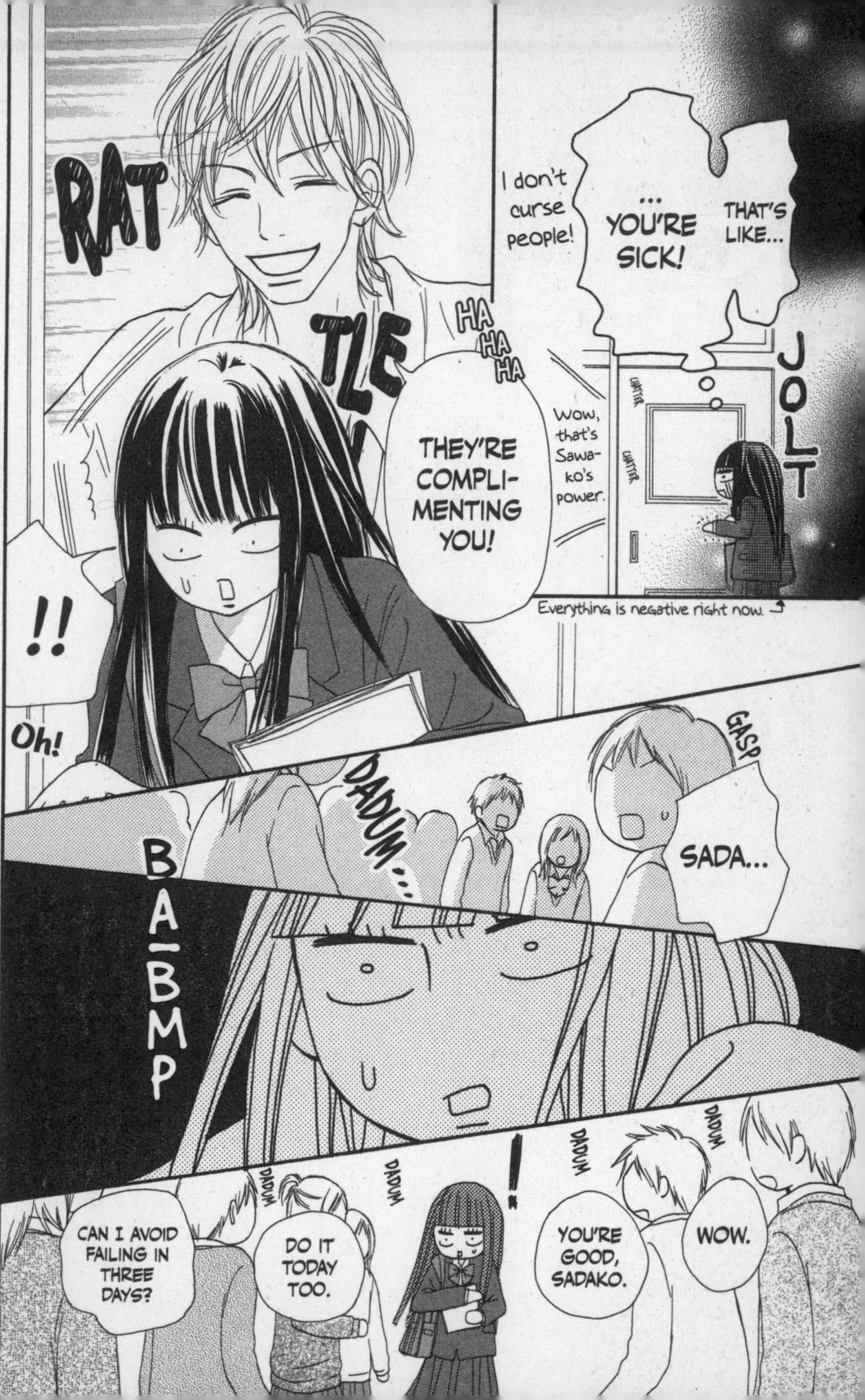

THAT'S LIKE...
...YOU'RE SICK!
I don't curse people!
JOLT
CHATTER
CHATTER
Wow, that's Sawa-ko's power.
Everything is negative right now.
RATTLE
HA HA HA
THEY'RE COMPLI-MENTING YOU!
!!
Oh!
GASP
SADA...
DADUM...
BA-BUMP
DADUM
WOW.
DADUM
YOU'RE GOOD, SADAKO.
!
DADUM
DO IT TODAY TOO.
DADUM
CAN I AVOID FAILING IN THREE DAYS?

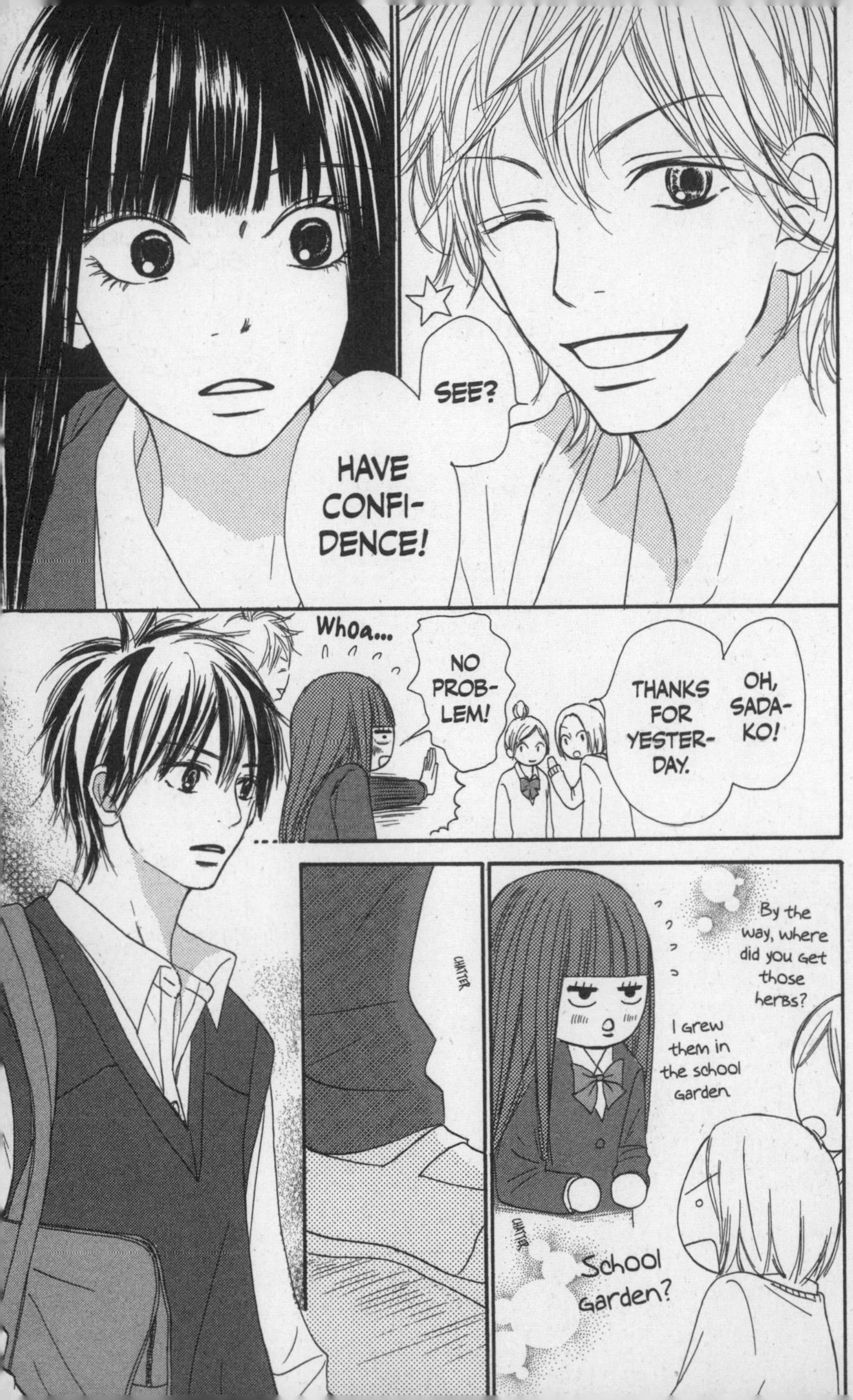
SEE?
HAVE CONFIDENCE!
OH, SADAKO!
THANKS FOR YESTERDAY.
NO PROBLEM!
Whoa...
...
By the way, where did you get those herbs?
I grew them in the school garden.
CHATTER
School garden?
CHATTER

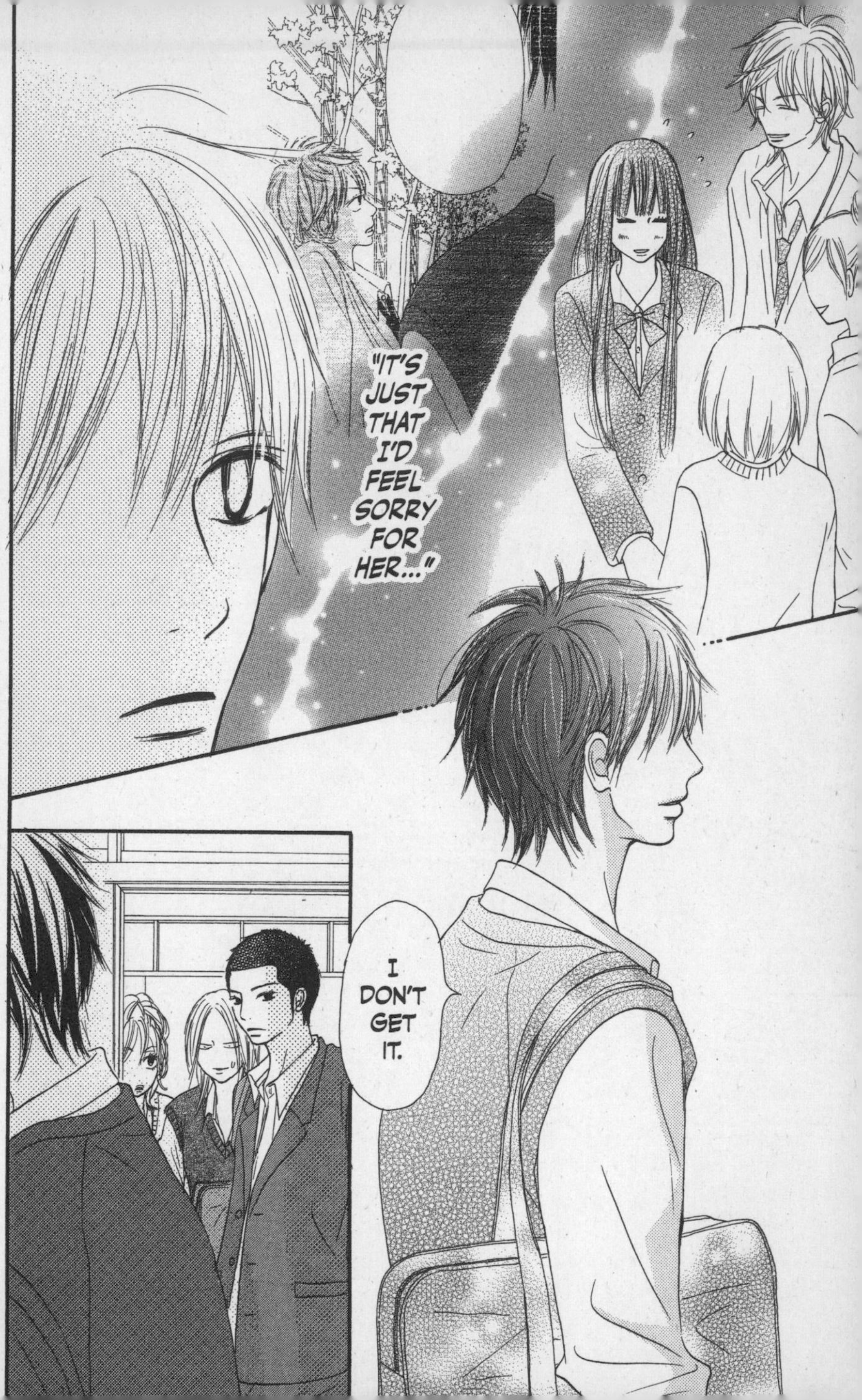
"IT'S JUST THAT I'D FEEL SORRY FOR HER..."
I DON'T GET IT.

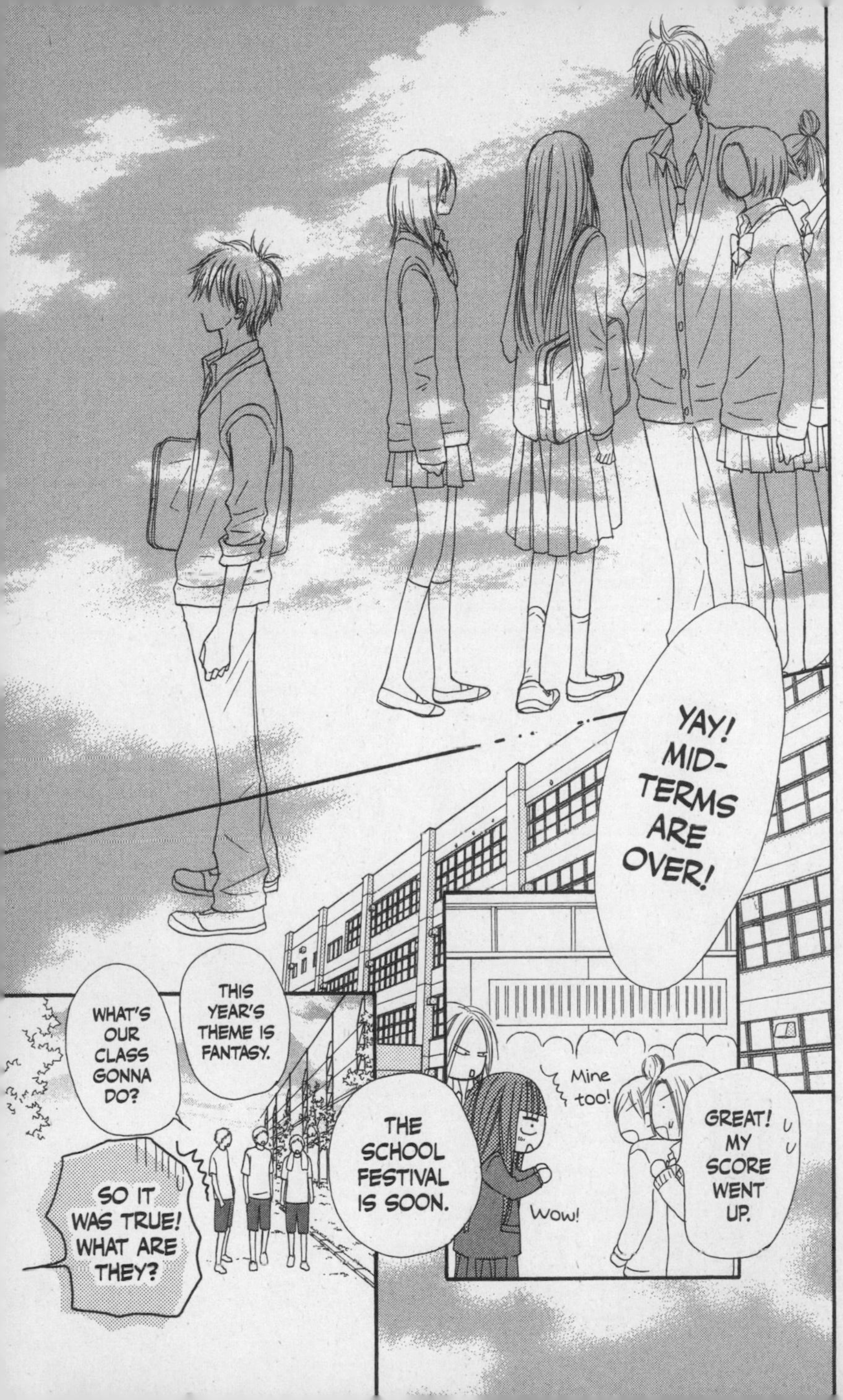
YAY! MID-TERMS ARE OVER!
GREAT! MY SCORE WENT UP.
Mine too!
Wow!
THE SCHOOL FESTIVAL IS SOON.
THIS YEAR'S THEME IS FANTASY.
WHAT'S OUR CLASS GONNA DO?
SO IT WAS TRUE! WHAT ARE THEY?

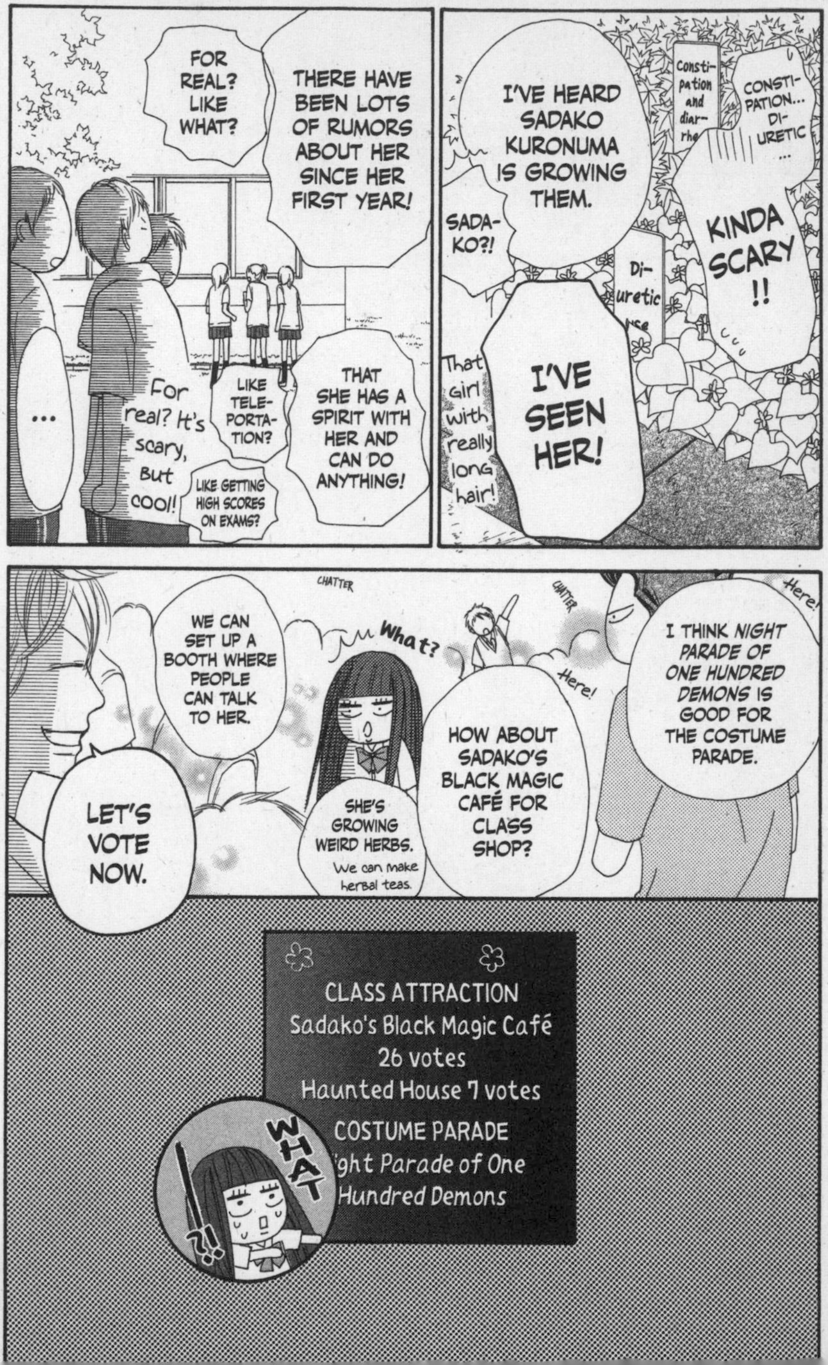
CONSTI-PATION... DI-URETIC...
Consti-pation and diar-rhe
KINDA SCARY!!
I'VE HEARD SADAKO KURONUMA IS GROWING THEM.
SADAKO?!
Di-uretic
I'VE SEEN HER!
That girl with really long hair!
THERE HAVE BEEN LOTS OF RUMORS ABOUT HER SINCE HER FIRST YEAR!
FOR REAL? LIKE WHAT?
THAT SHE HAS A SPIRIT WITH HER AND CAN DO ANYTHING!
LIKE TELE-PORTA-TION?
For real? It's scary, but cool!
LIKE GETTING HIGH SCORES ON EXAMS?
...
Here!
I THINK NIGHT PARADE OF ONE HUNDRED DEMONS IS GOOD FOR THE COSTUME PARADE.
CHATTER
Here!
HOW ABOUT SADAKO'S BLACK MAGIC CAFÉ FOR CLASS SHOP?
What?
CHATTER
WE CAN SET UP A BOOTH WHERE PEOPLE CAN TALK TO HER.
SHE'S GROWING WEIRD HERBS. We can make herbal teas.
LET'S VOTE NOW.
CLASS ATTRACTION
Sadako's Black Magic Café
26 votes
Haunted House 7 votes
COSTUME PARADE
ight Parade of One
Hundred Demons
WHAT ?!

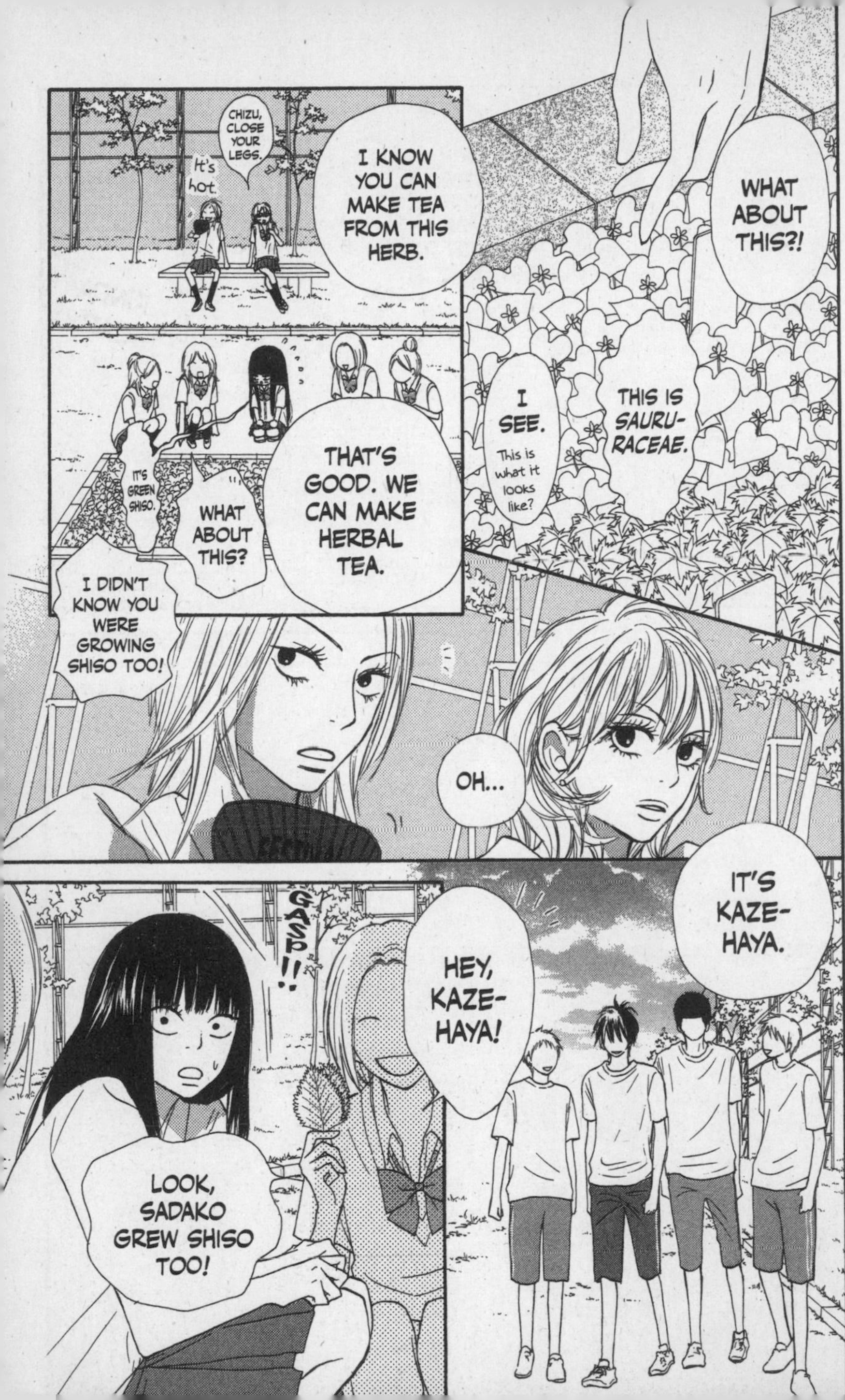
WHAT ABOUT THIS?!
THIS IS SAURU-RACEAE.
I SEE.
This is what it looks like?
I KNOW YOU CAN MAKE TEA FROM THIS HERB.
CHIZU, CLOSE YOUR LEGS.
It's hot.
THAT'S GOOD. WE CAN MAKE HERBAL TEA.
WHAT ABOUT THIS?
IT'S GREEN SHISO.
OH...
I DIDN'T KNOW YOU WERE GROWING SHISO TOO!
IT'S KAZE-HAYA.
HEY, KAZE-HAYA!
GASP!!
LOOK, SADAKO GREW SHISO TOO!

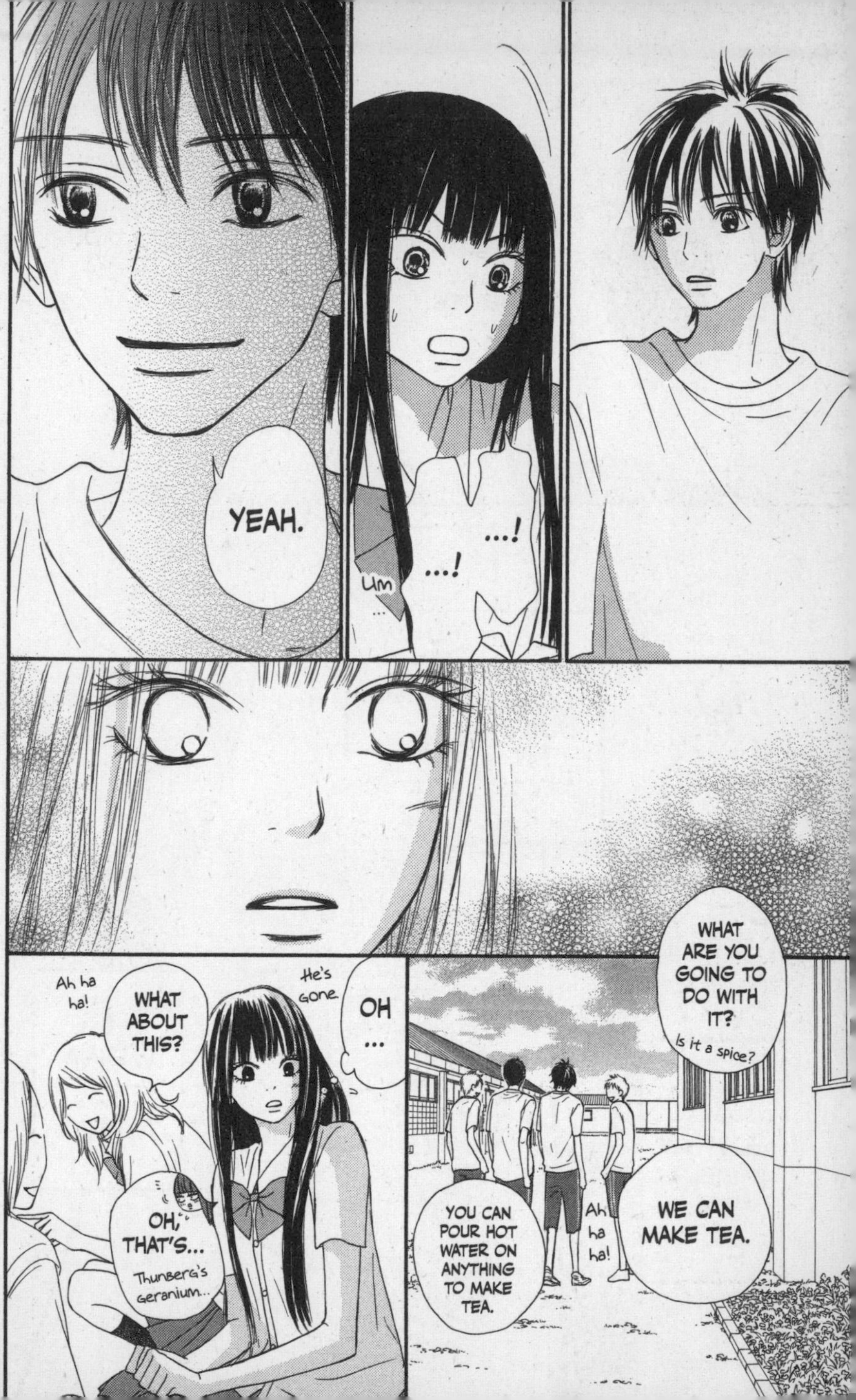
...!
...!
Um ...
YEAH.
WHAT ARE YOU GOING TO DO WITH IT?
Is it a spice?
WE CAN MAKE TEA.
Ah ha ha!
YOU CAN POUR HOT WATER ON ANYTHING TO MAKE TEA.
OH ...
He's gone.
WHAT ABOUT THIS?
Ah ha ha!
OH, THAT'S...
Thunberg's geranium...

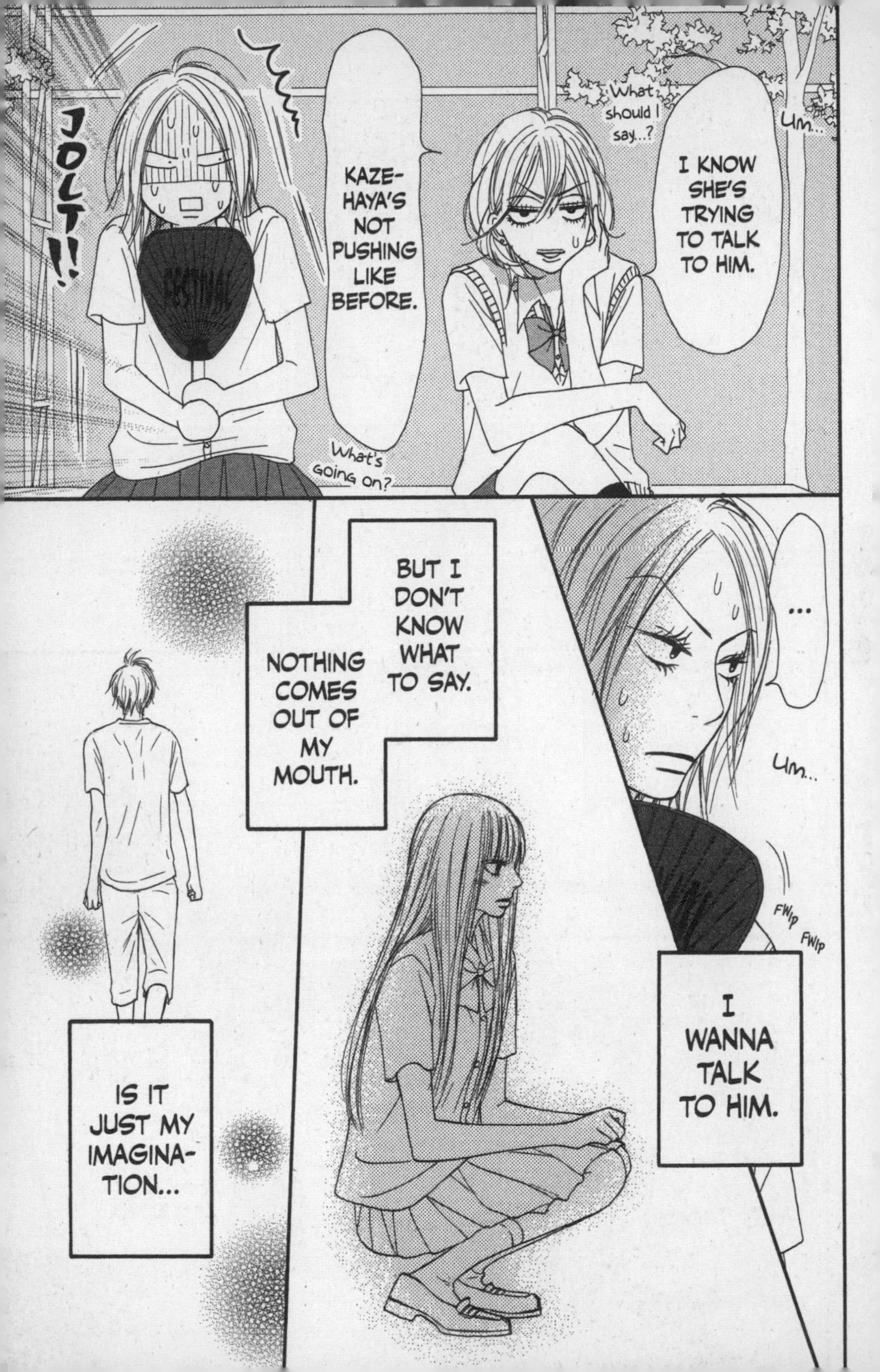
Um...
I KNOW SHE'S TRYING TO TALK TO HIM.
What should I say...?
KAZE-HAYA'S NOT PUSHING LIKE BEFORE.
What's going on?
JOLT!!
...
Um...
FWIP FWIP
I WANNA TALK TO HIM.
BUT I DON'T KNOW WHAT TO SAY.
NOTHING COMES OUT OF MY MOUTH.
IS IT JUST MY IMAGINATION...

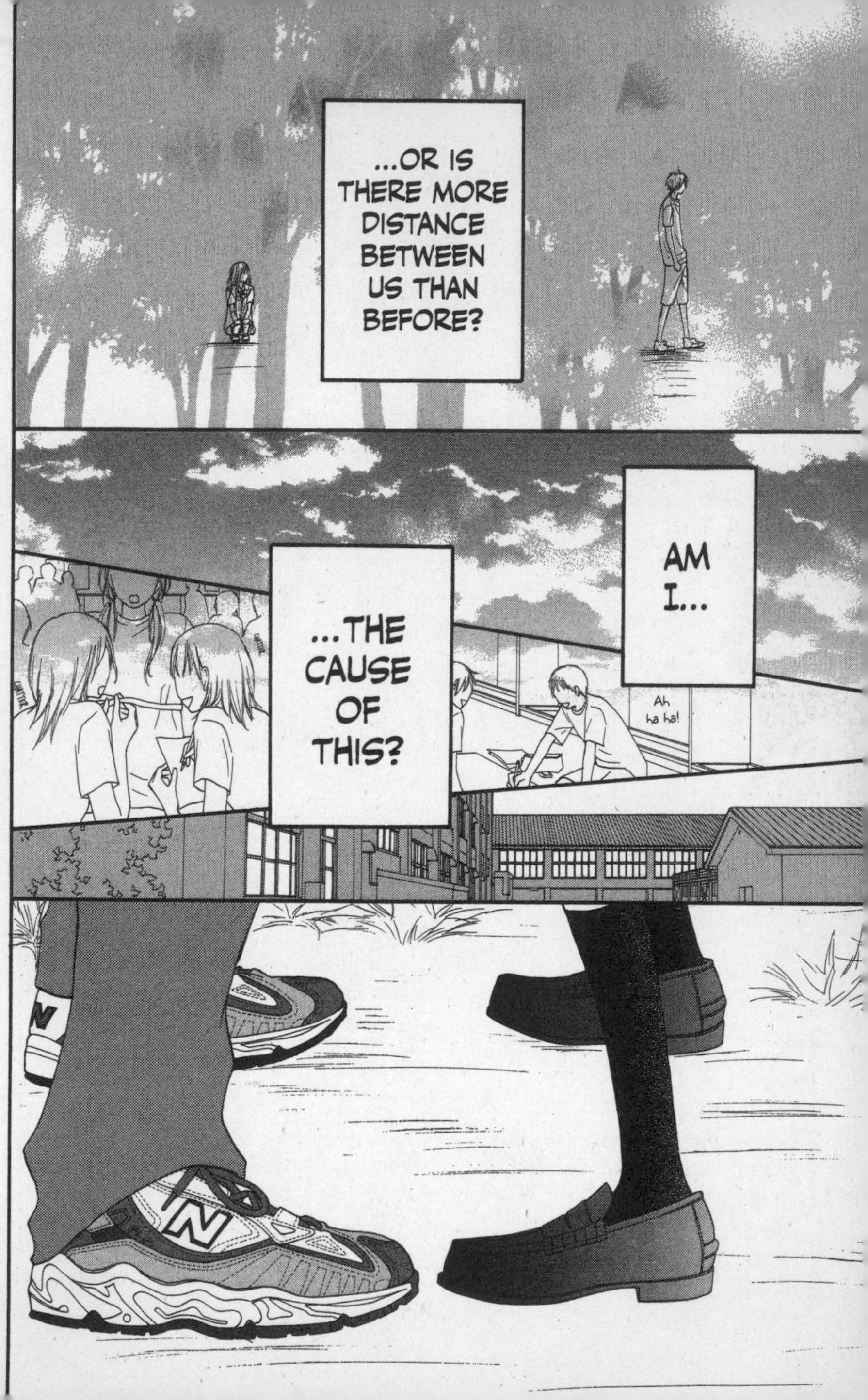
...OR IS THERE MORE DISTANCE BETWEEN US THAN BEFORE?
AM I...
Ah ha ha!
...THE CAUSE OF THIS?

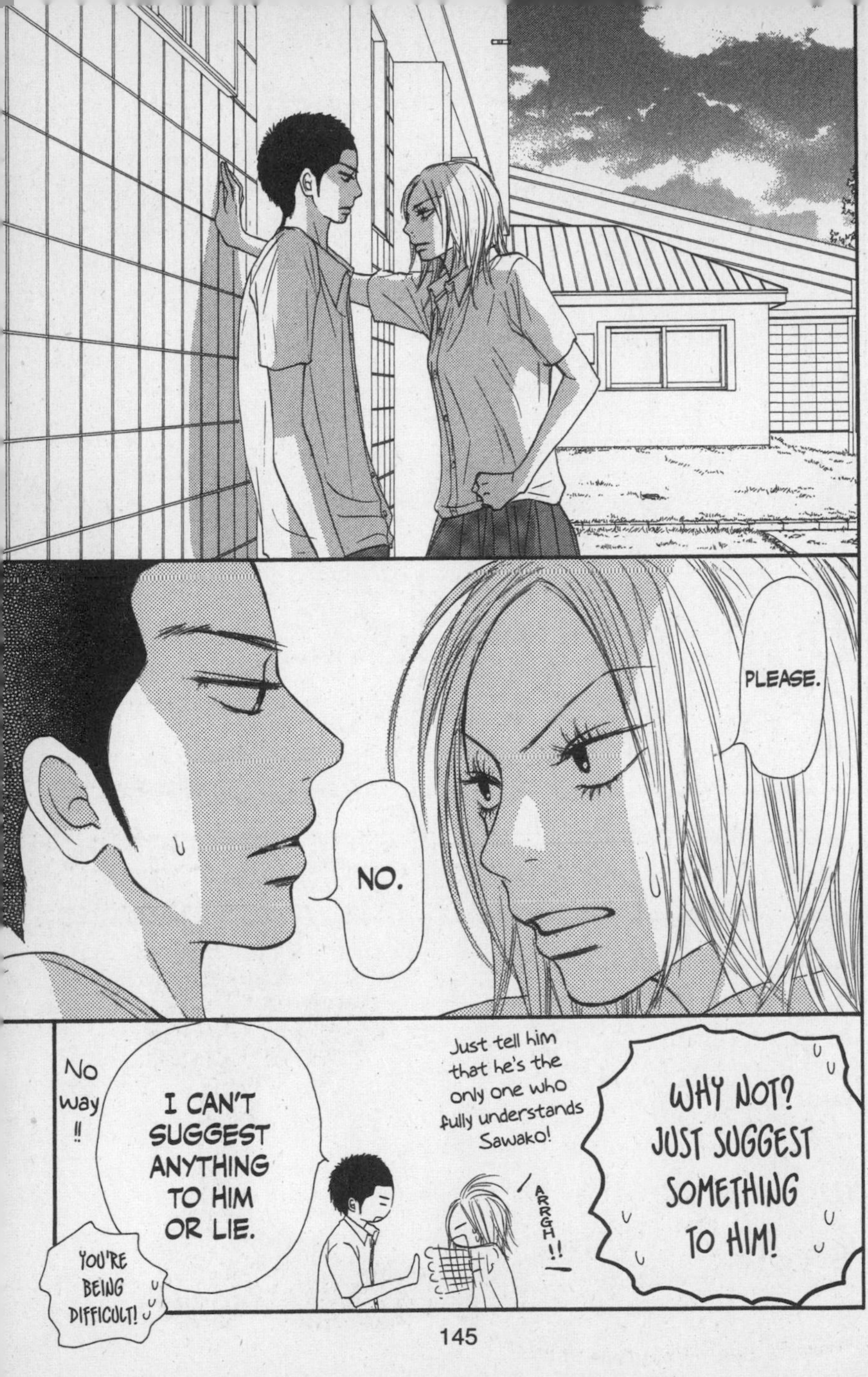
PLEASE.
NO.
WHY NOT? JUST SUGGEST SOMETHING TO HIM!
ARRGH!!
Just tell him that he's the only one who fully understands Sawako!
I CAN'T SUGGEST ANYTHING TO HIM OR LIE.
No way!!
YOU'RE BEING DIFFICULT!

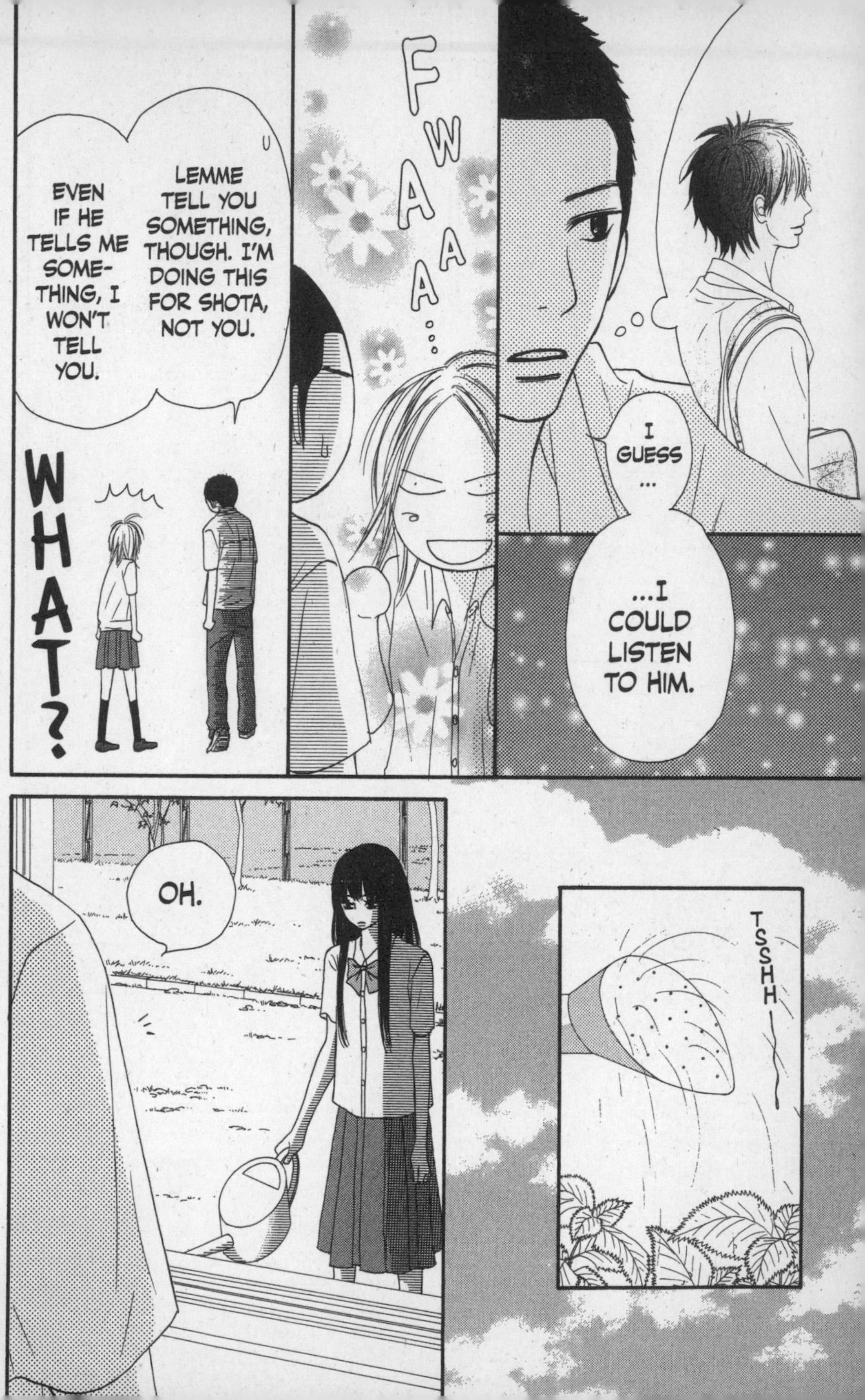
I GUESS ...
...I COULD LISTEN TO HIM.
FWAAA...
LEMME TELL YOU SOMETHING, THOUGH. I'M DOING THIS FOR SHOTA, NOT YOU.
EVEN IF HE TELLS ME SOMETHING, I WON'T TELL YOU.
WHAT?
TSSHH
OH.

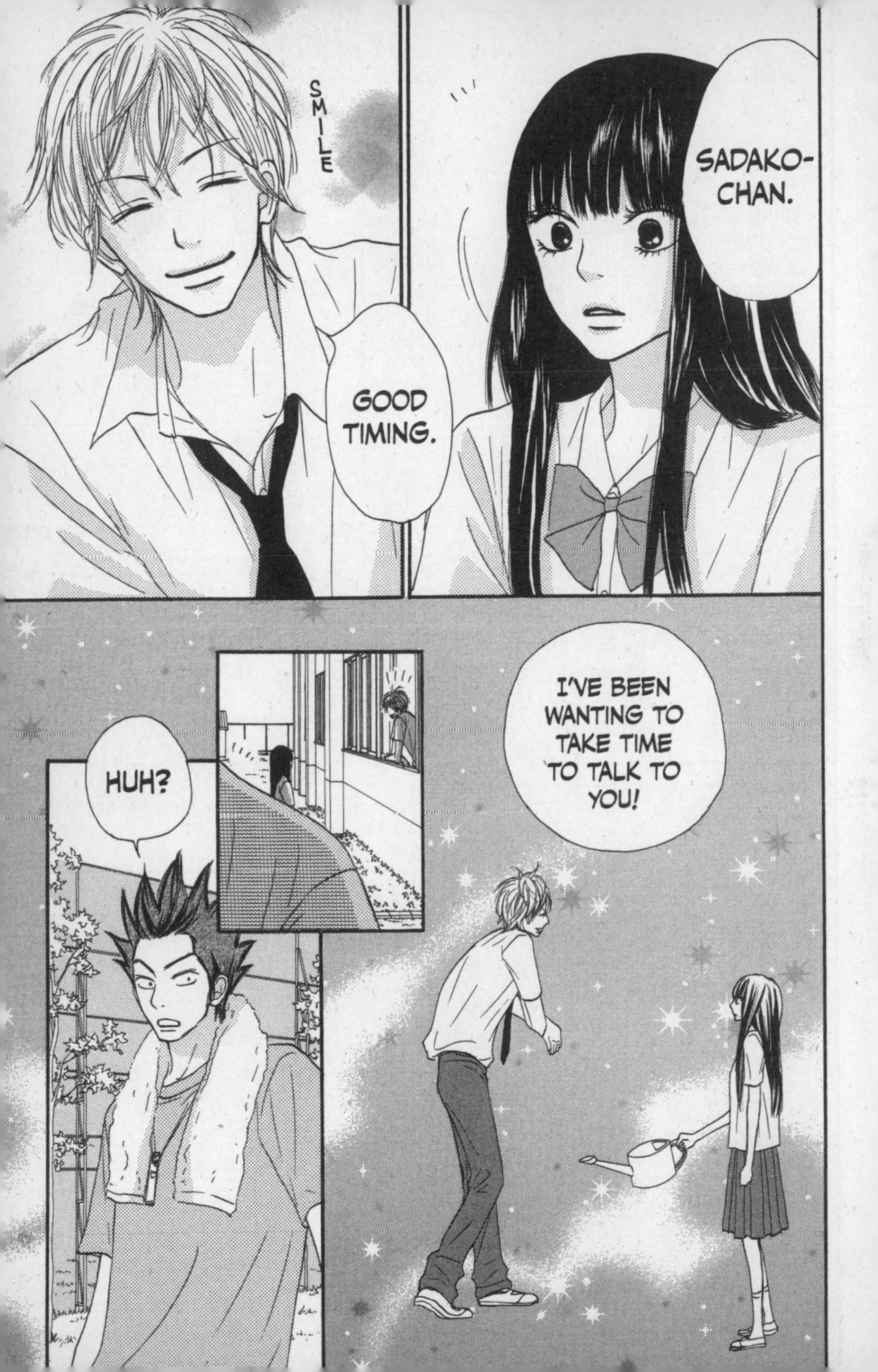
SADAKO-CHAN.
SMILE
GOOD TIMING.
I'VE BEEN WANTING TO TAKE TIME TO TALK TO YOU!
HUH?

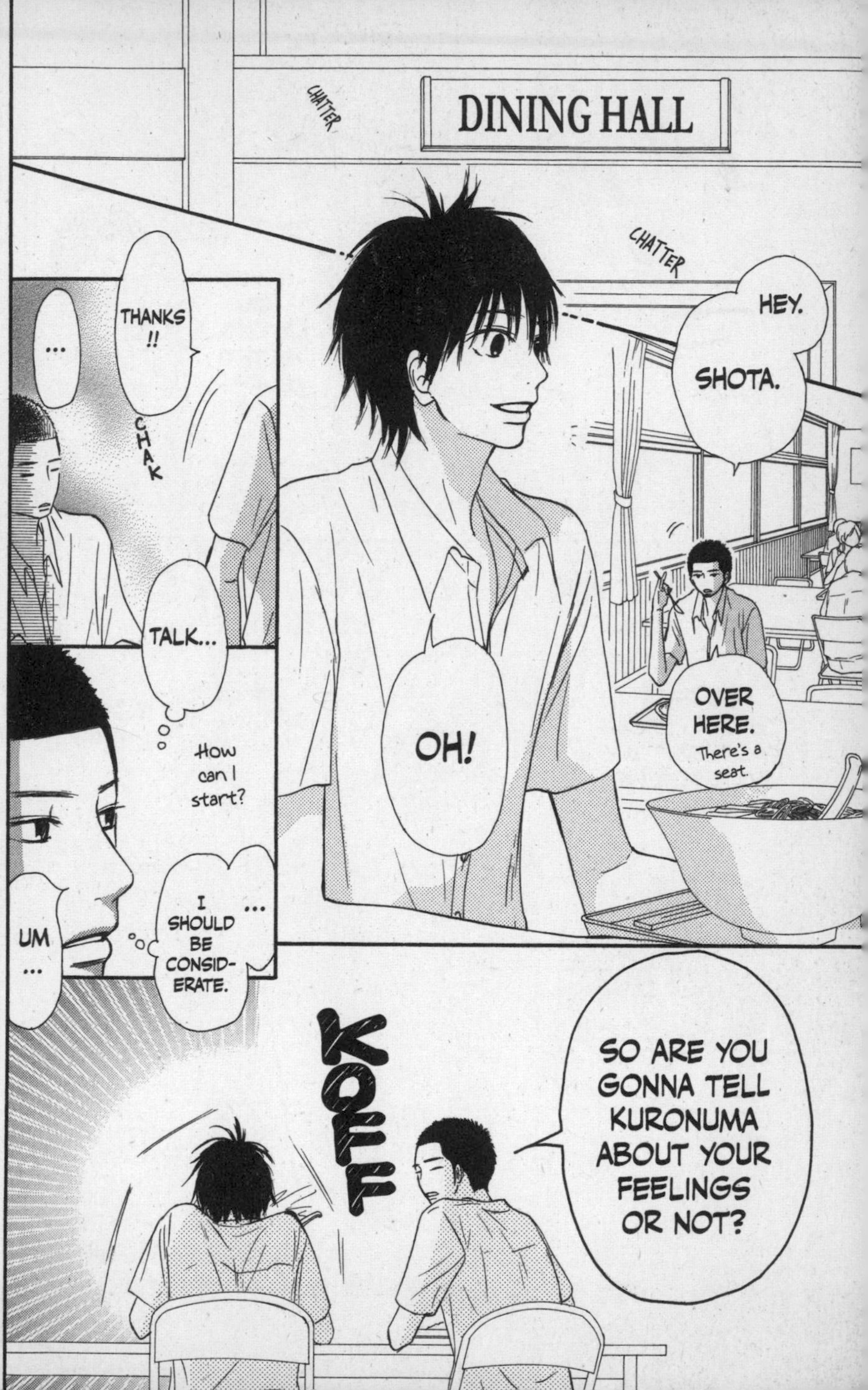
DINING HALL
CHATTER
CHATTER
HEY.
SHOTA.
OVER HERE.
There's a seat.
OH!
THANKS !!
...
CHAK
TALK...
How can I start?
... I SHOULD BE CONSID-ERATE.
UM ...
SO ARE YOU GONNA TELL KURONUMA ABOUT YOUR FEELINGS OR NOT?
KOFF

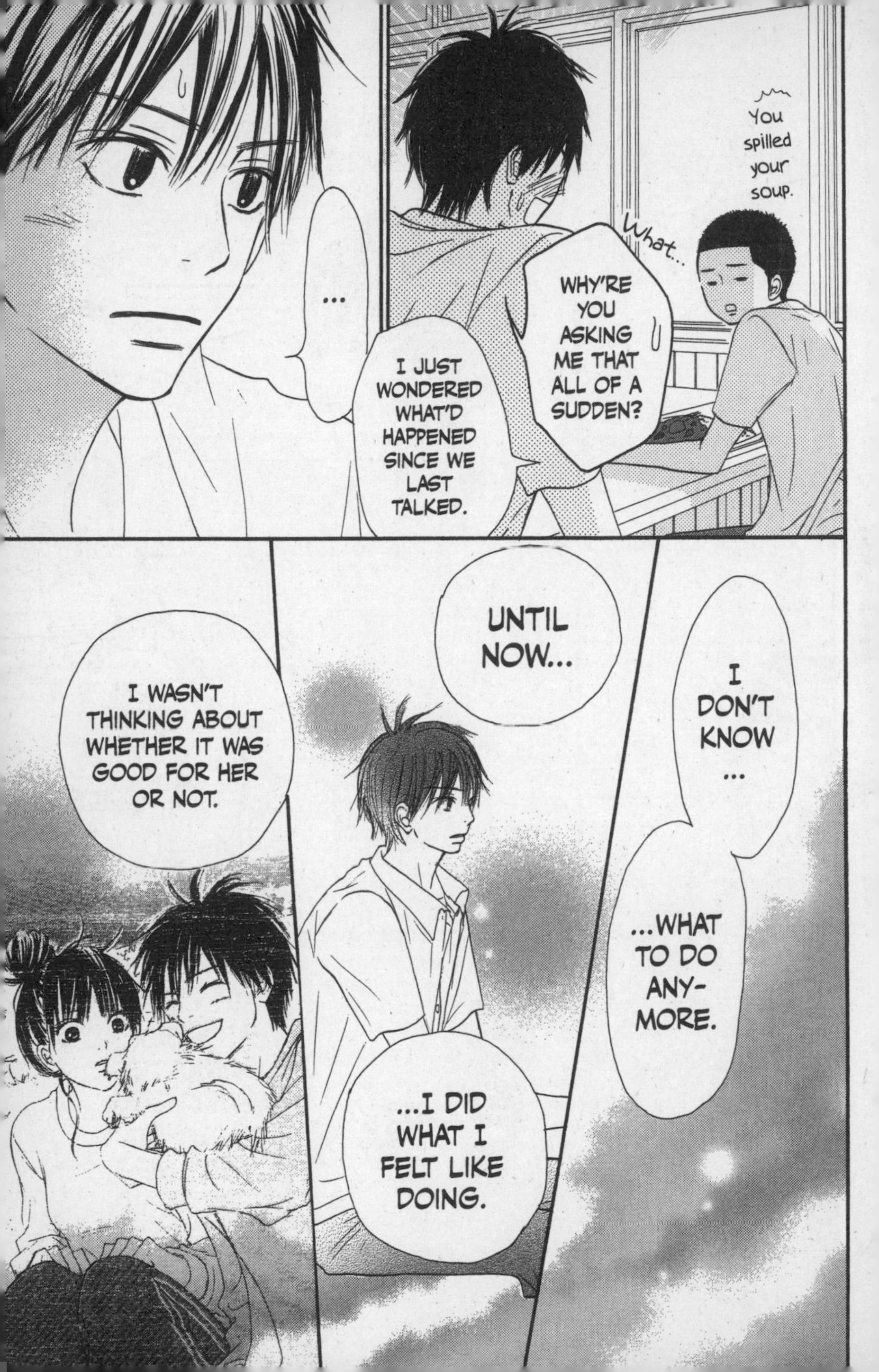
You spilled your soup.
What...
WHY'RE YOU ASKING ME THAT ALL OF A SUDDEN?
I JUST WONDERED WHAT'D HAPPENED SINCE WE LAST TALKED.
...
I DON'T KNOW ...
...WHAT TO DO ANYMORE.
UNTIL NOW...
...I DID WHAT I FELT LIKE DOING.
I WASN'T THINKING ABOUT WHETHER IT WAS GOOD FOR HER OR NOT.

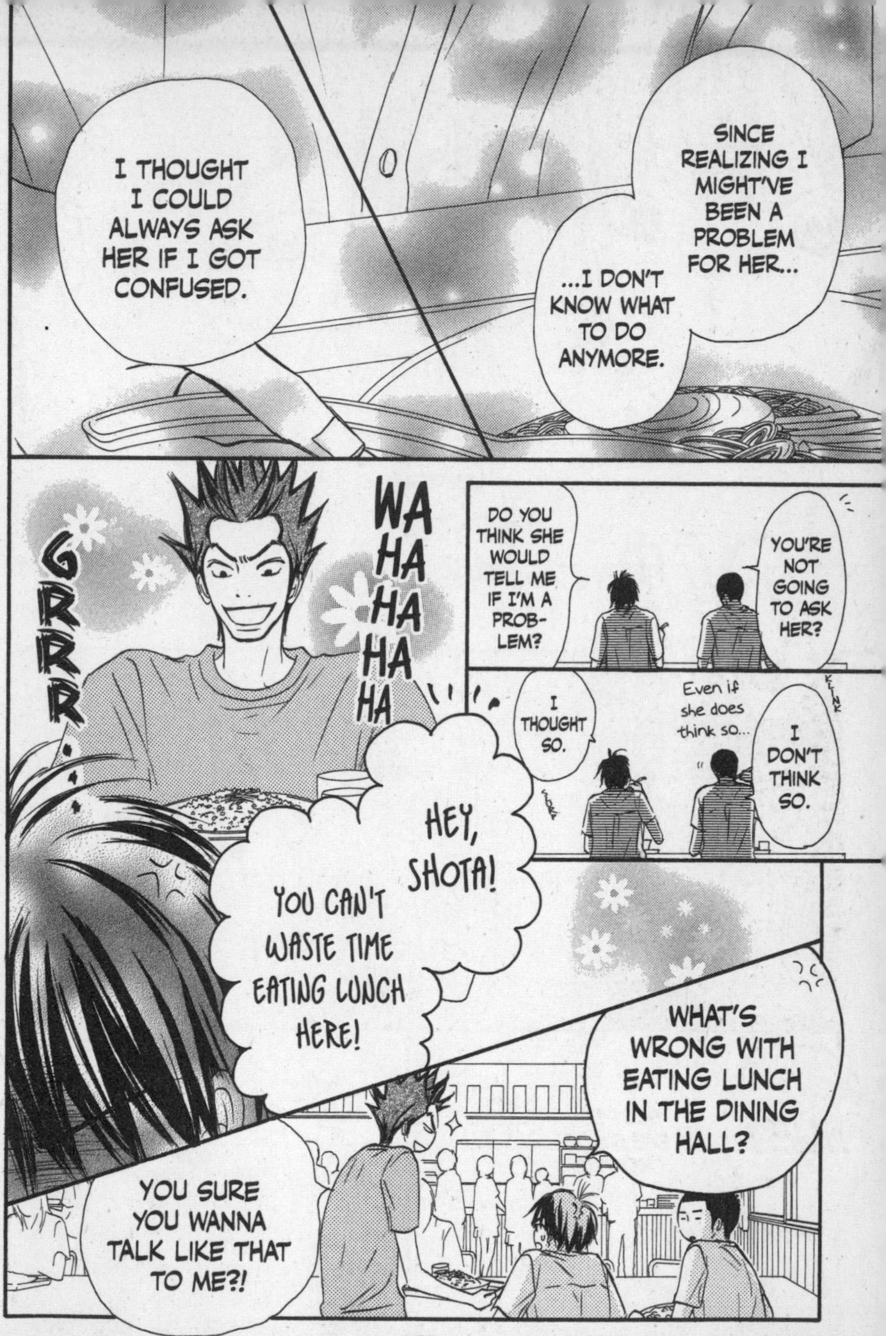
SINCE REALIZING I MIGHT'VE BEEN A PROBLEM FOR HER...
...I DON'T KNOW WHAT TO DO ANYMORE.
I THOUGHT I COULD ALWAYS ASK HER IF I GOT CONFUSED.
YOU'RE NOT GOING TO ASK HER?
DO YOU THINK SHE WOULD TELL ME IF I'M A PROBLEM?
I DON'T THINK SO.
KLINK
Even if she does think so...
I THOUGHT SO.
WA HA HA HA HA HA
GRRR
HEY, SHOTA!
YOU CAN'T WASTE TIME EATING LUNCH HERE!
WHAT'S WRONG WITH EATING LUNCH IN THE DINING HALL?
YOU SURE YOU WANNA TALK LIKE THAT TO ME?!

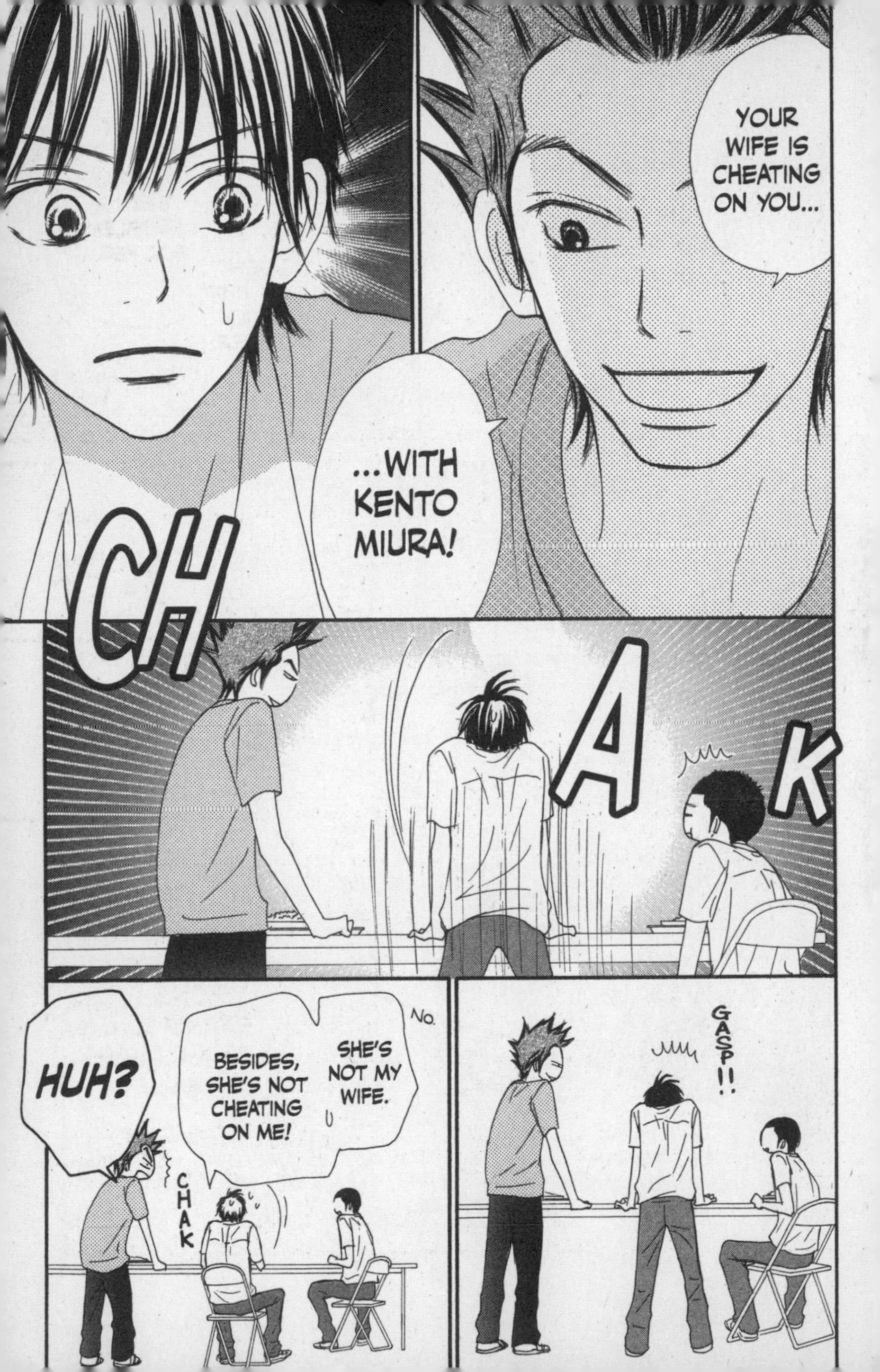
YOUR WIFE IS CHEATING ON YOU...
...WITH KENTO MIURA!
CHAK
GASP!!
NO.
SHE'S NOT MY WIFE.
BESIDES, SHE'S NOT CHEATING ON ME!
HUH?
CHAK

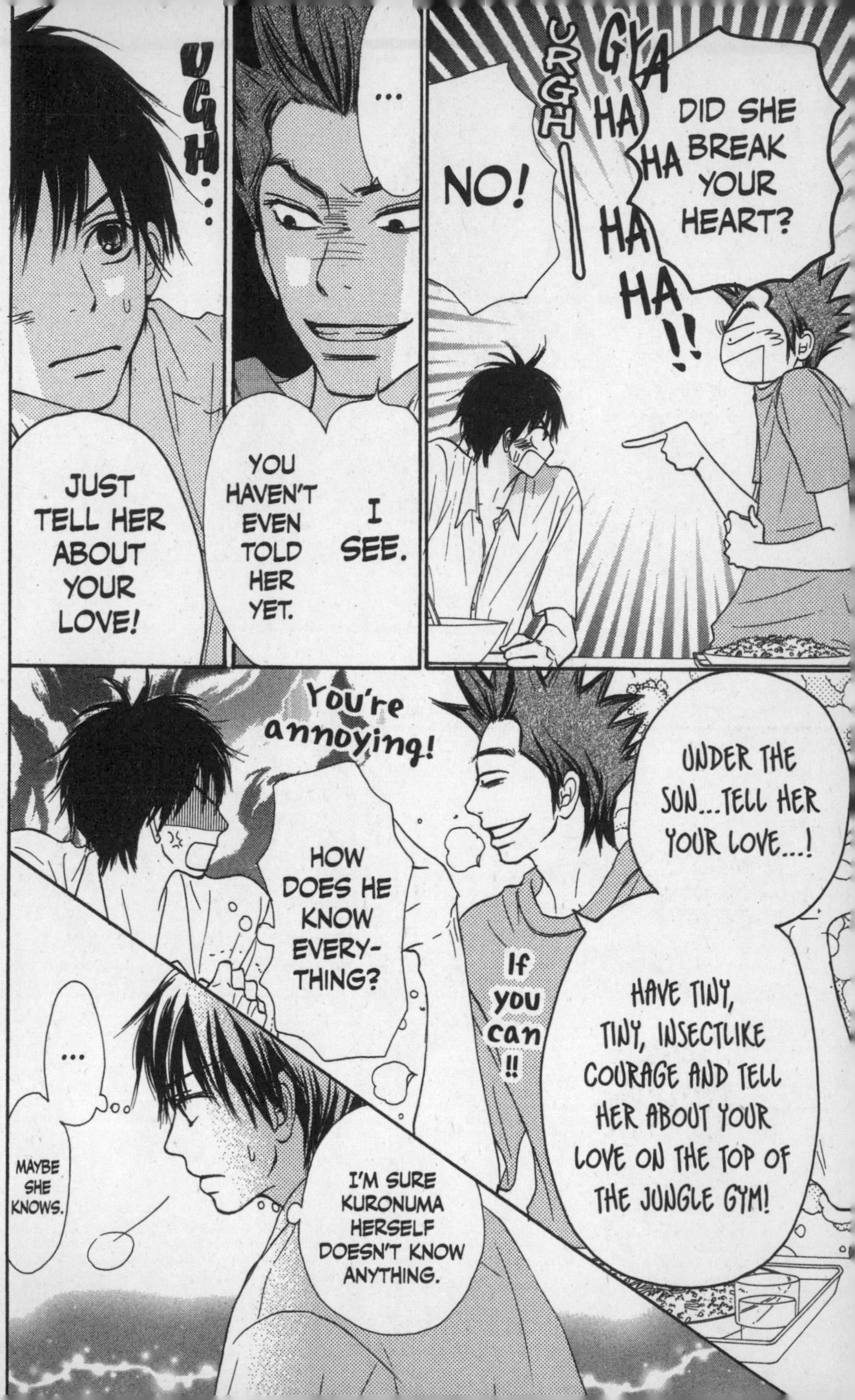
GYAHAHAHAHA!!
DID SHE BREAK YOUR HEART?
URGH
NO!
...
I SEE.
YOU HAVEN'T EVEN TOLD HER YET.
UGH...
JUST TELL HER ABOUT YOUR LOVE!
UNDER THE SUN...TELL HER YOUR LOVE...!
HAVE TINY, TINY, INSECTLIKE COURAGE AND TELL HER ABOUT YOUR LOVE ON THE TOP OF THE JUNGLE GYM!
If you can!!
You're annoying!
HOW DOES HE KNOW EVERYTHING?
I'M SURE KURONUMA HERSELF DOESN'T KNOW ANYTHING.
...
MAYBE SHE KNOWS.

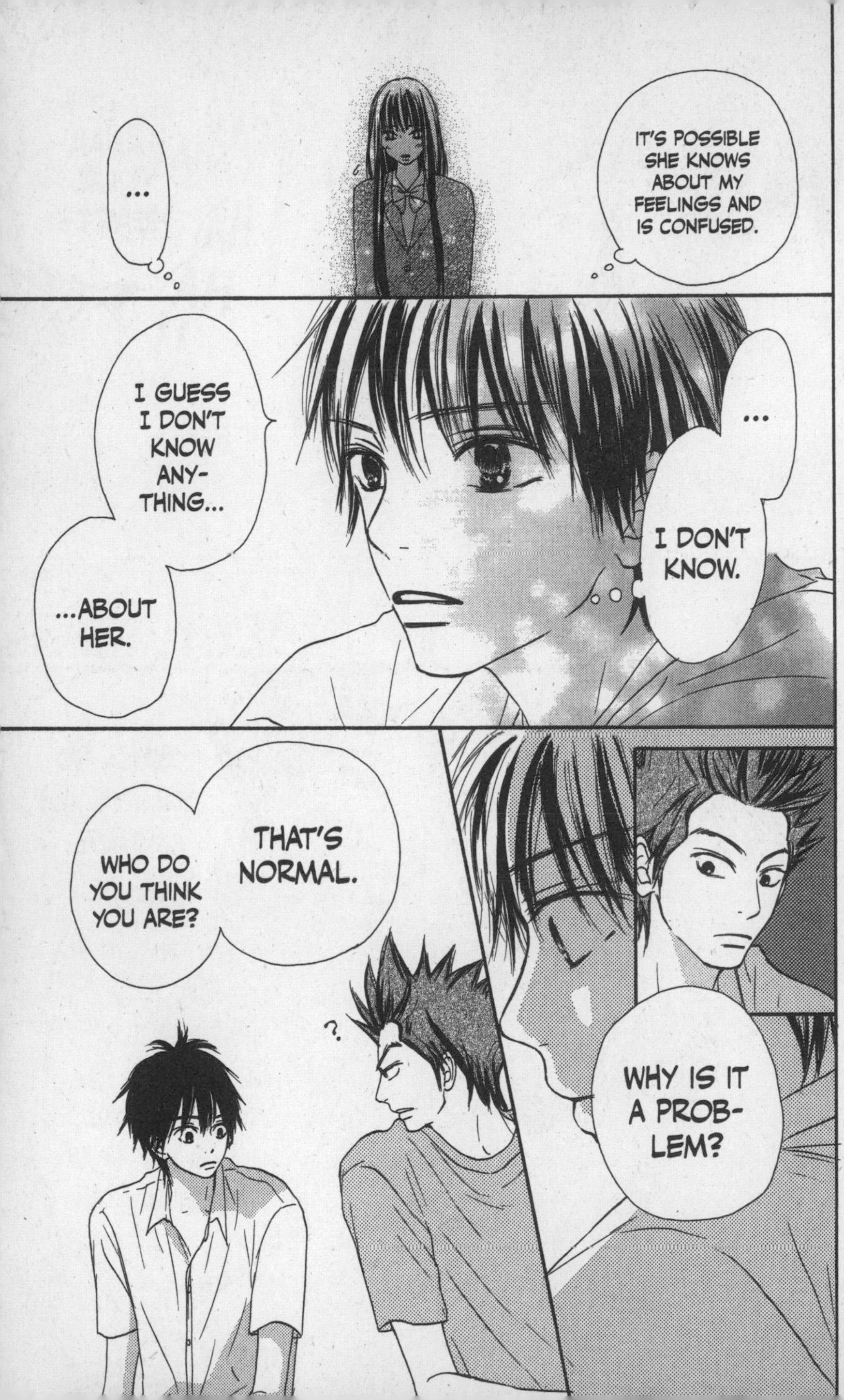
IT'S POSSIBLE SHE KNOWS ABOUT MY FEELINGS AND IS CONFUSED.
...
...
I DON'T KNOW.
I GUESS I DON'T KNOW ANYTHING...
...ABOUT HER.
WHY IS IT A PROBLEM?
?
THAT'S NORMAL.
WHO DO YOU THINK YOU ARE?

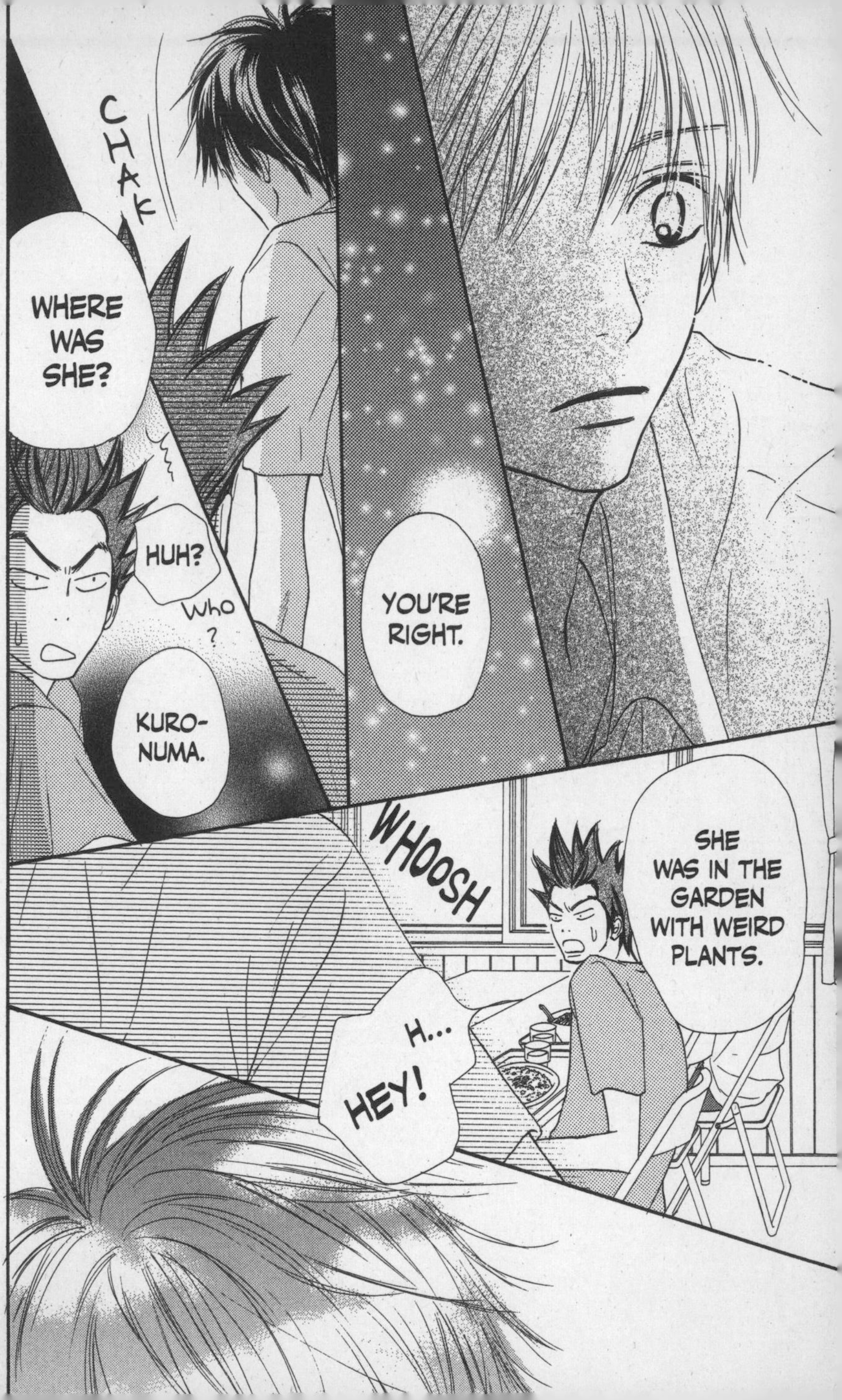
YOU'RE RIGHT.
CHAK
WHERE WAS SHE?
HUH?
Who?
KURO-NUMA.
SHE WAS IN THE GARDEN WITH WEIRD PLANTS.
WHOOSH
H... HEY!

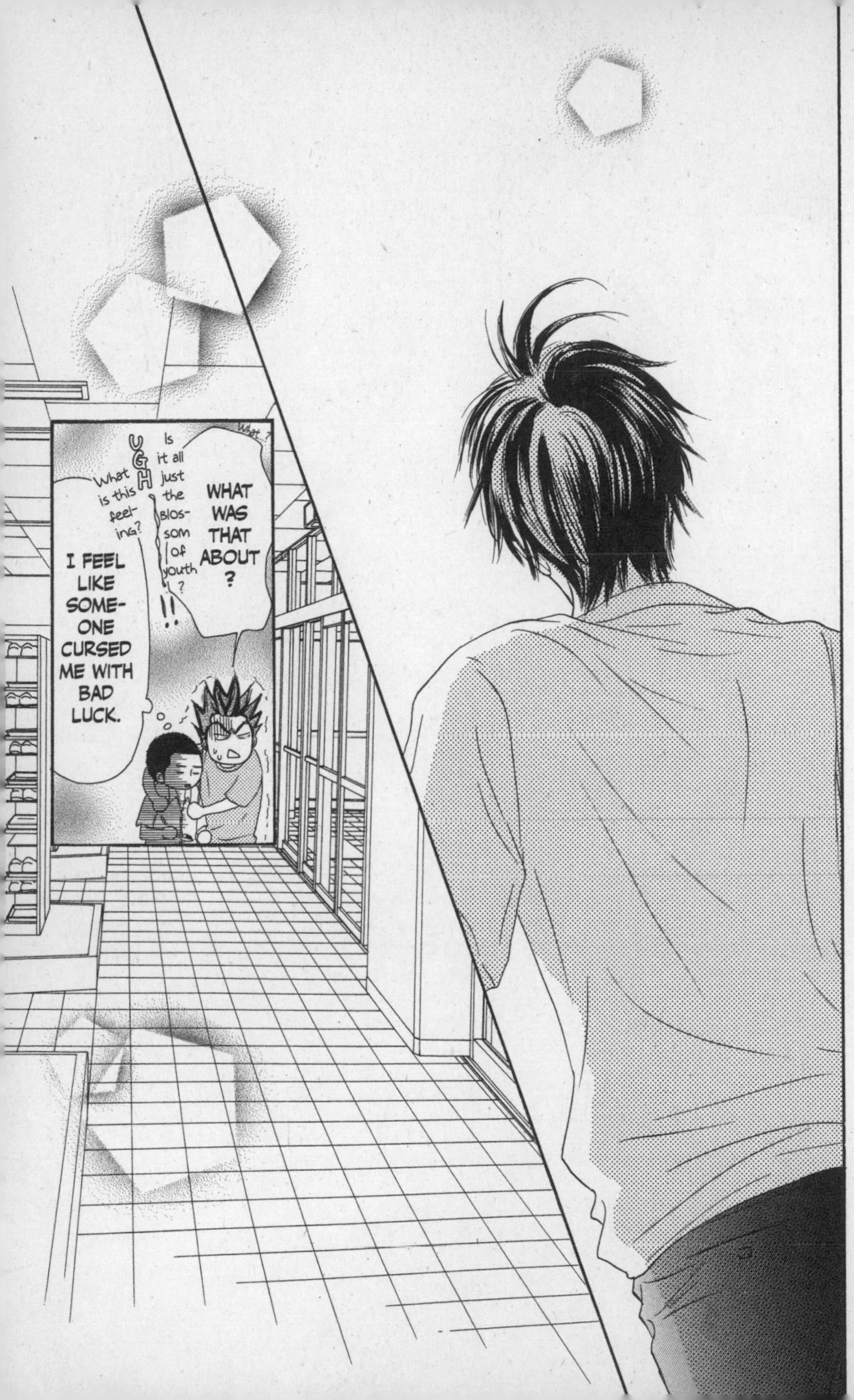
What...?
WHAT WAS THAT ABOUT?
Is it all just the blossom of youth?
UGH!!
What is this feeling?
I FEEL LIKE SOMEONE CURSED ME WITH BAD LUCK.

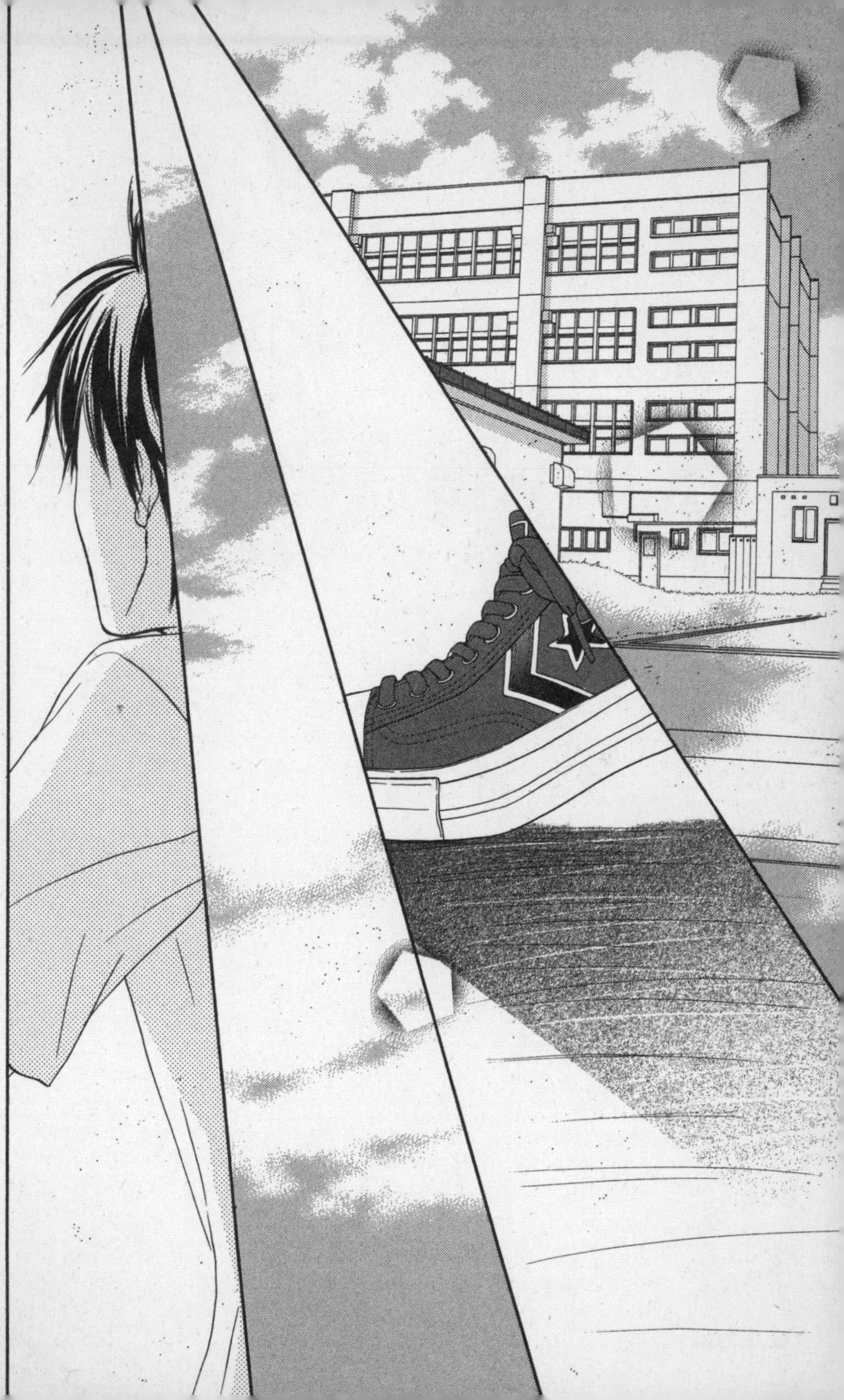

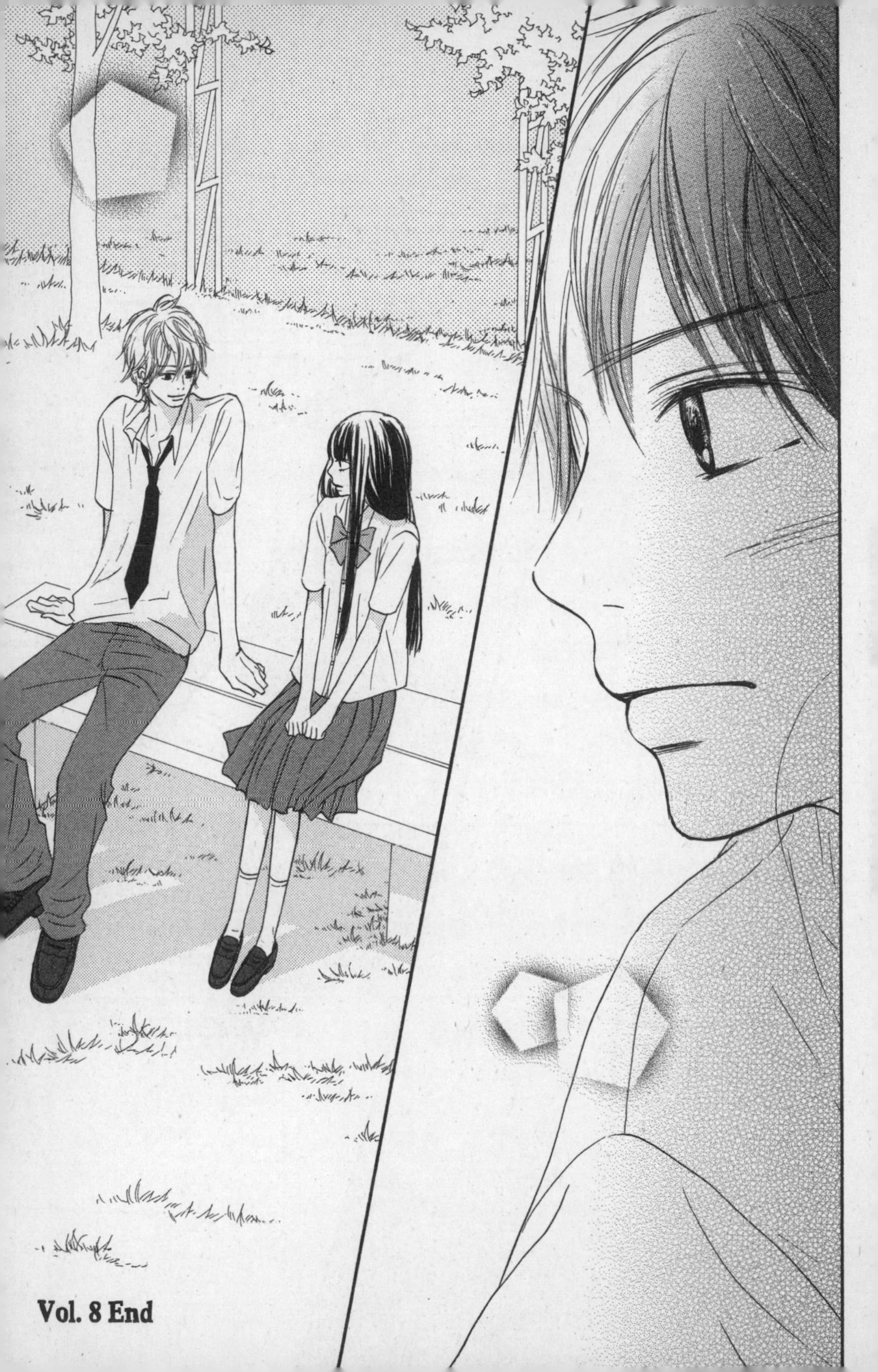

Vol. 8 End

SAWAKO AND HER FUNNY FRIENDS☆

Everyone answered!

Kimi Todo Friend Notebook

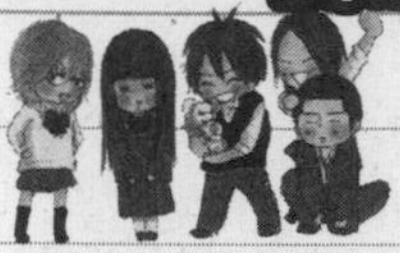

REVEALING PROFILES WRITTEN BY SAWAKO AND HER FRIENDS! THERE'S IMPORTANT PRIVATE INFORMATION! DON'T MISS IT! ♥

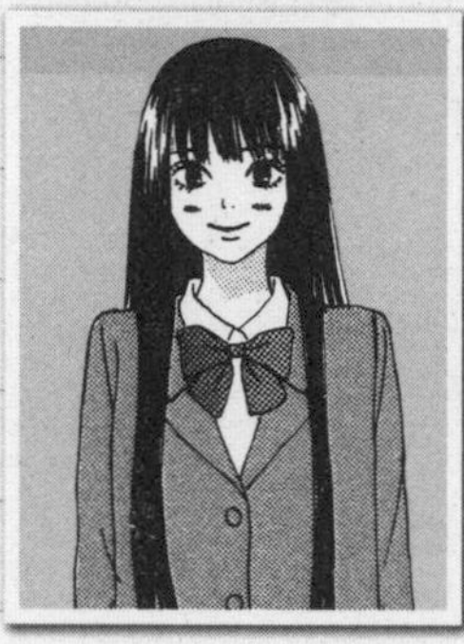

PROFILE The basics!

Name: Sawako Kuronuma, Female

Nickname: Sadako, Sawako ← Yay!

Birthday: December 31
New Year's Eve

Star Sign: Capricorn

Blood Type: O

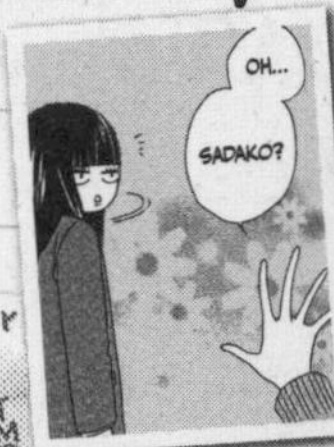

OH...
SADAKO?

Naturally, she's called Sadako!

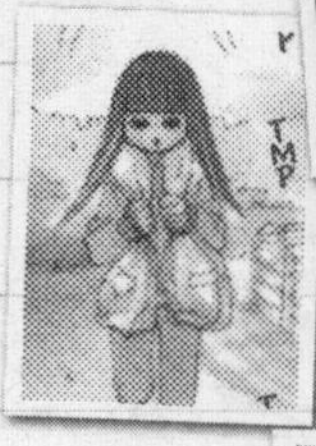

TMP

Good Girl!

DATA The details!

Hobbies: Feeding birds, picking up trash while jogging, cooking and needlework

Skills: Currently studying ghost stories and being the class garden officer

Favorite saying: One good thing per day.

Childhood dream: To become a ladybug ← When I was a baby...

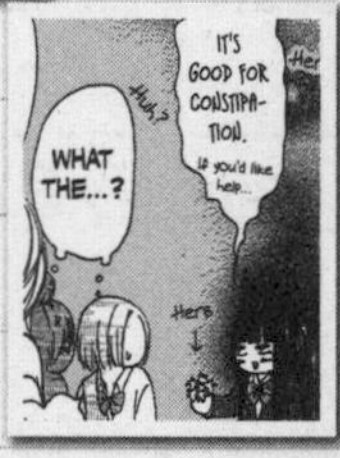

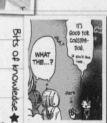

Her
IT'S GOOD FOR CONSTIPATION.
If you'd like help...
Huh?
WHAT THE...?
Hers

Bits of knowledge★

FAVORITES Anything at all!♡

I like my room because it has all my favorite and important stuff.

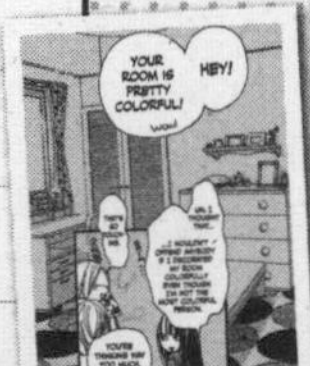

HEY!
YOUR ROOM IS PRETTY COLORFUL!

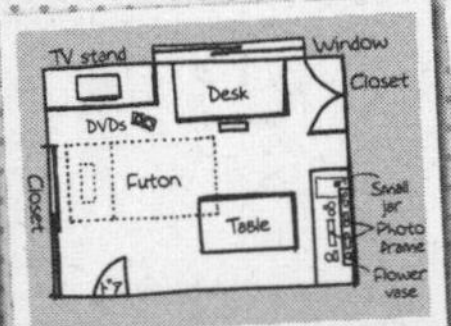

TV stand
Window
Closet
Desk
DVDs
Closet
Futon
Table
Small jar
Photo frame
Flower vase

The floor plan of Sadako's room—revealed for the first time!

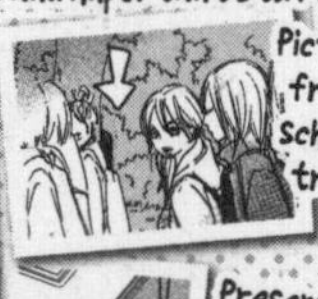

Picture from school trip

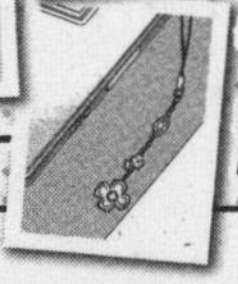

Present from Kaze-haya-kun

WORD A word, please!

WHAT IS ONE WORD THAT DESCRIBES YOU?

人

People are always helping me out.

Kanji for "person"

PROFILE

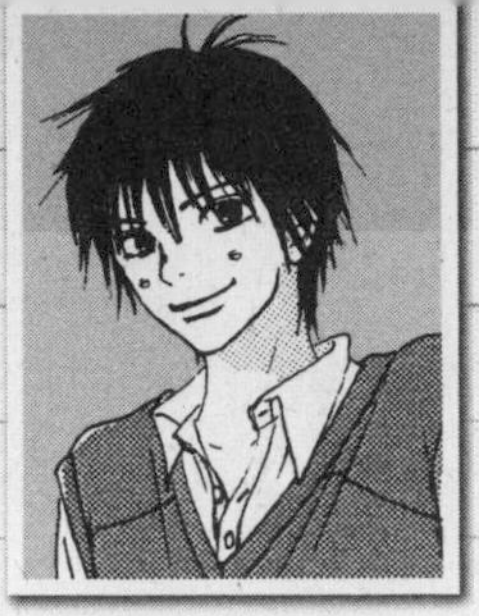

Name: Shota Kazehaya, Male

Nickname: Kazehaya

Most of the time. Ryu and Pin use my first name.

Birthday: May 15

Star Sign: Taurus **Blood Type:** O

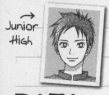

Junior High →

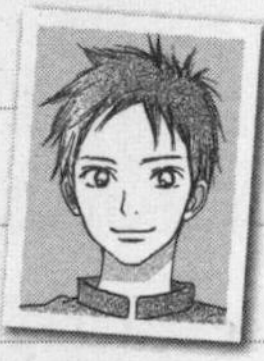

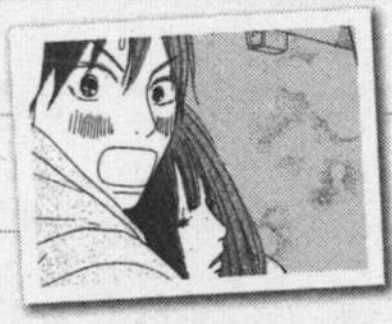

← Sorry, Kazehaya. We secretly took this photo! (—Chizu and Ayane)

FAVORITES

Maru's paws! They're soft and make me relax.

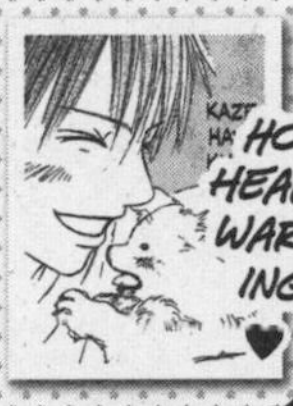

HOW HEART-WARMING! —♥

DATA

Hobbies: Hanging out with classmates, exercising and taking walks with Maru!

Skills: Sports

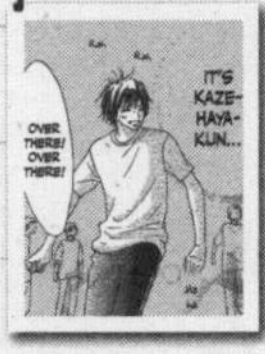
IT'S KAZE-HAYA-KUN...
OVER THERE! OVER THERE!

I love working out!

Favorite saying:

Nothing but the truth.

Childhood dream: To become a baseball player and get revenge on Pin when I grow up!

WORD

WHAT IS ONE WORD THAT DESCRIBES YOU?

焦

Kanji for "anxious"

I feel that way right now.

Special Edition

MARU ANSWERED TOO. KAZEHAYA-KUN WROTE FOR HIM.

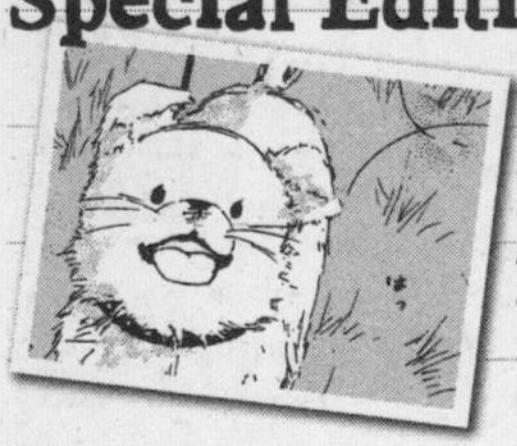

PROFILE

Name: Pedro Martinez

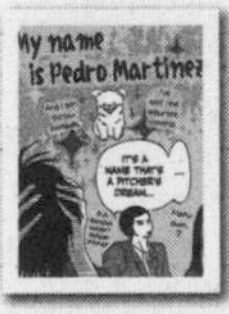
My name is Pedro Martinez
IT'S A NAME THAT'S A PITCHER'S DREAM...

Nickname: Maru

Date when found: Sometime in September

Star Sign: Dog... Is there such a sign? **Blood Type:** B Just guessing.

DATA

Hobbies: Sleeping, eating, playing and taking walks

Skills: Shaking hands (just learned) and jumping

Favorite saying: "Here's your food!" and "Let's go take a walk!"

FAVORITES

He's close to Ryu too!

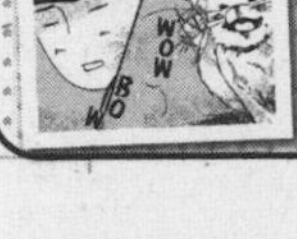
WOW WOW

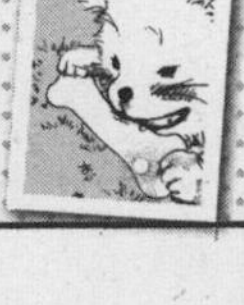

He was happy when Kuronuma gave him a bone.

PROFILE

Name: Chizuru Yoshida, Female

Nickname: Chizu, Chii **Birthday:** June 1

Star Sign: Gemini **Blood Type:** A

I am a well-organized person.

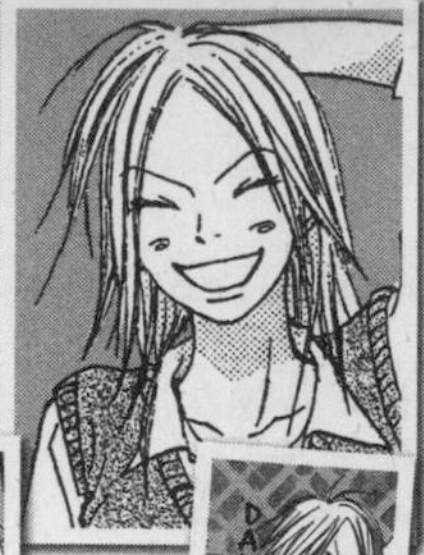

Red demon-God

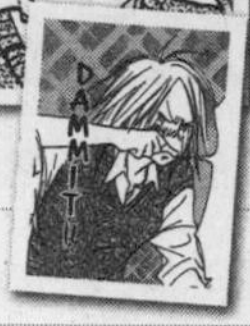
DAMMIT!

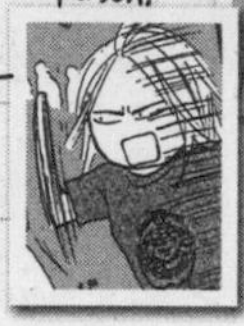

DATA

Hobbies: talking about ramen noodles, playing video games (at Ryu's house)

Skills: Anything involving moving my body!

Favorite saying: Eat moderately. **Childhood dream:** to become the wife of a ramen chef or of Toru

FAVORITES

Ramen at Ryu's is great! Ryu's dad is great!

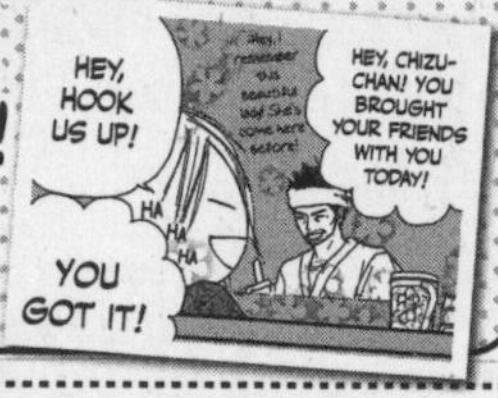
HEY, CHIZU-CHAN! YOU BROUGHT YOUR FRIENDS WITH YOU TODAY!
HEY, HOOK US UP!
HA HA HA
YOU GOT IT!

WORD

WHAT IS ONE WORD THAT DESCRIBES YOU?

仁義

Sorry, there are two words.

Kanji for "humanity and justice"

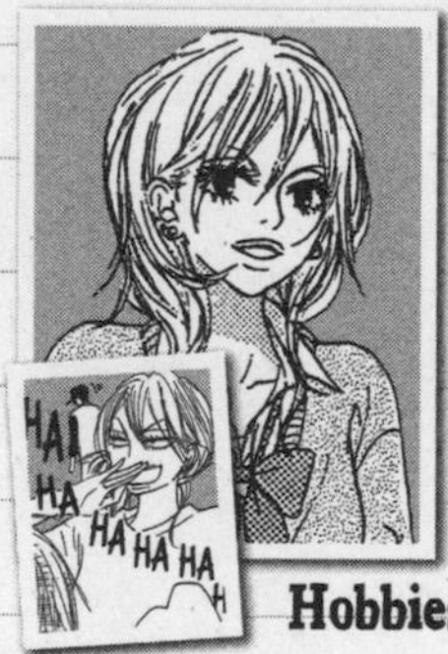
HA HA HA HA HA HA H

PROFILE

Name: Ayane Yano, Female

Nickname: Yano-chin, Ayane **Birthday:** March 3 ← Girl's Day

Star Sign: Pisces **Blood Type:** AB

DATA

Sawako's transforming?!

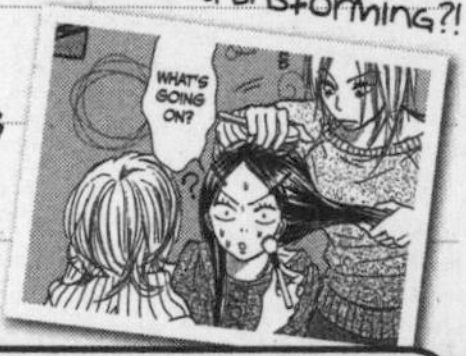
WHAT'S GOING ON?

Hobbies: Anything to do with cosmetics

Skills: Makeup (for both myself and others), Ghost stories

Favorite word: Beauty **Childhood dream:** To be a hairdresser

WORD

I'm a seeker of beauty.

WHAT IS ONE WORD THAT DESCRIBES YOU?

美

Kanji for "beauty"

FAVORITES

Face lotion that I asked Kurumi for, watching Kazehaya and Sawako.

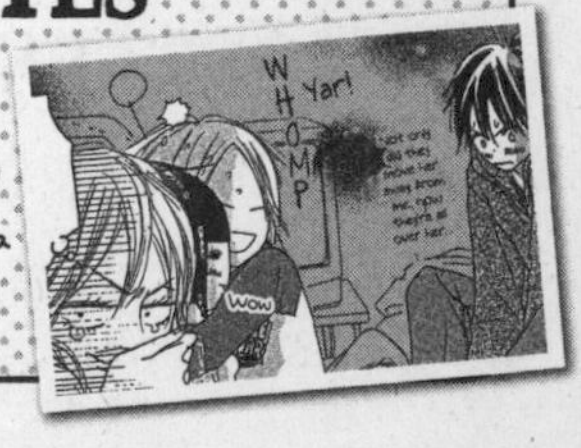
WHOMP
Yar!
WOW

PROFILE

Name: Ryu Sanada, Male

Nickname: Ryu **Birthday:** December 2

Star Sign: Sagittarius **Blood Type:** B

DATA

...
TAKAKO KURO-YAMA.

Hobbies: Playing baseball, working out

Skills: ~~Nothing special~~ ← Misremembering people's names! (—Chizu)

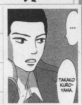

Favorite saying: Actions speak louder than words.

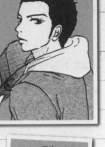

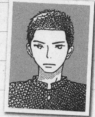

Hasn't changed since junior high. (—Chizu)

FAVORITES

Glove case that Chizu gave me on my birthday

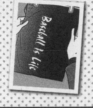

Baseball is Life

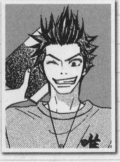

PROFILE

Name: Kazuichi Arai, Male

Nickname: Pin! (—Kazehaya) **Birthday:** July 25

Star Sign: Leo **Blood Type:** B

DATA

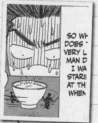

SO WH
DOES
VERY L
MAN D
I WA
STARI
AT TH
WHEN

Hobbies: Bullying Shota

Skills: Nothing is impossible for me!

Favorite word: Self-righteousness

FAVORITES

Kuronuma's power as an exorcist. It's real!

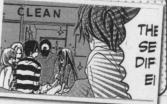

CLEAN
THE
SE
DIF
EI

Pin often senses ghosts. (—Ayane)

PROFILE

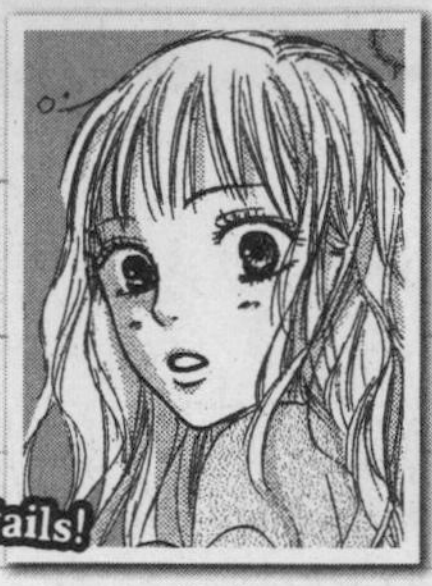

Name: Ume Kurumizawa, Female

Nickname: Kurumi **Birthday:** September 16

Star Sign: Virgo **Blood Type:** AB

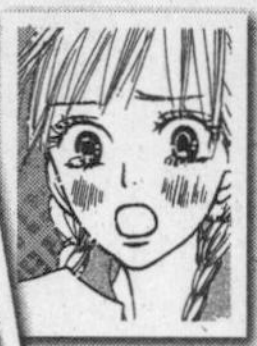

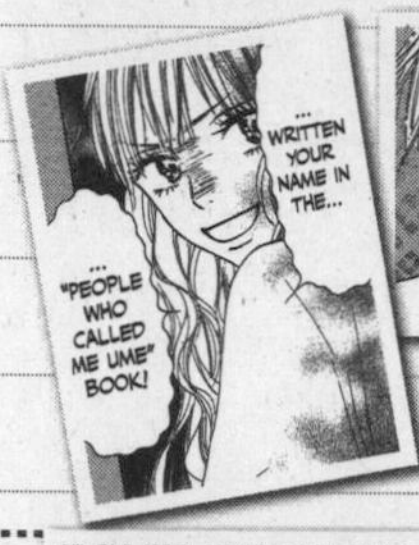
...WRITTEN YOUR NAME IN THE...
..."PEOPLE WHO CALLED ME UME" BOOK!

DATA

The details!

Hobbies: Making a list of "people who called me Ume"

Skills: Controlling gossip♥

Favorite words: Well-prepared

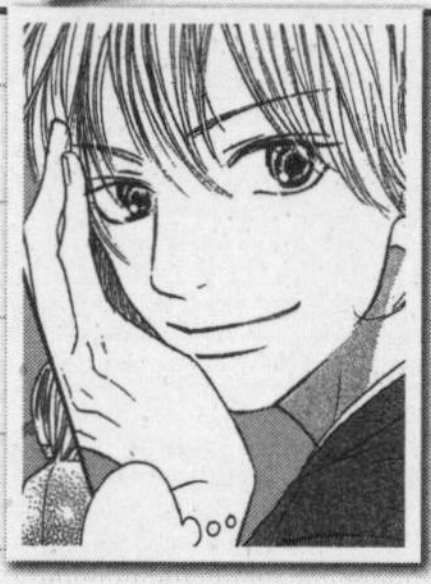

PROFILE

Name: *Kento Miura, Male*

Nickname: *Kento* **Birthday:** *February 6*

Star Sign: *Aquarius* **Blood Type:** *A*

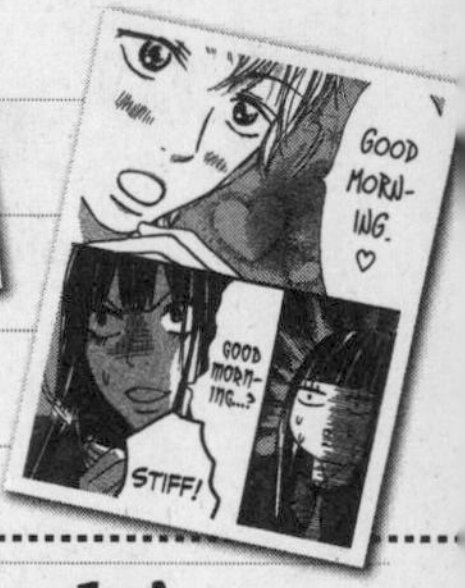
GOOD MORN-ING. ♡
GOOD MORN-ING...?
STIFF!

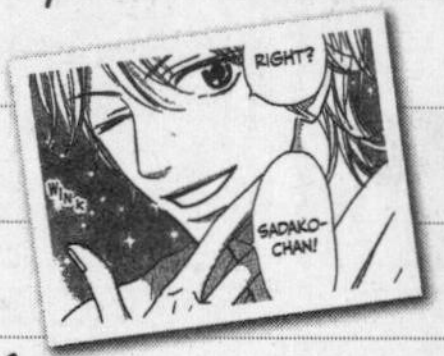
RIGHT?
WINK
SADAKO-CHAN!

DATA

Hobbies: *Supporting girls*

Skills: *I understand girls' feelings.*

Favorite word: *Philanthropism*

More and more funny friends!

Takahashi-san

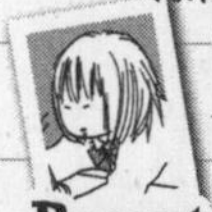

Name: Takahashi-san

Recent news:

Why do I feel there's a hole in my heart ever since Sadako and I went into different classes?

Joe-kun

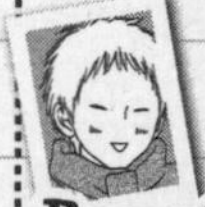

Name: Shoichi Jonouchi

Recent news:

I'm worried about my future with Yano.

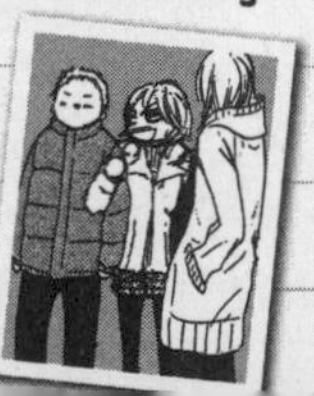

Ekko-chan & Tomo-chan

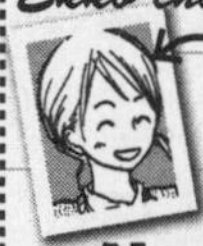

Name: *Eriko Hirano*

Name: *Tomomi Endo*

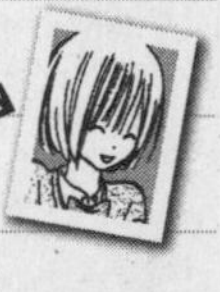

Recent news:

We're often asked if we're twins.

PRODUCED (AND INTERFERED WITH) BY PIN

Is that okay? —Ayane

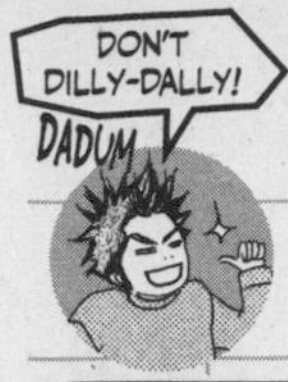
DON'T DILLY-DALLY!
DADUM

Friend☆Finder!

ANALYZE WHICH FRIEND IS BEST FOR YOU...

Start!

DO YOU HAVE MORE THAN THREE PIERCINGS?

Yes→Go to C

No→Go to 1

1 DO PEOPLE THINK YOU CAN SENSE GHOSTS?

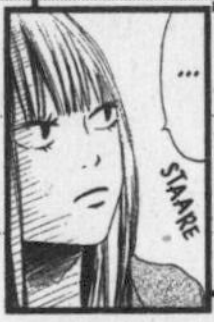
...
STARE

Yes→Go to A

No→Go to 2

2 DO YOU WANT TO BE REINCARNATED AS RAMEN NOODLES?

Yes→Go to B

No→Go to 3

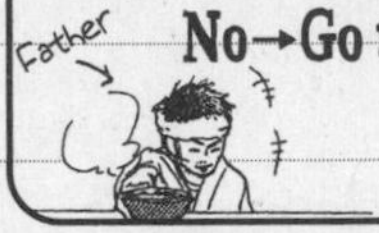
Father

3 DO YOU HAVE AN INSTINCTIVE SENSE FOR WHO IS THE RIGHT ONE FOR YOU?

Yes→Go to A

No→Go to 4

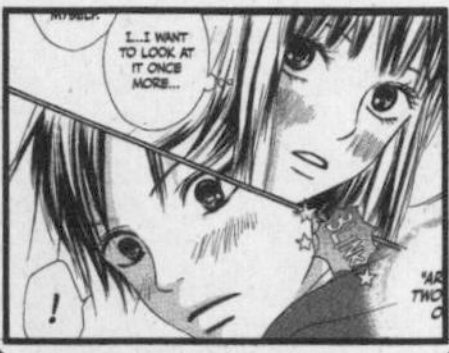
I...I WANT TO LOOK AT IT ONCE MORE...
!

4 HAVE YOU ALREADY BEEN HIT ON BY BOYS?

Yes→Go to C

No→Go to 5

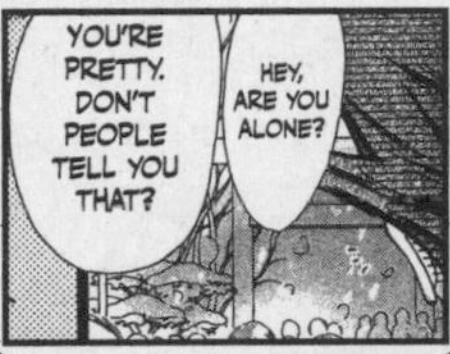
HEY, ARE YOU ALONE?
YOU'RE PRETTY. DON'T PEOPLE TELL YOU THAT?

5 IS THE COLOR OF YOUR CLOTHES FOR IMPORTANT EVENTS RED?

Yes Go to A

No Go to 2

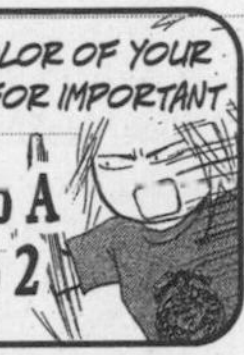

6 WHAT? NONE OF THE ABOVE FITS YOU? THEN JUST GO TO D.

YOUR PERFECT FRIEND

Result

A Sawako Kuronuma

SHE SENSES GHOSTS. SHE HAS A PURITY THAT MAKES THE PEOPLE AROUND HER FEEL WARM. KURONUMA SUITS YOU.

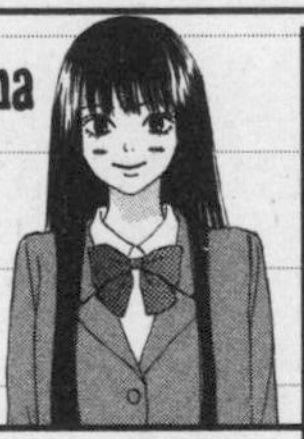

B Chizuru Yoshida

RAMEN AND THE COLOR RED BROUGHT YOU HERE. THAT MEANS YOSHIDA IS PERFECT FOR YOU!

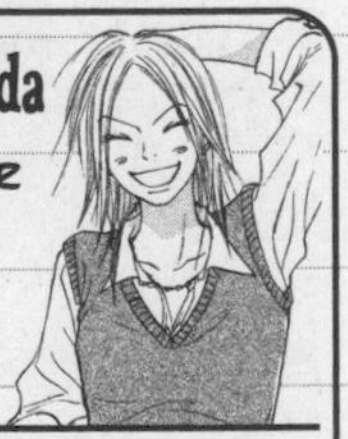

C Ayane Yano

ARE YOU A LITTLE DEVIL? THEN YANO IS GOOD FOR YOU. FOR A HIGH SCHOOL GIRL, PIERCINGS AND BEING HIT ON BY BOYS ARE TEN YEARS TOO SOON!

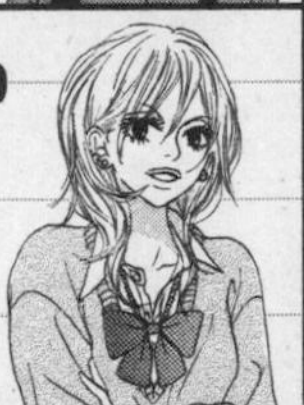

D Pedro Martinez

YOU HAVE QUITE A LOT OF COURAGE TO GO THROUGH ALL OF MY QUESTIONS. A FREE-SPIRITED DOG SUITS YOU!

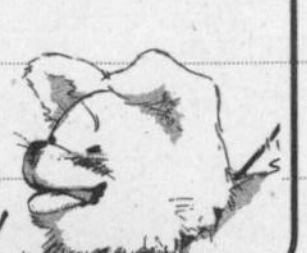

A dog? Can't you be more serious...on many levels?

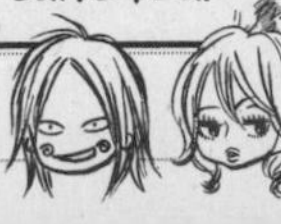

DRAWN BY SADAKO

Map of the School Area

SADAKO DREW A NEIGHBORHOOD MAP. CHIZU AND AYANE ALSO PROVIDED SOME INFO. ☆

CHIZU AND AYANE HELPED!

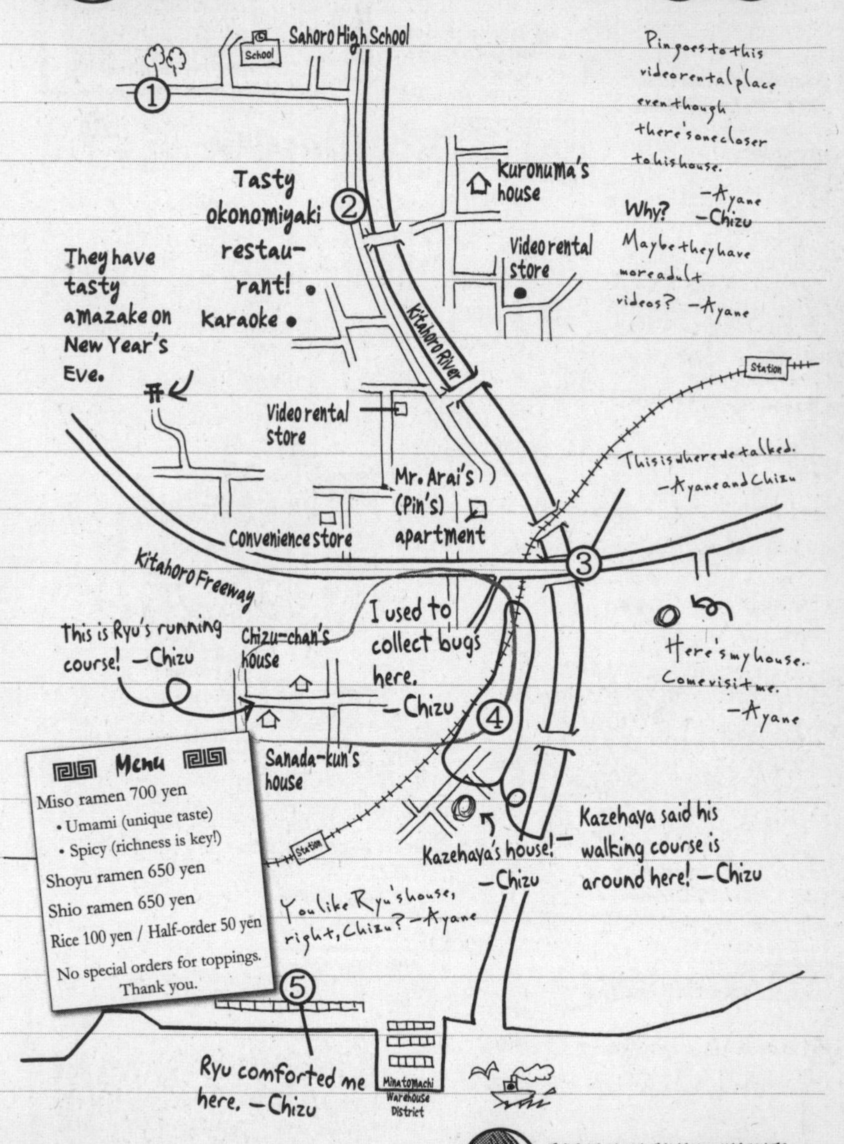
Sahoro High School
School
①
Pin goes to this video rental place even though there's one closer to his house. —Ayane
Why? —Chizu
Maybe they have more adult videos? —Ayane
Kuronuma's house
Tasty okonomiyaki restaurant!
②
Video rental store
They have tasty amazake on New Year's Eve.
Karaoke
Kitahoro River
Station
Video rental store
Mr. Arai's (Pin's) apartment
This is where we talked. —Ayane and Chizu
Convenience store
③
Kitahoro Freeway
I used to collect bugs here. —Chizu
This is Ryu's running course! —Chizu
Chizu-chan's house
Here's my house. Come visit me. —Ayane
④
Sanada-kun's house
Menu
Miso ramen 700 yen
• Umami (unique taste)
• Spicy (richness is key!)
Shoyu ramen 650 yen
Shio ramen 650 yen
Rice 100 yen / Half-order 50 yen
No special orders for toppings.
Thank you.
Station
Kazehaya's house! —Chizu
Kazehaya said his walking course is around here! —Chizu
You like Ryu's house, right, Chizu? —Ayane
⑤
Ryu comforted me here. —Chizu
Minatomachi Warehouse District

THIS IS HOW SAWAKO IMAGINES THE AREA. THERE MAY BE SLIGHT DIFFERENCES FROM WHAT IS REAL.